About the Book and Editors

Based on the proceedings of the seventh annual conference of the International Association of Energy Economists, this book examines prospects for world oil prices in both the short- and long-term future; the outlook for natural gas supply, demand, and price; the pace of U.S. electricity demand growth and the supply options likely to be used to meet that demand; and overall energy supply and demand with particular attention to countries other than the United States.

William F. Thompson, an economist for the Philadelphia Electric Company, previously worked for Westinghouse Electric Company and the Atlantic Richfield Company. He is the author of Economic Growth in the Future: The Growth Debate in National and Global Perspective and Choice Over Change: Economic and Energy Options for the Future. *David J. DeAngelo* is senior fuel planning economist at Pennsylvania Power & Light Company. He was previously a logistics simulation officer at the U.S. Army Logistics Center.

International Association of Energy Economists

Philadelphia, Pennsylvania
December 1985

edited by William F. Thompson
and David J. DeAngelo

Routledge
Taylor & Francis Group
LONDON AND NEW YORK

First published 1985 by Westview Press, Inc.

Published 2019 by Routledge
52 Vanderbilt Avenue, New York, NY 10017
2 Park Square, Milton Park, Abingdon, Oxon OX14 4RN

Routledge is an imprint of the Taylor & Francis Group, an informa business

Library of Congress Catalog Card Number: 85-52036

ISBN 13: 978-0-367-21409-8 (hbk)
ISBN 13: 978-0-429-26817-5 (ebk)

Contents

PART 2: LONG-TERM OIL MARKETS AND PRICES

PART 3: NATURAL GAS MARKETS AND PRICES

PART 5: ENERGY AND THE ECONOMY

Editors' Preface

This document contains most of the papers accepted for publication by the Planning Committee of the Seventh Annual North American Meeting of the International Association of Energy Economists on December 10-13, 1985 in Philadelphia, Pa. The conference, entitled "World Energy Markets: Stability or Continued Cycle?", included three plenary sessions and nine parallel sessions that focused on (1) oil, (2) natural gas, and (3) coal and electricity. A fourth theme, the outlook for world economic growth and energy consumption, was interwoven among the plenary sessions and several of the parallel sessions.

Short and long term prospects for world oil prices, the effects of changing U.S. policies on natural gas demand and supply, the future of the coal industry, and alternatives for future electric power generation were topics of primary interest in the parallel sessions. Approximately 30 papers were presented formally during the nine parallel sessions, spread over the three mornings of the conference. Extended discussions of these papers and summary presentations of the remaining papers took place in 18 roundtable sessions during the two afternoons of the conference.

In a break with procedures followed in recent IAEE North American annual meetings, the Planning Committee asked authors to provide their papers early in the autumn so that these Proceedings could be published in time for them to be available during the Meeting. In another break with past procedures, some papers with complex analytical foundations or analyses were allowed to exceed the normal 15-page limit by a few pages. We wish to thank the authors for their cooperation in meeting the early deadline for papers and for their general adherence to the paper preparation guidelines we distributed.

One disadvantage of publishing the Proceedings at the time of the meeting is that some of the plenary session addresses and the summaries of the roundtable discussions cannot be included. Fot that we express our regret to the speakers, the moderators and the discussants, as well as to the readers of this volume. However, the Planning Committee decided that the advantages of early distribution of the papers given at this important energy conclave outweighed the disadvantages. We hope that prompt, broad distribution of these papers will prove useful to both non-members and members of IAEE.

The editors are not responsible for any errors that may remain in this volume, although each paper was read carefully and all typographic errors noted were corrected. There was no effort to referee papers or do substantive editing, but the papers were screened at the proposal stage by the Program Planning Committee. The views expressed by the authors are their own and do not represent the official positions of either their own institutions or the IAEE.

William F. Thompson

David J. DeAngelo

1 The Political Economy of World Petroleum

Melvin A. Conant, Conant and Associates, Ltd.

It took a severe depression (1981-1983) to remind those of us particularly interested in the political environment of internationally traded oil that the economics affecting supply -- the terms of trade -- had been slighted, and even overlooked. And it is now increasingly the case that the politics of oil are being overlooked and even forgotten in the effects of market forces which, for many, are now of paramount importance. This is especially the situation within the U.S. administration in contrast to the perspectives of many other oil importers which have a longer memory. There is a history to oil, and a large part of its story is a rich mixture of the political and economic; ignoring or not even being aware of this still unfolding story -- either the political or economic ingredients -- can be self-wounding as we rethink the current and prospective forces acting upon world oil trades.

One cannot visit Tokyo, London, Bonn, or Paris and discuss the outlook for international oil without reference to the role of oil in relations between states; nor can one visit Mexico City, Caracas, Riyadh, Baghdad, or Teheran without awareness of the political background to oil. How different it appears to be in Washington at least in discussions with the so-called (and often self-styled) policy makers. But talk with some of the professionals in the intelligence community, or with the very few still found in the Department of Energy and of State and one can be on more familiar ground.

There exists, then, within the OECD community a division of opinion about the circumstances affecting international oil which by and large finds the United States on one side and other key oil importers somewhere else. Since this separation is caused by different appreciations of the oil scene, we should review the principal elements in their respective positions.

To those who still argue that the United States has no energy policy, what follows may seem to substantiate that view: the U.S. administration believes as if it were an article of faith that oil ought to be dealt with as is (or should be) any other commodity; its terms should be set by commercial forces -- the market. When this is not the case, as happened in 1973-1974 and governments move in to define those terms, eventually everyone loses. Government intervention turns access to oil -- especially to someone else's oil -- into a different game distorting the economics of supply into something of a political game. As this occurs, prices, profits and returns on investment are altered artificially; continuous and adequate supplies become increasingly subject to political considerations and governments feel obliged to intervene more and more. The "cure" then to whatever ails the oil trade is for governments to back off, to deregulate, and for most aspects of oil adopt a hands-off approach in which the dictates of government policy are replaced by those of the market.

There is much to be said in support of this view although there are some who remember how often earlier U.S. administrations intervened on prices and imports, usually at the behest of private oil interests. Few argue that the price of world oil as it quadrupled and tripled again had been defined by "the market" even in the different circumstances surrounding the surges of 1973-1974 from those of 1979-1980. But there is a presumption buried deep in this view of world oil which needs to be examined. If the role of government and of policy in oil matters grew exponentially when crudes were in tight supply, may there not come a time again in which the current situation of surplus throughout the system -- will be succeeded by a closer balance between supply and demand? Many oil analysts appear to believe this and indicate that the early- to mid-1990s may well find us contending once more with questions of supply, of import security, and possibly of rapid, real price increases.

It is this other, longer view which is held elsewhere in the OECD and oil exporting communities. In effect, it is held that in a time of surplus of a strategic commodity (not to be regarded as just a commercial one), it is easy enough, but risky, to rely upon market forces without a thought for the possibility of change or for a return to a condition in which the politics of supply intrude and distort the economics of oil trade.

It remains true, also, that most other oil importers link their oil needs to intergovernmental relationships notably in North Africa and the Middle East in which the role of the private sector is not separate from that of officialdom. In fact, a very large part of the history of oil is about the connections between oil companies and governments.

Actually, even for those most imbued with the notion that the economics of oil now are supreme and ought to continue to be if we are possessed of our senses, there are aspects of oil trade which contain more politics -- government policies and practices -- than is admitted: The near-demise of a U.S. synfuels industry, the collapse of a domestic shipbuilding industry, and the relaxation of laws and regulations influencing the choice of fuels other than oil; even the failure to date of government to propose ways and means whereby a number of financially-endangered utilities may keep/complete their nuclear programs has major energy impacts, including oil.

We speak often of the oil volumes now produced in non-OPEC free world countries (currently about 23 MMB/D versus a 14.5 MMB/D from OPEC) including many which are comparatively high-cost production, and in doing so we are saying implicitly, at least, that in acquiring this increased supply, we have thereby avoided much of the political trouble which OPEC suppliers, especially of the Middle East Gulf, have given us. It has been a quite deliberate act of many governments to look elsewhere for oil-- more expensive oil -- than to remain vulnerable to Middle East political instabilities. (Should the U.S. change its mind and in a year or so agree to export some North Slope oil to Japan, whatever amount Japan decides to buy will be defined in large part by Tokyo's political decision to purchase expensive Alaskan oil for reasons other than Japan's energy needs.)

But there are several other, quite important matters involving oil which should hold our attention.

The one most likely to hold our attention over the next three to five years is that of world oil pricing. Ought it to be subject only to market forces? And run the risks from a further decline in oil prices on companies, investors, banks, and governments in terms of falling revenue? Or is it more to the common advantage to find a process whereby oil prices would be sustained? Advocates of "pure" economic/market forces would answer that it would be a travesty if a price artifically set by governments should now be accepted as real. Other interests would hold that however regrettable were the oil price experiences of the 1970s and very early 1980s, there is now so much at stake in the oil price not going lower, especially over the short-term, that a reference to market forces prevailing is an altogether inadequate response to a deeply troubling and spreading phenomenon.

Here again the reactions of the U.S. administration differ from those of others -- allies and oil importers. The U.S. attitude can be summarized by the view that it is altogether beneficial that oil prices decline; how far? The market will inform when an equilibrium between supply and demand is, at long last, regained. When that occurs, a major benefit will be the boost given economies generally as energy costs are reduced, and import bills are less. (The once-widely discussed OPEC notion that economic growth will lead to higher oil consumption is not heard much of today as societies now have larger stakes in the use of alternative fuels.) To the extent that in the process substantial interests are put at risk -- e.g., governments which are financially strapped and banks with too large energy loan portfolios -- ad hoc measures may have to be taken to rescue them.

But it will be important to distinguish between those interests in trouble because of the general fall in commodities prices, the lackluster economic performance of the OECD community, and the record of governments' mismanagement of their economies, from the difficulties many governments have in borrowing additional sums -- all to be distinguished from difficulties caused by oil prices declining. Moreover, one has also to bear in mind that with oil prices tripling 1979-1980, and a strong U.S. dollar relative to other currencies for a large part of the time since then, it is still something of a mystery why OPEC members are in trouble: Nigeria, Indonesia, Venezuela, and now even Saudi Arabia. The point that a society adjusts itself quickly to much greater revenues and consequently higher standards of living is not a sufficient argument for others taking major measures to prevent those oil exporters from having to tighten their belts. After all, it was those oil exporters and their fellow OPEC members which caused the oil price to quadruple and which were far from innocent bystanders when it tripled again in 1979-1980.

Hence, the U.S. administration view reflects the consideration mentioned earlier -- that adhering to market forces is essential and will be to the general benefit. Those who counted on continuing to profit from OPEC's continued price increases which were quickly introduced in sales of domestically produced oil, will suffer from their miscalculations, as they should if we are to deal with market forces. This U.S. administration view is, of course, rooted not only in an appreciation of the market and how it works to the common good, but in political decisions thus reintroducing the theme of this essay: That the economic forces affecting oil are inextricably tangled with politics.

The United States is not altogether alone in espousing these views. Great Britain may come closer to the American perspective but its own interests as an important oil exporter are also reflected in a government whose revenues from oil (some 13 percent) are crucial; oil price declines put its conservative rule in a dilemma. Germany (FRG) shares some of the U.S. attitude but one would be mistaken to regard Bonn as the most useful European example of <u>laissez faire</u>; successive German administrations have not hesitated to inform the oil industry when Bonn was uneasy about the direction of forces.

Such a time could come again and FRG would have allies in its determination not to let declining oil prices reverse the progress made since 1974 in the greater use of fuels other than oil and the 10-12 percent reduction in energy input per unit of GNP (and a 20 percent reduction in oil input.) If lower oil prices reduce the public commitment to alternative energy sources, to conservation, and longer-term improvements in energy efficiencies, then governments will react. They could, of course, keep oil prices high by increasing fuel taxes but, it is argued, this is as difficult politically for them as it is for the United States. Keeping oil prices from declining might be more easily accomplished, incongruous as that may sound. As a result, it is from Europe and Japan that one hears increasingly of the need for a dialogue being restarted with OPEC joined by other oil exporters such as Mexico -- even Canada? -- and few will include the Soviet Union although its interest in high oil prices is certainly as great as that of other countries.

France might again initiate the process, as it did in 1975 with Saudi Arabia and which led to the unlamented Conference on International Economic Cooperation. From a variety of sources, different recommendations are being discussed. These range: (1) from an effort to establish price parameters between which oil prices could move "freely," (2) agreements on volumes to be obtained from oil exporters generally or particular supplies from certain sources, (3) to a commodity stabilization fund to help insure stable income to oil exporters, and (4) to create that elusive "basket of currencies" to help stabilize the value to oil exporters of the money earned from oil sales. In addition, there is a host of recommendations as to how OPEC might improve upon its discipline. Not one of these proferred measures would have the support of the U.S. administration -- each one serves mainly to sustain a price which has already been too high and kept there by artificial, non-market forces.

Moreover, every one of these measures requires as an essential condition of their being initiated and then implemented, the intimate involvement of governments. This is not a game in which the current U.S. administration has any interest and would, undoubtedly, strongly oppose. Such is the (still) large weight of the United States in economic and financial matters that its absence from a dialogue would probably -- but not necessarily -- doom the effort.

If the immediate need is for financial rescues, the U.S. role is widely acknowledged to be crucial. If the need is for a process through which Europeans find price stabilization, and in arrangements which reflect their broader range of historical economic and political links to the Middle East, then the United States should not be surprised if the present EC talks with the Gulf Cooperation Council and other Arab groups move more definitively than has been the case so far. Should this occur, the United States would have a more difficult situation to deal with: Can the U.S. stay out of an oil compact which might also include Japanese?

We tend to scoff at the possibility of such an oil impact, and point out the near impossibility of the EC agreeing on anything truly vital. Perhaps -- but we should be attentive to these efforts, and careful. There is more than enough sentiment in Europe that the link to the United States is losing some of its luster.

The Japanese emphasize the advantages to them of lower priced oil imports but they are as determined as other nations not to have their achievements at energy diversification and energy efficiencies undermined by cheap oil. They also see their interests served in the avoidance of sudden, large price changes. Finally, Japanese wonder if their present dependence on the Middle East Gulf for nearly 75 percent of their oil supplies can ever be different -- which argues for good relations with the Arab oil exporters for whom some kind of understanding about price has special importance.

But how might private sector oil companies and troubled banks react to an effort to sustain oil prices? The political pressures they could bring to bear would be considerable. Does the distinction drawn between the U.S. administration and European and Japanese views apply to the private sector? Both Shell and BP top management have been increasingly insistent that further price declines and a failure to meet with OPEC warn of disaster. There has been no such remark made publicly by U.S. oil company chief executives although we have every reason to think that Mobil, TEXACO, Chevron, ARCO, Phillips, Occidental, Ashland, etc. have to be as deeply concerned if for quite different reasons. Banks have referred to the problems created for (and, to be frank, by) them in their energy lending in the diminished flow of petrodollars and in the seeming inability of key oil exporters to make ends meet, contributing thereby to the general pressure upon banks as debtor obligations remain difficult to meet and in too many cases impossible to deal with except through deferral of payments, forgiveness, and outright suspension of further payments for several more years. Debt obligations are not being met in too many cases; the debts are being "rolled over." Oil prices are a factor in their difficulties in that some nations cannot meet their own import bills without further indebtedness; oil exporters cannot meet some of their other obligations as financial assets shrink. Saudi Arabia's holdings in foreign exchange have been reduced from about $24 billion in 1983 to $14 billion so far by June 1985; its overseas holdings were over $200 billion in 1983 and now less than half of that amount. OPEC as a whole has a net negative of $45-$50 billion in current account for 1982-1984. One may expect to find not a coalition of oil, banking, and investment firms moving together to press for undertakings about oil prices but acting separately through their own ways and means to accomplish that purpose.

There is, of course, a small chance (20 percent?) that OPEC can improve upon its act and that other interests will act not to increase downward pressures on price, holding it more or less at a possible $25/barrel. There is a much larger chance (50 percent) of pressure being placed on governments to support prices if the price is about $23/barrel; and there is a 20 percent chance of a free fall to below $20/barrel. In either of the two latter situations, the politics of oil -- meaning government intervention -- is likely to be of greater influence than that market forces will be allowed to prevail.

There are two other issues -- among many -- in which political considerations will greatly influence the oil outcome.

First, it is widely noted that a significant number of large and small oil companies are in deep financial trouble, including a high proportion of the service industry. We know already that in budgets for exploration and development we are witnessing a drop in outlays. U.S. drilling costs in 1983 were about $40 billion; in 1984, they were $27 billion. We know also that U.S. finding rates have generally been disappointing -- and that a very high proportion of drilling has been for field extensions/development and not for exploration per se. In 1983, 2,092 wells were drilled in the U.S. but 35,115 wells for field development or extension. In 1984, the proportion was 2,421 to 41,095. And we ought to be reminding ourselves daily that without a vigorous drilling effort, and greater overall success than we have had in the past twenty years, our import requirements could rise and dependence return on Gulf supplies.

Thus the worsening financial situation of a critically important U.S. industry raises the issue of the value to the U.S. national interest of its being sheltered from the repercussions of the anticipated further decline in oil prices. However this may be done, it is clearly a political act in behalf of a group of private interests better known for its insistent advocacy of "free market forces." We have probably not heard the last of an import fee per barrel of crude, or one also imposed on product; if it is described as a source of additional revenue to be applied to the federal deficit, and not as protection for a beleagured domestic industry, it will be clear enough that the real purposes served embrace both considerations. In view of the U.S. administration's insistence on market forces prevailing, and the President's reiterated opposition to new taxes, a political choice will have to be made on the import fee option which could also be described as being in the national interest.

Second among the politics of oil is the issue of mergers/buyouts -- in what circumstances are the national interests affected by what appears to some to be a dubious kind of business practice? With TEXACO, Mobil, Chevron, ARCO, Phillips and smaller companies either the pursuers or the pursued, it is clear enough that a further decline in oil prices could impact on the ability of these companies to meet their debt obligations incurred in launching a takeover or in avoiding one. Three of the companies mentioned would be listed among the giant enterprises of the world. If one or more of them have increasing difficulties in meeting their debts incurred for non-capital reasons, and becomes either a target once again or suffers a sharp decline in its energy role, is the national interest affected?

Some will say so while being at a loss to prescribe the actions which would be necessary, yet bearing in mind the precedents set by the rescue of Chrysler and the Continental Illinois Bank.

There are, therefore, at least three issues whose fundamental origins lie in an economic circumstance: the decline of the oil market price. In each case, if remedies are sought, a political decision will have to be made. At a previous IAEE Conference, we thought about the prospect for oil cooperation or oil competition in the years ahead between Saudi Arabia, Iraq, and Iran. That question was discussed in light of the proposition that these three have common interests in high oil prices but also in the light of the extraordinary political difficulties each would have in any durable undertaking regarding oil. It is mentioned again as a quiet reminder that political aspects to oil may loom more important at one time than another but they do not ever disappear altogether. If one of us dismisses the political element, it may mean he is ignorant, or uncaring, about the long history of oil which in addition to its economic and financial contexts has never been without a political dimension.

2
Prospects for World Oil Markets

Stephen A. Smith, Data Resources, Inc.

No Room Left to Swing

As the summer of 1985 comes to an end, OPEC continues to face a now familiar array of problems. While the problems are the same, OPEC's position is not and the group finds itself at a very important threshold. The combined impact of further demand declines, continued non-OPEC production gains, and yet another anticipatory "price break stockdraw" is an OPEC production rate running at about 14 mmbd for the last four months with the Saudis only getting a little better than 2 mmbd. While this sustained low rate has had the effect of recently firming spot crude prices, it is coming at an extremely high cost to the Saudis.

At recent production rates, the Saudis have been drawing down their foreign exchange reserves at an unbelievably strong $1.5 billion per month. If sustained, this rate would exhaust all Saudi reserves in less than 60 months. This places the Saudis and all of OPEC at a significant "crunch point". Either demand for OPEC oil begins to move up, or non-Saudi production makes more room for Saudi production, or the Saudis will force their way in by cutting price. Recent and persistent rumors of possible Saudi "netback" pricing deals could be pointing to the "tip of the iceberg" of this price reduction process. The new, low Saudi production levels are now putting them in a position where they are indifferent to sharply lower prices with higher volumes versus today's very low volumes and "higher" prices. The reality of the new Saudi economics could add believability to heretofore hollow Saudi threats. The other possibility is that the Saudis have cried wolf once too often. Now that the wolf is truly at the door they may not be believed.

Big Problems With Demand

Ranking the factors underlying the current OPEC situation in order of their severity, the continuing decline in oil demands is in a class by itself. The declines are large, and surprising, and most disturbing of all to OPEC, they are occurring despite modest economic growth. In 1984, OECD economic growth was 5% and oil demands grew at 3%--resulting in a 2% decline in oil per unit of real GNP. This decline rate had been as high as 9% in 1981 but had steadily slowed to 2% in 1984. Then surprisingly, in 1985, 2.5% <u>growth</u> in real GNP is producing a <u>2.5% decline</u> in oil consumption, indicating a sharp reversal in what had been a slowing decline rate for oil per unit of GNP. Since long-term trend growth in OECD's real GNP is not likely to exceed 1985's growth by very much, a continuation of 1985's performance would lop an annual one million barrels per day off free world demands. This is unlikely, but it does frame the severity of 1985's demand decline. There seem to be about four culprits. First, there may be meager economic growth, but U.S. industrial production is flat at best. Second, an unusually larger number of nuclear power plants have come on-line both in the U.S. and Europe over the last year. Third, substantial natural gas gluts in both the U.S. and Europe are slowly cutting into residual fuel's market. Fourth, the end of the U.K. coal strike cut oil demands abruptly by 0.4 mmbd last April.

Big Problems From Non-OPEC Oil

On a smaller scale than the demand slide, but still big enough to be a major problem, total non-OPEC production keeps edging up. In some countries, "edging" means growth of 100 mbd per year. This includes the U.S., where a year-over-year gain of 1.3% amounts to 110 mbd, and the U.K., where a 5.3% gains means an additional 130 mbd. Other major rapid production gains have come from offshore development in Brazil, India, Australia and Norway. Finally, China's production is growing at about an 8% annual rate which adds about 200 mbd to world production. The only bright spot for OPEC of late has been the Soviet Union. It has become increasingly apparent that the Soviet Union has very serious and not easily correctable problems. Production is currently declining at an annual rate of about 3.7%, which means a loss of 450 mbd per year if it keeps up.

The Saudi Options

The Saudis will aggressively seek to reduce their deficit in the coming year. On the expense side, the Saudis can and will continue to squeeze domestic spending, but this is unlikely to save them more than about 10% or $4 billion from the current year's budget. Aside from hoping that OPEC's total volume will expand at current prices, there are only two politically realistic options on the revenue side: (1) they can engineer a major price cut to significantly expand OPEC volume, or (2) they can pressure non-Saudi OPEC to reduce their volume share. A third, and probably their best strategic option, is not politically workable--it would involve tightening cartel production and discipline enough to increase prices by $2 to $3 per barrel. This would have the benefit of easing the revenue squabble, restoring confidence, and not seriously changing the competitive position of oil. This option, however, is a bit like asking for ham and eggs when eggs alone might be a luxury. In other words, could OPEC have the discipline to defend $30 when supporting $28 has been "touch and go?" The more realistic options are continued Saudi pressure for share while holding $28 or a major price break engineered by the Saudis. The actual outcome could lie in between.

As total OPEC volume shrinks, the current volume allocation procedure is tending to drift towards a de facto "OPEC policy" of allocation by severity of economic need. In this scheme, the Saudis and Kuwaitis lose more, and others lose less. At the other end of the spectrum, a move to sharply lower prices would ultimately lead to higher OPEC export volumes. Production allocation within OPEC then gradually returns to a basis of allocation by productive capacity. In this situation, high capacity producers who are currently at low utilization rates would then increase their share of total OPEC revenue while other producers would lose. The "losers" suffer because all producers take a pro-rata "hit" from lower prices but only those producers with additional capacity to expand could expect to see "more-than-offseting" volume gains. Large non-OPEC oil exporters would lose the most since they have virtually no spare capacity. They would see only the price effect. Prominent on this list would be Mexico, the U.K., Norway, Egypt and the Soviet Union. Within OPEC, the largest losers would be small members who have been producing near capacity, such as Ecuador and Gabon and "high-potential" producers whose current production is constrained by war-related factors, i.e., Iran and Iraq. The overall equations are complex in that the Saudis lose indirectly if Iraq loses because of the key Saudi financial support role in funding Iraq's war effort.

The most important point related to the sharp recent drop in Saudi production levels is straightforward: as Saudi export volumes begin to approach zero, the importance of their acting to maintain "high" prices, declines. They are rapidly approaching a position where <u>their</u> potential volume gains from lower prices are likely to result in longer-term net revenue gains as compared with holding current prices. This does not imply that the Saudis would not be net revenue losers in the next two to three years, if prices were to break hard in 1985. It's really a question of the Saudis choosing to accept greater short-term financial pressure as a necessary trade-off to salvage their longer-term position. This is not a pleasant "bullet to bite" and, of course, they would prefer to exhaust other alternatives before taking such a drastic move. The unknown political consequences of such a move, particularly the response of Iran, are a second reason why the Saudis may choose to "wait it out" in hope of a volume upturn.

Option Two: Coerce Non-Saudi Discipline

The second option for the Saudis at this point is really just another attempt at what they have been trying to achieve all along. It clearly represents the path of least resistance for the Saudis. It involves threats of higher Saudi production (and therefore lower prices) as a mechanism to coerce other members to adhere to quotas.

Parodoxically, the more believable it becomes that the Saudis will choose to break price, the greater the odds become that they won't have to, at least for a while. This type of logic ultimately breaks down and prices would decline sharply if demand for OPEC oil continues to fall.

To implement this strategy, the principal task required of the the Saudis at this point is to convince non-Saudi OPEC that they, the Saudis, are now approaching indifference to sharply lower prices. Further, non-Saudi OPEC must be sufficiently convinced so that they do two things: first, they must adhere to current quotas, thus allowing any incremental OPEC volume gains to flow to the Saudis, which would allow the Saudis' production to move closer to their quota of 4.35 mmbd. Second, if OPEC's total volume continues to shrink in the next year or two, non-Saudi OPEC would have to be willing to accept, and adhere to, at least pro-rata reductions in quota. For example, if the total OPEC quota were reduced by 20%, to 12.8 mmbd, over the next two years, the new Saudi quota would then be 3.5 mmbd an a pro-rata basis. The Saudis could get by with 3.5 mmbd, but they are not likely to accept only 2 mmbd for a sustained period. There is every reason for non-Saudi OPEC to believe that recent Saudi threats should now be taken seriously. However, the Saudis have been "crying wolf" with intermittent threats for several years. Will anyone believe them now? The prospects don't look good.

Amidst this backdrop of OPEC desperation, there are actually a few positive signals for OPEC in late summer markets. First, total OPEC production remained at about 14 mmbd, or 2 mmbd below quota through August. It remained at this level because non-Saudi production held to quota while Saudi production was 2 mmbd under quota. On the basis of low OPEC production levels in May/June, and a lean world stock position, spot crude prices have been rising since mid-June. Past performances suggest that non-Saudi OPEC would have been cheating by August. Of course, August production numbers are not firm at this point, but if it is true that non-Saudi producers are still holding to quota, then there is some possibility that the new Saudi threats are being taken more seriously.

About the time of OPEC's late July meeting in Geneva, and again more recently, there have been persistent rumors of Saudi negotiations for "netback-based" pricing deals. We would be very surprised if the Saudis were not having such discussions. As previously discussed, they now have every reason to seriously consider pulling their support of current price levels, and netback pricing is the least transparent way of accomplishing this. Effectively, the Saudis could then say, "We didn't lower crude prices, the lower product prices did". They could also legitimately observe that they were merely following a practice initiated by other OPEC members. Lastly, if rumors of such a deal are leaked sufficiently, then the possibility of a resulting increase in non-Saudi discipline could mean that the Saudis would not have to follow through.

A combination of non-OPEC production gains, free world oil demand declines and additional stockdraw, is likely to push OPEC's crude production to about 15.7 mmbd in 1985. It could be as low as 15.0 mmbd. This is roughly a 2 mmbd decline from the 17.3 mmbd produced in 1984. This outcome occurs despite OECD economic growth of about 2.5% in 1985. Economic growth for 1986 and 1987 is unlikely to be much better and it could be worse. Since OPEC exports in 1985 are likely to be only 12.2 mmbd, then a two year replay of 1985's OPEC production decline suggests that exports could be off by 2 to 3 mmbd by 1987, or by 15% to 25%. Since prices would almost certainly decline sharply in this case, total OPEC export revenues could be as much as 30% to 40% lower by 1987. We don't expect this to happen, but it is the most likely scenario if OPEC's 1985 situation was simply mechanically extended for two additional years.

Near-Term Price Summary

Most of 1985's decline in oil consumption has been the result of continued growth in nuclear power, substitution of natural gas for residual fuel oil, and consumer stockdraw. We expect this process to slow considerably in 1986 and 1987. However, the point we wish to emphasize is that the demand trend reversal in 1985 has been both sudden and substantial. For OPEC, it raises the spectre of two to three more years of declining oil export volumes. It comes at a time when prices have held only because the Saudis have cut their production to only slightly better than 2 mmbd. For OPEC, the moment of truth may have arrived. Their "call" has been drifting steadily lower, most members have serious financial pressures already, and their swing producer has run out of incentive and room to swing.

In summary, there are simply too many potentially negative factors to warrant any reversal in the gradually eroding price path of the last few years. Non-OPEC production appears likely to continue to edge up--the only question is "how much". We show free world consumption edging up by enough to offset non-OPEC production gains and therefore, the base case shows a slight increase in OPEC production. But there is a substantial downside demand risk stemming partially from macroeconomic uncertainty but primarily from uncertainty regarding the momentum of the oil substitution process. Much of the uncertainty has downside risk for price.

We have chosen to represent this risk by two further breaks in the official marker price: one break from $28 to $26 at the beginning of 1986, a second break to $24 at the beginning of 1987. Could the marker hold at $28? Absolutely--but a lot of things would have to work out right. Could the marker break deeper, say to $20? Absolutely--if free world demand declines and non-OPEC production gains of 1985 each persisted for two more years. Our base case forecast of a $24 bottom represents a hedge to straddle the most likely range of possibilities.

Long-Term Price Outlook

The long-term outlook for oil prices depends in large measure on the degree of OPEC's success in maintaining nominal oil prices over the next three to four years. The large excess of OPEC production capacity and the financial hardship of many members are likely to continue to exert severe downward pressure on price for the next two to three years. If OPEC suffers only modest declines in nominal prices to the $23 to $25 range by 1987/1988 as our base case expects, then OPEC's total "call" will begin to move slowly upward. We see the late 1980s and early 1990s as a period of transition. During this period OPEC volume is no longer declining and in fact, is edging upward albeit at a slow rate. This upturn in exports should given OPEC enough confidence to take a few nominal price increases. However, a narrowing but still substantial excess capacity situation is likely to keep markets competitive so that significant <u>real</u> price increases remain unlikely. Our base case forecast expects a $26 nominal market price by 1990 and $37 by 1995. In 1985 dollars, these represent $20 by 1990 and $22 by 1995.

By the mid-1990s, OPEC's volume expansion should be gaining momentum. The "high-absorber" producers should be at capacity and therefore the "spare capacity" producers will be limited to the major five Persian Gulf producers. A key uncertainty is the extent to which the capacity of Iran and Iraq will have expanded by this period. The Saudis will attempt to balance the needs of the high-absorbers and other Gulf producers with the dynamics of longer term price/volume relationships. The concentration of excess production capacity under Saudi control will still afford them absolute veto power over the upward pricing demands of the capacity-constrained high absorbers. As demand continues to expand in the late 1990s, and spare Saudi capacity begins to decline, they must price so as to (1) take into account the lagged nature of volume responses to price increases, and (2) the uncertainty with respect to OPEC's total capacity, particularly the uncertainty surrounding Iran and Iraq.

We expect prices to run up sharply in the 1995 to 2000 period. Our base case shows $70 in nominal terms by 2000, which equates to $32 in 1985 dollars. This implies a 7% real annual growth rate for the 1995-2000 period. In real terms, however, this level still only represents only about 75% of 1981's price level.

Summary and Conclusions

OPEC's consistently demonstrated inability to adhere to adequately low production levels has created a market in which spot prices almost always undercut official prices. Recognition of this fact by buyers has led to steady pressure away from officially priced transactions, and toward spot-related transactions. This enormous structural change has created a market in which spot-related prices have become dominant, and in which retroactive official price changes merely ratify the lower prices which spot markets established as the "new reality". This gradual establishment of a price continuum, as compared with discrete levels of official prices, now permits prices to slip gradually lower with no single OPEC or non-OPEC action identifiable as the obvious cause.

<u>On a theoretical basis</u>, OPEC could realize the dangers inherent in such a decay process and take firm steps to tighten production. Their behavior of the last four years argues strongly against such a course. It is safer to argue that OPEC will need help from an expanding market to arrest the decay, and even then an adequate return to discipline is not assured. The strongest support for reversing the slide will come

partially from "backs-to-the-wall" OPEC cooperation, but most importantly from the demand/supply responses to the lower oil prices themselves. If OPEC discipline is irretreivably damaged at this point, and "every man for himself" prevails, then market-clearing somewhere below $15 should be expected. We would continue to assign relatively low odds to an abrupt collapse to this level in the next two years. OPEC has repeatedly demonstrated "crisis" discipline over the last few years. The problem has been that OPEC discipline has usually not been sustained past the immediate crisis. The new "continuous" nature of today's price decay presents OPEC with a more difficult challenge. Gathering the wagons in a circle to combat occasional pricing crisis is no longer an appropriate model. The attacks are no longer coming in rounds--it is now one unending attack. Nonetheless, we would look for intermittent rounds of OPEC discipline to result in price decay rather than abrupt collapse. Meanwhile, the steady slippage in price, both past and future, should be sowing the seeds for a price reversal, but probably not before the mid-1990's.

3
Short-Term Petroleum Outlook: Refiner and OPEC Behavior

William H. Brown, III, Kidder Peabody

Perspective

Since the historic OPEC official price reduction in March of 1983, intermittent speculation has suggested the probability of a total "collapse" in the price of internationally traded crude oil. An offical price reduction was terra incognita for the Organization, since every price movement had been upward due to two sustainable supply disruptions in the 1970's. Oil market behavior under a substantial surplus in productive capacity was a relative unknown. Price adjustments have been required over the last two and a half year period in order to recognize commercial realities; however, these price adjustments have been made without the market ever "collapsing".

Several "actors" critical to the short-term international petroleum cycle in an era of surplus capacity suggest that further adjustments, when required, will continue to be made over time, and yet the market is unlikely ever to "collapse". There are basically five steps to this cycle. Oil market psychology turns negative at any given point in time due to excess supplies on the market and a weakening in product prices if industry overestimates required days' supply of inventory. Refiner margins are squeezed, pressuring crude producers for an adjustment in price, but OPEC members still generally recognize the short-term price inelasticity of the petroleum market. As a result, no "collapse" occurs but rather incremental adjustments to raw material cost either officially or unofficially. Once crude prices are reduced, the fear of further price reductions leads to an accelerated inventory draw by refiners before and after the price adjustment in order to avoid holding devalued excess inventory. Lean inventories and a "hand-to-mouth" purchasing strategy by refiners cause prompt delivery product prices to rise, thus improving the downstream market. Thus, the short-term pressure on crude prices is eased, until the next cycle begins and oil market psychology once again turns negative, a reasonable probability given excess productive capacity.

Over the last two years, several factors within an overall excess capacity have distorted petroleum price relationships and promoted a negative psychology. One example was the U.K. coal strike, creating incremental heavy fuel oil demand by U.K. electric utilities, with excess gasoline supplies the byproduct result. The market effect was compounded moving into late 1984, as seasonal requirements by electric utilities rose in addition to the increment required by the UK electric utilities precisely when US gasoline demand declined on a seasonal basis.

Pressure on light crudes worldwide resulted in the reductions by the British National Oil Corporation, Nigeria and Norway. The OPEC meeting in December of 1984 called for an adjustment in differentials, with the net result a narrowing of the light-heavy relationship. Sheikh Yamani was adament in opposing a larger increase in heavy crude oil prices, exhibiting foresight as the UK coal strike ended in the spring of 1985. The timing of the end of the strike was less than fortuitous for the petroleum market, since it corresponded with weak manufacturing activity in the United States, depressed bunker fuel oil demand due to lower OPEC output compared to the previous year, as well as ongoing substitution for under-the-boiler usage by alternative fuels. These factors pressured the heavy end of the barrel, culminating in price reductions by Mexico and a modest downward revision in heavy grades at the July OPEC meetings, an action aimed less toward commercial viability than political compromise.

Within this overall volatile environment dollar movements (generally upward) have adversely affected international petroleum markets due to the impact of constraining international oil company refiner margins and increasing the effective local currency cost of crude oil. While improving the purchasing power of OPEC members, the strength of the dollar has done little to improve the overseas health of the refining industry, and further reductions in the dollar price of crude oil have been avoided simply by a greater "tolerance for loss" by foreign refiners.

OPEC Versus Refiner Behavior:

Structural Versus Cyclical Demand For The Residual Supplier

While the above briefly describes the events over the last two and a half years, a multitude of factors have explained the effective path of world crude oil prices. Our analyses take into account a number of variables; we do not purely view OPEC as a residual supplier and Saudi Arabia in turn as the altruistic swing producer to explain price movements. We have observed that other key variables helped determine stability or instability in the petroleum market on a short term basis such as: movements in the usable commercial or "discretionary" tier of inventory; final end-use consumption of petroleum products versus refinery runs; and petroleum product pricing versus crude values. A key to the behavior of the oil market over the last three years is to differentiate between the structural versus cyclical demand for OPEC crude oil.

The "structural" demand for OPEC crude is defined as the annual average "normalized" requirement after taking into account: final end-use consumption trends, adjusting for conservative/substitution and economic activity; non-OPEC crude oil production which, with certain exceptions tends to flow close to or at productive capacity; and stable inventory behavior. The "cyclical" demand for OPEC crude is defined as the quarter-by-quarter variations in OPEC output due to: seasonal fluctuations in demand; discretionary inventory movements; tanker logistics and the economic discrimination between short and long-haul crudes; and random turns in oil market psychology.

Although OPEC was established in 1960, throughout the bulk of its history it has not even attempted to function as a true cartel, contrary to such characterizations in the Western press. It is only in the last two years, due to the emergence of surplus productive capacity that OPEC members individually and collectively have sought to protect the revenue stream by establishing a system of individual "quotas" for members, within an overall "ceiling".

The purpose of the quota system was not an attempt to specifically "target" OPEC production levels on a quarter-by-quarter basis. Its pure function was to serve as an estimate of the structual or "normalized" requirement for OPEC crude oil in the context of a reasonable projection of final world oil demand versus non-OPEC supply. Even though the real and nominal price of crude has declined compared to the late

1970's there are substantial incentives to substitute less efficient under-the-boiler oil usage with alternative forms of energy. For non-OPEC oil producers the current price still may provide an adequate exploration incentive. Over the last two years however, forward price expectations have been extremely low, and thus industry has accelerated development work to produce non-OPEC supplies at, or perhaps greater than, a maximum efficient rate in order to maximize the present value of estimated recoverable reserves.

Serving in this function, the "ceilings" established by OPEC have actually served as a reasonable proxy for reality. When the ceiling was 17.5 million barrels per day, the actual annual average OPEC crude output in 1984 deviated less than 100,000 barrels per day (BD). In late 1984, OPEC established a ceiling of only 16.0 million BD and while we believe the actual 1985 average production level will be somewhat lower, OPEC still has recognized the general order of magnitude of the anticipated structual change in the demand for its crude.

Within these normalized targets, however, OPEC has had to deal with the realities of quarterly fluctuations in offtake due to: refiner requirements, who have attempted to hit a "moving" target in terms of demand and required inventory; market psychology which, due to general excess availability, is more critical than in the past; and the influence of the oil trading and futures community. From the refiners' standpoint, the key is the usable commercial tier of inventory which is the smallest in absolute volume of the inventory tiers and yet fluctuates the most in terms of days' supply. The days' supply of these stocks interfaces with short-term final demand expectations, which are a function of anticipated weather, economic activity, and individual company market share as opposed to conservation/substitution, more of a structural demand variable. This interface of inventory and demand is necessarily coupled with future price expectations which, depending on market psychology, can either be substantially lower or even marginally higher on a short-term basis. These factors have a multiplier impact on stock movements and OPEC production, since the fear of a price collapse delays any stock building and forces the refiner into the strategy of lean inventories and hand-to-mouth purchasing practices. The fear of price collapse can, in and of itself, promote a positive turn in the marketplace since this strategy necessarily places a premium on short-term physical availability. This cyclical behavior results in a residual, quarterly and geographically segmented demand for OPEC crude oil, which according to a close analysis of data, suggest that Saudi Arabia never has nor never will serve as the pure swing supplier within the Organization. Preferential crude availability, depending on tanker transit time (short-haul crudes) or refiner requirements has placed a number of OPEC members in the "swing" supplier role.

Further complicating the international petroleum market in addition to the "OPEC/Refiner Interface" is the influence of the oil trading community and the emergence of futures markets, both of which ensure short-term volatility in petroleum product prices and a greater influence of psychology. The trading community is generally unconcerned with the absolute price level of either crude and products, but only the short term spreads between and among the two. Futures markets in turn are considered by some to be the new price determinate in world trade rather than OPEC. This latter assumption is faulted by the facts that OPEC has never set prices in the past but tended to follow market reality, and that futures markets have never accurately forecast oil prices. Current futures prices reflect the extreme short-term physical state of the petroleum market whereas forward prices merely reflect futures market "sentiment" at any given point in time.

A Quantification

As discussed above the usable commercial or discretionary tier of inventory is a substantial influence on the quarterly movements in OPEC production and price expectations. Although currently smallest in terms of total volume within the three tiers of inventory (the other two being the minimum operating volume required to keep the system in operation, and the strategic/compulsory volume of stocks held by companies and governments), in the second quarter of 1981 the usable commerical volume was an estimated 1.1 billion barrels, or 25 days of forward cover. This compared to a minimum operating volume of 3.4 billion and a strategic/compulsory volume of only 900 million barrels. Due to the attempt by industry to hit the "moving target" of progressively lower oil demand, there has been a concerted effort to reduce this usable commercial tier (built up in anticipation of the effects of the Iran-Iraq War) down to a more reasonable level. As inventories are based on anticipated demand and structual oil demand continued to fall below industry expectations, four years were required to bring the discretionary tier of inventory to the "reasonable" levels at present. Since quarter-by-quarter demand expectations have fluctuated and differed between companies, the downward adjustment in days' supply has been less than smooth. This has caused, in conjunction with intermittant turns in oil market psychology, a less-than-smooth adjustment in effective world crude prices. By the end of 1983, the usable commercial tier of inventory had reached an approximate 9 days level of forward cover. At that point in time we estimate that the total usable commercial volume was about 400 million barrels, substantially lower than the strategic/compulsory volume which had continued to be built up largely influenced by the US Strategic Petroleum Reserve. The days' supply hovered between the 8 to 10 days level until 1985, when extreme negative psychology pervaded oil markets once again. The downward trend in day's supply was interrupted in the second quarter of 1984, when the tanker war between Iran and Iraq escalated. A current standard input to our short-term petroleum outlook is a conservative 6 day usable commerical tier of inventory, exceeding by only one day the historic low reached immediately after the Iranian Revolution.

The price quantification of this cyclical inventory behavior can be illustrated by a cracking margin for West Texas Intermediate crude at Houston which traced short-term fluctuations in oil market psychology and the discretionary stock tier movement. Immediately preceeding the March 1983 OPEC price reduction, the WTI gross margin had declined to a -$1.50 per barrel. Following the official price decision, the margin improved through September, reaching a peak of almost +$2.40 per barrel. The temptation to produce and run and the incremental barrel was too great, however, as excess availability on world oil markets interfaced with a less-than-robust seasonal swing in demand causing the margin to collapse once again by December of 1983 to almost -$1.00 per barrel. Saving the margin on a short-term basis in early 1984 was the extreme cold weather that affected both refinery output in the US Gulf Coast as well as end-use requirements in the Northeast.

Following the end of the cold spell, however, excess availability caught up to the market. Ample supplies in conjunction with the the Saudi-Boeing barter deal (in spite of the increased tanker attacks in the Persian Gulf) and the UK coal strike which produced excess gasoline thus harming the premium end of the barrel, resulted in a continual erosion in refining margins, reaching a low of -$2.00 per barrel in December of 1984. In the US market in particular, thereafter, gasoline stocks were withdrawn on a contraseasonable basis in an effort to reestablish some equilibrium to the gasoline market; this factor combined with constrained refinery runs and the eventual end of the UK coal strike improved refining margins to near records levels in the second quarter of this year, thus easing short-term concerns of the future raw material cost.

Within this context of continued margin volatility, refiner perception, and the behavior of the usable commercial tier of inventory was the quarterly cyclicality in OPEC requirments. Particular commercial preferences as well as an overall depressed structual level of OPEC requirements has more geographically segregated world crude flows. Persian Gulf crudes have tended to flow to East of Suez markets, while crudes such as Nigerian have tended to remain competitive with other non-OPEC short-haul output such as the North Sea in its natural Atlantic Basin market. One fundamental reason is that lower structual oil demand and low future price expectations have relegated long-haul Gulf crudes to the barrel of last resort in the Western Hemisphere, while serving more as a baseload crude in the Far East due to lower availability of short-haul alternatives. This fact defies the conventional wisdom that Saudi Arabia has continued to accept the role as the pure swing supplier within OPEC and that market stability is due exclusively to Saudi "altruism". Production data on a quarterly basis for OPEC does not support this premise. The data reveal that a number of OPEC countries on an short-term basis have shared prorata general offtake levels. Several times in the last two and a half years, while Saudi Arabia has maintained a roughly 20-25% market share within OPEC other members, including those most revenue-constrained such as Nigeria, also have seen their production vary according to requirements in their respective geographical markets. Over the last two and a half years for example, Nigerian market share has fluctuated with approximately the same standard deviation as Saudi Arabian.

Geographical segregation, most OPEC members sharing on a quarterly basis refiner offtake, market psychology and the patterns of the usable commercial tier of inventory, indicates that a multitude of actors has promoted either price stability or instability. This behavior lies within a context of an overall downward trend over the last two years in the structual demand for OPEC crude oil.

Outlook

Recent OPEC meetings have been characterized by attempting to handle quarterly cyclical variations in OPEC production, which is more commonly referred to as "quota cheating." There is likely little method by which OPEC can regimentally handle the short-term fluctuations in requirements for its crude other than a monitoring of production levels. OPEC should still attempt to provide a rough framework of market expectations based on an annualized structual demand for its crude oil. This framework, if approached in a reasonable manner, should help prevent a general "collapse" in crude oil prices as the variables outlined above influence the system and the short-term cycle.

Over the next two years we believe the structural demand for OPEC crude oil will tend to rise modestly from its 1985 average. Non-communist world oil demand is expected to rise marginally, some 400,000 BD in 1986. Factors influencing this outlook will be higher bunker demand and the lack of estimated secondary and tertiary stock withdrawals that we believe occured in 1985 due to expectations for oil market "collapse". As an example, the distributor tier of inventory of heating oil in West Germany is substantial, generally equal to or exceeding primary stock capacity. In mid-1985 due to expectations of oil market collapse, dissecting demand data suggests that there was in fact a substantial withdrawal at the secondary level of inventory in Germany and other European countries, thus understating to a certain extent final oil "burn". The secondary and tertiary stock movements are a substantial influence on reported demand figures and thus should be taken into account when forecasting from current trends. Bunker consumption should rise due to the final stability in output from certain short-haul crude areas such as the North Sea. Even though North Sea production is expected to peak in early 1986, we believe that total non-OPEC production will rise due to increments from Colombia, North Yemen, Egypt, and selected other non-OPEC LDC's. The single most influential factor in terms of OPEC requirements, however, will be what we believe to be a lack of a net 400,000 BD stock draw that occured in 1985.

The dilemma for analysts is to take such a two dimensional supply and demand matrix and convert it into an expected price path. Official prices have tended to mean less in terms of representing the effective cost of crude oil traded. Due to complex countertrade, netback, and other pricing mechanisms, it is extremely difficult to ascertain the effective average world price of crude oil. As a result, we have attempted to forecast not official crude prices but monthly spot crude oil prices for such benchmarks as North Sea Brent through a proprietary model. Although there is a speculative trading element which can influence the price on an short-term basis, we have contructed a model using exogenous production variables from our supply/demand matrix which provides as an explicit output a monthly pattern of Brent spot prices. Thus far in 1985, the model has successfully called three critical turning points: The first was the weakening in spot prices in springtime due to our expectations of rising North Sea production versus rising Nigerian capacity utilization. The next was the bottoming out of spot prices in the early summer months due to the influence of North Sea production downtime for platform maintenance. These maintenance programs as well as a hand-to-mouth inventory pattern suggested to us that, thirdly, spot prices would rally for the months of August and September.

Thereafter, we believed that spot prices peaked and were due for a modest erosion through the end of 1985, contrary to the conventional wisdom that oil prices tend to firm in the seasonal peak demand months. Seasonal swings in non-communist world oil demand are less pronounced compared to historical experience due to the continued displacement of under-the-boiler heating usage of oil by alternative energy sources. A more modest upward seasonal swing in oil demand, coupled with incremental light crude availability as North Sea platform maintenance programs ended suggested that supply was more than adequate to meet expected seasonal demand. As a result, this interface projected a path of weakening spot prices through the end of 1985 and early 1986.

Although the structual demand for OPEC crude oil remains relatively weak, we believe a multitude of variables on the international petroleum market as quantified by our spot price forecasting model suggest to us that the international petroleum market is not due for a collapse in world crude oil prices but a modest further erosion followed by some stability in mid-1986. Although inventories will tend to be a factor, we have continued to assume that the usable commercial tier of inventory will be maintained as 6 days of forward cover. Since we expect that structual demand for OPEC crude will bottom out, there will be less pressure on general crude oil prices due to refiners' attempts to adjust inventories to hit a moving target of expected intermediate-term demand.

As a final sensitivity of oil market expectations, we have attempted to periodically quantify our estimative effect of a substantial weakening in manufacturing activity in the United States and elsewhere on the world price of crude oil and OPEC requirements. Since manufacturing activity remained relatively depressed throughout most of the summer months of 1985, we believe the oil market has already experienced to a degree behavior in this type of environment. As demand weakened seasonally, it is was not offset by more robust rail and truck traffic and other indicators of manufacturing activity which would help support continued modest improvements in global oil consumption. As industry recognized this pattern, cyclical demand for OPEC crude oil remained depressed, compounded by the downward adjustment of discretionary inventory levels to meet a lower expected demand. Throughout the summer months the weak manufacturing activity in the face of substantially higher non-OPEC production still did not result in a general oil market "collapse". If, like the 1974-75 recession, negative movements in manufacturing activity are still to come in the winter ahead, there could be sufficient seasonal improvement in world oil demand to counter the depressed economically-driven requirements for petroleum.

Thus, based on our expectations of the structual demand for OPEC crude oil, the likelihood of a substantial decline in international crude oil prices is less than periodically expressed in the general press. While the petroleum market will exist in a state of general fragility over the next several years, we believe increments in non-OPEC output will tend to be smaller, since a number of fields are producing at maximum capacity precisely in fear of oil price "collapse". As a result, later on in the decade we still anticipate a modest rise in the structual demand for OPEC crude, which in the interim, will still be influenced by a multitude of cyclical, short-term variables.

4

The Impact of a Dollar Decline on the U.S. Economy and Energy Industries

Mary L. Barcella, Bruce B. Henning,
American Gas Association

INTRODUCTION

The increase in the exchange value of the dollar over the past several years has exerted a strong negative influence on the U.S. economy, releasing a flood of imports into the United States, eroding the market share of many domestic industries, and placing U.S. exports at a severe competitive disadvantage. Many of the industries hardest hit by the rising dollar have been major energy users. These include the agriculture, steel, petroleum and chemicals industries. Therefore, energy demand has been adversely affected by the rise in the dollar.

The dollar is widely recognized to be overvalued, and has already dropped significantly from its February 1985 peak. Its value is generally expected to continue to decline gradually over the next several years. For example, the Wharton Long-Term Forecast of March 1985 projected a decline of 30% in the annual average trade-weighted value of the dollar during the next five years. While a gradual decline in the dollar would gradually produce benefits to the U.S. economy and to the energy industries, a more rapid decline could prove even more beneficial. This paper evaluates the implications of a rapid decline in the dollar for the U.S. economy, the energy producing industries and energy consumers.

METHODOLOGY AND ASSUMPTIONS

The economic impacts of a dollar decline were estimated using the Wharton Econometric Forecasting Associates (WEFA) Long-Term Model.[1] The WEFA Long-Term Forecast of March 1985 was used as the baseline forecast against which changes in the dollar value were evaluated. The WEFA forecast assumes that the dollar will decline gradually over the next five years, reaching a level 30% below its 1985 peak by the year 1990 (see Table 1).

In order to assess the effects of a more rapid decline in the dollar, an alternative scenario was run using the WEFA forecast as a baseline. The alternative assumed that the dollar declines as much during 1985 and 1986 as the WEFA baseline assumed for the entire 1985-1990 period. In 1986, the dollar value index assumed by A.G.A. is 26% lower than the WEFA baseline assumption (see Table 1).

In this alternative scenario, the dollar decline was assumed not to have any significant adverse impact on U.S. interest rates in and of itself. The increased economic activity resulting from the dollar decline would be expected to put some upward pressure on interest rates, but no additional increase was exogenously assumed in this scenario. The sensitivity of the forecast results to this assumption was evaluated by running a second alternative scenario that assumed exogenously that the dollar decline resulted in a large increase in interest rates, due for example, to a sudden withdrawal of foreign capital from the U.S. as the result of an international crisis of confidence in U.S. financial institutions. The results of the sensitivity analysis indicated that the favorable impacts of a rapid dollar decline would outweigh the negative impacts of a sharp increase in interest rates. Output from

Table 1. Historical and Assumed Future Trade-Weighted Value of The Dollar[a] Under Various Scenarios (1972=100)

Historical Values		
1980	86.9	
1981	99.2	
1982	115.7	
1983	127.0	
1984	140.9	
Assumed Future Values	**WEFA Base Case[b]**	**A.G.A. Dollar Decline Scenario**
1985	162.1[c]	140.9[c]
1986	155.9	115.0
1987	142.5	110.0
1988	127.3	105.0
1989	117.6	100.0
1990	114.1	100.0

a. Annual average value of the dollar against seven major currencies, on a trade-weighted basis, converted to an index (1972=100).

b. Wharton Econometric Forecasting Associates, Long-Term Forecast (Philadelphia, March 1985).

c. As a point of reference, the index for the first quarter 1985 was approximately 165. The WEFA forecast therefore assumes a moderate decline through the remaining quarters of 1985, while the A.G.A. forecast assumes a very rapid decline.

the ten largest energy-consuming manufacturing industries would hardly be affected. As a result, the energy consumption projections were virtually identical for the two dollar decline scenarios evaluated.

Impacts on U.S. energy markets were projected by incorporating the results of the economic analysis into the A.G.A. Total Energy Resource Analysis (A.G.A.-TERA) Model.[2] By using the A.G.A.-TERA modeling system, a rigorous detailed analysis was accomplished for each of the energy consuming sectors of the economy.

The A.G.A.-TERA Base Case 1985-I (Arlington, VA: American Gas Association, February 12, 1985) was used as the baseline for this analysis. The Base Case simulation is intended to represent a "most probable" future base on existing laws, regulations, and current economic outlook. The assumptions underlying this forecast included the following:

1. Regulated natural gas wellhead prices were assumed to follow the NGPA schedule, except where NGPA ceiling prices were estimated to exceed the prevailing market clearing price. In those cases, the gas price was assumed to equal the prevailing market price. All deregulated natural gas was assumed to be priced at the prevailing market price.

2. Projected rates of economic growth and inflation were taken from the economic projections report in A.G.A.'s Five-Year Economic Outlook (Arlington, VA: American Gas Association, December 21, 1984).

Since the economic assumptions underlying the A.G.A.-TERA 1985-1 Base Case were similar but not identical to the WEFA baseline projection, the A.G.A.-TERA simulation of the dollar decline scenarios was conducted by adjusting the economic variables in the A.G.A.-TERA Base Case by the percentage change from the baseline forecast indicated by the Dollar Decline simulations. Specific macroeconomic variables input to the TERA model include real value added by manufacturing industries (at the 2-digit SIC level), real disposable personal income, employment in specific commercial industries, number of households, non-energy consumer expenditures, and inflation.

In this analysis, it was assumed that a change in the exchange rate does not affect the dollar price of world crude oil sold in the United States. Since world oil trade is conducted in U.S. dollars, a decline in the exchange rate would reduce the purchase value obtained by exporting nations for this oil. On the other hand, the price of oil bought by consuming nations other than the United States would decline in terms of their native currencies. Over the longer term, this would tend to increase world oil demand. Whether OPEC would react by sharply reducing prices and increasing sales in order to maintain a certain level of oil revenues in the short run or by maintaining current production levels while waiting for an eventual upturn in world oil demand is highly uncertain. A "middle of the road" assumption of no change in the dollar price of oil was therefore adopted for this analysis.

ECONOMIC EFFECTS OF A RAPID DOLLAR DECLINE

A rapid decline in the value of the dollar could have very beneficial effects for U.S. economic growth over the next few years. The simulation indicates that in the absence of adverse interest rate effects, a 30% decline in the dollar over the next two years could increase real GNP by more than $100 billion (constant 1972 dollars) by 1988, giving a cumulative GNP increase of $390 billion during 1985-1990 (see Table 2).

Table 2. Projected Impacts of A Rapid Dollar Decline on the U.S. Economy and Natural Gas Industry

	Peak Year Differential	Cumulative Differential 1985-1990
Real GNP (billion 1972 $)	$ 107	$ 390
Personal Consumption (billion 1972 $)	$ 52	$ 164
Fixed Investment, Total (billion 1972 $)	$ 16	$ 45
Net Exports (billion 1972 $)	$ 41	$ 152
Real Disposable Income Per Household (1972 $)	$ 309	$ 735
Employment (million jobs)	4.7	4.7
Inflation (% change, GNP Deflator)	3.4	-
Federal Budget Deficit Reduction (billion nominal $)	$ 96.2	$304.6

Initially, the greatest impact would be on the trade balance, as a decline in the dollar made U.S. goods and services more attractive relative to foreign products. Real exports would exceed imports by 1986 with a sharp dollar decline. Without such a decline, real exports are projected to be lower than imports through the next five years.

While the higher cost of imports would cause consumers to curtail their expenditures temporarily under a rapid dollar decline, they would gradually substitute more U.S. products for imports. With faster income growth, consumers would spend $52 billion (constant 1972 dollars) more by 1989 than in the Baseline projection and $164 billion more cumulatively during 1985-1990.

Faster economic growth in the Dollar Decline Scenario would have additional benefits. The growth in world demand for U.S. products would lead to greater investment. Real disposable income per household would be $309 higher by 1990 (constant 1972 dollars) -- equivalent to $721 in today's dollars. More than four million additional jobs would be created by 1988 due to the revitalization of U.S. manufacturing.

On the negative side, the increased price of imports would drive the overall inflation rate to 7.5% by 1989, more than 3 points higher than the inflation rate that would be expected with a more gradual decline (assuming that the monetary authorities take no unusual steps to counteract the higher inflation).

Finally, the faster growth rate and higher incomes would generate more tax revenues, reducing cumulative federal budget deficits by nearly $305 billion over the 1985-1990 time frame.

The primary force behind this improved economic performance would be the increased output from U.S. manufacturing industries, which have borne the brunt of the high dollar value for several years. A fast dollar decline would increase real manufacturing output by $183 billion (constant 1972 dollars) cumulatively over the 1985-1990 period (see Table 3), accounting for nearly half of the increase in total GNP during most of this period. The primary metals, transportation equipment and

Table 3. Projected Impact of a Dollar Decline on Manufacturing Output (billion 1972 dollars)

	Peak Year Differential	Cumulative Differential 1985-1990
Total Manufacturing	$ 51.4	$ 183.0
Lumber	1.8	4.7
Stone, Clay, Glass	1.3	4.3
Primary Metals	6.8	24.3
Fabricated Metals	3.4	11.5
Transportation Equipment	10.1	31.9
Food	2.1	8.0
Paper	2.3	8.7
Chemicals	4.0	15.0
Petroleum Refining	0.6	2.3

chemicals industries would particularly benefit. Production of primary metals could be nearly $7 billion greater (constant 1972 dollars) by 1987 under a Dollar Decline scenario. This would represent an improvement of almost 40% over the Baseline forecast. In the transportation industry, peak year real output would be $10 billion (16.6%) greater under a Dollar Decline Scenario, and peak-year real chemical output would be $4 billion (11%) higher, in constant 1972 dollars.

ENERGY IMPACTS OF A RAPID DOLLAR DECLINE

The stimulation to the U.S. economy resulting from a lower value of the dollar in the Dollar Decline Scenario would cause an increase in energy consumption above Base Case levels in all years in this decade. Projected increases in energy consumption range from 0.84 quadrillion Btus (quads) in 1985 to 4.92 quads in 1988 or between 1.1% and 6.3% above Base Case energy consumption levels. The cumulative projected increase over the 1985 to 1990 period is more than 18 quads (see Table 4).

Consumption of all fuels would increase with the dollar decline. Of the total cumulative increase in energy consumption, 34% is projected to take the form of increased natural gas consumption, 28% increased coal use, 19% increased hydro and nuclear consumption, and 16% increased oil use. However, the projected market shares for each energy type, presented in Table 5, do not change a great deal between the two scenarios, since no change in the relative prices of different energy types was anticipated to result from the dollar decline. The minor changes in market share that are projected result from the patterns of economic stimulation provided by the decline in the dollar.

The major impact of the dollar decline would fall on the industrial sector, where cumulative energy consumption would increase by an estimated 13 quads, accounting for more than 72% of the total increase in energy consumption (see Table 6). In this sector, the market share of coal is projected to increase significantly, since the industries that would benefit most from a rapid dollar decline (e.g., primary metals, fabricated metals, and transportation equipment) are characterized by large steam demands from boilers, where most non-metallurgical coal use occurs.

The increase in industrial energy use would be larger in percentage terms than the increase

Table 4. Projected U.S. Total Energy Consumption Impacts by Fuel Type (Quadrillion Btus)

	Peak Year Differential	Cumulative Differential 1985-1990
Natural Gas	1.70	6.37
Petroleum[a]	0.83	3.02
Coal	1.59	5.15
Hydro and Nuclear	0.83	3.54
Total Primary Energy Demand[b]	4.92	18.12
Electricity[c]	0.72	2.11

a. Petroleum differential may be underestimated due to differences in gasoline consumption not calculated in A.G.A.-TERA.

b. Total Primary Energy Demand excludes net direct end use of electricity since the energy used to create this electricity is included as power plant demand. Individual fuels may not sum to totals due to rounding.

c. Net direct end use of electricity by consumer.

Table 5. Projected U.S. Energy Market Shares By Energy Type, 1988
(percent)

	Base Case	Dollar Decline
Residential		
Gas	54.5	54.9
Oil	15.6	15.4
Electricity	26.9	26.7
Other	3.0	2.9
Commercial		
Gas	39.6	40.4
Oil	29.9	29.6
Electriciy	28.4	28.0
Other	2.0	2.0
Industrial		
Gas	40.8	40.6
Oil	30.1	29.1
Coal	14.7	16.1
Electricity	14.3	14.2
Total Consumer Energy Demand[a]		
Gas	28.9	29.8
Oil	49.5	47.2
Electricity	13.8	13.9
Coal and Other	7.8	8.5

a. Fuel shares of final consumer demand. Excludes powerplant fuel demand and losses in electricity generation.

Table 6. Projected Total Energy Consumption Impacts By Sector (Quadrillion Btu)

	Peak Year Differential	Cumulative Differential 1985–1990
Residential	0.06	0.25
Commercial	0.23	0.62
Industrial	3.71	13.31
Power Plant[a]	1.03	3.79
Transportation & Other[b]	0.05	0.20
Total Consumption[c]	4.92	18.12

a. Power Plant consumption of primary energy is calculated as total consumption minus electricity sold.

b. Changes in the demand for transportation uses of gasoline are not calculated in this analysis.

c. Individual items may not sum to totals due to rounding.

in total manufacturing output (10.2% vs. 6.6% over 1985-1990) because of the pattern of changes in industrial growth. In other words, the dollar decline would disproportionately benefit the major energy consuming industries. These are the same industries which have been so negatively affected by the rise in the dollar over the past five years.

As a result, the energy/GNP ratio is projected to decline more slowly during the early years of the forecast in the Dollar Decline scenario than in the Baseline forecast (see Table 7). Nevertheless, by the end of the

Table 7. Projected Energy/GNP Ratio (Thousand Btu per 1972 $)

	Dollar Decline	Baseline
1985	44.3	44.0
1986	43.3	42.7
1987	43.0	42.6
1988	42.2	42.0
1989	40.8	40.9
1990	40.0	40.3

decade, a multiplier effect is expected to show results, by which the early growth in manufacturing output is transmitted to other, less energy-intensive industries. By 1990, the energy/GNP ratio for the Dollar Decline Scenario is projected to be slightly lower than that of the Baseline projection.

FOOTNOTES

1. Assumptions and simulations used for this analysis were prepared by the American Gas Association and do not represent the views of the Wharton Econometric Forecasting Associates, Philadelphia, Pa.

2. The A.G.A. - TERA system of computer models is a detailed long-run simulation of natural gas supply, transportation and markets. The model was developed and is maintained by the American Gas Association, under the guidance of a gas industry advisory committee. The Association is located in Arlington, Va.

5
Empirical Testing of the Rationality and Efficiency of the Crude Oil Market

Steven L. Green, **Vanderbilt University**
and The Federal Reserve Bank of Dallas
Knut A. Mork, **Vanderbilt University**

1. INTRODUCTION

How well do existing markets and institutions in the private sector convey proper signals for the production and allocation of crude oil? This question has important policy implications, because the argument for government intervention and regulation is stronger if the private sector does its job poorly. Drawing on techniques employed mainly in finance and macroeconomics, this paper describes empirical tests that will provide some indirect insight into how well crude oil markets function.

Since the publication of a famous paper by Fama (1970), economists have become increasingly interested in the dynamic efficiency of financial and other markets. A market is said to be dynamically efficient if the price in the market accurately reflects all available information that pertains to the value of the good in question. If a market is not efficient, "incorrect" price signals result in a misallocation of resources. This issue was first examined in the context of financial markets, with market efficiency implying that there can be no obvious bargains--i.e., securities with predictable abnormally high risk-adjusted yields. Market efficiency is a simple implication of investor rationality: an obvious bargain will be in great demand, and this demand will drive its price up until the implied return no longer is abnormally high. The testable restrictions implied by this theory have in fact received some support from the data for financial markets.

Macroeconomists soon incorporated the insights of the efficient markets literature into their models. The first application was to the modelling of expectations. In contrast to these conventional models that attributed expectations to some ad hoc rule of thumb, so-called rational expectations models--like that of Sargent and Wallace (1976)--assumed that agents base expectations on all available relevant information. The second application was to the treatment of long-term contracts in macroeconomic models--e.g., Fischer (1977). The rational-expectations approach viewed contracts as forward looking and thereby reflecting all available information about events likely to occur over the time periods they cover. If the spot market for a good is dynamically efficient, and if contracts are based on rational expectations, then contract prices should reflect expectations of future spot prices. Because the crude oil market is dominated by contracts, it is this aspect of the rational expectations/efficient markets idea that may be employed to provide some insight into how well crude oil markets function.

2. THE CRUDE OIL MARKET AND MARKET EFFICIENCY

For some time, oil-market analysts have been interested in the relationship between spot and contract prices for crude oil. Verleger (1982) hypothesized that the members of OPEC set their official (contract) prices in response to the movements in the spot market, with a lag. This view has been challenged by Bohi (1983), who considers the relationship between the two prices more as a correlation than a causal relationship.

The implications of assuming that oil market participants employ all available information in forming contracts may be detailed as follows. Let S_t denote the spot market price in period t, and let C_t denote the contract price for delivery in period t, where the agreement for delivery is made in period t-n, n > 0. Define the operator E_{t-n} as the rational expectation conditional on all information available in period t-n. Suppose that, as a simplification, we can assume that crude oil contracts are non-contingent agreements to trade a specified quantity at a given price. Now consider the relation between C_t and $E_{t-n}S_t$, i.e., the relation between the contract price and the expectation at the time the contract is signed of what the spot price will be at the time of delivery. Suppose $C_t > E_{t-n}S_t$. In this case, speculators would contract to sell at C_t in the hope of being able to buy at the lower spot price to fulfill the contract and therefore make a profit. This speculative activity would raise the supply of oil in the contract market and put downward pressure on C_t. Conversely, speculators would buy in the contract market if $C_t < E_{t-n}S_t$, and this would put upward pressure on C_t.

The opportunity for speculative profit will vanish if and only if

$$C_t = E_{t-n}S_t. \quad (1)$$

Equation (1) says that crude oil contracts are efficient and therefore reflect all available information regarding the value of crude oil at the time of delivery. Grossman and Haraf (1983) use a relation equivalent to (1) in testing the efficiency of contracts in the Japanese labor market.

The above argument relies on the presence of explicit speculation to drive C_t and $E_{t-n}S_t$ toward equality. Although the major oil companies should have the right incentives to engage in this activity, the presence of explicit speculation is not in fact crucial to the argument in support of relation (1). If $C_t > E_{t-n}S_t$, then actual ultimate users of crude oil should be reluctant to buy at the higher contract price, opting instead to take their chances in the spot market. This implies reduced demand for contract crude oil. Conversely, producers of crude oil should be reluctant to sell at C_t if $C_t < E_{t-n}S_t$, which will reduce supply in the contract market and put downward pressure on the contract price.

3. EMPIRICAL TESTS OF CRUDE OIL CONTRACT EFFICIENCY

The hypothesis of crude oil contract efficiency given by relation (1) above is easily embedded into a regression equation of the form

$$S_t = a_0 + a_1C_t + a_2X_{t-n} + e_t, \tag{2}$$

where S_t and C_t are defined above, X_{t-n} is a vector of variables of potential relevance in predicting oil prices, and e_t is a regression error term. Taking expectations of both sides of (2) conditionally on the information available at time t-n yields:

$$E_{t-n}S_t = a_0 + a_1C_t + a_2X_{t-n} + E_{t-n}e_t. \tag{3}$$

Here, $E_{t-1}a_0 = a_0$ follows from the fact that a_0 is constant and $E_{t-n}a_1C_t = a_1C_t$ and $E_{t-n}a_2X_{t-n} = a_2X_{t-n}$ follow from the fact that C_t and X_{t-n} are known in period t-n. Clearly, (3) is consistent with (1) only if (i) $a_1 = 1$, (ii) $a_0 = 0$, (iii) $a_2 = 0$, and (iv) $E_{t-n}e_t = 0$. Each of these conditions will now be considered in turn:

$a_1 = 1.$ (i)

This condition is necessary for the contract price to be an unbiased predictor of the spot price.

$a_0 = 0.$ (ii)

Provided $a_2 = 0$, this condition ensures the zero mean of the difference between the spot and the official price. This particular constraint may be unnecessarily strict, as discussed in the next section. Thus, a small violation of (ii) should be interpreted with caution. However, a large, significant value of a_0 may be interpreted as a violation of rationality.

$a_2 = 0.$ (iii)

This condition is essential. If information available at the time the contract price was determined could have helped improve predictions about the market-clearing price, then the parties to the contract must have wasted information. The formal analogy between this and similar constraints imposed in other rational-expectations models is obvious (see, for example, Hall, 1978).

e_t is "white noise," i.e., $E_{t-n}e_t = 0.$ (iv)

This constraint will be violated, for example, if the error term is serially correlated. It is closely related to (iii) in that, under serial correlation, lagged residuals could help predict the differential between the two prices. It is also of some independent importance. Since price differences spell arbitrage opportunities, they cannot persist in an efficient market. While we must allow for random mistakes, systematic persistence is incompatible with efficiency. The above arguments also imply, although not in an exact sense, that

$\text{var}(e_t)$ must be small. (v)

This implication follows from the argument that large price differentials should be closed quickly by speculation. Of course, this constraint cannot be tested rigorously. However, to some extent, it should be possible to judge whether or not the results are reasonable.

4. ALTERNATIVE HYPOTHESES

Any test of market efficiency is implicitly a joint test of market efficiency <u>and</u> of the validity of the structural model of the market employed for the test. The model we use of the oil market rests on several assumptions, both explicit and tacit, the violation of any one of which could result in the rejection of some or all of the above hypotheses. The first important assumption is that transactions costs are quantitatively unimportant. If they are of significance, then C_t must differ from $E_{t-n}S_t$ by a sufficient amount in order for speculation to become profitable. In this case, C_t could fluctuate relative to $E_{t-1}S_t$ by an amount that depends on the magnitude of transactions costs. Note, however, that if transactions costs are constant over time, then the wedge between C_t and $E_{t-1}S_t$ might also be constant. In this case, the hypothesis that $a_0 = 0$ in relation (3) may be rejected, but all the other hypotheses should hold.

The second implicit assumption employed above was that speculators are risk neutral and hence willing to take on risk with no compensation in the form of expected return. If, alternatively, speculators are risk averse, then $C_t > E_{t-n}S_t$ ($C_t < E_{t-n}S_t$) will be required to induce them to sell (buy) contract crude oil. If non-speculative demand and supply are not equal, then speculators must make up the difference, and risk averse speculators must be compensated in expected value terms to take such a position. Depending on the position speculators take, C_t can be greater or smaller than $E_{t-1}S_t$. If the risk premium--i.e., the wedge between C_t and $E_{t-1}S_t$--is constant over time, then, again, the hypothesis that $a_0 = 0$ in (2) might be rejected while all the other hypotheses should hold. In this case, speculators would be taking the same position over most (or all) of the sample period. Alternatively, the risk premium could vary over time, and if it is correlated with some member of the vector X_{t-n} in (2), then the hypothesis that $a_2 = 0$ could be rejected.

The speculation arguments in section 2 all assume that crude oil contracts are non-contingent agreements to trade a given amount at a specified price. While contracts in many markets do in fact take such a form, recent contracts in the world oil market have typically been little more than an agreement to trade. The difference between contract and spot transactions is that contract sales are made at the supplier's official price, perhaps with some modifications to evade OPEC rules. While the contract price may be changed by the supplier during the contract period, it changes infrequently and in a much more "orderly" fashion than the spot price.

This institutional structure has implications for the length of the lag n in the above mode. While it was referred to as the duration of the contract, it really reflects the time elapsed since the last reconsideration of the official price. Casual observation suggests that the length of this time has been variable over recent years. While the members of OPEC have announced price decisions at their regular meetings, extraordinary meetings have been held; and sometimes individual members have announced official price changes (or what amounted to official price changes) independently of OPEC. Finally, some producer countries are not members of OPEC.

While the appropriate value for n thus is both uncertain and variable, it would seem sufficient to make it large enough so that at the official price may have been reconsidered at least once during the last n periods. Such a specification will bias the results against a false rejection of the rationality hypothesis. Perhaps a six month lag would satisfy this criterion.

Each of the factors mentioned in this section could account for rejection of the hypothesis of crude oil market efficiency as embodied in the restrictions on equation (2). If such rejection does occur, then research into the reason for the apparent lack of market efficiency is in order. One simple technique, which may provide some insight into these issues, is to test for structural change by examining contract efficiency over various subperiods. This technique is indicated by the observation that the crude oil spot market has become larger, and thus, perhaps, more efficient, over time.

5. DATA REQUIREMENTS

The study obviously requires data for spot and official prices. The data sources used by Verleger and Bohi should be adequate. For the official prices, care must be taken to correct for surcharges and discounts, or else errors in the variables could bias the results. For the spot prices, a choice exists, at least for the most recent period, between crude-oil spot prices and spot values, derived from the spot prices of petroleum products. The spot value is attractive because the spot market for products has been better established and organized, at least until recently. On the other hand, the model presented in Section 3 incorporates the stochastic fluctuations in the spot market for crude oil. Actual spot prices for crude oil may thus correspond most closely to the model specification.

Daily price observations would, perhaps, be ideal. However, the improvements in the results are not likely to be worth the considerable effort involved in obtaining daily quotes. On the other hand, since the oil market has moved quickly at times, the observations should not be too far apart. Monthly observations would seem adequate. The estimation sample should, as usual, be as long as permitted by the availability of the data; but it may also be interesting to carry out the tests on subsamples of tight or slack market periods.

The vector X of lagged variables includes lagged spot and contract prices, but also other related variables, such as production, consumption, and inventory levels. Furthermore, it may be desirable to include general economic indicators, for which monthly data may not be available.

It may become necessary to estimate a quarterly version of the model for this purpose.

A specific grade or grades of crude oil must be chosen. Several alternatives are available. Arabian light is important as the OPEC market price, and it would be interesting to investigate the discrepancy that existed for some time between the official prices of this and similar grades. African light is also of interest because of the frequent and irregular changes in official prices. Finally, it might be interesting to study the market of oil from a non-OPEC member. Perhaps two or three grades should be studied.

6. CONCLUDING REMARKS

At the time of this writing, results of the tests described above are not yet available. A complete version of this paper including those results should be available from either author on request by the publication date of this proceedings volume.

Even in the absence of test results, it is useful to speculate on what they will be and how they should be interpreted. From casual reading of the data, we would, in fact, be highly surprised if the data fail to reject the restrictions placed on relation (2) by the notion of contract efficiency. If the failure to reject does occur, the conclusion must be reached that the crude oil market does appear to operate more efficiently than was apparent (to us) *a priori*.

If, as expected, the data do reject the restrictions, care must be taken in the drawing of conclusions. It may be the case that the relatively simplistic application of the efficient markets idea abstracts too greatly from institutional realities of the crude oil market. Rejection of the hypotheses should lead to further research--such as the split sample tests mentioned above--to isolate the cause of the rejection. If the cause or causes can be identified, then the workings of the contract oil market will be better understood. If they cannot be identified, then the ability of the market to convey appropriate price signals for production and allocation is called into question. This result should lead to research on the desirability and feasibility of government intervention and regulation.

REFERENCES

Bohi, D. R. (1983). "What Causes Oil Price Shocks?" Mimeographed, Resources for the Future (January).

Fama, E. F. (1970). "Efficient Capital Markets: A Review of Theory and Empirical Work." Journal of Finance, 25: 383-417.

Fischer, S. (1977). "Long-Term Contracts, Rational Expectations, and the Optimal Money Supply Rule." Journal of Political Economy, 85: 191-205.

Grossman, H. I. and W. S. Haraf (1983). "Shunto, Rational Expectations, and Output Growth in Japan." Working Paper, Brown University.

Hall, R. E. (1978). "Stochastic Implications of the LIfe Cycle - Permanent Income Hypothesis: Theory and Evidence." Journal of Political Economy, 86: 971-987.

Sargent, T. J. and N. Wallace. (1976). "Rational Expectations and the Theory of Monetary Policy." Journal of Monetary Economics, 2: 169-183.

Verleger, P. K. (1982). Oil Markets in Turmoil. Cambridge, MA: Ballinger.

6
Rational Expectations, Inventory Adjustments, and the Short-Run Dynamics of the World Oil Market

Knut A. Mork, Vanderbilt University
Steven L. Green, Vanderbilt University
and The Federal Reserve Bank of Dallas

1. INTRODUCTION

This paper seeks to contribute to the analysis of the short-run functioning of the world oil market. Inventory behavior in the presence of supply and demand shocks is a key element of the analysis.

The literature in this area has focused on the dramatic events in 1978-80. As the supply of Iranian oil was interrupted, spot prices rose dramatically. At the same time, worldwide demand for petroleum products increased, and oil companies scrambled to rebuild their low inventories.

Verleger (1982) has constructed an econometric model of the dynamics of this process. He assumes that refiners base their expectations about future prices on a geometrically distributed lag of past spot prices. He then finds that refiners' inventory behavior is destabilizing and argues for government intervention in the form of a steep, temporary tariff.

Bohi (1982) offers an alternative understanding by focusing on the apparent increase in demand by the final users of petroleum products. He conjectures that this increase was a result of hoarding because of the uncertain supply situation. However, he argues that the refiners mistook the temporary hoarding response for a permanent demand increase and started to add to inventories in order to accommodate the perceived larger volume of flows. Bohi regards this episode as an example of an expectations error, which cannot be expected to be repeated in the future, but not as an indication of irrational behavior or irrational expectations.

Badger and Belgrave (1982) argue that neither refiners nor the OECD governments understood at the time that the building of inventories was counterproductive for market stability. However, according to these authors, by the time of the outbreak of the Iran-Iraq war, they had learned their lessons. Then, inventories were drawn down, and a dramatic price escalation was avoided.

The rationality of oil company behavior and expectations is a key issue in this debate. Yet, to our knowledge, no attempt has yet been made to analyze the short-run functioning of the world oil market in the context of a rational-expectations model. This paper presents the results of such an attempt. Two results stand out. First, the rationality of expectations does not imply full and perfect knowledge about all the relevant facts at all times. In particular, a rational refiner may very well be confused as to whether a given change in demand is permanent or transitory. As a consequence, refiners tend to react to transitory demand increases as if they were partly permanent. Second, the rational-expectations model is very rich and can explain a wide range of responses under different circumstances. Even so, the assumption of rational expectations imposes empirically testable constraints.

2. THE MODEL

Our model of the short-run functioning of the oil market is derived from the rational-expectations model of the market for a single good analyzed by Muth (1961). We add three important features to Muth's model. First, we allow for stochastic disturbances on the demand side as well as the supply side. Second, to Muth's specification of speculative inventory holdings, we add a "transactions motive" to reflect the need for refiners to hold working inventories. Third, we allow for a richer specification of the dynamic behavior of the stochastic disturbances. The structural equations are as follows:

$$C_t = \beta p_t + v_t \quad (1a)$$

$$Q_t = \gamma E_{t-1} p_t + u_t \quad (1b)$$

$$I_t = kE_t C_{t+1} + \alpha(E_t p_{t+1} - p_t) \quad (1c)$$

$$Q_t = C_t + I_t - I_{t-1} \quad (1d)$$

The symbols are explained as follows. C_t is the demand for petroleum products, Q_t is the supply of crude oil, I_t is the level of inventories held by refiners, and p_t is the price of oil (or its natural logarithm). The operator E_t denotes expectations formed at time t. The variables u_t and v_t are stochastic disturbances that will be discussed further below.

The model does not distinguish between spot and contract prices or between the prices of crude oil and petroleum products. Furthermore, it ignores volume changes in the refining process, and it does not distinguish between inventories of crude oil and petroleum products. For the purpose at hand, these simplifications seem acceptable.

Demand and supply are written as deviations from their equilibrium values with zero disturbances. Otherwise, the interpretation of the demand equation is obvious. The supply function reflects a one-period production and transportation lag. The inventory equation consists of two parts. First, refiners want to hold "normal" inventories in proportion to their expected future deliveries in order to keep the system flowing smoothly. This is the transactions motive. Second, refiners hold inventories for speculative purposes in proportion to the expected change in prices. Discounting of the expected future price is ignored in the equation.

The demand equation is simplified in two ways. First, observable exogenous variables affecting oil demand (such as GNP) are ignored. Second, it ignores lagged adjustments to price changes. Finally, the modeling of supply is simplified by ignoring depletion and assuming the oil market is competitive.

The disturbance to supply, u_t, is assumed to follow an autoregressive process with an innovation term denoted e_t. The demand disturbance is assumed to be the sum of a permanent and a transitory component:

$$v_t = \sum_{i=0}^{\infty} \varepsilon_{t-i} + \eta_t \tag{2}$$

The model is driven by the three innovations e_t, ε_t, and η_t. These are all assumed to have zero means and constant variances over time (denoted σ_e^2, σ_ε^2, and σ_η^2, respectively), and to be uncorrelated with their own lagged values and those of the two other disturbances. We also assume that ε_t is uncorrelated with e_t and η_t; but we do allow for a contemporaneous correlation between e_t and η_t.

The rationale for this correlation is similar to the argument by Bohi referred to in the introduction. A negative supply shock may sometimes lead to hoarding by the final users, thus producing a transitory increase in demand. Ideally, this behavior should be modeled explicitly, and we may do so so at a later stage of our research. For the time being, in an attempt to keep the complexity of the model at a manageable level, we approximate by allowing for a correlation between e_t and η_t in the stochastic specification. The covariance, denoted $\sigma_{\eta e}$, is assumed to be negative.

3. CONFUSION OF PERMANENT AND TRANSITORY CHANGES IN DEMAND

In accordance with the theory of rational expectations, we assume that refiners know and understand the true model of the oil market, and that this model coincides with the one in equations (1) - (2). They are then able to infer the values of e_t and v_t from the observations of the endogenous variables. However, the model does not allow a refiner at time t to distinguish unambiguously between the permanent and the transitory components of v_t. If a demand shock occurs at the same time as a supply shock, the refiner is not completely without a clue, because a supply shock is a signal that at least part of the demand shock is transitory. Furthermore, in hindsight, it may be possible to tell which demand shocks were permanent and which were transitory. However, at the time, it is not possible to know for sure.

In this environment, refiners have to make educated guesses as to the likely duration of a given shock. These guesses are based on the past occurrences of permanent and transitory shocks (measured by their relative variances), the most recent supply innovation, and the covariance between the supply and demand shocks.

The predictions thus made are important for the refiners as well as for the market, becuase refiners need to make sure that their inventory levels are adequate to meet future demand. If a given increase in demand is believed to be permanent, refiners should add to their inventories in order to ensure the continued smooth flow of the system. If it is transitory, the optimal policy is likely to be a temporary drawdown. The possibility of error is obvious, even if the refiners act rationally.

The optimal prediction can be derived from the model. The problem can be formulated as predicting next period's disturbance given information about current and past disturbances. If the current disturbance is believed to be transitory, the prediction for next period should be zero. If it is believed to be permanent, the prediction should equal the most recent disturbance. Following Muth (1960), we derive the following formula:

$$E_{t-1}v_t = (1 - \mu)\sum_{i=1}^{\infty}\mu^{i-1}(v_{t-i} - \phi e_{t-i}). \quad (3)$$

Here, ϕ is the theoretical regression coefficient of η_t on e_t ($\phi = \sigma_{\eta e}/ \sigma_e^2$). The parameter μ is a monotonically increasing function of the ratio $(1 - r^2)\, \sigma_\eta^2/\sigma_\varepsilon^2$, where r is the correlation coefficient between η_t and e_t. The numerator of this expression may be interpreted as the variance in η_t that is not explained by e_t. If the ratio is zero or infinity, μ takes on the value zero or one, respectively. If it is positive, but finite, $0 < \mu < 1$. It is easy to see that the formula obeys the criteria just stated.

An Appendix available on request from the authors derives the quasi-reduced form solution for the model, where the price of oil and the level of inventories are expressed as moving averages of the indirecly observable disturbance terms v_t and e_t.

4. EXPLORATION OF INVENTORY AND PRICE BEHAVIOR DURING 1978-79.

It is useful to explore the predictions of the model for the dynamic responses of inventories and prices to supply- and demand shocks. While the discussion is valid for any shock, we are particularly concerned with the model's ability to reproduce the events of 1978-79, when a supply shock was accompanied by inventory buildups and a prolonged period of rising prices.

For an unanticipated reduction in oil supplies ($e_t <$ 0), the model predicts an immediate drawdown of inventories, followed by a gradual and monotonic increase until the original level is restored. This response is strengthened by the transitory increase in demand that can be predicted from the supply side. Since this response is known to be transitory, it causes no complications. However, as long as the correlation between the two types of shocks is less than perfect, the actual demand disturbance may deviate from what can be predicted from the supply shock. The deviation may go either way. As an example, intended to parallel the events of 1978-79, we consider the case where the increase in demand is larger than what could be predicted from the supply shock. The oil refineries then have to determine the extent to which they should treat the unexpected demand increase as permanent or transitory. According to the argument made in Section 3, they treat it as part transitory, part permanent.

Figure 1 illustrates the implications of the model for the case of an unexpected demand increase of 100 mmb per month. The demand increase is assumed to be transitory, although this information is not available to the refiners at the time. The example assumes $k = 3$ (a working inventory of 3 months' supply), $\beta = 0$, $\gamma = 500$, and $\alpha = 1{,}000$. The quantity variables are assumed to be in units of mmb/month, while prices are in logs.

Regardless of the value of μ, the immediate inventory response is a drawdown of the same magnitude as the shock. This result follows directly from the lag on the supply side and the zero demand elasticity. However, the

Figure 1

Inventory Behavior After Demand Shock

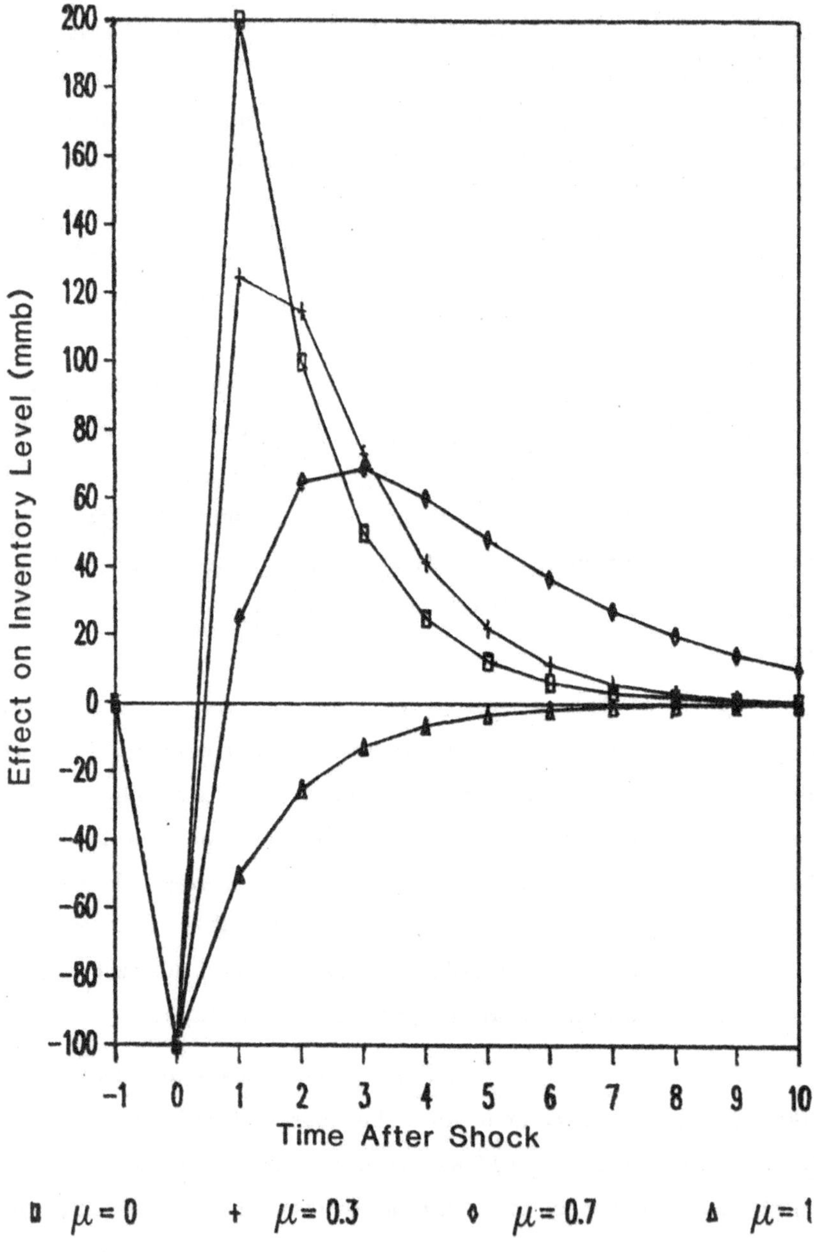

pattern in the following months depends crucially on how likely it is that the perceived demand increase is permanent or transitory, as reflected in the value of μ.

The simplest case occurs when it is known that all shocks are transitory, so that $\mu = 1$. Then, the inventories are rebuilt gradually after the initial drawdown, until the original level is restored. At the other extreme, if all shocks are believed to be permanent ($\mu = 0$), the initial drawdown is followed by an even larger buildup, so that inventories exceed their original levels by twice the amount of the demand increase. However, over time, as it becomes apparent that the demand increase does not in fact persist, inventories will be reduced gradually back to their original levels. Interestingly, all of the intermediate cases show the same "overshooting" of inventory levels. As long as there is <u>some</u> probability that a given shock may be permanent, that shock sets off a dynamic response which eventually will ensure the appropriate increase in working inventories in case it <u>is</u> permanent.

The implications for prices are shown in figure 2. Immediately, the price increases for any value of μ, since the inventory drawdown needed to clear the market will not take place unless the refiners face the right incentives. If all shocks are believed to be transitory ($\mu = 1$), the immediate price increase is followed by a gradual return to the original price level. This result is to be expected, as the gradual refilling of inventories leads to a positive, though declining pressure on prices compared to their original levels.

Figure 2

Price Behavior after Demand Shock

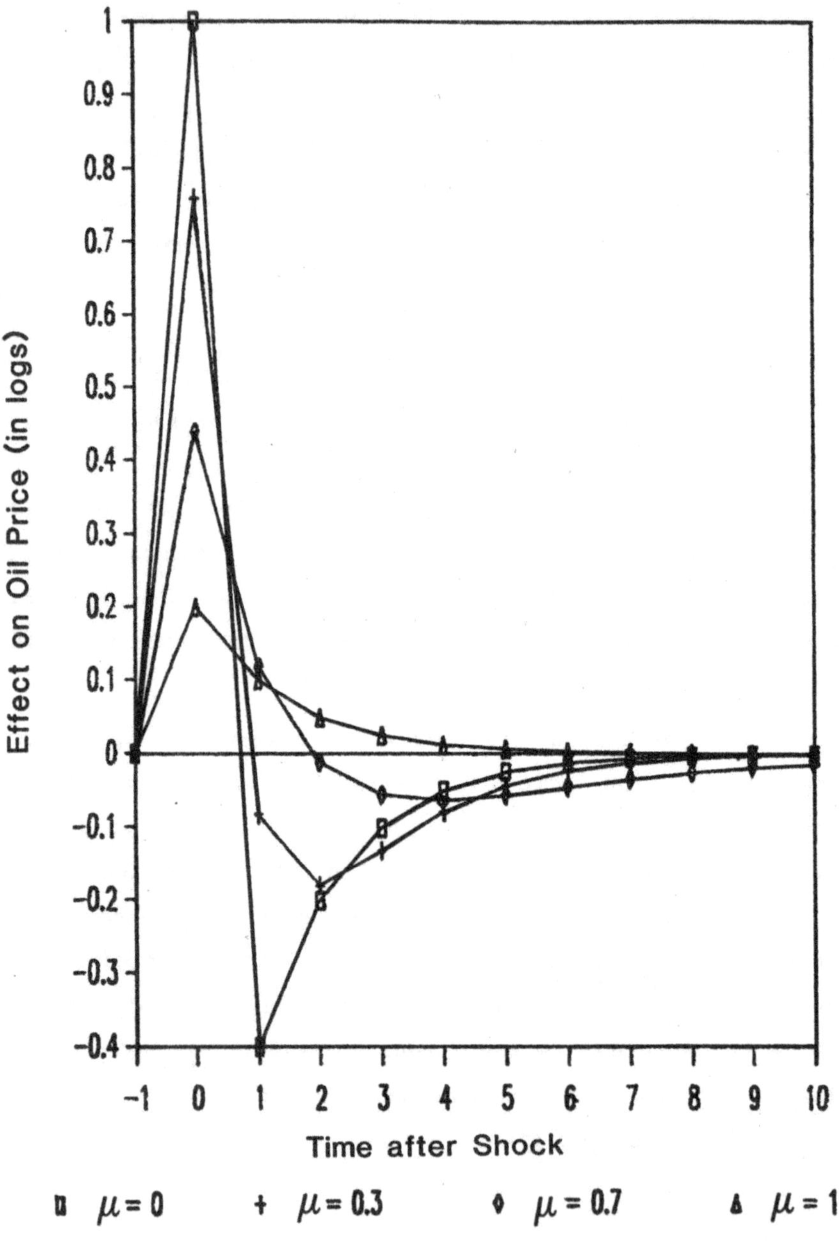

If there is a possibility that the shock may be permanent, inventories will be raised above their original levels at some point. This buildup creates a demand pressure that is strong enough to maintain the price above its original level in some cases. However, in this model, it is not strong enough to produce a rising price path over time. There are two reasons for this. First, supply rises as well as demand in response to expectations about potentially permanently higher demand levels. Second, the confusion about the duration of the damand shock leads to a chronic overprediction of the price level. Since supply responds to the expected rather than the actual price, this effect enhances the price-softening effect from the supply side.

It seems quite possible, however, that a slightly extended model could produce a quite different price path. In particular, consider a model where the unexpected demand response lasts for more than one period while still being temporary. As in the above model, refiners would start building up inventories in response to such a disturbance. Furthermore, in the extended model, this buildup would take place at the same time as the surge in final demand. During this time, we would expect to observe a substantial escalation of prices.

Such an extension of the model would not involve any new principles, although it would complicate the algebra. Rather than pursuing it, the next section explores ways to implement rational-expectations models empirically.

5. TOWARDS AN EMPIRICAL IMPLEMENTATION

Equations (1a) - (1d) in principle describe a class of models. The various members of the class are distinguished by the specification of the stochastic processes driving the exogenous variables u and v. The empirical test of any member of this class is a test of the validity of the stochastic processes as well as the structural model itself.

Hansen and Sargent (1980) outline a general methodology for formulating and estimating dynamic linear rational-expectations models. Sargent (1978) applies this methodology to estimation of labor-demand schedules. In principle, it can be applied to the class of oil-market models defined by (1a) - (1d). However, such an application will have to deal with two difficult problems, one theoretical and one empirical.

The theoretical problem involves derivation of an estimable system of observable variables. In general, all relevant variants of the model (1a) - (1d) can be solved as infinite-order vector autoregressive processes or infinite-order vector moving-average processes in the observable variables. The challenge is to specify the conditions under which they may be written as finite-order processes, which can be estimated. An example of such a dimension reduction is presented by Hansen and Sargent (1980:13-16).

The empirical problem involves isolating the vector of observable variables that are useful in predicting u and v. This exercise is important because the theory implies that rational agents use all available information when forming expectations. A procedure for isolating this vector has been developed by Hansen and Sargent (1980: 21-25).

6. CONCLUSIONS

We have explored the use of rational-expectations models for analysis of the short-run functioning of the world oil market. The results are highly suggestive. First, the use of such models seems appropriate because the participants in this market are well-informed professionals who bet their own money on the predictions they make. Second, the hypothesis that these participants sometimes behave erratically, as has been claimed in the debate about the events of 1978-79, can only be tested within the context of a rational-expectations model. Erratic behavior should lead to the empirical rejection of any such model. Third, the implications of the model are both reasonable and appealing. In particular, the model seems well capable of explaining the apparently puzzling inventory behavior of the 1978-79 period.

REFERENCES:

Badger, D. and R. Belgrave (1982). "Oil Supply and Price: What Went Right in 1980?" London: Policy Studies Institute.

Bohi, D. R. (1983). "What Causes Oil Price Shocks?" Mimeographed, Resources for the Future (January).

Hansen, L. P. and T. J. Sargent (1980). "Formulating and Estimating Dynamic Linear Rational Expectations Models." Journal of Economic Dynamics and Control 2: 7-46 (February).

Muth, J. F. (1960). "Optimal Properties of Exponentially Weighted Forecasts." Journal of the American Statistical Association 55(290).

____________ (1961). "Rational Expectations and the Theory of Price Movements." Econometrica 29(6).

Sargent, T. J. (1978). "Estimation of Dynamic Labor Demand Schedules Under Rational Expectations." Journal of Political Economy 86: 1009-1044 (December).

Verleger, P. K., Jr. (1982). Oil Markets in Turmoil, Cambridge, MA: Ballinger.

7
The Costs and Benefits of a Gasoline Tariff

Roy Boyd, U.S. Federal Trade Commission[1]
Carol A. Dahl, Louisiana State University

INTRODUCTION

The past several years have witnessed a marked growth in the refining capacity of many foreign crude petroleum suppliers. The completion of Saudi Arabia's Yanbu refinery in 1984 was only the latest in a series of moves by producers in the Mideast and South America to invest in their energy sector. Continued expansion and increased refined product exports by these countries are expected well into the 1990's with the largest share of these products sent to the world's developed countries.

The possibility of increased U.S. imports of refined petroleum products occurs at a time when various unrelated factors have been causing significant changes in the U.S. refinery industry. Decreases in overall demand for gasoline and other refined petroleum products in the United States have led to over 100 plant closings and significant employee layoffs since 1981. In light of such developments, independent refineries and large integrated oil companies alike have sought some sort of government protection from foreign competition. The suggestion has been made to increase the tariff on gasoline from $0.025 per gallon to $0.10 per gallon. Given the growing concern and emotional response to foreign encroachment on the U.S. refinery industry, such proposals are likely to receive substantial attention and heated debate. To date, however, no quantitative analyses have measured the potential costs and benefits of such an action. Therefore, careful quantitative analysis should prove highly valuable in any such debate.

In our quantitative analysis we first briefly review the current problems of the U.S. industry and the expansion of foreign refinery operations. Second, we present our model of the refined petroleum sector and use it to measure losses from a gasoline tariff. Third, we measure the value of employment gains from such a tariff. We conclude by comparing the costs of these employments gains with their benefits and find that their costs to both consumers and to society as a whole are quite substantial.

OIL REFINING: U.S. PROBLEMS AND FOREIGN EXPANSION

The past five years have witnessed a drastic curtailment in U.S. demand for petroleum products. During that time aggregate demand for fuel oils declined by 296 million barrels. Gasoline consumption also decreased, and even though it rebounded slightly in 1983 to 2.5 billion barrels, it remained 300 million barrels short of its pre-74 level. Not surprisingly, since 1981 the U.S. refinery industry has had 104 closings, trimming aggregate capacity by more than one-sixth to 16,074,000 barrels per day. U.S. refineries are currently running at 75 percent of capacity, and it is estimated that they will not achieve desirable returns until operating rates rise to 85-90 percent and aggregate capacity is trimmed by another 1.5 to 2 million barrels per day. (Oil and Gas Journal 11/19/84, p. 44)

In the past, closings have generally involved independent refineries and small 'tea kettle' operations resulting from advantages under the U.S. entitlement program. Many recent closings, however, have involved the majors and have resulted in a significant loss of employment. In September 1984, for example, Texaco announced a halving of its Port Arthur, Texas plant, causing a loss in capacity of 100,000 barrels per day and a lay-off of over 1,400 employees.

In addition to these demand related problems, U.S. refineries now face the prospect of new competition from overseas. This new threat does not come from traditional rivals in the OECD countries, but rather from the third world oil producers themselves. As shown in table 1, refinery capacity among third world producers in the Middle East and South America has climbed steadily since the beginning of the decade. Furthermore, planned increases in refinery capacity indicate that this trend should continue unabated to the end of this decade and well into the next. These projections indicate that by 1990, third world oil producers will increase their refining capacity by 1,896,000 barrels per day.

Downstream processing capacity is favored by these nations for a number of reasons. Other investment opportunities tend to be more limited. The hydrocarbon sector can be more easily segregated from other sectors of the economy allowing more gradual transition. Further, these highly visible projects will not tend to contribute to domestic inflation. (Fesharaki and Isaak 1982)

The latest tangible results of these Middle Eastern efforts are the two newly-opened Saudi Arabian refineries at Yanbu and Jubail. Each of these plants has a refining capacity of 250,000 barrels per day and employs the latest in hydrocracking technology. Each cost approximately 1.4 billion dollars to construct, and each is a joint venture undertaken by the state-owned Petromin Company and large Western oil firms. Although the construction cost of

Table 1 New Foreign Capacity
(1000 of barrels per day)

	Country	Capacity Increase 1980-1984	Total Capacity by 1988
1	Saudi Arabia	200	825
2	Libya	0	220
3	UAE	0	170
4	Kuwait	0	156
5	Mexico	0	350
6	Nigeria	87	100
7	Brazil	96	55
	Total	383	1,876

Sources: Oil and Gas Journal, December 26, 1983, October 29, 1984, and March 4, 1985

refineries in the Gulf is about one third more than the cost of comparable facilities in the U.S., their capital costs are greatly reduced by low interest government loans. They have lower operational expenses because they can use low cost natural gas to power their facilities, and they have lower regulatory expenses. Projections by Fesharaki and Isaak (1983, pp. 122-125) indicate that their total cost will be quite competitive on the world market.

As in the U.S., demand for petroleum products in Western Europe has declined over the past several years. High unemployment and the lack of a strong economic recovery have led to a loss in OECD refining capacity similar to that experience in the United States. Anxious to find new markets, OECD as well as OPEC refiners now see the U.S. East Coast as a potentially lucrative market. In response to these threats U.S. producers have called for import restrictions. Although no specific policies have been suggested yet, the president of Ashland Oil stated that a 10-12 cent per gallon tariff ($4.20-$5.04 per barrel) would be "equitable." The effects of the 10 cent per gallon tariff increase are quantified in the next section.

QUANTITATIVE EFFECTS OF A 10 CENT PER GALLON GASOLINE TARIFF

We focus on the market for gasoline in the U.S. because it is the most important refined petroleum product in the United States. Further, it is the one most often mentioned in connection with trade restrictions. For purposes of our analysis, we make the fairly realistic assumptions that gasoline is a final and homogeneous product and that the U.S. (given its small share of imports) is a price taker on the world gasoline market. Thus, foreign supply to the U.S. is horizontal in the relevant range.

In order to measure the gasoline tariff's effect, it is necessary to have data on prices and quantities as well as supply and demand elasticities. The gasoline price used is the weighted average import price of leaded and unleaded gasoline in 1983, $33.86 per barrel.

U.S. imports of gasoline were 83.4 million barrels, U.S. demand was 2,452 million barrels, and U.S. supply was 2,368.6 million barrels.[2] The elasticity of gasoline demand for the U.S. is based on per capita estimates of -0.61 reported in Dahl (forthcoming), while a supply elasticity of 1.28 is obtained from Richardson and Mutti (1976). The rest of the world demand elasticity of -1.61 comes from Pindyck (1979), while the rest of the world supply elasticity of 1.47 comes from Yang and Hu (1984).[3]

Graphically we represent the initial market in figure 1. As refinery capacity in the Middle East expands in the latter half of the 1980's by 1,876,000 barrels per day (as projected in table 1) the world supply curve moves outward to Sw' lowering the world price by $0.59 to $32.75 per barrel and the U.S. wholesale gasoline price to that same level. Under these new circumstances, foreign gasoline imports increase substantially from 83.4 to 163.8 million barrels per year. This gain comes largely at the expense of domestic producers whose production decreases by 54.7 million barrels to 2,313.9 million barrels per year.

As our base case in figure 2, we assume the above projections for the latter half of this decade. We then introduce our alternative tariff policy of a $4.20 per barrel ($0.10 per

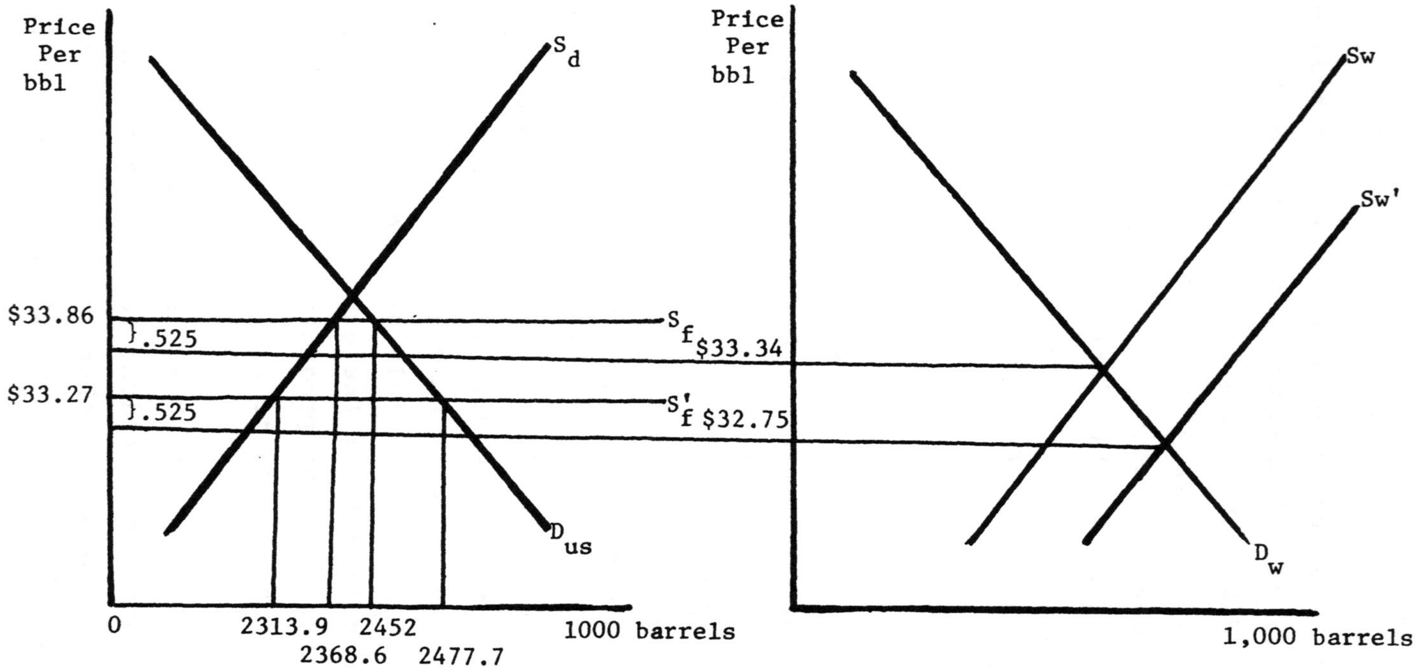

Figure 1: The U.S. and World Gasoline Market Situation

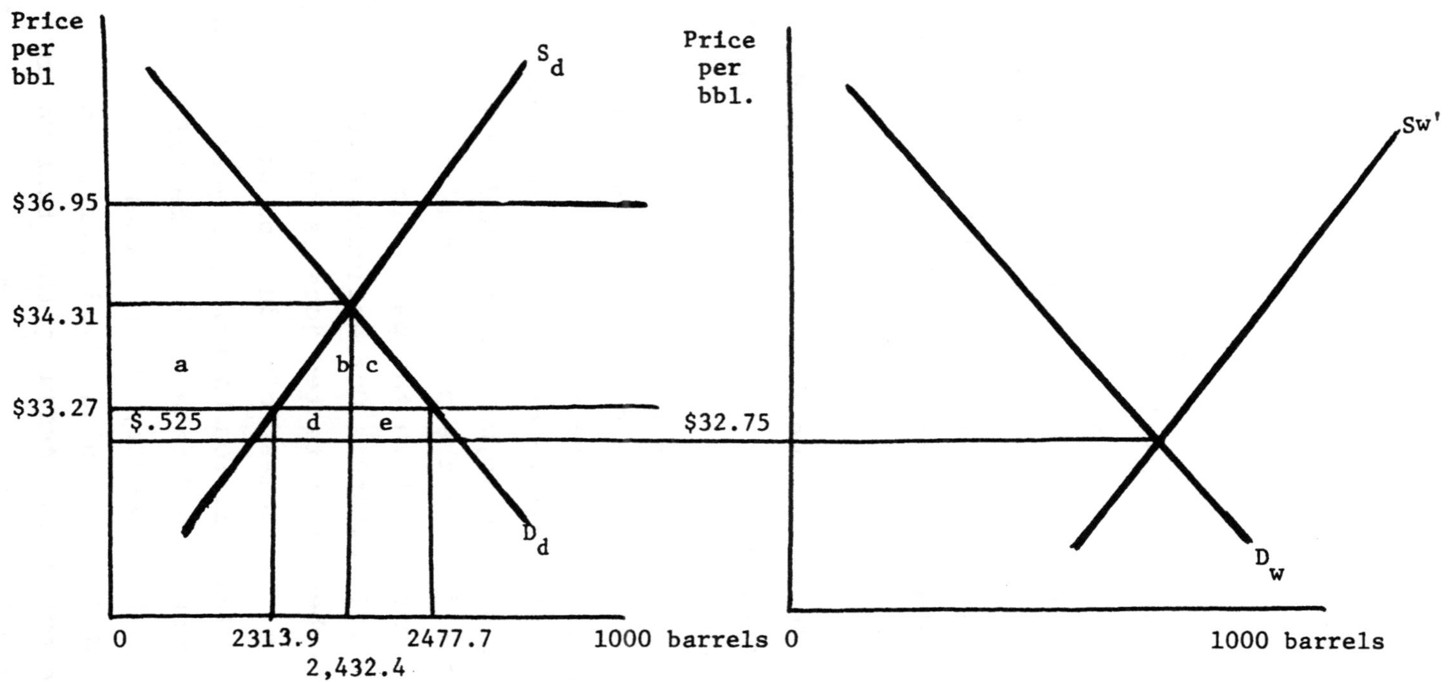

Figure 2: The U.S. Market after a Tariff Increase

gallon) tariff, which turns out to be prohibitive.

Under this tax the price of imported gasoline rises to $36.95 per barrel. Domestic consumption decreases from 2,477.6 to 2,432.4 million barrels per year. Gasoline imports fall to zero and domestic production rises from 2,313.9 to 2,432.4 million barrels per year. In fact, the same outcome would be generated if the existing tariff were raised by only $1.04 per barrel (roughly tripling the present tariff).

The four basic welfare effects from this tariff increase shown in figure 2 are: (1) the redistribution effect (area a), (2) the production loss (area b), (3) the tariff revenues effect (area d + e), and (4) the net consumption loss (area c).

The last welfare effect to be considered is the gain in employment that would accrue from a tariff. If the proposed tariff is granted, employment in the petroleum refining industry will expand. Our estimate of the actual number of protected jobs is based on our projection that domestic production will increase 118.5 million barrels per year. From annual production data and the number of workers in the industry, each worker is responsible for refining 14,934 barrels of gasoline per year. Assuming that this ratio would be maintained suggests that production of

118.5 million barrels of gasoline per year would result in an additional 7,935 jobs.

Following the methodology of Tarr and Morkre, (1980, pp. 16-19) the benefits of imposing the tariff are taken as the amount by which the earnings of the recalled workers are higher than they would have been had they not been recalled and instead found jobs in other industries.[4]

The costs and benefits of this increase in tariff rates would have the consequences listed in table 2. The first set of numbers listed gives the welfare losses or benefits for one year. The second set gives the losses or benefits accruing over a six year period and discounted back to the present.[5]

As shown in table 2 the present value of losses to consumers from imposing the proposed tariff increase over six years is over $12.9 billion while the present value of the losses to the economy over this same period are over $814 million. This estimated cost to the economy is especially significant given that imports initially represent less than 10 percent of 1983 domestic consumption. Thus, the elimination of a relatively small foreign sector could result in large welfare loss to the domestic economy.

Since all foreign gasoline imports would be cut off, all existing tariff revenue of over $438 million would be lost. Thus, a gasoline

Table 2. Welfare Following the Requested Tariff
(thousands of 1983 dollars)

Welfare Effects	Year 1	6 Year
Total Redistribution	$2,456,584	$12,529,063
Total Consumer Loss	2,530,222	12,904,632
Net Tariff Revenue Loss	85,989	438,561
Production Loss	23,510	119,906
Net Consumer Loss	50,128	255,663
Loss to the Economy	159,627	814,129
Employment Benefits	29,327	149,575

tariff would not be a panacea to an already beleaguered U.S. Treasury.

Our estimates of the benefits from increased employment tend to be rather modest given the capital intensive nature of petroleum refining. The six year employment benefits are less than $150.6 million. Comparing these benefits with the above costs shows that each dollar of employee benefits costs consumers $86.28 and costs the economy as a whole $5.44. In terms of the 7,935 jobs created, the proposed 10 cent per gallon tariff would cost consumers $1,626,300 per job, would cost the economy as a whole $102,600 per job, but would only benefit each worker $18,850 per job.

The redistribution effect is large. The real gainers from the tariff would be domestic refiners who stand to gain over $12.5 billion dollars over a six year period. Given this large redistribution effect, it is expected that gasoline tariff proposals would be subject to intense lobbying efforts by both consumer and producer groups to protect their respective interests.

CONCLUSION

The above analysis for a gasoline tariff shows that for a domestic supply elasticity of 1.28 and a domestic demand elasticity of -0.61, the net costs of a 10 cent per gallon gasoline tariff are fairly large compared to employment benefits. Consumer losses are large as are domestic refiner gains while the U.S. Treasury loses tariff revenues.

Starting from our above base case and a prohibitive tariff, if demand is less elastic than we have hypothesized, then consumers as well as total societal loss would be less. If supply is less elastic, then societal loss would be more while the redistribution effect would be less. In a nonprohibitive tariff case, the less elastic are domestic supply and demand, the more likely are tariff revenues to increase.

FOOTNOTES

1. The authors wish to emphasize that this paper does not necessarily reflect the views of the U.S. Federal Trade Commission or any Commissioner.

2. Price and import data are taken from U.S. Imports for Consumption and General Imports (1983). Domestic supply and demand quantities are taken from the Basic Petroleum Data Book (1984).

3. The U.S. demand elasticity is from yearly time series data and is considered long run. The U.S. supply elasticity also relies on time series data for the U.S. No elasticity is available for foreign supply. Therefore, we chose the most elastic U.S. supply curve available given that these new refineries are state of the art and should be very flexible. Further very elastic foreign demand and supplies were chosen to lessen the domestic welfare losses.

4. We approximate the real, risk free, social rate of discount by the real yield on longer term government securities in 1983 of 6.9 percent. We round up and use 7% for all subsequent discounting.

5. Louis S. Jacobsen (1978) has estimated the earnings losses of workers displaced from a number of manufacturing industries, including oil refining, to be 12.4 percent of their earnings in the first two years and 12.5 percent in the subsequent four years of displacement. The average total compensation of a refinery worker in 1983 was $29,806 per year (See API Basic Data Book, 1984).

REFERENCE

Petroleum Institute. 1984. Basic Petroleum Data Book Petroleum Industry Statistics. Washington, D.C., May.

Dahl, Carol A. forthcoming. "Gasoline Demand Survey," Energy Journal.

Jacobsen, Louis S. 1978. "Earnings Losses of Workers Displaced from Manufacturing Industries." In The Impact of International Trade and Investment on Employment. Washington, D.C.: U.S. Department of Labor.

Pennwell Publications. Oil and Gas Journal. Tulsa, Okla.: Pennwell Publishing Company various issues.

Pindyck, Robert S. 1979. The Structure of World Energy Demand. Cambridge, Mass.: MIT Press.

Richardson, J. David and Mutti, John H. 1976. "Industrial Displacement Through Environmental Controls: The International Competitive Aspects." In Studies in International Environmental Economics. ed. by Inga Walter. New York, N.Y.: John Wiley and Sons.

Tarr, David G. and Morkre, Morris E. 1980. The Effects of Restriction of U.S. Imports: Five Case Studies and Theory. Bureau of Economics Report to the Federal Trade Commission. Washington, D.C.: U.S. Government Printing Office.

U.S. Department of Commerce, Bureau of Census: 1983. U.S. Imports for Consumption and General Imports. Washington, D.C.: U.S. Government Printing Office.

Yang, Bong-Min and Wu, Teh-Wei. 1984. "Gasoline Demand and Supply Under a Disequilibrium Market." Energy Economics. October.

8
Economic and Legal Considerations for Oil and Gas Producers in Declining Markets

Joe Dancy, Chris Pearson, Andrews Davis Legg
Bixler Milsten & Murrah,
Vickey Dancy, Kornfeld, Franklin & Phillips

INTRODUCTION

In an environment of declining crude oil and natural gas prices, producers of oil and gas are facing numerous legal problems directly related to the industry's current economic woes. The interaction of these legal and economic parameters directly affects the nation's degree of oil and gas self sufficiency, and thus its national security. This paper will discuss two legal concepts in light of current economic considerations: (1) the duty to produce crude oil in paying quantities; and (2) the duty to market natural gas.

THE DUTY TO PRODUCE IN PAYING QUANTITIES

A. CRUDE OIL PRODUCTION. The number of producing oil wells in the United States increased to a twenty year high in 1984, with approximately 616,000 producing oil wells in operation as of December 31st.[1] During the last decade higher crude oil prices, and the increased drilling activity caused by the first and second oil shock, increased the number of producing oil wells in the United States by approximately 22%.

Although the number of oil wells has increased, the average production rate per well in the United States has declined from a level of 18.3 barrels per day in 1974 to 14.2 barrels per day in 1984.[2] This production rate per well is relatively anemic compared to Saudi Arabia's average production rate in 1983 of 6,500 barrels per day.[3]

As a result of the relatively low production rate and the maturity of the producing fields, a majority of the oil wells in the United States are economically marginal. Many of these wells have been classified as "stripper" wells, which are defined as those wells that on the average, produce less than 10 barrels per day. Of the 616,000 producing oil wells in the United States approximately 457,000, or 75%, are classified as "stripper" wells.[4]

The average stripper well produces less than three barrels of oil per day.[5] Even with their relatively low production rate, in 1984 stripper wells contributed approximately 1.2 million (16%) of the 7.5 million barrels of oil produced each day from on-shore wells in the United States.[6] Stripper wells also have a relatively long life-span, averaging 25.8 years, and account for a significant portion of on-shore reserves.[7] A summary of stripper well statistics is illustrated in Table 1.

Table 1

United States Stripper Well Production

Year	Total Number of Oil Wells	Number of Stripper Wells	Average Oil Well Production[a]	Average Stripper Well Production[a]
1975	500,000	368,000	16.8 b/d	2.93 b/d
1980	548,000	395,000	15.9	2.77
1981	557,000	409,000	15.4	2.85
1982	580,000	416,000	14.9	2.90
1983	603,000	441,000	14.4	2.87
1984 (est)	616,000	457,000	14.2	2.87

Source: Energy Information Administration, "Annual Energy Review 1984" (1985); Interstate Oil Compact Commission, "The Impact of Tax Simplification Proposals on Oil & Gas Production," (1985).

[a] barrels per day

From a geological standpoint, most oil reserves in the United States are found at depths of less than 12,000 feet. Below this depth the pressures and temperatures tend to form natural gas if hydrocarbons are present. Because of the shallow nature of the oil reserves, the ready market for crude oil, and the extensive drilling activity, most basins in the United States have been intensely explored for oil. Even by the year 1900 approximately 17,000 wells were being drilled annually in the U.S., a drilling level which has not been reached by any other free-world country to this date.[8] As a result current exploration activities conducted onshore are facing a mature province from an exploration standpoint. Most of the marginal stripper wells exist in these mature, developed fields.

B. CRUDE OIL PRICES. The average price of crude oil has declined over the last few years, and many experts are predicting a continued slide in the price of crude oil. This has made the marginal status of many of the stripper wells even more so.

The price paid to the producer at the wellhead for the crude oil is relatively free to adjust to reflect market changes and conditions. Prices are adjusted relatively frequently for oil as compared to natural gas prices which are dictated by long term contracts.

In Oklahoma, from a high of $35.22 per barrel in 1981, we have seen the average price slip to $26.30 per barrel during the first four months of 1985. As is illustrated in Table 2, a similar trend has occurred nationwide.

Table 2

Crude Oil Prices

Year	Average U.S. Price Per bbl	Average Oklahoma Price Per bbl	Value of Oklahoma Production
1981	$31.77	$35.22	$5.34 bil.
1982	$28.52	$32.73	$5.19
1983	$26.19	$29.84	$4.73
1984	$25.87	$28.46	$4.79
1985 (4 mo.)	-	$26.30	-

Source: Texas Railroad Commission, "Oil & Gas Statistics," (1985); Oklahoma Corporation Commission, "Production Report," (1985).

Most of the lifting and related producing costs have remained relatively constant during this price decline. As a result, the net proceeds received per barrel of oil produced have declined concurrently with crude oil prices. Therefore, stripper wells that in recent years were marginally profitable may now or in the near future fail to produce oil in "paying quantities" as that term is legally defined. The failure to produce in paying quantities is significant because, under certain circumstances, it may result in termination of the oil and gas lease.

LEGAL CONSIDERATIONS: DUTY TO PRODUCE IN PAYING QUANTITIES[2]

A. DEFINING PRODUCTION. The language contained in the "habendum" or "term" clause of an oil and gas lease is of great importance as they set forth the duration of the lessee's interest in the premises. The typical habendum clause provides that the lease shall remain in force for a specified primary term and as long there-

thereafter as oil, gas, or other hydrocarbons are "produced in paying quantities" from the leasehold.

Under a strict interpretation of the habendum clause any interruption in production however slight or short, would, absent some special lease provision, put an end to the lease for failure to produce in paying quantities. The overwhelming majority of courts have rejected the literal approach and stated that in deciding whether a lease may be cancelled for lack of production is determined on the basis of a subjective test that considers the duration and cause of the cessation of production as well as the diligence or lack of diligence exercised in resuming production. Applying such a subjective test, a lease will continue in existence so long as the interruption of production in paying quantities does not extend for a period longer than reasonable or justifiable in light of all the circumstances involved.

B. <u>DEFINING "PAYING QUANTITIES"</u>. The courts have encountered considerable difficulty in determining whether production on a given lease is or is not in "paying quantities." The basic definition of the term is easily stated: the phrase means that the lessee must produce in quantities sufficient to yield a return, however small, in excess of lifting expenses even though well drilling and completion costs might never be repaid. The definition is not, however, so easily applied.

Given the above formula one must, in order to determine whether a well is producing in paying quantities, compare the lessee's income from the property with the lifting expenses. In arriving at the amount of income that has been realized, the lessee's share of production or share of receipts from the sale of oil or gas is taken into account. On the debit side one must consider all lifting expenses. The term "lifting expenses" includes those expenses that are directly related to lifting operations. Numerous courts, in deciding the issue of whether a given well is producing in paying quantities, have set forth items which are or are not considered to be directly related to lifting operations. Due to the fact that lifting costs on natural gas wells are relatively negligible as compared to oil wells, most questions involving the duty to produce in paying quantities involve oil wells.

Items Held Not Directly Related To Lifting Operations

The following items are not directly related to lifting operations and therefore may not be used to calculate whether a given lease is producing in paying quantities:

a. The Costs of Drilling and Equipping a Well. The costs incurred in drilling a producing well are not items to be considered in computing production in paying quantities. The lifting of oil marks the commencement of production and production-related expenses.

b. District Expenses. Where the producing entity is a large corporation, a district office may handle all matters concerning day-to-day operations of the well. It has been held that such administrative costs, though perhaps a practical necessity, are too remote in relation to producing operations to be included in a determination of whether a well operates at a profit.

c. Administrative Overhead. Administrative expenses, defined as that indirect expense attributable to the cost of accounting, interest, postage, office supplies, telephone, depreciation of office equipment, and all other indirect expenses of the oil company regarding production shall not be considered in determining whether a well is producing in paying quantities.

d. Depreciation of Casing, Tubing, and Christmas Tree. The depreciation of casing, tubing, and christmas trees are not directly related to lifting costs.

e. Depreciation Of Lifting Equipment Where The Equipment Is Not Utilized In Connection With Lifting Operations. Items which are not utilized in connection with operations on the well may be subject to depreciation in the accounting sense of the term, however, their mere proximity to the wells does not make their depreciation an item of expense chargeable against production proceeds in determining whether the well is a producer.

f. Depreciation On Equipment Used In Drilling And Completion. Because the costs of drilling and equipping a well are not considered to be expenses directly related to lifting operations, it follows that depreciation on such items is not to be considered in determining whether a well is producing in paying quantities.

Items Held Directly
Related to Lifting Operations

Courts have held that the following items are directly related to lifting operations and therefore may be used to calculate whether a given lease is producing in paying quantities:

a. Depreciation of Non-Recurring Capital Expenditures for Lifting Equipment. Depreciation of items classified as non-recurring capital expenditures have been allowed by most courts where the court is satisfied that the expense in question is not a maintenance item but clearly a replacement of original lifting equipment occasioned by catastrophic failure or justified by improved production technology.

b. Depreciation of Equipment Used in Lifting Operations. Depreciation of equipment used in lifting operations is regarded as a production expense and thus may generally be considered in determining whether a well is producing in paying quantities. Courts reason that while depreciation is not strictly an out-ofpocket lifting expense, the value of production related equipment does have a value that is being depleted through its continued operation.

c. Other Miscellaneous Lifting Expenses. In addition to the items set forth above, courts have stated that lifting expenses may include the cost of: royalties payable to the lessor; salaries paid to pumpers; electricity; operating pumps; supervision; repairs; telephones; license permit fees; taxes; maintenance and repair of road and gates; and other incidental operating expenses.

C. PERIOD OF TIME TAKEN INTO ACCOUNT. The courts have encountered some difficulty in determining what period of time may be used in calculating whether production is in paying quantities. Obviously, the fact that production fluctuates from day to day means that the determination must be made on more than a single day's production. Courts have stated that the period considered must be a relatively long period of time or a time which is "reasonable and proper." The courts have, however, been reluctant to set forth a specific time frame from which data may be taken to determine if a well is producing in paying quantities. Periods used in such determination have included one month, four months, fourteen months, two years, and the entire life of the lease. The courts have, in the past, even considered future production and the price obtainable from such production in making a present determination as to whether a lease should be cancelled for failure to produce in paying quantities.

THE DUTY TO MARKET NATURAL GAS

A. INTRODUCTION. At the end of 1984 there were approximately 230,000 producing natural gas wells in the United States, up approximately 60% from the 144,000 gas wells producing in the United States in 1977.[10] This increase in the number of natural gas wells is directly related to the increase in the price of natural gas, which rose from an average of $0.79 per thousand cubic feet (mcf) in 1977 to an average of $2.63 per thousand cubic feet in 1984.[11] A summary of U.S. natural gas statistics is illustrated in Table 3.

Table 3

U.S. Natural Gas Statistics

Year	Total Gas Wells	U.S. Gas Reserves Per Well[a]	U.S. Consumption[b]
1977	144,000	989 mmcf	19.52 tcf
1981	193,000	746	19.40
1982	209,000	702	18.00
1983	219,000	672	16.83
1984	230,000 (est)	-	17.48

Source: Interstate Oil Compact Commission, "History of Production Statistics," (Dec. 1984).

[a] Non-associated gas, million cubic feet

[b] trillion cubic feet

B. NATURAL GAS PRICES. Natural gas, unlike oil, has traditionally been sold under long term contracts of 10 years in length or more.[12] As a result, the price received for gas sold under these long term contracts has slowly escalated, in accordance with the terms of the existing gas contracts. This price increase has occurred even with the excess deliverability of natural gas experienced in the United States during recent years. The average price received per thousand cubic feet of natural gas peaked in Oklahoma in 1983, and will peak nationally in 1985, for several reasons.

First, many gas contracts executed in recent years contained clauses which allow the purchaser to redetermine the price of gas at periodic intervals should the price of natural gas be deregulated. That contingency became a reality for selected categories of natural gas as of January 1, 1985, and it has been estimated that as of that date approximately sixty percent of flowing natural gas will no longer be regulated under the Natural Gas Policy Act of 1978 (NGPA).[13] Recent gas contracts also contain "market-out" clauses, under which the price can be adjusted to reflect current market conditions.

Secondly due to the excess supply of natural gas, recent gas purchase contracts are generally for shorter periods of duration than those of traditional long term contracts. As a result they are more frequently negotiated, and recent contract prices have been rapidly falling due to the excess deliverability of natural gas, estimated to be around 4.2 trillion cubic feet in 1985.[14]

Thirdly, due to the fact that large quantities of gas are shut-in, a number of producers have obtained permanent or temporary releases from existing long term gas contracts, and are marketing that gas on a short term basis at reduced prices.

A summary of the trends in the price of natural gas is illustrated in Table 4.

Table 4

Natural Gas Prices

Year	U.S. Average Price/mcf [a]	Oklahoma Average Price/mcf [a]
1977	$ 0.79	$ 0.79
1981	1.98	1.87
1982	2.46	2.73
1983	2.59	2.80
1984	2.63	2.67
1985	-	2.56 (1st qtr.)

Source: Texas Railroad Commission, "Oil & Gas Statistics," (1985); Oklahoma Corporation Commission, "Production Report," (1985).

[a] Price per thousand cubic feet.

These factors led to an environment where the price per thousand cubic feet being currently offered by purchasers is well below levels offered in the recent past. Such a price decline adds a new twist to the producer's duty to market the gas. This duty to market the natural gas, imposed by law, has serious implications for the producer.

LEGAL CONSIDERATIONS: DUTY TO MARKET NATURAL GAS[15]

Under an oil and gas lease, the producer has a duty to market the natural gas or oil discovered. This is so even though most leases do not expressly require or provide for the marketing of the oil or gas. This duty to market is implied by law, and is referred to as an "implied covenant".

When the oil or gas is marketed by the producer, the mineral owner will receive a royalty from production in accordance with the terms of the lease. The producer has total control of the negotiations for the sale of the oil or gas, and the terms of the contract under which the oil or gas is sold. The royalty owner derives royalty benefits from the contract negotiated by the producer. The royalty owner, while not a party to the contract negotiated by the producer, is a direct beneficiary thereto.

In most cases the duty to market is easily satisfied with regard to oil as crude oil can be easily stored at the well site and can be economically transported by pipeline or truck to an available market. Gas on the other hand is difficult to store, a pipeline is required for transportation and may have to be built, the gas may need to be compressed or dehydrated, and in general gas is more difficult to market. For this reason the duty to market, and the breach thereof, usually involves natural gas.

In most situations the producer and the royalty holder will have a similar interest in obtaining the highest possible price for the natural gas being sold. The recent financial problems experienced by the oil and gas industry may result in situations where the producer has different objectives than the royalty holder. The producer, in order to maximize current cash flow in an attempt to service bank debt or pay operating expenses, may agree to sell natural gas at prices which in light of recent transactions appear to be below market value. The royalty owner, on the other hand, may want to maximize the return from his royalty payments.

In the era of steadily increasing natural gas prices during the 1970's, the courts in some instances required the producer to obtain a gas contract with the "highest price" or "best price and terms" that were available. Considering the recent decline in natural gas prices and the natural gas overdeliverability problem now being faced by the industry, these decisions have caused uncertainty with regard to the extent of a producer's legal duty to market the gas.

In response to the recent changes in the natural gas market, other courts have stated that the producer has the duty to obtain a gas contract which is "fair and representative" of other gas contracts negotiated at the same time in the same field. A producer who does not obtain a gas contract that is "fair and representative" may be liable to the royalty owner for underpayment of royalties. Likewise, if the court requires the producer to obtain "the highest price" under a gas contract, the producer will be liable to the royalty owner should the producer execute a gas contract at a lesser price.

This problem is especially acute when a producer is selling the gas to a related entity, such as a pipeline subsidiary. The courts will closely scrutinize the transaction to insure that the price being paid is fair and reasonable. If the price being paid is not fair and reasonable, the royalty owner can recover damages, and possibly punitive damages, against the producer and/or purchaser.

At the present time, a reasonably prudent producer, due to the overdeliverability of natural gas, has numerous options to choose from in attempting to satisfy the duty to market. If the producer does not have a gas contract it may: (1) ratify the terms of an existing gas contract covering the unit; (2) negotiate a new long-term gas contract with an interstate or intrastate pipeline; (3) "spot market" its gas under relatively short term contracts; (4) sell gas under a pipeline's Special Marketing Program (SMP); (5) attempt a direct sale to an industrial customer; or (6) shut-in the well and wait for a better market.

If there is an existing gas contract, the producer has additional alternatives: (1) renegotiate the price terms of the contract after deregulation; (2) renegotiate take levels in return for other considerations; (3) if the "market-out" provision is employed, the producer may have the option of marketing the gas elsewhere; (4) the producer may request a total or partial release from an existing gas contract in order to market the gas elsewhere.

With all the various alternatives in today's natural gas market, it may be difficult, if not impossible, to identify what would be a "fair and reasonable" contract for the sale of natural gas. Worse, because normal procedures and practices have broken down in the present market, an effort to contract for the sale of gas may not appear to be diligent to a judge or jury not familiar with the severity of the marketing problem, thereby creating liability for the breach of the marketing covenant.

A number of suggestions can be made to protect the producer. First, in the new economic environment relating to natural gas, with falling natural gas prices, the producer should closely investigate a number of different marketing alternatives. Secondly, the producer should document its efforts to market the gas should its diligence be questioned later. Thirdly, the producer should attempt to investigate market transactions to determine if similar contracts have been entered into recently in the same area. These steps will reduce the producer's exposure to liability by establishing that the gas contract was reasonable at the time it was executed, and that the producer acted in a prudent manner.

CONCLUSION

The downturn of oil and gas prices has serious legal implications with regard to oil and gas production activities in the United States, and consequently the level of energy security. With regard to oil, any decrease in prices may result in the plugging of thousands of economically marginal wells for failure to produce in paying quantities as legally defined. Secondly, because of the unstructured nature of the current natural gas market, the duty to market natural gas could create serious problems and liabilities for natural gas producers.

FOOTNOTES

1. Energy Information Administration, "Annual Energy Review 1984," p. 91 (April 1985).

2. Id.

3. Exxon, "Middle East Oil," p. 3 (Dec. 1984). This rate per well would have been exceeded except for demand constraints for crude oil on the world market.

4. Interstate Oil Compact Commission, "Impact of Tax Simplification Proposals on Oil & Gas Production," (Jan. 1985).

5. Id.

6. Id.; Energy Information Administration, supra.

7. Interstate Oil Compact Commission, supra.

8. Merklein & Asner, "U.S. Oil & Gas: The Economic Realities," World Oil (Jan. 1983), p. 159.

9. R. Hemingway, The Law of Oil and Gas §6.4 (1983); 2 E. Kuntz, The Law of Oil and Gas §§26.5-26.7 (1964); C. Pearson, "Production in Paying Quantities: A Review of Oklahoma Law," 56 Okla. Bar Journal 1186 (May 1985).

10. Interstate Oil Compact Commission, "History of Production Statistics," (Dec. 1984).

11. Energy Information Administration, supra at 137.

12. Energy Information Administration, "Structure And Trends In Natural Gas Wellhead Contracts," (Nov. 1983).

13. Federal Energy Regulatory Commission, "Monitor," (Oct. 4, 1984).

14. Interstate Oil Compact Commission, "Natural Gas Deliverability Study," Sept. 1985. This figure includes projected imports from Canada and Mexico as estimated by the American Gas Association.

15. C. Pearson and J. Dancy, "Negotiating and Renegotiating the Gas Contract: Producer Duties to Third Parties," 56 Okla. Bar Journal 1948 (Sept. 1985).

9
Worldwide Oil and Gas: Permanent Instability

M. A. Adelman, Massachusetts Institute of Technology

INTRODUCTION

Since the first price explosion of 1973, a strong consensus has ruled public and official opinion. The old price levels were insupportable because of the pressure of growing consumption on scarce resources. Higher prices were inevitable. The cartel at most merely hastened the process, which still continues.

The difficult decade will pass. In the 1990s the industry will emerge from the dark thorny wood into the sunny upland meadows. The market will tighten, prices rise again, and the world will again worry about energy supplies enough for our needs.

In my opinion, this is very unlikely. Oversupply is permanent, and severe downward pressure on prices will last as long as we can foresee.

To be sure, the price may rise again, to record heights, at any time. Let the cartel members screw their

This paper summarizes work now in progress, supported by the National Science Foundation, grant #SES-8412971, and by the Center for Energy Policy Research at M.I.T. I am indebted to Michael C. Lynch for valuable assistance. The opinions expressed here are those of the author alone, and do not necessarily reflect the views of any other person or group.

courage and cohesion to the sticking place, and cut production hard for a month or two. Then just as in 1974 and 1979, spot markets will explode, cartelists will ratchet up their list prices, governments and corporations will flock to beg for special deals and "assurances" of supply. Another energy "crisis" will be upon us, just as phony as the last two.

But soon afterward, markets will be oversupplied and prices again will fall. To explain why, we must begin with the theory of mineral depletion, which, acknowledged or not, underlies every prognostication.

MINERAL DEPLETION IN GENERAL

1. Mineral reserves are renewable. They are constantly renewed by investment of billions every year in finding and development. But if the cost of finding-developing-extracting rises above the price of the nearest substitute, the mineral is no longer sought, found, and developed. The activity disappears. This implies a second principle.

2. Mineral resources are inexhaustible. We never get to the end of them; rising cost stops us. It would not matter or help if there were an infinite stock of any mineral--never mind that the earth, "the great globe itself," is finite. The economic problem--rising cost--would be unchanged. "Exhaustible resources" is an empty phrase; only cost matters.

3. The price of any mineral is the uncertain fluctuating resultant of two strong opposing forces: on the one side, diminishing returns as we use up the best deposits first, then go from good to bad and bad to worse. In the other corner is knowledge, the usual winner. But each

mineral is a case unto itself. It is a powerful delusion that "non-renewable" resources must increase in price over the long run. Mostly they drop.

4. "User cost" of development production. Cost includes the using-up of assets on hand. Reserves are an asset. No sensible owner will sell off any asset today if the price does not cover its discounted present value, which is the lesser of (a) the present value of its future replacement cost, or (b) the present value of future profit on selling it. Future values are notoriously difficult to calculate for any type of asset: buildings, equipment, stockpiles, or mineral reserves. But forecasts are made and corrected as information accumulates.

Thus, if the price of oil were really ruled by impending future scarcity, there would be no present glut, no fear of price collapse. Owners would be content to hold the asset and wait.

Nearly three years ago, Petroleum Intelligence Weekly reported an industry consensus: It would take a price drop to less than $10 per barrel to begin choking off production. In 1983, the $100 to $200 per barrel was being reluctantly put behind. But suppose many in the industry really believed that the price of oil was going even to $40 in 1995, as DOE now says it expects. Long before the price dropped to anywhere near $10 it would be far more profitable to stop production and hold for the higher price. There are many in the oil industry who believe in $40 or more in 1995, but they are not going to bet on it.

Their actions speak their thoughts: The current price level is unrelated to real scarcity, present or future. Their reasons are partly on the side of demand, partly of supply.

STAGNATING CONSUMPTION

In the industrial countries, oil intensity, the amount consumed per unit of gross national product, began to decline immediately after the first oil shock, and accelerated after the second. It is now down by about a third from 1973. In the United States, the shrinkage continued through the first half of 1985 despite a considerable decline in inflation-adjusted oil prices since 1981--about 21 percent for residual fuel oil, 24 percent for diesel-light heating oil, 31 percent for gasoline.

I do not expect such a continued rate of decline in oil-intensity. But I think it will long decline, because it is the replacement of less-efficient with more-efficient facilities, and of more energy-intensive goods and services with less-intensive. The capital stock of society, tangible and intangible (the latter more important), turns over slowly. Admittedly the brisk investment boom since 1981 did speed up the process (see Figure 1 at end of paper).

But the investment in more energy-efficient capital is diverted from economic growth. It is one reason for the disappointingly slow growth rate since 1973. The shock to the world monetary-financial system is another, as is the debt load that inhibits growth in much of the less-developed world. Consumption has not declined as much as in the industrial countries, but the difference is exaggerated by lumping the OPEC nations in with other less-developed countries. All these depressants will persist, and prevent any near-term resurgence to the pre-1973 growth rates.

<u>Supply: Competitive, Monopolistic, In-between Sectors of the World Petroleum Industry</u>

In the competitive sector, producers sell all they can

produce, and there is no excess capacity. In the monopolized sector (OPEC plus Mexico), the producers produce only what they can sell without breaking the price. There is great excess of installed capacity. But there is far greater excess of potential capacity.

For example, in Kuwait, there has been some exploration for non-associated gas for local power generation. Apparently they found "only" an oil field, currently estimated at between 25 and 35 billion barrels, with development cost so low that the new field will replace at least some of current production. That was found inadvertantly in a tiny country. What would they find if they deliberately tried to find oil, and over a larger area?

The more the cartel nations raise the price, the less the demand for oil, and the less they invest and produce. So there is a clear inverse relation between price and production.

In the competitive sector, quite the other way, the higher the price, the more it pays to invest and produce more.

The competitive sector includes the United States, the United Kingdom, the Soviet Union, and some others. For any competitive area in isolation, it is prudent to assume slowly falling reserves and production. But prudence is not necessarily truth. For all of them taken together, it is an error. It confuses reserves, the ready shelf inventory, with the ultimate resource.

U.S. oil output has, to the surprise of many, stabilized, and even increased a little in the last five years, even excluding Alaska. Reserves are being replenished almost completely, partly by small discoveries, partly by continued growth of the oil-in-place in old fields, and by improved recovery.

Soviet oil output has begun a slow contraction, and is maintained at high and rising marginal cost. But I expect continued high exports, because prices are so high that the Soviet economy benefits more by exports than it is hurt by deprivation of oil. Moreover, gas will be substituted for oil.

But in addition to the monopoly sector and the competitive sector, there is also a large in-between sector, where there is no adherence to the cartel, yet output is less, perhaps very much less, than would maximize wealth. In fact, there is a lot of this oddball behavior in the competitive nations too.

The in-between sector has so wide a variety of countries and sectors that no summary can be accurate. But we can discern a few factors common to all. One is the aversion to the oil industry and its "obscene profits." Even a reasonably courageous politician will not risk the dreadful accusation that he is soft on large and especially foreign oil companies. Better therefore to fix ceiling prices, tax to distraction, and in negotiating to demand the earth, get nothing, but escape the accusation.

We arrive at an upside-down result. The higher the price, the greater the potential "obscene profits," the greater the fear of allowing them, the greater the restrictions and the higher the taxes, and the less investment and output.

These sentiments are powerfully reinforced by the delusion already mentioned: that oil and gas are "non-renewable resources," fixed in supply, which must grow ever more scarce and expensive. Higher prices will not elicit more supply. The United States paid heavily for such beliefs and policies; oil prices were not decontrolled until 1981, and gas prices are only gradually being freed.

The belief in ever-increasing scarcity had its brightest hours around 1980. It is still powerful, but reason like cheerfulness has been breaking through, and the upside-down effect works in both directions. Lower oil and gas prices are inducing more investment and production.

The best example is Canada, where lower world oil prices, and plentiful natural gas in the United States helped scrap the National Energy Program of 1980. Oil prices have been allowed to rise toward market levels, and Canada is again a net exporter. Having refused natural gas sales at $5 per mcf, Canada is now selling briskly at $3. The terrible gas scarcity that so frightened the Carter Administration has been succeeded by a demand for protection against cheap Canadian gas, and the lament of an American gas producer: "Pierre Trudeau, where are you when we need you?"

Columbia, which had let the industry dwindle by overtaxing it, changed course a few years ago and is again a net exporter, having found much larger fields than ever known. Argentina is struggling to follow their example. Egypt has a similar history.

In Europe, the Netherlands has reacted to lower gas sales and prices by perceiving that their reserves are somewhat larger than previously stated, and promoting larger gas exports instead of trying to reduce deliveries. Norway, having once scorned $6.00 per mcf, was willing to bargain about $4.20 per mcf, yet lost the sale. The French, of all people, have just tabulated European new-contract city-gate prices as somewhere around $3.50. If translated into lower consumer prices, it means a large sales volume.

The U.K. tax system was made more flexible when prices declined, and the result was more drilling. Oil production was supposed to peak before 1990; Exxon now estimates there will be exports past the turn of the century. In 1980, Malaysia restricted oil production to about 5.25 percent of reserves; late last year, they permitted 9 percent; shortly before this, they had resolved differences with oil companies, who will increase output.

None of these developments is massive or dramatic, but their importance is disproportionate because they bear not on the whole world industry but on the monopolistic sector.

Natural gas needs special mention. Reserves are largely the unintended result of the search for oil. They are very large in relation to production, and still growing. Natural gas is mostly in the in-between sector, evolving toward competition. Prices are artificially high, set as a percentage of oil. If gas were governed by supply and demand, prices would decrease considerably in Europe, and increasing consumption would back out oil, as it is doing in North America.

Gas development in Asia will be slower for lack of a comparable network of pipelines and distribution infrastructure. But a recent compilation of pending Asian gas projects shows they will soon back out 1.3 mbd of oil consumption.

Natural gas is a sleeping giant. I do not expect the giant to awaken fully, but he is visibly stirring. The growth of natural gas, like the increased production in the competitive and in-between oil sector, will decrease the demand for the output of the cartel, to which we now turn.

The Cartel of the OPEC Nations and Mexico

In the good old days, the companies did their considerable best to avoid or minimize competition, but from 1945 to 1970 the inflation-adjusted price fell by about two-thirds. It was a masterful retreat.

This spontaneous coordination by the companies worked also in the first half of the 1970s, as the means whereby the nations operated their newly formed cartel. Those who asked rhetorically how there could be a cartel without some means of output division were not looking.

Total output was fixed as simply the companies' total sales, at current prices. The division of the market among producer nations was the uncontrollable result of who their resident oil companies happened to be.

It was a sloppy solution, which could never be incorporated into a model, since it optimized nobody's anything. But it worked, mostly.

By the late 1970s, the governments had expelled the companies, or reduced them to the status of contractors and resident buyers. Thereby the cartel nations themselves had to decide total output, and its division. They may have decided, privately, that expelling the companies was a mistake.

In a coalition, weakness is strength, and small is beautiful. Small members can be free riders, and collect the benefits, while not reducing output. Others will assume the burdens they evade, because it is in their interest to do so.

But the dominant member of the alliance, whether the Saudis in OPEC, or the United States in NATO, does not have this option. If he sheds the burden, the coalition vanishes, to the ruin of all. But he cannot let himself be taken for granted. He must make the others believe that there is a limit to how far he can be pushed.

In this game of mutual intimidation and bluff, the outcome is unpredictable. Even in 1974-78, there was enough excess capacity in the cartel to force them to by-pass the companies now and then, in the attempt to improve market share. Starting in late 1980, there were four attempts to share out production. The fourth worked.

In January 1983, Sheik Yamani broke up an OPEC conference. He made his colleagues look over the side of the cliff, which concentrated their minds wonderfully. He has not had the same success since. Yet at the risk of being called an optimist, I am impressed by how little ground the cartel has given, in relation to what they might have. But whatever their degree of success, they are hard to live with.

The Clumsy Cartel. Even if the cartel avoids the brinkmanship of 1973 and 1979, they cannot fine-tune with coarse instruments. Output decisions must be made in ignorance. There are no recent data on world consumption, and now even the production figures are discredited, and must be audited. Estimates of primary inventories, held by oil companies, are only within wide bands of error; "downstream" inventories held by consumers are a statistical black hole.

Spot markets will react strongly to supposed inventory changes that are negligible in relation to total supply/demand. This would not have mattered much in past years, when the oil industry operated roughly 90 percent on term contracts. They provided stability, with the spot market providing the needed balancing-off of excess supplies and demands. As with financial markets, each buyer and seller could acquire a balanced "portfolio" of inflows and outflows, and make constant marginal corrections. That is gone today, and dealings are all spot or spot-determined, with "contracts" being at best rights of first refusal. Term contracts have disappeared because the producing nations have made it abundantly clear that deliveries will not be made at contract prices if they are below spot prices, but that contract prices will be enforced when they are above spot.

The cartel nations have repeatedly tried to starve the market into using up the--unknown--discretionary inventories. As every sailor knows, when you take in a slack line too quickly, you risk a strain and breaking the line. It is impossible for the cartel to surmount repeated oversupply crises without ever creating shortages and panic. Only chiseling and cheating by cartel members have prevented another panic. Another one could happen any time.

CONCLUSIONS

The cartel has not lost control of the market. But they raised the price far too high on the second round. The verdict is crushing: Their real dollar revenues in 1983 and 1984 were below 1978, and 1985 will be worse. Only the unlooked-for appreciation of the dollar has softened the blow.

Yet they dare not reduce the price because benefits are too slow and uncertain, and they have not been able to live within their means. A declining dollar, and continuing mild increases in the prices of industrial goods, will tighten the budget and foreign-exchange squeeze further.

Thus the cartel nations are extremely vulnerable.

Prices to consumers cannot be raised without further loss of sales. Therefore any increase in consumer-country taxes, such as the oil import fee now being considered in the United States, will be borne by the cartel nations. Furthermore, if there were a drastic fall in price, development investment would dwindle in the competitive sector, but explode in the Persian Gulf and other low-cost areas. The only way for the Saudis to save anything from the wreck would be to dust off their 1973 plans to produce 20 million barrels daily, which at $10 per barrel would be far more than they earn today at $25. Their neighbors would do the same, hating every moment of it, but with no choice but to increase production drastically.

Silver linings. But the cartel has the strength of its weakness. Political instability has bestowed the great good fortune of the Iran-Iraq war. The next piece of good luck can be contrived. I cannot foretell who will attack, invade, and occupy whom. Even a complete cartel breakdown might be only temporary. The rewards of monopolizing the industry are so great that the most violent desperate efforts will be made to restore it.

Smooth transition in any direction does not seem likely.

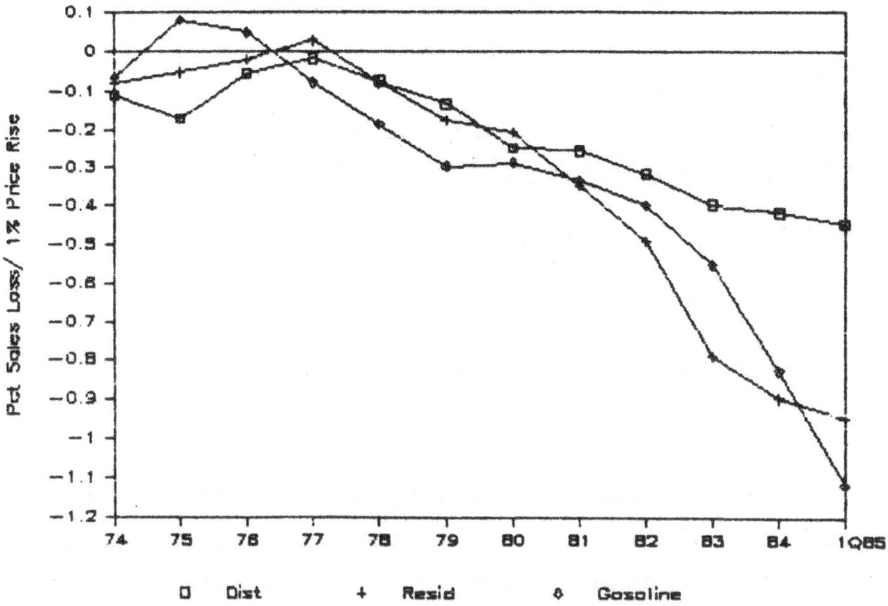

Figure 1. Apparent Product Demand Elasticities

The graph compares normalized consumption (gasoline and distillate divided by GNP, residual by industrial production) with normalized price (divided by GNP: Implicit Price Deflator). Each year's price and quantity is then compared with 1973. Distillate and residual seem to be approaching a limit, but not gasoline. Data for first-quarter 1985 preliminary.

10
The Long-Term Implications of Oil as a Commodity

Phillip K. Verleger, Consultant

OIL BECOMES AN ECONOMIC COMMODITY

Oil is gradually losing its status in world markets. Once upon a time oil was thought to be something special. Its price and supply were the topic of negotiations between world leaders. Consuming nations offered special concessions to producing nations in order to obtain "preferential access." Discussions between multinational companies and OPEC or among OPEC members themselves were the subject of prolonged debate at the highest levels of government. Every meeting of ministers was covered by hundreds of reporters and the pronouncements of any attendee, including those from the smallest, most insignificant country, would receive excruciatingly detailed coverage in major journals from every corner of the world. All of this has, however, come to an end.

Today, few world leaders spend time negotiating special agreements on oil (except perhaps for leaders of LDCs attempting to obtain oil on generous credit terms or for free). Agreements to provide oil on the basis of "preferential access" have become economic burdens to those countries still forced to accept oil on such a basis. Senior government officials in consuming countries pay scant attention to the actions of the members of the cartel. Newspapers, radio, and television give the comings and goings of the ministers minimal time and space, and the number of reporters covering the comings and goings of the ministers has been reduced to a hard-core group of OPEC followers. Oil has, in short, lost its glamour.

The change is not, however, just cosmetic. In the last five years oil has gone through a metamorphosis: it has lost its special status and become just another economic commodity. This emergence of oil as a commodity has important implications for all types of oil companies -- both integrated and nonintegrated -- as well as for consumers and governments. Some implications of oil as a commodity are investigated here.

To understand the nature and importance of the change, we begin by describing the characteristics of commonly traded commodities and attempt to note the manner in which oil has taken on the attributes of these commodities. We then seek to identify the changes in industry structure that can be credited (blamed) for causing the metamorphosis of oil.

Finally, we attempt to assess the status of the evolution of oil towards a true commodity.

GENERAL CHARACTERISTICS OF TRADED COMMODITIES

The theoretical and empirical behavior of commodity markets has been the subject of countless economic treatises. The list of distinguished economists who have written on the subject includes Keynes, Hicks, Houthakker, and Samuelson. In general, economists have been fascinated with the impact of price volatility and the role of inventories, as well as with the parts played by the principal protagonists: hedgers and speculators. Much of the applied literature has been written in the context of description and analysis of futures markets and the relationship between futures markets and cash markets. However, many of the conclusions apply to those commodity markets that exist without a parallel futures market.

An examination of the research on commodity markets leads one to the conclusion that widely and successfully traded commodities enjoy three or four basic characteristics. Hieronymus (1982, p. 21) lists three characteristics common to successfully traded commodities. "First, they are all bulk commodities that can be described and the separate lots of which are more or less interchangeable. Second, none of the commodities has been processed or manufactured to the point of being a product identified with the processes of a articular firm; in general they are bulk commodities but are not, in a strict sense, raw materials. Third, prices are variable and relatively competitively determined."

The U.S. Commodity Futures Trading Commission (the U.S. Government's regulator of the commodity industry) has adopted a longer and more precise list of six criteria to define a commodity that may be eligible for futures trading, a list that actually dates to Baer and Saxon (1948). These criteria require that a commodity meet the following conditions:

- First, the commodity must be sold in homogeneous units. A trader buys or sells a commodity according to established grades, not specific lots or identifiable units.
- Second, the commodity obviously must be susceptible to standardization. Trade in a commodity cannot take place unless units can be standardized and grades established so that units can be made interchangeable.
- Third, the supply and demand must be large. Hieronymus notes that trading in small markets is often unsuccessful because speculators with large financial resources may gain control of either supply or demand so that the market "ceases to be natural and free" and becomes instead "merely a battleground for contending speculative factions" (Hieronymus, 1982, p. 20).

- o Fourth, the supply of the commodity "should flow naturally to the market" unimpaired by artificial restraint imposed by governments or private organizations.
- o Fifth, supply and demand must be uncertain. Baer and Saxon suggest that prices may be readily adjusted without the intervention of market machinery if supply and demand are known with certainty. A market is required, however, where both supply and demand are large, uncertain, and subject to wide variations from year to year.
- o Sixth, the commodity must be storable so that forward and futures contracting can take place.

Since trade exists in some commodities that do not satisfy all of these criteria, one must conclude that these conditions do not represent necessary and sufficient conditions for the existence of markets. For instance, trade in grains is large and well established despite significant government intervention. Daily trade in foreign currencies, currently estimated to be in the range of hundreds of billions of dollars, takes place despite periodic central bank intervention. Further, trade in eggs, broilers, and live hogs is well established despite the obvious perishable nature of the commodity. Thus, these criteria provide only a framework for evaluating the comparability between various markets. In this context they provide a useful basis for assessing the evolution of the oil market.

FACTORS CONTRIBUTING TO THE EVOLUTION

The evolution of this market from the controlled environment of the period prior to 1973 into the relatively free market of the 1970s can be traced to a number of factors. Changes experienced in the 1970s appeared to:

- o Affect the flow of the oil to the market;
- o Make the level of supply and demand uncertain; and
- o Contribute to an increase in price volatility.

The nationalization of the producing interests belonging to the multinational companies, together with changes in the process by which crude prices were set, caused multinational oil companies to reduce their activity as distributors of crude oil and created the opportunity for entry by other firms such as Japanese trading companies. The variation in the level of supply and demand increased simultaneously with the nationalizations. During the 1970s and 1980s, year-to-year variation in consumption rose as a consequence of more erratic economic activity, higher real prices of oil, and vacillating regulations relating to fuel choice. At the same time, new sources of supply from the North Sea, Mexico, Alaska, Malaysia, and other countries were put on the market.

Volatility in prices increased due to the revision of tax regimes in consuming countries (principally the introduction of the windfall tax in the United States and the Petroleum Revenue Tax in the United Kingdom) and the creation of a crude oil futures market. The introduction of trading in crude oil futures increased volatility in prices by drastically cutting the cost and risks of speculation.

Changes in the Flow of Oil to the Market

Changes in both the pattern by which oil is moved from the well to the market and the economic incentives affecting oil production have represented a major force in the evolution of oil as a commodity. These changes have included alterations in traditional relationships between producing countries and the multinational oil companies, discoveries and developments in other lands, and changes in economic incentives to lift oil. In the 1960s and early 1970s the multinational oil companies were joined in a partnership with the producing nations under which they shared any increase or decrease in revenues due to fluctuations in price or volume. This partnership had become a distant memory by the 1980s.

The Decline in Market Shares. The seven major multinationals accounted for most of the oil sold in international trade until 1969.

The companies covered by Adelman include the traditional seven majors (Esso, B.P., Gulf, Mobil, Standard of California, Shell, and Texaco) and C.F.P. (Compagnie Francaise de Petroles). According to Adelman, in 1969 C.F.P. accounted for 4.7 percent of the liftings from OPEC, leaving the seven majors with 76.1 percent of OPEC sales.

In his calculations, Professor Adelman segregated the world market by separating the North American market from the rest of the free world. While this distinction may seem arbitrary, his choice makes sense because the United States had become an economically isolated market by 1958. Imports were limited by a mandatory quota, while domestic production was tightly controlled by various state regulatory agencies.

Vernon (1983) has recently updated Adelman's calculations to 1979. His calculations indicate that in that year the seven major oil companies distributed only 24 percent of OPEC production, while the share of oil distributed directly by producing country exporting companies had increased from zero to 69 percent in the same time period. In the same year, calculations made by this author from Petroleum Intelligence Weekly data indicate that OPEC accounted for 84 percent of the oil distributed to the free world market, excluding North America.

By 1983 the share of the market controlled by the seven majors further decreased, as had OPEC's share. Rough estimates of market shares indicate that the equity production controlled by the seven majors accounted for approximately 14 percent of OPEC production and 14 percent of non-OPEC, non-North American output. In addition, the majors appeared to have purchased another 11 percent of OPEC-controlled production. At the same time, OPEC's share of free world production outside North America had declined to 59 percent.

The Demise of Joint Agreements. The loss of market share incurred by the major oil companies was accompanied by the demise in joint producing agreements. The joint arrangements that were of concern to Adelman in 1972 seemed to have become a thing of the past by 1984. The change in the industry may be noted from Tables 1 and 2. Table 1, taken from The World Petroleum Market, displays the distribution of crude production in 1969 by exporting countries distributed by major producing company. Adelman notes "in the tables, the eight large companies are arranged as much as possible according to their important joint ventures" (Adelman, 1972, p. 81). Table 2 presents the author's attempt to make the same calculation for 1984.* It may be noted that the problem of joint production agreements had, by this time, mostly become an artifact of history.

---

*Adelman notes "There are numerous small discrepancies among all these sources and it is impossible to reconcile them fully." The same comment applies here. Volumes of production are assigned to companies listed in the Oil and Gas

Table 1

Production of Principal Crude Oil Companies and Producing Countries in the World Oil Market, 1969 — First Half (Thousand Barrels per Day)

	Esso	Mobil	SoCal	Texaco	BP	Gulf	Shell	CFP	Others	Total
Persian Gulf										
Iran	208	208	208	208	1,192	298	417	178	394	3,223
Iraq	181	181			361		361	361	76	1,520
Qatar	23	23			45		203	45	9	348
Abu Dhabi	49	49			236		99	167	21	620
Kuwait					1,254	1,254				2,508
Saudi Arabia	870	289	870	870						2,898
Oman							256		45	301
Other									453	453
SUBTOTAL	1,331	750	1,078	1,073	3,087	1,462	1,335	751	999	11,871
Africa										
Libya	683	126	181	181	155		119		1,561	3,006
Algeria							85	249	602	936
Nigeria					168	200	168			536
Other						36	63		406	505
Indonesia*	25	25	285	285			138		90	848
Venezuela	1,472	112	56	171		383	916		424	3,534
TOTAL	3,511	1,013	1,600	1,692	3,433	2,081	2,824	1,000	4,082	21,236

*Includes Brunei and Sarawak.

SOURCE: M. A. Adelman. 1972. The World Petroleum Market. Washington, D.C.: Johns Hopkins University Press: pp. 80-81.

Table 2

Production of Principal Crude Oil Companies and Producing Countries in the World Oil Market, 1984 — First Half

	Esso	Mobil	SoCal	Texaco	BP	Gulf	Shell	CFP	Others	National Oil Companies	Total
Persian Gulf											
Iran										2,164	2,164
Iraq										1,152	1,152
Qatar	7	7			15		15	15	107	250	416
Abu Dhabi	15	15			36		36	36	183	482	803
Kuwait										983	983
Saudi Arabia										4,951	4,951
Oman									1	403	403
Other				35					724	839	1,598
SUBTOTAL	22	22		35	51		51	51	1,015	11,224	12,470
Africa											
Libya									686	481	1,167
Algeria										617	617
Nigeria		176	28	28		173	715		252		1,372
Other				10		182	16	11	538		756
Indonesia*		95	305	305			173		815		1,693
Malaysia	246						216				462
Venezuela										1,820	1,820
Ecuador				216					27	4	247
TOTAL	268	293	333	594	51	355	1,171	62	3,333	14,146	20,604

*Includes Brunei and Sarawak.

SOURCE: Oil and Gas Journal 82, 53. December 31, 1984.

The demise of joint producing agreements has undoubtedly increased the competitive pressure between exporting countries. In the 1960s and 1970s exporting countries experienced great difficulties when they attempted to increase their share of the market because the operators (usually working under a joint agreement) would actively discourage or would refuse to increase liftings. (The experience of Iran in 1952 provides a classic example of this phenomenon.) By 1984 the situation had changed: in many cases the country was the sole operator and could vary production as it wished, effectively reducing constraints on the volume of oil moved to the market.

Increase in Non-OPEC Production. The expansion of production in new areas of the world represents the second factor that contributed to an increase in the flow of uncontrolled oil to the market. OPEC accounted for almost 90 percent of non-North American free world production in 1973, but less than 65 percent of this output in 1983.

(Footnote continued)
Journal Worldwide Report. In some cases the production is shared between two or more companies. In other cases, the production is shared with the government. In Table 2 these distinctions have been ignored except in the case of the well known production sharing agreements. Data published in company annual reports will differ from the totals shown here because companies include only the share of production which is actually owned by a company.

The primary increase in output has come from Egypt, Mexico, Norway, and the United Kingdom. Each of these countries has followed vigorous market efforts to make sure that the maximum possible volume of oil was produced and sold every year. Further, the role of the majors was considerably circumscribed in these new producing countries, although they have played a major role in developing fields in the United Kingdom and Norway.

The Change in Economic Incentives. The decline in the share of crude moved by the multinational oil companies is generally attributed to the nationalization of the concessions by exporting countries. However, the loss of ownership need not have caused an almost total withdrawal by the majors from marketing crude produced in lands where they were formerly active; indeed, the companies remained several years after nationalizations. As late as 1978 the seven majors were marketing approximately 4 million barrels a day to third-party buyers, according to *Petroleum Intelligence Weekly*. Thus, the seven majors still accounted for 46 percent of the market outside of the United States if their sales to third parties are added to the 13 million barrels a day of product these companies reported distributing. However, during 1979 most of the crude sales to third parties were dropped because such sales had become unprofitable.

The major impetus to the termination of third-party sales was the financial loss incurred by the majors during 1977 and 1978. This loss was followed by restrictive conditions imposed at the peak of the 1979 Iranian crisis which prevented sellers from profiting during the tight market.

The Increase in Volatility of Supply and Demand

The increase in the variance of consumption represents the second change in the structure of the market. (Hieronymus's point that no organized market machinery was required if supply and demand for a commodity were both certain was noted above.) In the case of the oil market, the variance in consumption and sources of supply increased after 1973, and particularly after 1979.

The increased volatility in the level of consumption may be noted in several ways, the most obvious of which may be by simple trend analysis. From 1960 to 1973 both United States and total free world consumption were highly correlated with a simple time trend. The standard error of the fitted trend line was 400 thousand barrels per day for the United States and 1,160 thousand barrels per day for the free world. This relationship collapsed after 1973 for obvious reasons. From 1974 to 1983 the correlation coefficients dropped from the mid-90s to zero, no trend is exhibited, and the standard errors triple to 1,248 thousand barrels per day for the United States and 3,515 for the free world.

A second indicator of the increased uncertainty as to supply and demand may be noted from the errors made in projecting future petroleum consumption. Presumably, if future levels of supply and demand are certain, then forecasting errors should be small. However, a comparison of projected levels of consumption with actual realizations illustrates the degree to which forecasters have missed the mark and, by implication, the uncertainty present in today's oil market.

The Increase in the Volatility of Prices

The increase in price volatility represents the final major structural change that has caused petroleum to evolve into a commodity. As Hieronymus (1982, p. 21) notes: "When supply and demand are large, and both uncertain and subject to wide fluctuations from season to season or year to year, a condition exists where the forces of supply and demand on free markets are constantly changing. This interplay of uncertain economic forces produces the constant fluctuations in price which must exist in any successful futures market."

A comparison of data on the fluctuation of prices during the period from 1960 to 1972 and 1979 to 1984 indicates that the volatility in prices has increased substantially. The analysis of volatility in prices is made by comparing the average price level to the standard deviation in prices. Volatility was analyzed for three periods: 1960 to May 1967, 1968 to 1971, and 1978 to 1984. Data for the first two periods were taken directly from The World Petroleum Market, with the last seven months of 1967 excluded due to the transitory impact of the Middle East crisis that year. The measure of volatility used here is the ratio of the mean of the price series to its standard deviation. These measures could be criticized because they fail to correct for an underlying trend in prices. However, the data for the early period exhibit no trends, and the trend in prices between 1978 and 1984 has been decidedly erratic -- indeed, the uncertainty as to the trend has contributed to the change in the industry. Results are shown in Table 3.

The increase in the variance of heavy fuel oil prices since 1971 is particularly noteworthy since heavy fuel oil accounted for the largest share of product sales in Europe prior to the 1973 embargo, and because a high portion of residual fuel oil was sold at spot-related prices.* The increase in the variance of gasoline prices is also noteworthy.

CHANGES THAT WILL PERPETUATE THE SHIFT

The three changes in the oil market can be directly or indirectly traced to actions of the exporting countries. Nationalizations of company interests and reductions in the incentive to handle third-party sales clearly caused the change in the flow of oil to shift. Increases in prices caused by exporting country mismanagement of supply contributed to economic recession,

---

*See Adelman (1972, p. 367) for market shares.

conservation, and fuel substitution, which made oil consumption more uncertain. Finally, the inability of exporting countries to control production contributed to the volatility of prices. Each of these three actions is, in theory, reversible. However, the events of the last 10 years have led to other changes in the market, changes that are both difficult to reverse and that make a return to the past almost impossible. The most dramatic of the changes concerns thé approach to the taxation of resources in consuming countries and the creation of a futures market in crude oil.

Changes in Taxation of Resources in Consuming Countries

The oil industry in the United States operated under a system of taxation that was highly favorable to resource production until 1976. Producers of resources benefitted from percentage depletion and from special regulations that permitted them to expense intangible drilling expenses. Percentage depletion directly affected the price of oil because the structure of the tax system encouraged producers to artificially inflate the price of oil to reduce tax liabilities.

The tax reform legislation which passed in 1976 repealed percentage depletion for the major oil companies and drastically limited the benefits received by independent producers. Further legislation enacted in 1980, the Windfall Profit Tax, created an incentive for the producer to minimize the wellhead value of crude oil because, under present law, income earned from resource production of oil is almost always taxed at a higher rate than income earned from refining.

Tax regimes adopted in the United Kingdom and Norway appear to offer private companies similar incentives to cut the price of oil.

The Creation of the Futures Market

The second major change in structure has occurred with the introduction of a futures market in crude oil. Trading in futures in crude oil began in March 1983 on the New York Mercantile Exchange (NYMEX). The NYMEX contract calls for delivery of 1,000 barrels of West Texas Intermediate crude oil (or one of nine alternative types of crude) to Cushing, Oklahoma, a landlocked location in the middle of the United States whose only justification is that it is located at the intersection of several major crude pipelines.

The creation of a futures market in crude oil appears to have had two impacts on the world oil market, both of which undermine price stability and enhance the commodity characteristics of petroleum. First, the futures market has permitted independent refiners in the

United States to break away from the system of posted crude oil prices which historically prevented them from setting widely divergent prices. Second, the market has contributed to a drastic reduction in the cost and risk of speculation against oil prices. (See the CRA Petroleum Economics Monthly, February 1982.)

CONCLUSION

The world petroleum market has gone through a series of transformations since 1972. Oil has emerged as a commodity. The process began when exporting countries took control of their own resources, and it was then furthered when the multinational oil companies elected (or were denied) the opportunity to be the marketing agents for the exporting countries. Then, discoveries in non-OPEC areas reduced OPEC's control over the flow of oil to the market. Finally, the price increases of 1973 and 1979 changed the relationship between oil consumption and economic activity, causing supply and demand to become more volatile. Simultaneously, the adoption of new tax systems in the United Kingdom and the United States reduced producer interest in stable prices, effectively increasing price volatility. Lastly, the creation of a futures market in petroleum created a mechanism that opened the oil market to a much larger number of participants.

The consequence of these changes is a much more open and transparent oil market. Prices change daily and are duly reported in many different sources, and control appears to have passed from a few organizations to the market. It is difficult to determine whether price movements will be wider in the long run, but, it is clear that price changes will be more frequent than they were in the past.

Short of nuclear war, the transformation of the industry could be reversed only through a return to something like the system of preferential agreements between the multinational companies and the producing countries which existed prior to 1972. The complete downstream integration by producing countries could help stabilize the market, but more likely such integration would further destabilize the market.

Some countries, such as Kuwait, have started down the road to downstream integration. Many officials of OPEC countries seem to think that this type of downstream integration will prove to be the cartel's salvation; however, I would reach a different conclusion. First, downstream integration makes it far more difficult for the cartel to monitor and police production decisions by each country. Production beyond agreed quotas can be hidden more easily if the producer is marketing a wide range of products. Second, even in the absence of this effect, downstream integration is not enough. Instead, the market stability that existed in the 1950s and 1960s resulted from the maintenance of sufficient surplus capacity to meet any unexpected surge in demand. At the same time, the joint production agreements provided multinational companies with the ability to exert control over total output, both among themselves and within exporting countries.

To achieve a return to the market stability of the past, producers need to exert control over output in a fashion that will achieve the effect of the market structure that existed in 1972. Both prices and consumption need to be stabilized. Uncertainty must be eliminated. Oil will not be "decommoditized" simply by ending the current glut because the return to a tight market will not eliminate uncertainty -- instead, prices will once again spiral upward. Oil can only be removed from the list of economic commodities through the establishment of joint producing agreements and the maintenance of sufficient surplus capacity in producing countries. This is an outcome that seems beyond the ability of the members of OPEC.

REFERENCES

Adelman, M. A. 1972. The World Petroleum Market. Baltimore, Md.: Johns Hopkins University Press for Resources for the Future.

__________ 1980. "The Clumsy Cartel." The Energy Journal 1: 1.

__________ 1982. "OPEC as a Cartel." In OPEC Behavior and World Oil Prices, ed. James Griffin and David Teece. Boston, Mass.: George Allen and Unwin.

Baer, Julius B., and Olin Saxon. 1984. Commodity Exchanges and Futures Trading. New York: Harper Brothers.

Hieronymus, Thomas A. 1982. Economics of Futures Trading. New York: Commodity Research Bureau.

Vernon, Raymond. 1983. Two Hungry Giants: The United States and Japan in the Quest for Oil and Ores. Cambridge, Mass.: Harvard University Press.

11
The World Energy Outlook

William D. Hermann, Chevron Corporation

Among the assignments falling to the Economics Department at Chevron is the task of accounting for every BTU of energy burned worldwide and forecasting energy use into the future. Even though a retrospective look at previous forecasts is always very humbling for the ego, we believe we are improving our ability to piece together all the complicated relationships and reach more accurate conclusions concerning their future paths and trends.

One of the most difficult problems in forecasting energy supply and demand balances is to estimate the relationship between energy requirements and the output of goods and services in various economies of the world. The amount of energy employed per unit of output differs among countries as a result of traditional living patterns, climate, previous access to energy and its historical relative cost. The inherited infrastructure of each country reflects these historical patterns.

Early attempts to compare the efficiency of energy use among countries simply calculated the per capita gross national product (or income) and per capita energy consumption and used the ratios of these two variables as a measure of each country's energy efficiency. Countries such as Sweden and West Germany appeared particularly efficient in providing a high per capita income relative to their use of energy. The U.S. and Canada, on the other hand, appeared to use a great deal more energy given their level of per capita incomes.

However, this analysis is seriously oversimplified. For example, floating currency rates have implied marked changes in per capita incomes when measured in any common currency such as the U.S. dollar, when, in fact, no significant change in living standards has occurred. Such an uncontrollable variable can introduce difficulties in the analysis and produce highly distorted results.

To avoid the problems of currency value fluctuations it is possible to use an internal index which measures the standard of living in any given country in terms of the ratio of average incomes to a standard basket of purchases. Such a purchasing power index has been calculated for 45 cities around the world by the Union Bank of Switzerland.

When this purchasing power index is compared with per capita energy consumption in each of the countries, the correlation is much more satisfactory. The U.S. and Canada no longer appear to be so profligate in their use of energy. It leads to the obvious and understandable conclusion that the use of energy increases as the standard of living improves. Put another way, the higher the quality of life, the greater the energy requirement to support it.

Even though there is a definite linkage between our standards of living and energy consumption, it is by no means frozen. Improvements in efficiency of energy utilization are both possible and desirable. In fact, if we use the three years 1971 to 1973 as a base of 100, the ratio of total energy use per unit of real GNP in a sample of industrial countries has fallen to a range of 70 to 85. For example, in Japan the ratio has fallen to 70, in the U.S. to 75, and in France to 85.

Last year, in the U.S., we actually consumed 37 million barrels per day of energy in terms of oil equivalent. Had the 1973 energy/GNP ratio prevailed, we would have consumed nearly 48 million barrels per day, a saving of about 11 million barrels per day in total energy use, nearly 30%. We expect this trend to continue at a slightly slower pace in the foreseeable future. In other words, while energy conservation is expected to persist, economies will continue to provide higher standards of living using less energy per unit of output.

Reduction in the consumption of gasoline in the U.S. provides a good example of price-induced conservation. Gasoline consumption had been increasing at a rate of about 4% per year in the post World War II period, reaching a peak of about 7½ million barrels per day in 1978.

In spite of the increased number of automobiles and trucks on the highways, we now expect gasoline consumption to average about 6 million barrels per day in the year 2000.

Even though the number of vehicles is expected to increase by about fifteen percent (from about 130 to 150 million), and the number of miles driven per vehicle to remain stable, the improvement in efficiency will be more than offsetting. This is expected to result in an overall saving of twenty percent in the consumption of gasoline by the year 2000 compared to the peak year of 1978.

The prolonged rise in the value of the dollar relative to other currencies has also had a significant impact on both petroleum importing and producing countries. For importing countries whose currencies have weakened relative to the dollar, the main effect has been to raise consumer prices contributing to slower economic growth and reduced demand for oil. For producing countries, the reduced demand for oil has resulted in lower revenues which has led to weaker economic performance. However, the oil producing nations have partially offset their lower dollar revenues by shifting purchases away from the United States toward countries whose currency values have declined relative to the dollars.

The official price of Saudi Light crude oil - the market crude - has fallen from $34 per barrel to $28 in the past two years. In the U.S. this has meant benefits in terms of reduced outflow of dollars as well as placing downward pressure on inflation rates. However, since oil is traded in dollars worldwide, our industrial trading partners have been forced to pay higher prices in terms of their own currencies. For example, the French franc averaged 4.22 to the dollar in 1980 and by 1984 it had fallen to an average rate of 9.26. This deterioration of the franc had the effect of more than doubling the price of oil for the French economy. In varying degrees, the other European countries have suffered similar increases in the price of oil during the past four years.

Viewed from the perspective of the oil producing countries, however, the increased value of the dollar has prevented their purchasing power from falling as far and as fast as might be supposed. By changing the source of their purchases from the United States to the countries with falling currency values, the oil producing countries have avoided a precipitous drop in purchasing power. Even though OPEC production fell by ten million barrels per day between 1980 and 1984, and the average price was about the same, the real dollar value of their imports changed only slightly. After adjusting for exchange rates, inflation and trade patterns, the real value of their imports fell only from $83 billion in 1980 to $78.5 billion in 1984. While the drawing down of currency reserve holdings accounted for a small proportion of their purchases during 1984, most of the maintenance of OPEC's purchasing power stemmed from the increased value of the dollar and their shifting of purchases to relatively weak currency countries.

A closer look at our forecast for energy supply, prices and consumption should begin with a bit of history. In 1973, we forecast oil demand would grow from 49 million barrels per day in the non-Communist world to over 100 million barrels per day by 1985. By 1978, demand had risen by only 3 million barrels per day and our current estimate for 1985 is only 47 million barrels per day. The reason for these vast differences is the giant leap in price.

In 1978, oil supplied 55 percent of the non-Communist world energy needs, with natural gas and coal each supplying about 18 percent and nuclear and hydroelectric power together supplying the remaining 10 percent. While oil's share was expected to grow, it actually declined by 5 million barrels per day, and total energy consumption grew by only about 5 percent. Market forces gradually worked their will as millions of individuals made intelligent decisions to cut energy consumption in the face of higher prices.

After thorough studies of recent history which provide, among other insights, a much greater appreciation for the lags between a price shock and its market response, we believe our latest thinking on the relationship between supply, demand and prices is, if not correct, at least logical. We are now forecasting more modest growth in energy consumption which we believe is closely linked to the price forecast through a better knowledge of demand elasticities. We now expect consumption to grow at the relatively slow rate of just over 1 percent per year. By the end of the century, oil will supply only 40 percent of all energy consumed, down from roughly 50 percent today. Natural gas consumption is expected to grow at a rate of almost 3 percent per year, coal at slightly more than 3 percent per year, with nuclear power at almost 6 percent per year. However, we do not expect any new nuclear plants to come on line other than those currently planned or under construction.

Even with the low growth rates in our forecast, the non-Communist world will consume 9 million barrels a day more oil in the year 2000 than it does today. Most of this increased supply will come from OPEC. Even though two new major sources, Mexico and the North Sea, have emerged since 1973, OPEC has approximately two-thirds of the world's proven oil reserves. In fact, over half the world's reserves are in the Middle East, where we expect most of the growth in oil production to occur.

With OPEC looming large in the supply picture, it should come as no surprise that our price forecast is greatly influenced by our estimate of demand for OPEC oil. Even a casual review of the oil price shocks of 1973 and 1979, will reveal that OPEC was pushing the limits of its capacity to produce crude oil. Incited by the Yom Kippur War of 1973, the Arab member governments initiated an oil embargo which demonstrated OPEC's power in a tight market. From 1973 to 1978, production growth slowed because of reduced demand stemming from higher oil prices. The gap between production and capacity widened and prices stabilized. However, the Iranian Revolution and the Iran-Iraq War removed a large increment of OPEC capacity in 1979 and 1980, resulting in another jump in prices. Demand slackened even more, bringing current production down to less than 15 million barrels a day from a maximum OPEC production rate of 31 million barrels a day.

We tend to believe that as long as demand for OPEC oil is below about 20 million barrels a day, prices will be extremely weak. When production exceeds approximately 26 million barrels a day, or 80 percent of capacity, prices will strengthen. In between these limits, OPEC can comfortably maintain fairly stable prices in real terms.

With OPEC production well under 20 million barrels a day currently, we would not be surprised to see another small decrease in official prices this year. Over the next few years, we expect prices to stay constant in nominal dollars, and to decline in real terms as inflation erodes the dollar's value. Towards the beginning of the next decade, rising oil demand will pull OPEC production back up into the 20 to 26 million barrel per day range. Prices will then begin to rise with inflation, remaining constant in real terms. Then, towards the end of the century, as we see the gap between production and capacity closing, we expect oil prices to begin rising in real terms -- in other words, faster than inflation. In the twenty-first century, higher real oil prices will begin to make alternate energy sources attractive. We estimate that oil from shale or coal can be produced for $60 to $70 a barrel in today's dollars.

The outlook for oil prices and production has important implications for the United States. U.S. petroleum reserves are relatively small compared to the rest of the world, yet at the moment, we are producing 9 million barrels a day. We are the second largest producer in the world, led only by the Soviet Union. However, oil production in the United States is a mature industry. Even with enhanced-recovery techniques, the development of heavy crude in California, and likely new finds, U.S. oil production will inevitably decline. With U.S.

oil demand rising an estimated half a percent a year, we expect domestic production to cover only 50 percent of consumption by the year 2000.

Obviously, declining U.S. production is a serious national issue. It is further complicated by the fact that this forecast assumes considerable offshore exploration and development within limits necessary to protect environmentally sensitive areas. If offshore activities were to be prohibited indiscriminately, we could become dependent on imported oil for 80 percent of our total consumption by the end of the century.

12
The World Oil Market to the Year 2000

Charles K. Ebinger, Center for Strategic and International Studies, Georgetown University

Introduction

While the newspaper and magazine headlines of 1985 have been dominated by the pending collapse of oil prices, the long anticipated breakup of OPEC and the demise of the nuclear power industry, an emerging crisis has been developing which threatens U.S. and global economic security, Third World development and societal cohesion, as much as the oil price and supply shocks of the 1970s. This crisis centers on the illusion permeating Washington that the energy crisis is over and that the future energy needs of the U.S. and the rest of the world are secure. Nothing could be further from reality. It was just a few years ago that energy forecasters predicted that energy supplies would remain tight for the rest of the century. Studies done by the petroleum industry predicted that world oil production would reach at least 90 million barrels per day before peaking between 1985-1995. Actual production in 1985 will be closer to 57 mmbd. Almost all long-term assessments by industry, consultants and academics forecast rising oil prices that would lead to the development of high cost alternative energy sources, such as shale oil, and coal liquefaction and gasification. Under this scenario, the Energy Security Act predicted that U.S. shale oil production would hit 2 million barrels per day by 1992. Today, it is apparent that we will be lucky to hit 30,000 b/d. In almost all these scenarios, nuclear and coal fired power plants were to be built on a massive scale. Instead, today we have a nuclear power industry on the brink of financial chaos and coal, despite major improvements in new clean burning technologies, is under intense scrutiny as a major contributor to the growing internationalization of acid rain. Finally, almost all prognoses released during 1979-1982 envisaged that little spare oil producing capacity would exist anywhere in the world by the mid to late 1980s. Because of this fact, it was believed that the oil industry would rush out and search for new sources of oil in high cost areas, such as the frontier regions of the Arctic and the Outer Continental Shelf.

Although reasonable from the vantage point of 1979 or 1980, these assumptions were misdirected. What is most surprising is the fact that despite the abysmal record of almost all forecasters, our views continue to be solicited. Nonetheless, just as the "herd" instinct of constrained energy supplies pervaded the industry a few years ago, today, a similar consensus is emerging; namely, that oil and energy demand will be depressed for the next ten to fifteen years, OPEC will remain under pressure and energy supply security is no longer a major public policy issue. While some analysts clearly differ on how far prices will slide over the next two years, there are only a few lonely voices that now argue that a major crisis, rather than just a tightening market, may loom ahead in the decade of the 1990s.

While in the last several months there have been indications that oil prices might once again be heading downwards posing new strains on OPEC and on much of the international financial community, too many analysts are focusing, though understandably, on the short-term market and neglecting the medium term (5-10 years) implications of current developments.

Recent concerns over falling oil prices in the short-term have been triggered by the following events: (1) the end of the British coal strike, which has further reduced fuel oil demand by 275-300 mbd, (2) still hotly contested proposal by the Reagan Administration to end purchases of 50,000 b/d for the Strategic Petroleum Reserve beginning in September, 1985, (3) further gains by natural gas, coal and nuclear power at the expense of oil in Western Europe's and to a lesser extent, the United States' industrial market, (4) enhanced sales of natural gas liquids (500,000 b/d) most of which is outside the OPEC crude oil quota system, (5) the coming onstream of three large export refineries in Saudi Arabia, Algeria and Libya of over 800,000 b/d of capacity, and the prospect that an additional 1.1-1.4 mmbd of OPEC refining capacity (outside the OPEC quota) will be built in the 1985-1990 period, (6) the construction of Shell's large petrochemical plant (250,000 b/d) in Saudi Arabia, which will by late 1986 use natural gas feedstocks, currently being flared, thus backing out more crude oil, (7) cheating on OPEC quotas by Nigeria and others through a variety of mechanisms (countertrade) that are placing additional sizeable volumes of crude oil on the market, (8) an end to inventory build-ups by some of the major oil companies, (9) further slippages in demand in the first eight months of 1985 in Western Europe, Japan, and the United States, which has led several major oil companies to revise their world oil demand figures down dramatically, (10) rising volumes of product exports from non-OPEC, as well as the OPEC producers noted above. These developments have led to an additional 1 mmbd of closings of U.S. refinery capacity since 1983 and the prospects of still more, (11) continued rises, above those projected, in non-OPEC oil production of 800,000 b/d in 1985 against a projected demand growth of 300-400 mb/d, and the anticipation that new non-OPEC production will come on stream in the future, (12) fluctuating exports by the centrally planned economies of barter oil from client states (Angola), and OPEC (Saudi Arabia, Libya, Iraq, Algeria), adding further to market instability, (13) continued conservation, (14) market aberrations unleashed by the burgeoning futures, cash forward and spot markets and (15) the flow of large volumes of sub-octane gasoline, gasohol and ethanol into the United States, which has considerably added to price volatility in the oil products market.

These events, combined with the emergence of more Iraqi oil export outlets (700,000 b/d) in the near future, presage growing downward pressure on oil prices during the rest of 1985 and 1986. If the above events are coupled with a significant slowdown in world economic growth in the last half of 1985 and 1986 an official OPEC price drop to the $22-23/bbl level or even lower remains a stark possibility. Likewise, were the Iran/Iraq war to come to an abrupt halt (which seems unlikely) further pressures by these two nations to increase exports by as much as 3 mmbd in one year to rebuild their economies could prove the *coup de grace* for oil price stability. Iraq has already demanded an increase in its quota of 800,000 b/d, which can only be partially met by Saudi and Kuwait reductions in the production of "war relief" crude. The key trouble period for OPEC will occur between the fall of 1985 and mid-June 1987 with the stocking policies of the oil companies in the fall of 1986 being a good harbinger of things to come. In any case, there seems almost no plausible scenario, barring a political catastrophe in the Middle East, that could lead to OPEC demand being above the 16-17.5 mmbd range through the third quarter of 1987.

In contrast to the above rather somber view for anyone in the oil, energy and especially the U.S. refining industry, there are some disturbing trends that may make the "short" term market the wrong place to focus one's attention, as a harbinger of future prices. Market observers have been severely humbled. After the events of 1973-74 and again after the fall of the Shah in January 1979, they seem to have forgotten the lessons of basic economics; namely, that the higher the price of a commodity the less demand there is for it. As an energy commodity rises in price, people will pursue other "energy" alternatives. With the advantage of hindsight, the changes in the pattern of energy usage have been staggering. Between 1979-84, oil imports plummeted 34 percent in Western Europe, 40 percent in the United States and 26 percent in Japan. As Christopher Flavin notes in a recent Worldwatch Report, these three countries accounted for 31 percent of the decline in world petroleum trade.[1] In the OECD nations, energy consumption fell by 36 percent between 1973-1979. In contrast to this situation, oil consumption in the rest of the world rose by 7 percent between 1979-84 despite the impact of the global economic recession.[2]

While these gains are extremely impressive, they have not occurred without massive costs: (1) the mothballing or closing down of nearly 7-7.5 mmbd of refinery capacity worldwide, (2) the looming prospect of major bankruptcies of some electric utilities, which embarked on high cost coal and nuclear power plants to meet increases in demand projected in the early 1970s that never occurred, owing to consumer resistance to high prices. Forbes Magazine estimates that the United States may have squandered $100 billion in the nuclear power sector alone, (3) a near depression in parts of the oil service sector, (4) a massive restructuring and truncation of the gasoline marketing business, which raises profound national security concerns about the ability of the U.S. refining industry, if current trends continue, to meet oil demand in the event of a major military mobilization in even a "secondary" conflict theater. It would be extremely ironic if the Strategic Petroleum Reserve, on which the American taxpayers have already spent $15 billion dollars, could only be partially used owing to inadequate domestic refining capacity. With several refineries in Western Europe (dedicated to NATO use) having recently closed, the Western Alliance could suffer grave consequences if the 4.5 mmbd future drawdown capability of the Strategic Petroleum

Reserve could not be used to resupply Western Europe in a variety of conflict scenarios, (5) a massive rise in the debt burden of many oil industry giants incurred in the course either of acquisitions or in fighting off unfriendly suitors. Not one dollar of this debt has added one drop of oil or gas to the nation's oil and natural gas reserve base, and (6) the scuttling of 24 LNG projects destined for the U.S. market.

Furthermore, falling energy prices, according to Bankers Trust[3] have led to a plummeting in U.S. expenditures for oil and natural gas drilling, from $40 billion in 1982 to $27 billion in 1984 and an estimated $24.3-23 billion in 1985. Clearly, if oil prices fall further, oil and gas drilling in once promising frontier areas in Alaska, the OCS, the North and Norwegian Seas, and elsewhere will fall, leading to declining reserve/production ratios as oil demand picks up in the 1990s. Far too few policymakers seem to understand that given the long lead times necessary to develop new oil fields, 1990 is already energy history. If a project is not at least under way today, it will not be in the marketplace by 1990.

The consequences of these facts are profound. While the elasticity between the price of oil and oil demand are determined by a wide variety of factors (taxation regimes, etc.) and are the subject of intense academic debate, if oil prices fall precipitously in the short run, it appears likely that at least high cost conservation measures, such as the replacement of energy inefficient machinery, which has not yet been amortized, will be delayed if not postponed. Clearly, generalities on this subject are dangerous since consumer perspectives on both the short and the long term direction of energy prices, as well as non-economic factors, affect all consumer investment decisions.

Nonetheless, to the extent that oil prices fall to a level in the short run that generates consumer complacency, as appears to be happening in the United States with renewed interest in medium sized cars, we will begin to lock ourselves into rising dependence on imported oil later in the 1990s. The reason for this centers on the fact that with almost all non-OPEC oil production on the market that can be produced without driving prices downwards, any incremental demand for oil will be demand for OPEC oil. If conservation efforts stagnate, new oil and gas exploration expenditures continue to be cut back, and oil prices crash to a level that places other higher cost energy investments (nuclear, coal) at risk, demand for OPEC oil will accelerate in the early rather than the mid 1990s.

It should be emphasized that those analysts who believe that a collapse in world oil prices would be a boon for the world economy are naive in their assumptions. Even if existing oil investments in high cost areas, such as the North Sea or in Alaska, were not scrapped or made uneconomic either owing to the complexity of the governing taxation regimes or because the economics of the particular field make it less expensive to operate the field at a small loss rather than to close it down completely, new investments would be curtailed. In any event, those analysts who generalize about how oil production in high cost areas will be affected at various price levels should be wary since the economics of a field brought into production during the high inflation years of 1979-80 will vary greatly from those brought into production in earlier years. Despite these caveats, it is clear that at prices of $20 or less per barrel, new investment in frontier oil production will fall off precipitously.

Still another issue that energy forecasters have neglected is the fact that when a price for commodity rises dramatically over a short period of time, demand can fall so rapidly that prices fall owing to the availability of too much productive capacity being available relative to the changed market circumstances. In this situation, there is obviously little incentive to develop new productive capacity when demand has shrunk, unless the investments are already well underway.

In this regard, John Lichtblau's article "OPEC's Challenge: Surviving Until the Mid-1990s" in the May 13, 1985 issue of the Petroleum Intelligence Weekly, is of interest.[4] While Mr. Lichtblau notes that the displacement of OPEC crude by non-OPEC crude since the late 1970s occurred as the result of several unique factors; namely, the near simultaneous opening up of the three largest oil finds outside OPEC in the post-war period - the North Slope, the North Sea and Mexico's big output rise, he fails to note that most of this new production was the result of exploration expenditures made before the first oil shock of 1973-74. Since 1973-74, the growth in "new" non-OPEC production while significant, has been far less dramatic. While this statement may appear at variance with the recent report in the July 15, 1985 issue of the Petroleum Intelligence Weekly, that Norwegian and other non-OPEC oil production has risen much more rapidly than forecast, the PIW goes on to warn that the higher peak production levels may also presage a steeper decline in non-OPEC oil production in the early 1990s. Indeed it appears that this may already be the case for oil production in Egypt, Malaysia, Norway and the United Kingdom.

While nearly 6.5-7 mmbd of non-OPEC crude supplies have been added to the world oil market since 1979, there is little reason to be sanguine about this development. By 1988-89, North Sea production will begin to decline, followed by the North Slope in 1990. Some new production in the Third World will come on stream, but it is impossible to see this amounting to more than an additional 1-1.5 mmbd between now and 1990.

The fact that these events are occurring against the backdrop of (1) a World Bank projected growth in OPEC and Third World oil demand of 5-7 mmbd by 1995, (2) declining East-bloc oil production and exports, (3) major declines in the oil reserves of the United States (25%), the USSR (25%) and Western Europe (5%) (despite the North Sea) over the last decade, (4) sagging U.S., Australian and United Kingdom production (1.7 mmbd by 1990 and 2.5-3.5 mmbd by 1995), (5) the prospect of major reductions in the growth of coal and nuclear power in much of the OECD nations after 1992 in the absence of major new orders and solutions to the acid rain and nuclear environmental issues, (6) the transfer by the OECD nations of many of its smokestack industries (steel, basic chemicals, cement, glass, etc.) abroad, which could presage faster than anticipated rises in energy and oil consumption in parts of the Third World, and (7) EIA projected U.S. oil imports of 7.38 mmbd in 1990 and 9.44 mmbd by 1995 (52.4% of consumption), gives little reason for complacency. Moreover, too few policy-makers in Washington seem to be paying attention to the effect that falling oil prices in the short-run may have on medium-term energy supplies. Between 1963-73 world oil production grew by 25.5 mmbd at a cost of $76.2 billion ($3,000/bbl of productive capacity). In contrast, between 1973-83 world oil production grew by 6 mmbd at a cost of $420 billion ($70,000/bbl of productive capacity). What these figures clearly tell us is that it is becoming more expensive to find oil, the risks are rising exponentially and we are finding less of it.

Given the uncertainties of the short-term market, the following conclusions can be drawn. First, as long as fears of a price collapse or slow price erosion persist commercial inventories will remain lean, and investments in new exploration and production both in and outside OPEC will fall, leading to an erosion over time in global reserve/production ratios. Consequently, it appears likely that by the mid-1990s, OPEC's real productive capacity will not be the 31 mmbd produced in 1979 but closer to 25 mmbd. This reduction will occur for several reasons: (1) sagging oil reservoir investments in the wake of falling petrodollar revenue, (2) the emergence of a truncated OPEC as four or five OPEC members use their oil for internal consumption, and (3) neglect of oil facilities.

Furthermore, if oil prices fall dramatically, the economies of Indonesia, Mexico, Venezuela, Ecuador and Nigeria could be thrown into political and social upheaval either endangering current oil production or leading to reduced investments in oil facilities.

If one accepts the direction of this analysis, it is apparent that by 1995, demand for OPEC oil could hover in the 23-24 mmbd range, thus straining OPEC's productive capacity at 25 mmbd. In such a scenario, a political upheaval in any major oil producing country could send oil prices skyrocketing. This prognosis would be disturbing enough simply on the basis of supply and demand analysis, but unfortunately OPEC's oil pricing and production decisions do not occur in a vacuum but as we have seen in 1967, 1970, 1973-1974 and 1979 are deeply influenced by political events exogenous to the oil market. Likewise even in major non-OPEC oil producing nations such as Mexico, political unheaval could send shudders through the world oil market.

It is this fact more than any other that leaves us dangerously exposed to another oil price shock during the early 1990s. The specter of another Arab-Israeli war, the spread of the Iran/Iraq war, the coming to power of anti-western Islamic fundamentalist regimes in Iraq, Kuwait, Saudi Arabia or the UAE or even terrorist attacks against major oil installations are all factors that could tear asunder the pragmatic assumptions of our supply and demand forecasts. They also raise serious questions about the wisdom of enhanced product import dependency from this volatile region.

Likewise those who automatically and complacently assume that OPEC and especially the Gulf producers, will tailor their production levels to meet world oil demand in the 1990s, do so at their peril. The question we should be asking is what if Saudi Arabia decides to avoid the financial excesses of the past and produces only 5-6 mmbd over the next decade? What if a new generation of leaders concerned about the erosion of their society's values brought on by modernization and westernization decide that their black gold belongs to Allah and should remain in the ground?

It is these factors, as well as the continued fragility of the international financial system largely brought on by the oil shocks of the 1970s that generates the need for continued policy action on the energy front. Those who dismiss the IBRD's projections of the growth of Third World energy demand as grossly inflated should ask themselves what the energy implications would be if the major debtor nations either repudiated their debts or, as a bloc, followed the new Peruvian model and announced that repayments will be limited to a percentage of export earnings. If the nations of Asia, Latin America and Africa could reduce their burden of debt servicing and resumed economic growth at the levels of the early 1970s, what impact would this have on global oil supplies, especially if oil prices fell to $20 or less? Far too few analysts in the United States have paid enough attention to the social and political chaos that IMF austerity measures have imposed on the mass of the population in the Third World. With large birth rates of 3.5-4% per annum, and a GDP/energy coefficients of one or greater, it is apparent that any constraints on energy supplies will lead to declining levels of personal energy consumption and thus falling living standards. Already in much of the Third World, basic living standards are below those that prevailed in the early 1970s.

The World Energy Market After 1995

While the above analysis suggests that the halycon days of OPEC may return in the mid 1990s, this in no way suggests either that OPEC's troubles are over in the short run or that as we move towards the turn of the century that oil's role as a major fuel will remain predominant. The major uncertainties that plague both short and long term energy projections are:
(1) assumptions about world economics growth,
(2) changing relationships in the GDP/energy coefficient in response to changing energy prices, (3) the inability to project exogenous factors (political or social upheavals) that impact on world oil markets.

Clearly, if oil prices fall dramatically ($15/bbl) in the short to medium term, this will have an impact on the global crude oil and petroleum production supply/demand energy balance of the 1990s. The key question that makes further prognoses fraught with uncertainty is how long prices at $15/bbl could stay there before demand rose once again as coal, nuclear and other higher cost energy alternatives came under price pressure. Those analysts who have recently argued that rising oil product imports into the United States, pose no threat to U.S. national security[5] have been too influenced by current market trends (slowly eroding prices) and have neglected the potential impact on the U.S. refining industry of a collapse in crude oil prices in the short run followed by rising volumes of crude oil and petroleum product import dependency in the 1990-1995 period. Those market forecasters who discount the prospect of crude oil prices falling to $15-20/bbl in the short run should note the recent statements of Saudi officials threatening to place large additional volumes of oil on the already "glutted" world market and recent "conversations" between high level Kuwaiti officials and senior U.S. government personnel indicating that $17/bbl oil is now viewed as a distinct market possibility.

The energy market after 1995 will be heavily influenced by (1) the impact of the short to medium term market on energy development, (2) world economic trends, (3) changing environmental policies, (4) breakthroughs in energy technology.

If the oil price stagnates or slowly erodes, it appears that global oil demand will begin to creep back in the early to mid 1990s. As the market tightens there will be renewed interest in a wide variety of energy technologies such as biomass energy (wood, energy from waste, alcohol fuels), small scale hydro and a wide variety of solar and geothermal technologies. While generalizations are dangerous, it would appear that increasingly world energy demand will be met by a wider diversity of energy technologies than is generally the case today. These technologies will be more geared to meet end use energy needs in as efficient a way as possible. For example, in the transportation sector it seems likely that by 2000-2010 cars running on CNG, methanol, ethanol, electricity, etc., may find enhanced market niches, thus displacing petroleum for perhaps 10%-15% of the U.S. transportation market.

Likewise, solar heating and cooling technologies, as well as photovoltaics will gain a market share at the expense of large scale coal and nuclear fired plants. As oil prices pick up, cogeneration will grow dramatically and it appears that worldwide natural gas use will rise exponentially, especially in the Third World.

If on the other hand, oil prices fall below \$20/bbl in the short run and stay there 2-3 years, interest and investment in high cost oil and other alternative energy technologies will fall leading to potential shortfalls in global energy supply/demand and a potential for a ratcheting upwards in oil prices in the 1990s.

What emerges from the above analysis is that it is in the interest of the entire global community to avoid large swings upwards or downwards in oil and energy prices. Large price swings by generating uncertainty lead to the inefficient allocation of resources by private investors.

Similarly, governments must on the basis of the best information available to them avoid wide fluctuations in energy policy. Ideological rhetoric either for an energy "free market approach" (which has never existed) or for government management (which has never worked) needs to be rejected for some basic policy goals which can then be fine tuned.

If energy is perceived to be a long term security problem then policies such as filling the SPR or aiding the development of alternative technologies need to be pursued across administrations. While conservatives will bewail government intervention citing the extreme cost of such actions and liberals will assail the hardships sometimes unleashed by "free market" policies, both groups must remember that there are real financial costs associated both with implementing policies, as well as not implementing them. The question is merely who in the society pays for these policies when the bill comes due.

In summary, while OPEC is clearly under assault, the rumors of its death are premature. Until the global community begins to recognize energy as a long term problem and that few energy options are "cost free," all of us will remain susceptible to the vagaries of wide price swings both upwards and downwards. The time for a global energy conference involving OPEC, the OECD, the CMEA nations and the Third World to discuss these problems is here. Those who profess that such a meeting can only lead to "government intervention" in the marketplace should travel to those parts of the Third World which have been ravaged by two oil shocks, both directly (economically) and indirectly (socially, politically, environmentally). The world can no longer afford laissez faire energy policies. Let's get on with the job!

FOOTNOTES

1. Christopher Flavin, "World Oil" Coping With the Dangers of Success," Worldwatch Paper 66, July 1985, p. 13.

2. Ibid, p. 12.

3. Energy Viewpoint, Vol. IV, Number 2, Bankers Trust Company, July 24, 1985.

4. Petroleum Intelligence Weekly, May 13, 1985.

5. The Changing Structure of World Refining Industry: Implications For U.S. Refining Industry. Paper prepared for U.S. Department of Energy by OPEC Downstream Project Resource Systems Institute, East-West Center, Honolulu, Hawaii, January 23, 1985; Exxon Company, U.S. Statement on Petroleum Product Imports Submitted to Senate Energy and Natural Resources Committee, Subcommittee on Energy Regulations and Conservation, June 4, 1985; Outlook For Light Product Imports Into the United States. A report of the Petroleum Industry Research Foundation, New York, June 1985.

13
Precursors for High and Low Future World Oil Prices

Anthony J. Finizza, Peter B. Jaquette,
Atlantic Richfield Company
Dale M. Nesbitt, Robert A. Marshalla,
Decision Focus Incorporated

1.0 INTRODUCTION

The past fifteen years have demonstrated how strongly corporate and government decisions are influenced by expectations of future oil prices. Many analysts have pointed out that investment, research and development (R&D), and regulatory decisions are strongly affected by highly uncertain and often erroneous estimates of future prices.

Uncertainty about future prices imposes substantial risks on energy decision makers. Yet we know of few respectable efforts to understand and quantify these risks. Rather, the most common approach is to project (usually by consensus judgment but occasionally by modeling) recent price trends into the future. Often colored by a great deal of inertia based on recent events, such projections provide an incomplete basis for effective decision making under uncertainty and for understanding how the economic forces are likely to play out in the world oil market.

The objective of this paper is to take the first step toward developing what is truly needed: a credible probability distribution over future world oil prices. Our discussion extends that of Gately (1984), which is focused on point forecasting.

An important first step in developing a probability distribution over future oil prices is to determine what are the "tails" or extreme values of that distribution. The low tail characterizes the lower bound on future oil prices and in an important sense the maximum degree of risk faced by agents in the energy system. A company seeking a risk-averse investment and R&D strategy should devote considerable effort to characterizing this low tail.

By contrast, the high tail bounds the largest bonanza that can befall domestic producers. In an important sense, it tells producers how large a potential prize they stand to obtain from any particular investment, which they must balance against the potential losses from that investment. In an equally important sense, the high tail presages the degree of political pressure that is likely to be brought to bear on the government to intervene in the energy system--the higher the price, the more pressure for government intervention.

This paper will quantify the probability distribution over future oil prices using two models of the world oil market--the Decision Focus Incorporated World Oil Model, described in Marshalla (1979) and Marshalla and Nesbitt (1984), and the Gately (1983) model. By using explicit models, we feel can achieve a higher degree of consistency, appeal more directly to economic science, and therefore attain more accuracy than by relying on subjective guesswork.

2.0 PRECURSORS FOR HIGH OIL PRICES-DFI MODEL

The centerpiece of the DFI model is a two part behavioral model of the OPEC cartel, the two parts being the core cartel and the competitive fringe or noncore. The model calculates time paths of oil prices, costs, revenues, supplies, and demands throughout a 60 year horizon. In the model, the core cartel, acting as a unified bloc, is assumed to set oil prices. Fringe members and non-OPEC producers all act as price taking, profit maximizing producers. The core supports its chosen price strategy by acting as a residual supplier, producing whatever levels of output are necessary for the world market to equilibrate at the desired price. The price policy that the core perceives to be in its own best interest is the price path that maximizes the present value of future profits from oil production. In selecting this price path, the core takes full account of how its selection will affect the behavior of all other producers and consumers and thereby takes account of the true demand it faces. Bohi and Toman (1984) state that a dominant firm pricing approach such as DFI's is perhaps the most descriptive of the world oil market.

2.1 Low Discount Rate

Our results suggest that the most powerful variable facing oil suppliers is the interest rate they face. It seems appropriate to regard discount rates facing producers as the rate of return they can receive on low-risk corporate or government securities. (We will use the terms discount rate and interest rate interchangeably.) Low discount rates mean that the return on a dollar invested in such securities is relatively low, implying that there is limited value to having a dollar available sooner rather than later. If oil in the ground is appreciating faster than the discount rate, the producer is better off to defer exploration, development, and production activities to the future. Such deferment causes prices to be high in the near and intermediate term.

Interest rates have a profound effect not only on producers but also on consumers. High real interest rates retard economic growth and thereby retard oil consumption, and low real interest rates have the opposite effect. Thus, low real interest rates give a double-edged impetus to oil prices--stimulating oil demand and discouraging oil production. High real interest rates have the converse effect.

During the postwar era, real interest rates have been in the range of 1-2 percent or lower. The 1970s saw low (and at times negative) real interest rates and simultaneously high oil prices. Our results suggest these events were far from coincidental. Since the late 1970s, real interest rates have shot up to the range of 4-6 percent. If such high rates persist (or more properly if people's expectations of interest rates at these high levels persist) for the indefinite future, oil prices will be soft for a long time to come. Only if real interest rates retreat to historical levels can future oil prices be high.

2.2 High Degree of Intracartel Cooperation

In order for world oil prices to be high, none of the larger OPEC states can act as a price taker; all must cooperate.

2.3 Other Precursors to High Oil Prices

The remaining economic variables that tend to favor higher oil prices are presented in summary form because they are substantially less important than the first two variables mentioned--interest rates and cartel cooperation.

2.3.1 High Demand. If the level of oil demand for any given price is high, oil prices will tend to be higher. If demand is robust across a broad range of oil prices (i.e., inelastic demand), prices will tend to be firm because there is relatively more rent to be earned by OPEC from cartelization. Perhaps surprisingly, the magnitude of oil demand is less important than interest rates or the degree of intra-cartel cooperation, at least across the ranges tested. Nonetheless, robust oil demand is a necessary precursor to high future oil prices.

2.3.2 Limited Oil Resource Availability. The extent of the oil resource base both within and outside OPEC countries is uncertain. If the extent of the oil resource base is lower or the cost of proving and producing that resource base is higher than current expectations in either OPEC or non-OPEC countries, the future time path of production cost will be higher and prices will be correspondingly higher. Within a reasonable range of uncertainty over oil production costs and quantities, there is less sensitivity of oil price to the size and cost of the oil resource base than one might think. This finding implies that increasingly detailed surveys of the world resource base are less important in forecasting future oil prices than other activities such as understanding interest rates or incentives for cartel cooperation.

2.3.3 Policy or Physical Constraints. It has been quite popular to argue that physical capacity limitations are key driving forces within OPEC. Some have argued that OPEC will never add capacity beyond today's roughly 30 million barrel per day level. Some have argued that producers in non-OPEC as well as OPEC countries cannot increase or decrease production because of physical constraints or political limitations. To the extent that such constraints will exist and will limit oil production relative to an economically optimal level, they will tend to drive oil prices upward.

2.3.4 Wars, Disruptions, or Other Noneconomic Events. Traumatic occurrences such as wars, disruptions, or other short-term events usually cause near-term prices to skyrocket, and they cause expectations of near and long-term prices to be higher.

2.3.5 High Backstop Price. The term backstop price has come to mean the price of the next best source relative to conventional crude oil that can be produced in comparable quantities. The next best source can represent another physical source of oil (or a substitute) or the cost incurred by doing without. If the backstop price is high, oil is relatively more valuable (compared to the alternative) and therefore should command a higher market price. It is clear that a high backstop price is a precursor to high future oil prices.

3.0 PRECURSORS FOR LOW OIL PRICES—DFI MODEL

3.1 High Interest Rate

A high interest rate implies that there is very high value to having a dollar available today (for investment purposes) rather than later. If oil in the ground is appreciating more slowly than the interest rate, the producer is better off to turn his oil into dollars today than to hold the oil in the ground for the future. High interest rates stimulate current production at the expense of future production, causing prices to be low in the near and intermediate term. Our results imply that high real interest rates ALONE are enough to guarantee that future oil prices will be low.

We should point out that the DFI model calculates the pricing strategy for core OPEC that maximizes the present value of profits from oil production in the face of an assumed interest rate--there is no way for OPEC to do better. We note further that OPEC makes less money (in a present value sense) from oil production if interest rates are high than if interest rates are low.

High real interest rates have a differentially larger impact on non-OPEC competitive producers than they do on core OPEC (monopolistic) producers. Core OPEC producers have market power, which they can use to partially mitigate the deleterious effects of higher real interest rates. Competitive producers have no market power, meaning they must bear the full brunt of higher real interest rates.

3.2 Low Degree of Intracartel Cooperation

While our results suggest that full cooperation among cartel members is a necessary precursor to sustain high oil prices, they also suggest that disintegration of the cartel does not necessarily imply a return to very low prices. In short, the "good old days" of the 1960s are gone forever. Our results further imply that the most significant variable in the "good old days" was not the birth of an oil cartel; indeed even in a competitive market the owner of the oil resource can expect to command huge Hotelling scarcity rents. Rather, the most significant variable was the nationalization of the resource, allowing governments rather than multinational companies to garner scarcity rents. While monopoly rents are far from insignificant, they are substantially smaller in magnitude than the scarcity rents. Our results also suggest that monopoly rents are potentially large enough to encourage continued cooperation among the most significant OPEC players.

3.3 Other Precursors to Low Oil Prices

3.3.1 Low Demand. If the level of oil demand for any given level of price is low, oil prices will tend to be lower. If demand is elastic, due either to substitution possibilities or to income effects, prices will tend to be lower because there is relatively less benefit to OPEC from monopolistic practices.

Indeed, if demand is low enough, the ability of OPEC to sustain a cartel will be seriously eroded--there will simply not be enough aggregate demand to allocate among the OPEC members. Such an event would likely precipitate the partial disintegration of the cartel, with only the "hard-core" OPEC states remaining as the core. The sheer magnitude of resource owned by Saudi Arabia suggests that there will always be a core cartel even if it is Saudi Arabia acting alone.

3.3.2 High Resource Availability. If the extent of the oil resource base is higher or the cost of production is lower than current expectations in either OPEC or non-OPEC countries, the future time path of production cost will be higher and prices will be correspondingly lower. Assuredly, a major low-cost discovery, whether or not it occurred within an OPEC country, would put downward pressure on oil prices. However, the size of such a discovery would have to be astronomical in order to lead unconditionally to low world oil prices.

3.3.3 Low Backstop Price. Suppose OPEC foresaw the advent of a technology that could produce liquid fuels in large quantities for $30/bbl. In such a situation, future escalation of oil prices would necessarily be limited--they could never escalate past $30/bbl. Slower escalation would tip the produce/hold decision in favor of producing today, which would put substantial downward pressure on oil prices. Thus, the very possibility of lower-priced long-run substitutes would be sufficient to guarantee low oil prices regardless of whether the cartel exerts any market power or interest rates are low. We perceive a great deal of uncertainty in the price of oil substitutes.

3.3.4 Protectionist Policies. Representative protectionist policies against imported oil include tariffs levied against imported oil, quotas restricting imports above certain levels, or subsidies for domestic sources to render them price-competitive with imported oil. Such policies tend to depress demand for oil from oil exporting countries, thereby reducing their "market share," their market power, and thereby the price of oil.

3.4 Concluding Comment

Unlike our findings for high oil prices, it is not necessary for a number of events to occur SIMULTANEOUSLY in order for oil prices to be low. Indeed, high real interest rates alone are sufficient to guarantee that oil prices will be low. Dissolution of the cartel is sufficient to guarantee that oil prices will be low unless interest rates are low. This is in sharp contrast to the finding that low real interest rates and full intracartel cooperation must occur SIMULTANEOUSLY in order for future oil prices to be high.

4.0 DFI MODEL RESULTS

This section summarizes eight model scenarios from which the assertions of the previous sections were derived. Figure 1 summarizes these scenarios, which are designed to analyze interest rates from one to six percent real given either full cartel cooperation or no cooperation (competitive world oil market). These eight scenarios are designed to span the range from high oil prices (full cartel, one percent interest rate) to low oil prices (no cartel, six percent interest rate). Table 1 shows the profit-maximizing price strategy for core OPEC in each of the scenarios represented in the figure.

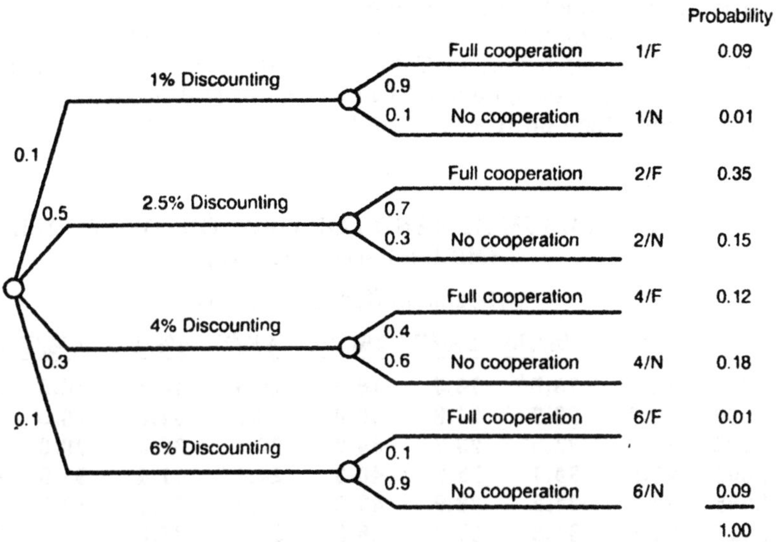

Figure 1. Probability Distribution Over DFI Model Scenarios

Table 1

PROFIT MAXIMIZING OPEC PRICES-DFI MODEL
(1984 Dollars per Barrel)

Scenario (from Figure 1)

	1%/F	1%/No	2%/F	2%/No	4%/F	4%/No	6%/F	6%/No
1985	$26.00	$26.00	$26.00	$26.00	$26.00	$26.00	$26.00	$26.00
1990	45.00	40.70	32.00	27.00	25.30	19.70	17.30	14.60
1995	46.90	41.10	34.40	28.30	27.80	20.90	18.60	15.60
2000	48.10	41.80	36.80	28.60	30.40	21.60	20.10	16.20
2005	48.90	43.80	38.60	31.70	32.30	24.00	22.70	17.80
2015	50.80	48.10	43.30	39.60	38.10	33.10	30.50	27.30
2035	57.40	56.50	57.10	56.00	56.70	55.50	55.10	55.30

The six percent interest rate/no cartel case calls for a significant softening in world oil prices even relative to today's prices. Indeed, if today's high real interest rates are maintained and OPEC ceases to exert market power, oil prices can be expected to drop below $15 per barrel in the next five years and remain at that low level through the turn of the century.

Table 2 shows the demand that will be faced by OPEC at the market clearing prices in Table 1. Note that in the high interest rate/no cartel cases, demand for OPEC oil will increase rapidly and remain very high until well after the turn of the century.

Table 2

EQUILIBRIUM DEMAND FOR OPEC OIL-DFI MODEL
(Million Barrels per Day)

Scenario (from Figure 1)

	1%/F	1%/No	2%/F	2%/No	4%/F	4%/No	6%/F	6%/No
1985	16.5	16.5	16.5	16.5	16.5	16.5	16.5	16.5
1990	22.9	28.7	21.8	30.0	19.9	32.0	25.9	35.0
1995	24.2	33.5	23.7	34.7	22.1	36.3	29.0	38.6
2000	25.9	34.1	25.5	40.3	24.4	41.4	31.6	42.7
2005	27.3	34.2	28.9	40.0	28.4	42.2	32.0	44.0
2015	31.6	34.3	35.2	26.3	36.1	36.5	33.9	36.3
2035	31.7	32.1	33.0	31.0	34.3	31.4	36.1	33.4

The six percent/no cartel case represents the lower tail of our probability distribution over future oil price. The assumption that real interest rates will remain as high as four to six percent for the indefinite future is unprecedented. Furthermore, the assumption that no member of OPEC will ever exert any market power seems unrealistic. Certainly Saudi Arabia acting alone will have at least some degree of unilateral market power, and it would be difficult to argue that such market power would never be exercised.

Turning now to the other extreme, the low discount rate/full cartel cases show substantial near-term firming of oil markets. Such firming comes about because there is much less incentive for non-OPEC and OPEC countries to produce today rather than hold; monopoly practices retard production and thereby drive up prices; and demand is potentially stimulated by low interest rates. It is interesting that the combination of the first two of these three phenomena does not lead to prices higher than those shown in Table 1. The high price cases, which represent the upper tail of our probability distribution over future oil prices, shows a real price in the year 2000 of approximately $48.00/bbl, about twenty percent higher than the all-time real price peak in 1979-80.

Notice in Table 2 that even in the higher price cases, demand for OPEC oil can be expected to rebound in the next five years. This reflects the fact that at prices between $25 and $35 per barrel, there will be significant world consumption of oil, and OPEC can expect to achieve at least as large a market share as it enjoys today. If it acts as a bloc, OPEC can realistically maintain its current share until non-OPEC producers have substantially depleted their resources.

If intracartel cooperation is complete, notice that OPEC production will not reach today's installed capacity of 30 million bbl/day until after the year 2000. This finding forewarns that full cooperation might remain a difficult task for OPEC during the next 20 years, just as it has been during the past two or three. By contrast, if intracartel cooperation breaks down altogether, OPEC countries can expect to produce at capacity as rapidly as possible and non-OPEC producers to decrease production as their oil becomes noncompetitive, i.e., by 1990. The four noncartel cases emphasize just how low oil prices can go and just how large OPEC's market share can be at those low prices.

We have made no attempt to be exhaustive with regard to all the economic variables that could potentially affect future oil prices and quantities. Marshalla and Nesbitt (1985) have conducted a more exhaustive analysis that supports the basic conclusions here.

5.0 PRECURSORS FOR HIGH OIL PRICES—THE GATELY MODEL

The Gately model (Gately, 1977) is a simple target capacity utilization construct where oil prices are determined endogenously following a rule-of-thumb. In our implementation of the model, real prices rise when the market is tight (above 85 percent OPEC capacity utilization), prices decline when capacity utilization is low (below 75 percent), and prices hold constant when capacity utilization is between these levels.

This paper utilizes a two-fuel variant of the Gately model in which energy is modeled as the combination of oil and non-oil, which depend on economic growth and current and past prices. Non-OPEC energy supply (both oil and non-oil) are functions of present and past prices. Fuel substitution is handled using cross price elasticities. At equilibrium in the oil and non-oil markets, the demand for OPEC oil is the difference between world demand and non-OPEC supply. OPEC capacity utilization is calculated as the ratio of OPEC demand and an exogenous estimate of OPEC capacity.

Because of the model's simplicity, the precursors of high or low oil prices can be stated in terms of the proximate determinants of capacity utilization: (1) economic growth, (2) energy efficiency (a function of the model's price elasticities), (3) non-OPEC energy supply, and (4) OPEC capacity. Relaxation of the pricing rule to allow market clearing prices in the absence of the OPEC cartel permits inclusion of another precursor, (5) cartel cooperation.

5.1 High Demand

High oil demand, the concatenation of high economic growth and low energy efficiency gains, is the most leveraging factor for high oil prices for precisely the reasons cited in Section 2.3.1. Since the Gately model approach is silent on the real discount rate effect, it is not surprising that demand assumes the dominant role. A critical demand issue is whether Lesser Developed Countries (LDCs), particularly those in the Pacific Basin and Latin America, will continue their industrialization in an oil-intensive fashion. Little evidence is available to support arguments either way.

5.2 Low Non-OPEC Supply

If the resource base for non-OPEC oil and non-oil resources is lower than current expectations, the demand for OPEC oil will be greater, implying a higher OPEC capacity utilization. Given fixed capacity (in the short run), this translates into higher oil prices. Since the response of non-OPEC supply to price is relatively weak and requires a long lead time, this factor is of secondary importance as a precursor for high oil prices.

5.3 Decreased OPEC Capacity

Since the Gately model targets capacity utilization, divergence in expected and actual capacity will have a significant effect on oil prices. A decline in capacity, for example, due to an extension of the Iran/Iraq war, a spread of fundamentalist Islamic thought, or a widespread war would have a sharp upward bias to oil precursor for high oil prices than for low oil prices.

6.0 PRECURSORS FOR LOW OIL PRICES—GATELY MODEL

This section addresses factors complementary to those in Section 5--events that presage low oil prices.

6.1 Low Demand

Low demand, either from prolonged worldwide economic stagnation or strong energy efficiency gains, would foreshadow low oil prices. Weak economic growth could be the consequence of widespread trade restrictions leading to constricted trade which could stymie industrialization of LDCs, misguided economic policies (emanating from the U.S.), or financial debt crises. Strong efficiency improvements might occur from widespread technology transfer. Happily, the two underlying factors of demand are not complementary: weak economic growth, operating through low capital stock turnover, does not foster strong efficiency gains.

6.2 High Non-OPEC Supply

A major hydrocarbon discovery (unlikely) or emergence of cost-effective technology to convert gas to liquid would be a precursor for low oil prices. As stated in Section 5.2, this factor is deemed unlikely to be a major factor in low oil prices.

6.3 Increased OPEC Capacity

A large increase in OPEC capacity above today's level would depress prices. It is difficult, however, to find the economic incentive for such a move, unless it were coupled with the next precursor.

6.4 No Cartel Cooperation

If OPEC and non-OPEC members behave similarly--both producing as rapidly as possible--we would see strong impetus favoring low oil prices. In the Gately framework, unlike the DFI construct, higher cost non-OPEC oil producers would choose to endure substantially lower prices rather than shut in their capacity. This implies that much lower prices would be required to clear the market because of the significantly larger supply of oil.

7.0 GATELY MODEL RESULTS

This section summarizes six model scenarios designed to span the range from high oil prices (high demand, OPEC cooperation) to low oil prices (low demand, no OPEC cooperation). See Table 3.

Table 3

OPEC OIL PRICES-GATELY MODEL
(1984 Dollars per Barrel)

	High Demand		Most Likely Demand		Low Demand	
	Full Cartel	No Cartel	Full Cartel	No Cartel	Full Cartel	No Cartel
1985	26.00	26.00	26.00	26.00	26.00	26.00
1990	22.20	19.20	21.30	16.10	19.00	13.20
1995	41.20	37.60	25.80	23.50	19.30	16.40
2000	52.50	52.20	37.00	36.00	19.30	18.20
2005	50.70	48.60	32.30	30.80	17.20	17.90

The low demand scenarios exhibit a significant decline throughout the period in prices from today's level. It is interesting to note that under the no cooperation variant, oil prices fall to the $13 level, a result similar to the DFI analysis.

In the two most likely demand cases, oil prices fall sharply before recovering to levels higher than today's prices, reflecting tightening OPEC capacity utilization in the late 1990s following an initial period of slack capacity.

Oil prices weaken even in the two high demand cases. In these cases initial low prices stimulate demand, reinforcing the high demand assumption of the case. This stimulus causes OPEC capacity to be reached early in the 1990s, resulting in a sharp rise in prices.

Notice that the greatest price difference is between pairs of demand scenarios, supporting the assertion made earlier that oil demand, the combination of economic growth and energy efficiency, is the most leveraging factor. Also, for any given pair of demand scenarios the price difference between full and no cartel narrows as time progresses.

8.0 PROBABILITY DISTRIBUTION—DFI MODEL

Figure 1 represents the probability distribution over interest rates and cartel cooperation given interest rates. As shown at the right, the figure represents a probability distribution over scenarios. Using this probability distribution, the corresponding probability distributions over 1995 and 2000 oil prices is:

Probability	1995	2000
0.09	$15.60/bbl	$16.20/bbl
0.01	18.60	20.10
0.18	20.90	21.60
0.15	28.30	28.60
0.12	27.80	30.40
0.35	34.40	36.80
0.01	41.10	41.80
0.09	46.90	48.10
mean	29.60	31.10
standard deviation	8.30	8.80

In the year 2000, the expected or mean oil price is therefore $31.11/bbl, and the standard deviation is $8.77/bbl. Notice that the distribution is skewed slightly below the mean, the five outcomes below the mean price having a combined probability of occurrence of 0.55. This skewness is consistent with the observation that for high prices to occur, several simultaneous events must occur (e.g., low interest rates and full intracartel cooperation) but for moderate or low prices to occur, only a single precursor event is necessary.

Confining our attention to the year 2000, suppose we were considering an investment such as a tertiary oil project that would be profitable as long as the oil price were larger than $29/bbl. The mean oil price in the year 2000 as determined by the model ($31.11/bbl) is higher than $29/bbl, implying that the investment will be profitable in a mean or average sense. But will the company pursue the investment, particularly in light of the fact that there is a 43 percent probability that the price will be lower than $29/bbl? Given that most investments require substantial out-front capital exposure, many companies would be expected to shy away from investments with a 43 percent probability of losing money even if the expected profits are positive. That is, many companies can be expected to behave in a risk-averse fashion.

It is interesting to note that if decision makers had access only to the mean or expected future price (a typical situation when corporations make only point forecasts), they might well compare the breakeven price of $29/bbl with the mean price of $31.11/bbl and decide that the project is worthwhile. On the other hand, given the probability distribution above, the corporation would know that the project is a $2.11/bbl winner on average but is extremely risky--a 43 percent chance of losing money. On that basis, the corporation might well decide to direct its resources toward investments with better returns relative to risks.

9.0 PROBABILITY DISTRIBUTION—GATELY MODEL

Figure 2 represents the probability distribution over oil demand and cartel cooperation given OPEC capacity. Using this distribution, the corresponding probability distributions of oil prices for the years 1995 and 2000 are:

Probability	1995	2000
0.11	$16.40/bbl	$18.20/bbl
0.04	18.30	19.30
0.28	23.50	36.00
0.42	25.10	37.00
0.03	37.60	52.20
0.12	41.20	52.50
mean	$25.70	$36.30
standard deviation	$6.80	$9.30

In the year 2000, the mean is slightly higher than the DFI mean, and the standard deviations is slightly larger. The distribution for 1995 is skewed below the mean while the distribution for 2000 is skewed slightly above the mean.

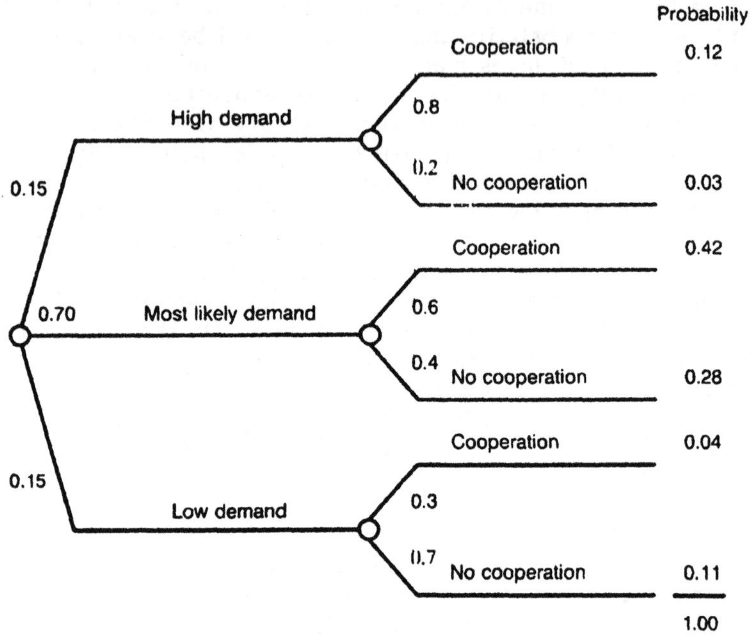

Figure 2. Probability Distribution Over Gately Model Scenarios

10.0 CONCLUSIONS

Our analyses conclude that the lowest credible price (approximately $15/bbl) is higher than many analysts have forecasted. "Price crash" cases with prices falling to the level of OPEC production costs are simply not going to occur. Furthermore, extremely low prices are likely to be transient indeed, persisting for only a brief period of time.

The highest credible price (approximately $50/bbl) is lower than a number of analysts have forecasted. There is virtually zero probability that oil prices will achieve the $60, $80, or $100 per barrel estimates made during during the 1970s and early 1980s.

Furthermore, the probability distribution over future oil prices is not symmetric between the low and high tails. Rather, it is skewed toward the low end (particularly in the near term) because it takes fewer precursor events for low rather than high prices to occur.

What should non-OPEC producers do to make more effective decisions? Rather than continuing the typical practice of adopting a single conservative (i.e., low) point estimate of future oil prices against which to evaluate potential investment and R&D strategies, companies should use explicit probability distributions such as those developed here to quantify downside risk and properly trade it off against upside profit potential. Only by so doing can companies ensure that they are not missing an attractive opportunity (in a risk return sense).

REFERENCES

1. Bohi, D. and Toman, M., "Analyzing Nonrenewable Resource Supply," Resources for the Future, Johns Hopkins University Press, 1984.

2. Gately, D. R., "OPEC: Retrospective and Prospects, 1973-1990," European Economic Review, May 1983.

3. Gately, D. R., Kyle, J. R., and Fischer, D., "Strategies for OPEC's Pricing Decisions," European Economic Review, 1977.

4. Gately, D. R., "A Ten Year Retrospective: OPEC and the World Oil Market," Journal of Economic Literature, September 1984.

5. Marshalla, R. A., An Analysis of Cartelized Market Structures for Nonrenewable Resources, Garland Publishing Inc., New York, 1979.

6. Marshalla, R. A. and Nesbitt, D. M., "Future World Oil Prices and Production Levels: An Economic Analysis," The Energy Journal, forthcoming 1985.

7. Marshalla, R. A., and Nesbitt, D. M., "The Decision Focus Incorporated World Oil Model: Model Structure and Methodology," Decision Focus Incorporated working paper, 4984 El Camino Real, Los Altos, CA 94022, March 1984.

8. Nesbitt, D. M., "A Theory of Supply Cartels with Application to OPEC," Decision Focus Incorporated working paper, 4984 El Camino Real, Los Altos, CA 94022, 1984.

14
Economic Theory and World Energy Markets in the 1990s

David A. Huettner, University of Oklahoma

I. INTRODUCTION

Over the past decade, world energy markets have proven to be a laboratory for energy economists eager to test their theories on problems of widespread interest. A brief review of these theories and their success and failure over the past decade would have at least two uses. First, economists should weed their fields occasionally and cultivate only the best crops. Second, successful theories when applied to current energy markets could offer useful insights to the behavior of these markets in the 1990s.

Given these objectives Section II of this paper will briefly review the dominant theories of the past decade. Section III will utilize the best of these theories and some general rules of thumb to provide an overview of world energy markets in the 1990s.

II. DOMINANT ENERGY MARKET THEORIES OF THE PAST DECADE: SUCCESSES AND FAILURES

Turning first to failures, perhaps the least useful economic theory has been that of exhaustible resources. While the stock of world energy resources may someday be fully identified and prices may rise inexorably with interest rates, at present, technological change, unexpected discoveries, investment program changes and demand shifts produce conditions incompatable with the basic assumptions of exhaustible resource models. Augmentation of exhaustible resource models for these factors would, in effect, convert them to renewable resource models but perhaps analysis should move in this direction until the conditions assumed by exhaustible resource models are satisfied.

A second theory advanced occasionally by industrial organization economists over the past decade is that the low cost OPEC producers would utilize limit pricing to deter entry and maintain their dominant market share. Since limit pricing theory has had a generally poor record in predicting producer behavior in industrial markets, its failure to describe energy market price and output trends is perhaps not surprising.

A closely related theory used frequently over the past ten years has been the dominant producer competitive fringe theory. While this theory enjoyed some fleeting predictive successes, it has failed over the past decade to predict major real price movements and the rapidly dwindling OPEC market share.

One of the more interesting outgrowths of the 1970s has been the revival of cartel theory. Competition among modelers has yielded many variants and offered insights into intra-cartel conflicts. Overall, these models have not predicted the full sweep of events over the past decade and have certainly not been useful for longer term investment decisions.

Another class of models worthy of note could be described as large scale simulation models. These models have improved understanding of the role of short and long run elasticity of demand, investment, and government policy and have often outperformed other models in extrapolating existing short run trends. Prediction of long run energy market movements, however, has proved elusive even for large scale simulation models.

What then have been the successful energy models of the past decade? In my estimation, the more successful models have been those taught in Economics 101. Certainly the full sweep of events of the past decade was captured by these models and those who truly believed that markets would function. Once the overall nature of the forest was outlined by these simple models, one could return to the trees and fill in the details with large scale simulation models.

The most useful Economics 101 concepts proved to be simple supply/demand models, elasticity of demand, and substitution. The 1974 OPEC price shock was easily modeled as an upward shift in the supply curve. The pressing question in 1974 was how high would the price of oil go? Given the low marginal and average costs of the dominant middle east producers, their short run profit maximization problem was virtually identical to revenue maximization. An astute Economics 101 student knows that short run revenue is maximized when short run elasticity of demand equals -1.0. Two limits to OPEC prices were immediately obvious: short term elasticity of demand and substitutes. Events quickly indicated that short run demand elasticity was going to limit OPEC prices to levels below $50--the cost of substitutes available on a large scale in a five to seven year time horizon.

Longer run price movements would clearly depend on the supply and demand curve shifts that would occur beyond a five to seven year time horizon. The five to seven year time horizon was a minimum indicated for any sizeable turnover in durable goods on the demand side and for any large scale increase in both non-OPEC oil supplies and non-oil substitutes. Certainly the demand for oil would shift down in the long run as end user stocks of energy consuming appliances and equipment were updated with more efficient and/or nonoil based stocks. Equally certain was the fact that both oil and non-oil supply would increase. The long run combination of a downward shift in oil demand and an upward shift in oil supply strongly suggested that the oil prices achieved in the first five to seven years after 1974 would be the peak prices and that subsequent real price movement would be downward.

The pleasant surprise of the past decade is that markets performed as rapidly as could be expected despite much counter productive tinkering by governments around the world--particularly Washington.

III. ECONOMICS 101 AND WORLD ENERGY MARKETS IN THE 1990S

If models taught in Economics 101 offered valuable insights in the past decade, what then do they offer for world energy markets in the 1990s? Certainly the indications are clear that end-user demand shifts will continue to be an important factor. In addition, coal and nuclear power will continue to replace the bottom half of the barrel in most industrial countries. Coal will be particularly attractive given the cost-effective, clean burning techniques developed over the past decade.

On the supply side, the 1970s taught us that the best direct substitute for OPEC oil was non-OPEC oil. The 1990s will show that the best substitute for remaining oil uses is natural gas. World proved reserves of natural gas doubled over the past decade while proven oil reserves showed no increase. Russian proven gas reserves also doubled and now exceed Saudi Arabia's oil reserves on a Btu basis. Over thirty countries with no oil resources have now discovered natural gas and the World Bank is working with 20 undeveloped countries to expand local gas use at prices one-third or less than that of imported oil. The United States has a temporary gas surplus; Canadian gas exports to the United States are increasing; and Mexican gas exports to the United States are likely by the late 1990s. The current slowdown in U.S. gas drilling should end about 1990 and, when drilling picks up, there should be little repeat of the mid-1970 debate over whether gas supply will respond to price incentives.

At present, world proved reserves of natural gas are nearly equal to those of oil on a Btu basis. World proven gas reserves will soon surpass those of oil, on a BTU basis, and natural gas should make major inroads into remaining oil uses throughout the 1990s.

If coal and natural gas make major inroads into oil end uses, what are the prospects for oil supply in the 1990s? We know that a major decline in oil exploration worldwide began in 1983, that this condition continues today, and that the supply impact of this decline will not be evident until after 1990. Moreover, this exploration decline has been felt in the major non-OPEC oil provinces. Russian and Mexican exploration has slowed. North Sea production will peak about 1990 yet North Sea exploration has slowed too. US exploration has also slowed and the drilling that continues will be confined to Alaska, the Gulf and selected onshore basins given the impending lease moratorium off the West coast and the dry holes off the Atlantic coast. The 100,000 to 300,000 barrel per day discoveries in Brazil, Columbia and other countries could assume a more important role over the next decade in a delicately balanced market. OPEC itself will undoubtedly experience increased internal problems in the 1990s as Iraq and Iran increase production in a post Khomeni termination of conflict.

The question of whether non-OPEC oil will continue to gain oil market share depends on the rate of growth of oil consumption. Overall, simple supply/demand analysis suggests that oil consumption will increase only slightly over the next decade, that OPEC's production will not increase until at least 1990, and that OPEC's share of world oil output will increase very slowly through the 1990s. These output predictions suggest further modest but orderly decline in real oil prices over the next few years followed by stability of real price through 1990. Gradual increase in real price to a level above the current level is unlikely (barring major political upheavel) before the early 1990s.

Since oil is priced in dollars, one must consider the future course of the dollar to determine oil price trends outside the United States. The dollar's strength reflects the often noted influx of capital to the United States as well as the less noted slowing of U.S. bank loans overseas. Two factors suggest continuation of a relatively strong dollar. First, ongoing shifts in the U.S. electorate should provide conditions attractive to foreign capital well into the next decade. Second, major U.S. banks will spend the next decade repairing their balance sheets rather than dabbling in foreign aid. Given these assumptions, the U.S. dollar should retreat only gradually from current levels to balance trade deficits. While this will result in gradual oil price declines for most countries, the declines will prove too modest a reduction from the current levels to slow the growth of coal, natural gas and nuclear power evident outside the United States.

The continued low market share for OPEC oil indicates that refinery margins will remain depressed worldwide over the next decade. With substantial excess refining capacity, middle east refined products will continue to be sold at crude oil price levels. Stocks will be held to minimum levels to cut inventory costs. Surplus production, refining and tanker capacity plus brief spot market price increases will replace storage tanks.

Extrapolation of existing economic and political trends plus some basic geographic factors add further detail to the Economics 101 model predictions above. The United States and Italy should be the only major industrialized countries to substantially increase oil imports over the next decade. U.S. imports will increase two to three million barrels per day by the mid 1990s with Mexico supplying much of the increase. European economies will continue the slow growth rates of recent years and will turn increasingly to barter for Russian gas as internal political dissent dissipates their ability to compete in international markets. Norwegian gas production will not increase rapidly in the face of stiff Russian competition. Britain will fail to revi its economy and management/labor relationships before North Sea production peaks and the gover ment's ability to placate dissent with largesse is ended. Natural gas will continue to increas its market share in a British economy that will grow very slowly during the 1990s. Japanese growth rates will slow as heavy industrial production shifts to other Asian countries. Coal a nuclear power will fuel most of this growth, however. South American governments will contin to limit oil imports and promote development of all indigenous energy forms given their crushin foreign debt burdens. These debts will be repu diated gradually through negotiated suspension principal payments, etc. to avoid an international debt crisis (and stockholder revolts a major U.S. banks).

Use of Economics 101 models leads to the broad bush predictions offered above for the 1990s. These predictions of basic market paran eters could now be fed into large scale simulation models to flesh out the necessary details. Even at this level of detail, however, one can recognize that the Economics 101 predictions ar at odds with several recent forecasts predictin sizeable real oil price increases by the early 1990s.

One must remember, however, that commodity markets are, by nature, generally depressed. Supply too easily exceeds demand when fixed investments are extremely long lived, suppliers and substitutes are numerous and products are extremely homogenous. Energy markets are commodity markets and for this reason Economics 101 models may focus at the correct level of detail for long run analysis.

15
On the Pricing of Oil: The Effects of Market Fragmentation

Thomas J. Woods, Gas Research Institute

INTRODUCTION

Prior to 1973, oil consumption in the non-communist world grew at a relatively steady rate, with almost no shift among regional markets. Demand for particular petroleum products, from residual fuel oil to gasoline, also grew across the board. Growth in oil production, however, occurred largely in one group of countries, which came to be called the Organization of Petroleum Exporting Countries (OPEC).[1] This led ultimately to a sellers' market, which provided the opportunity for oil prices to increase to levels that frequently exceeded the actual costs to discover and produce oil. By 1981, oil prices had increased almost an order of magnitude.

Such an increase in oil prices had major effects upon oil markets. In industrialized countries, oil ceased to be the fuel of choice for new facilities and for some existing facilities as well. Fuel switching and conservation further reduced the demand for oil. Economic growth for industrialized countries and many non-OPEC countries slowed significantly.

At the same time, increased oil prices provided incentives to look for new oil, often in regions with little or no known oil production. As a result, oil production outside of OPEC began to grow. In the face of falling demand, the increased oil production outside of OPEC created downward pressures on oil prices. Today, the oil market has become a buyers' market, and oil producers are struggling to hold existing prices.

The changes in oil consumption and production have not occurred across-the-board. Rather, both the consumption and the production parts of the oil market have fragmented into separate segments, each with its own growth patterns. The trends in these market segments indicate that the buyers' market for oil may not be a short-lived phenomenon. The purpose of this paper is to assess the outlook for world oil prices in light of the trends in the segments of the oil market.

Oil Consumption

World oil consumption increased rapidly through 1973, almost on a recession-free basis. Since 1973, the growth in world oil consumption has slowed and, since 1979, it has declined. By 1984, world oil consumption had fallen back to its 1976 level. In the non-centrally planned economies (CPE),[2] the decline has been more severe. The 1984 oil consumption in the non-CPE countries has declined almost to 1972 levels. And, oil consumption is now anything but recession-free.

The declines in non-CPE consumption have occurred in two general groupings of nations, the members of the Organization for Economic Cooperation and Development (OECD)[3] and the "non-oil-producing," less developed, countries (NOIL).[4] These countries accounted for about 80 percent of non-CPE oil consumption in 1984. In the OECD countries, oil consumption in 1984 has fallen back to almost 1970 levels. In the NOIL countries, consumption may have fallen back to pre-1970 levels.

Growth in oil consumption has continued in the remaining non-CPE countries, that is, OPEC and the oil-producing less-developed countries (OIL)[5]. In 1984, these accounted for about 20 percent of non-CPE oil consumption, up from about 8 percent in 1973. While oil consumption may continue to grow in most of these countries, the effect will be quite modest when viewed in terms of overall non-CPE oil consumption. The extent to whether increased consumption will be the major factor in weakening the current buyers' market for oil will rely principally on the long-term trends in OECD consumption.

Petroleum Products

The fragmenting of the general trends in oil consumption into different groupings of countries was more than matched by the fragmenting of growth rates for individual petroleum products. Prior to 1973, demand grew across the board for petroleum products, and virtually all products traded on the world market had a positive markup relative to world oil prices. The price spike in 1973-74 affected the demands for individual petroleum products in significantly different ways. The demand for petroleum products ceased to grow across the board.

The greatest effects of increased oil prices occurred in the consumption of fuel oil. Fuel oil became so expensive that it ceased to be a fuel of choice for new stationary uses. At the same time, the margins for fuel oil relative to world oil prices became negative. Prior to 1973, they had been positive. This severely affected refinery profitability and reduced the incentives to produce fuel oil.

Fuel oil consumption in non-CPE countries essentially stopped growing after 1973, even though growth in overall petroleum consumption resumed after 1975. As a result, fuel oil began to account for a rapidly decreasing share of non-CPE oil consumption, which is illustrated in table 1.

The decline in the fuel oil consumption exceeds the total decline in petroleum consumption between 1974 and 1984. Between 1979 and 1984, the decline in fuel oil consumption can be said to account for more than 75 percent of the total decline in petroleum consumption.

Table 1. NCPE Consumption by Product Groups
(million tonnes)

Product	1974	1979	1984
Gasolines	582.4	651.4	625.9
Middle distillates	627.4	747.5	706.0
Fuel oil	696.0	706.5	499.8
Others	343.0	383.1	362.6
Total	2248.8	2488.5	2194.3

Source: British Petroleum.

With the modest prospects for increased consumption of the other petroleum products, the extent to which overall petroleum consumption will grow, at least in the near term, will be significantly affected by the outlook for fuel oil consumption. If fuel oil consumption continues to decline, overall oil consumption might continue to decline, even though consumption of other products might increase. In the first seven months of 1985, declines in U.S. fuel oil consumption have offset increases in the consumption of other products such that overall U.S. oil consumption has declined.

The extent to which fuel oil consumption might decline in the long term can be seen by looking at fuel oil consumption in the United States and Canada. Because of natural gas, coal, and nuclear energy consumption, U.S. and Canadian fuel oil consumption accounts for only 11 percent of total oil consumption. Fuel oil consumption in the remaining OECD countries accounts for 27 percent of total oil consumption. The remaining non-CPE oil consumption is 34 percent fuel oil. Thus, there is significant potential for further decline in fuel oil consumption.

If the fuel share of oil consumption outside the United States and Canada were to approach 20 percent of total oil consumption, this would amount to almost 9 percent of non-CPE oil consumption in 1984. If the share were 11 percent of total oil consumption, this would amount to almost 15 percent of non-CPE oil consumption in 1984. In the future, substantial quantities of new gas supplies will be available in Western Europe and other non-CPE countries. A major share of these new gas supplies will go towards displacing fuel oil and some middle distillates.

In the CPE countries, fuel oil consumption continued to grow through about 1980, although its share of total oil consumption in the CPE countries declined. By 1982, fuel oil accounted for 30 percent of total oil consumption, a slightly higher share than in the non-CPE countries.

The CPE countries have substantial gas reserves, and their use of natural gas has begun to increase. In 1980, natural gas accounted for 18 percent of total primary energy consumption in the CPE countries. By 1984, the natural gas share had grown to 21.6 percent. Future CPE fuel oil consumption should decline as gas, coal and nuclear grow. This could reduce the overall demand for oil and compensate, at least in part, for declines in USSR oil production.

If the CPE fuel oil share had declined to 20 percent of total oil consumption, this would amount to about 14 percent of 1984 CPE production. In the long term, if CPE fuel consumption fell to the U.S. and Canada shares (11 percent), this would amount to almost 24 percent of current CPE production. While these declines in fuel oil shares might seem severe, it should be noted that, between 1976 and 1982, the fuel oil share of CPE oil consumption declined from 32 percent to 30 percent. Thus, a declining fuel oil share of the product mix in CPE consumption is consistent with current trends in the CPE countries. This reduced fuel oil share should be able to compensate for near-term declines in CPE oil production. If declines in CPE production could be held to 1 to 2 percent per year from 1984 levels, an aggressive displacement of fuel oil and some distillates in the CPE countries might be able to compensate for declines in oil production through a good part of the 1990s as well.

Oil Production

Figure 1 presents the trends in world oil production. The production is divided among CPE countries, OECD countries, OPEC, and non-OPEC countries. Figure 1 shows that world oil production grew quite rapidly through 1973. Following a decline in oil production in 1975, oil production began to grow again, but only at about half the rate of the 1965-73 period. Most of the growth in world oil production from 1975 to 1979 occurred in the CPE countries. Since oil production peaked in 1979, oil production has declined 15 percent by early 1985.

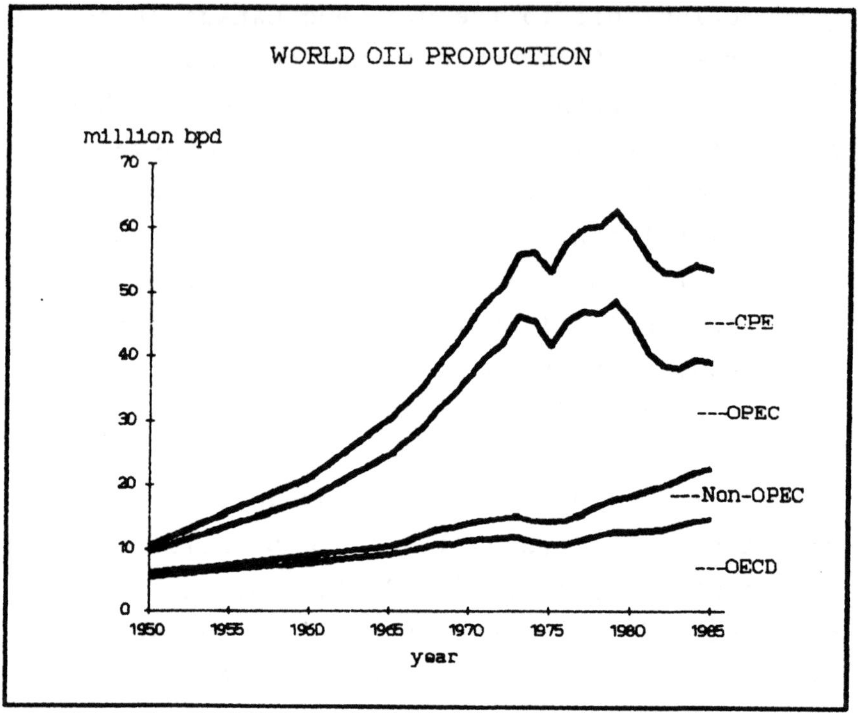

Figure 1. World Oil Production

Non-CPE production trends through 1973 were dominated by increased OPEC production. Between 1970 and 1973, over 88 percent of increased non-CPE production came from OPEC. Since the 1973-74 price spike, however, OPEC's role in world oil production has changed markedly. Between 1973 and 1979, OPEC provided only slightly more than 3 percent of the increase in non-CPE production. Between 1979 and early

1985, the decline in OPEC production exceeded the overall decline in non-CPE production by more than 50 percent.

Since 1973 the major change in non-CPE production has been the shifting of growth in oil production from OPEC to non-OPEC and OECD countries. Today, as a result of the increased prices for oil brought about and sustained by OPEC, OPEC is no longer the marginal source of oil. As of early 1985, non-OPEC countries accounted for 58 percent of total non-CPE production, up from 33 percent in 1973. Increased production from non-OPEC countries has occurred principally from the North Sea and Mexico. However, growing oil production is also occurring in other countries such as Brazil, Egypt, and India, which have large domestic oil consumption levels as well. Some of these non-OPEC producers may not become net exporters, but their increased domestic production should substantially reduce their need for imported oil.

The outlook for non-OPEC production in the near term is for continued growth perhaps on the order of as much as 1 to 2 million barrels per day (bpd). North Sea production will probably remain constant or perhaps even grow as a result of new discoveries and enhanced recovery projects in producing fields. United States production should remain stable as a result of continued infill drilling, new offshore oil production in the Lower-48 States, and modest increases in Alaska production. New production from Colombia should enter world markets in about one to three years. As world demand grows, it seems reasonable that Mexican production will increase to capture its share. Production in Brazil and India should continue to grow for a few more years. Other countries--such as Yemen, Syria, and the Sudan--may become factors by the late 1980s or early 1990s.

In the 1990s, the outlook for increased production in the non-OPEC countries is more speculative. Depending upon the success of improved recovery of oil-in-place, non-OPEC production could remain in the 20 to 24 million bpd range through 2000. Another critical factor in maintaining this production is the extent to which production in the North American Arctic regions will occur.

The effects of prices on future production is hard to gauge, but the effects may not be as severe as they might first appear. The rapid increase in oil prices, while it provided windfall profits to private producers, provided even larger "profits" to governments. Thus, future declines in oil prices will tend to be felt more in national treasuries than in exploration and production activity. Non-OPEC countries, with their more costly producing areas, would find their budgets squeezed severely. Producers, on the other hand, would experience only modest near-term impacts. For example, a drop of $5.00 per barrel in oil prices would cost the British government $4.50 and the producer $0.50 (Oil and Gas Journal, 1985). Thus, the near-term incentives for production and exploration would not necessarily be cut very much by further modest declines in oil prices. In the longer term, lower oil prices would have an effect, although some of this could be ameliorated if cost factors such as taxes, royalties, and well expenses were adjusted downward.

It should be noted that between 1969 and 1979 the real costs to find and produce new gas in the United States increased by a factor of 4.3. Only about one-third of this increase was due to depletion of the U.S. resource base. The remainder was due to increased government taxes and increased drilling and production costs that captured some of the "windfall" arising from the 1973-74 oil price spike.

Outlook for Oil Prices

The world oil market can be currently characterized as a buyers' market, the result of declining demand and rising non-OPEC oil production. The declining demand has been accompanied by a substantial erosion in refinery profitability. At current official prices, gross refinery margins are positive only for the most sophisticated refineries. Such refineries produce very little fuel oil. As a result, refinery economics will work to reduce the fuel oil share of refinery outputs. Short of oil prices declining to a level that would (1) make fuel oil a fuel of choice for new boilers and thus a growth market and, (2) be low enough to give fuel oil a near-positive or positive margin relative to crude, it is very unlikely that the reductions in fuel oil shares of total oil consumption will stop in the near to mid-term.

The extent to which fuel oil consumption will decline is hard to judge. In 1984, fuel oil accounted for only 11 percent of total U.S. oil consumption. In the first seven months of 1985, fuel oil has only accounted for about 7 percent of total U.S. petroleum deliveries. Based on the U.S. fuel oil consumption shares, world fuel oil consumption could decline substantially. This reduced fuel oil consumption is almost equivalent to current production from OECD countries. Therefore, it appears that the largest new source of oil in the 1980s and 1990s may be the oil freed up by falling fuel oil use.

In terms of overall demand, it appears that falling fuel oil use could counteract most, if not all, of the growth in world oil consumption of other products for a substantial period of time. At some point, the growth in non-fuel oil demand should begin to exceed declines in fuel oil demand, or fuel oil consumption should bottom out. At that point, growth in world oil consumption should begin to pick up. The odds of this occurring in the near term are quite small. In the mid term (1990s), noticeable growth in oil consumption outside of OPEC should resume, but if the world economy remains soft, growth sufficient to tighten world oil markets will probably not occur until well into the 1990s.

The outlook for non-OPEC oil production is quite good in the near term; in the 1990s, it is a bit more uncertain. However, because demand will probably grow quite modestly, substantial increases in the demand for OPEC production should not occur until the 1990s. Therefore, it seems that the buyers' market for oil should be a fairly long-lived phenomenon.

Until the sellers' market returns on the order of what it was in the late 1960s, the outlook for large increases in real oil prices is very limited. On a supply/demand balance basis, current oil markets appear to resemble more closely the world of the 1950s and early 1960s, when oil was a buyers' market. This does not mean that oil production in the near term will not be profitable. It just means that the opportunity for windfall revenues to government, producers, and other participants in the oil production process will not reappear for a substantial period of time.

FOOTNOTES

1. OPEC members: Ecuador, Venezuela, Iran, Iraq, Kuwait, Qatar, Saudi Arabia, United Arab Emirates, Algeria, Libya, Gabon, Nigeria, Indonesia.

2. CPE countries: China, USSR, Albania, Bulgaria, Cuba, Czechoslovakia, East Germany, Hungary, Kampuchea, Laos, Mongolia, North Korea, Poland, Romania, Viet Nam.

3. OECD countries: Austria, Belgium, Denmark, Finland, France, Greece, Iceland, Ireland, Italy, Luxembourg, Netherlands, Norway, Portugal, Spain, Sweden, Switzerland, Turkey, United Kingdom, West Germany, Australia, New Zealand, Japan, Canada, United States.

4. NOIL countries: All non-CPE countries other than OPEC, OECD, and OIL countries. These countries include some oil producers such as Angola and Brunei.

5. OIL countries: Argentina, Brazil, Colombia, Egypt, India, Malaysia, Oman, Syria.

REFERENCE

July 22, 1985. "Keller: Market Jitters Won't Trim Much from Crude Oil Price." Oil and Gas Journal 66.

16 Crude Oil Trading and Price Stability

R. Glenn Hubbard, Harvard University
Robert J. Weiner, Harvard University and ICF, Inc.

Petroleum is the world's largest market in value terms--accounting for up to one-third of international trade in recent years--and receives commensurate attention in the economics, business, and policy literature. The discussion here is consequently restricted to petroleum trading--the buying and selling that occurs in an auctioneerless market--and to economic analysis thereof.

Like many mineral industries, petroleum can be divided into vertical stages. Production entails extracting crude oil from existing reserves, development of newly discovered sources, and exploration. Refining is processing the crude oil by heat and chemical means into products that can be readily used. Distribution consists of marketing these products together with service to consumers through gasoline stations, fuel oil deliveries, etc. Each stage involves at least one transaction, which can be a spot or contract trade, or an intracompany transfer.

Before 1970, virtually the entire international petroleum trade was conducted through the channels of the "majors" or "seven sisters"--vertically integrated firms that functioned as a tightly-knit oligopsony in relations with reserve owners, and a tightly-knit oligopoly in selling refined products. Short-term price fluctuation was minimal; a very thin arm's-length market served to balance local excess supply and demand stemming from the vagaries of nature. Prices fell gradually as entry eroded the majors' position.

The price of oil rose sharply several times in the early 1970s, culminating in the enormous increase of 1973-74 that followed the oil embargo and sharp production cut by several large exporters (notably Saudi Arabia) in the wake of the Yom Kippur War. At the same time, oil-exporting countries began to nationalize their oil concessions, which had been owned by the majors. The state-owned companies, however, had little expertise in petroleum trade, and sold their "participation crude" (nationalization was partial) to the concessionaires, who were obliged to "buy back" the oil they had produced in order to maintain their equity positions. This change in ownership served to redistribute rents, but had little effect on market structure.

After the 1973-74 disruption, the majors and other large refiners sought to "secure supplies" through long-term (typically five-year) contracts with state-owned exporting companies. These contracts were for fixed prices and volumes (sometimes with small quantity tolerances), with the understanding that the contract price (known as the official government selling price, or GSP), would be adjusted periodically, typically at OPEC semiannnual meetings. Like many contracts, agreements to sell crude oil on a long-term basis are lengthy and detailed, devoting considerable attention to matters of product quality, financial, legal, and logistical arrangements, and contingencies. The use of the term "contract" here necessarily abstracts from the bulk of these non-price provisions, except when they have economic implications for trading and market adjustment.

Crude oil trading did not develop until the embargo. Although oil market liquidity ruled out the possibility of any targeted country's being cut off, considerable reshuffling of cargoes took place among the majors, in effect replicating a market allocation of the diminished supply. The experience of single-cargo trading provided the basis for transport divisions of the majors to spin off trading companies in the mid-1970s. The spot market remained thin, accounting for 3-5 percent of total trade according to industry estimates.

A similar supply shock due to the Iranian Revolution of 1978-79 produced another large, rapid price increase. The shock also advanced the dis-integration of the petroleum trade. In 1973, the seven largest companies ("the majors") alone handled roughly three-quarters of the crude oil moving in international trade (excluding the Communist bloc and intra-OECD trade, where the institutions are quite different). By 1978, this figure had fallen to about half, and by 1979 to about 40 percent. Some reduction came from within the majors' distribution systems, but the main structural change was the end of the role of integrated companies as resellers to third parties. Third-party sales were replaced by direct contracts between exporters and a variety of smaller purchasers, primarily independent refiners and traders, but also governments (see Table 1), and by spot-market sales. The industry literature described this change in the marketing and distribution of crude oil as reducing market flexibility, the idea being that the majors played a market-like equilibration role.

When contracts signed in the mid-1970s came up for renewal, buyers were reluctant to enter into further long-term agreements, for several reasons. First, the value of "supply security" was questionable, given the frequency of contract abrogation. Many exporting companies (Aramco in Saudi Arabia being a notable exception) had abrogated their contracts, and sold some of their contracted supplies on the spot market.

Second, the non-price provisions of these contracts had become increasingly onerous. Most contracts included "destination restrictions" that limited the resale of contract purchases, and often prohibited them altogether unless the exporter's permission were obtained. Monitoring these restrictions was costly but feasible; proof of compliance was through a certificate of cargo discharge at the tanker's destination. Industry reports of cheating suggest that the practice was risky and costly, entailing either purchase of forged certificates, or discharging and immediately reloading the cargo (Parra 1980).

Third, Saudi Arabia, the largest oil exporter, had honored its contracts, and enforced the no-resale provision. The oil-exporting company (Aramco, jointly owned by four of the majors: Exxon, SoCal, Texaco, Mobil), complied, and did not resell the crude oil, instead refining it and selling the products produced on spot product markets. The increased availability of spot supplies served to diminish the value of "security" obtained through term contracts.

The effects of these upheavals in buyer-seller relationships have become manifest in the last 2-3 years. Although contract terms are considered proprietary, it is possible to piece together their general outline from trade literature and conversations with participants. Contracts are typically very short: fixed quantity for one year, fixed price for 30 days. Buyers and sellers don't hesitate to walk away from negotiations. For example, Sonatrach, the Algerian state oil company known for its hard-line commercial attitude, negotiated 15 contracts for the sale of crude oil at official prices in January 1981. By the end of 1982, only one long-term contract remained in force, and crude oil exports had fallen more than 50 percent. Similarly, many of the customers of the Kuwait Petroleum Company and Petromin (Saudi Arabia) suspended or reduced their contractual commitments on grounds that official prices were too high. The Abu Dhabi National Oil Company's 3-5 year contracts expired by 1981, and were replaced by one-year contracts.[1]

Expansion of spot trade has paralled the decline of term contracts. Various industry estimates have placed the fraction of internationally-traded crude oil moving as spot cargoes at 30-40 percent and the remainder of the trade, with the exception of Aramco and some remaining concessions, as traded on contracts adjusted so frequently (through negotiation or through links to spot prices) as to make them effectively indistinguishable from spot trade from the standpoint of market adjustment. A recent industry survey (Petroleum Intelligence Weekly, 24

June 1985) found that of the 23 largest oil-producing countries, all but four linked their contract prices to the spot market.

The distinction between flexible contracts and spot trade must be based on transactions-costs, since the security value of such contracts is close to nil for both buyer and seller. In response to this question, the purchasing manager for a very large U.S. refiner indicated that his contracts served as "base load," with demand variation being handled through the spot market (interview, May 1985). Thus despite the change in contracting regime -- from years to one month or less, the roles played by spot and contract markets remain roughly the same.

Unfortunately, although estimates are plentiful, hard numbers on spot market volumes are scarce. Unlike in the copper market, spot trading of petroleum does not take place on an organized exchange, but rather through a loose network of producing and refining companies, brokers, traders, and transporters linked via telephone and telex. Much of the trading actively was originally centered on Rotterdam, a major oil port and refining center close to the industrial markets of Northwest Europe. "Rotterdam market" is some-times used to refer to the spot market, although today Rotterdam is but an important regional center in the worldwide spot trade. Entry into this market is easy, but not free -- a single cargo of one-half to one-and-a-half million barrels can be worth 10 to 50 million dollars. Potential entrants require a bank letter of credit for at least this much in order to buy and sell.

One U.S.-based major refining company now makes one-quarter of its crude purchases from governments, all through term contracts, and three-quarters from private companies, of which about half is bought spot (interview May 1985). Another, with fewer historical links to producers, buys all of its imported crude on the spot market (interview, March 1985). Table two below provides figures for Japan, whose government has long been concerned with security of energy supply.

While it is difficult to determine how typical the Japanese spot-contract split is of other importers, the time-pattern is quite striking. The data provide casual support for industry accounts that the spot market grew during the shocks of 1979-1980 (Iranian revolution and Iran-Iraq war), and is larger now than before. Although these statistics are not made public in the United States, a survey of the 31 largest refiners (which account for 90% of imports) produced similar numbers, as shown in Table 3.

Oil-industry reaction to the decline of term contracting is mixed regarding anticipated profit, but clear in terms of market stability -- a Walrasian market is seen as more risky than one in which supply and demand are "guaranteed." One trade-journal article (Roeber 1985) described term contracts as "redolent of stability, continuity, and reliability," and spot trade as "greedy, frantic, and somewhat sweaty." Producers view the vertical regime change as a threat to their market power. A goal of any pricing model should be to examine these assumptions, which are counterintuitive from the standpoint of economics, where the ability of a market to adjust quickly is seen as reducing instability.

The underlying reasons for the rapid and dramatic change in vertical structure--from "almost no spot" to "almost all spot" trade in a decade--are not entirely clear. De Kuijper (1983) showed that the equilibrium fraction of spot trade can be unstable, so that if some players switch away from contracts, a stampede may ensue. Such an explanation is plausible, but does not address when and why such regime changes occur. A less dramatic alternative is that the nature of market shocks has changed, affecting the optimality of contracting. An implication of the model developed below is that contacts will be more prevalent in markets characterized by demand shocks than in markets characterized by supply shocks. Another possibility is that the forced exit of the majors and entry by unintegrated state-owned oil companies, combined with costly reintegration, provides part of the explanation. These hypotheses are not mutually exclusive, nor easy to disentangle empirically.

The outpouring of books and articles occasioned by the "crisis" has focused on medium- and long-term issues, and somewhat surprisingly, has virtually ignored the crisis aspect--the violent short-term market fluctuations. Economic models of the oil market have stood steadfast on Walrasian grounds, and have performed systematically poorly in capturing short-term responses to exogenous shocks (see Stanford University 1982).

The causes of the market responses to the supply shocks of the 1970s (which were not great in quantity terms) are disputed. Among the purely economic explanations offered are 1) increasing marginal (user) costs due to the failure of new discoveries to match rapidly increasing demand ("running out"), 2) cartelization of the market by OPEC, 3) supply shifts due to replacement of oil companies as decisionmakers by nationals with lower discount rates, and 4) movement from low- to high-price equilibrium along a backward-bending supply curve. These explanations are all theoretically and empirically plausible without being completely satisfying. Nor are they mutually exclusive, although each has its vocal adherents and detractors.

Spot prices substantially exceeded contract prices during both disruptions, and were slightly below them over much of the intervening and succeeding periods. The attached figure shows recent spot and contract prices for the most widely traded crude oil, Mideast Light.

The role played by the two-price system is also a matter of (somewhat less coherent) debate. While descriptive accounts abound, analytical work has been confined to a short piece by Verleger (1982), a critique by Bohi (1983), and a couple of extensions.

The former approach is strictly neoclassical. Since the spot market performs the clearing function, spot prices are treated as marginal in the usual economic sense, with the attendant positive and normative implications. The price adjustment story is that of Fisher, Cootner, and Baily (1972). A negative supply shock causes excess demand in the spot market. Rising spot prices signal purchasers to accumulate inventories in anticipation of profit based on spot-contract price differentials. This excess demand causes producers to adjust contract prices upward. The two-price system is simply assumed away.

This formulation does nicely in fitting curves; the few empirical oil market models that do not ignore the issue entirely typically treat spot prices as determined by supply and demand, while relegating contract prices to the position of suitably lagged spot prices (Nordhaus 1980; Verleger 1982; Hubbard and Weiner 1983).

The objections to this view are two. First, it is incoherent. A model in which agents are both rational and behave according to the story is hard to imagine. Second, and equally important, it is uninteresting. There is no attempt to explain contracting as part of the market adjustment process. It renders trivial the relationship between spot and contract prices. It fails to consider the volume passing through the spot market, a market that is often quite thin.[2] A few barrels sold at a high price will have little or no impact on contract prices (nor will the world economy, or that of any individual nation, be perceptibly harmed). This neglect of the size of the spot market appears especially strange--considering that according to most tales from the world oil market, spot prices increase when contract purchasers are cut off, and forced onto the spot market.

The alternative advanced by Bohi addresses the first objection. Calling the above theory "fatuous," he argues that the arm's-length market is marginal only in its small size, thinness, and "peculiar function," and is therefore best ignored. He states (1983, p.25) that the spot market is a "peripheral adjunct that is influenced by, instead of responsible for, events in the petroleum market" , but cautions that his proposed alternative (hoarding of refinedproducts by consumers, which shifts the demand curve outwards) is not fully satisfactory theoretically or empirically, concluding that the determinants of world oil prices are not yet fully understood.

Granger-Sims causality tests of the relationships between spot and official prices carried out by Bohi and others (Fitzgerald and Pollio 1984; Lowinger and Ram 1984) show that spot prices help predict future contract prices, but not vice-versa. The interpretation of these tests, however, is problematic. Bohi's tests on refiner's marginal acquisition costs of crude oil, official prices, and petroleum product prices at the consumer level found Granger-Sims causality all around, leading him to conclude that these prices were determined simultaneously. None of these prices helped predict future spot prices, implying that either "the spot price determines all other prices, or more plausibly, the process generating spot prices is substantially different from that generating other prices" (p.25).

Bohi opts for the second interpretation on grounds of incoherence of the theory supporting the first. The other two papers view the tests as upholding the theory. The tests themselves--regressions of reduced-form equations of various current prices on various lagged prices and nothing else--are unable to distinguish between the two views. An important task for this study is to test whether the industry folklore regarding the changing relative sizes of contract and spot markets can be detected in price behavior, using a structural model to predict the effects of such a change.

The current received wisdom and the alternative are deficient in their unidirectional treatment of causality--the spot market affects the contract market (Verleger), or vice-versa (Bohi, de Kuijper)--whereas simutaneous equilibrium would seem natural. A careful examination of the relationship between the two markets is in order. Such is the goal of our ongoing research.

THE HUBBARD - WEINER MODEL

The rest of this paper summarizes our basic model, and illustrates the role of a multiple-price system in adjustment to transitory skocks. We examine the relationship between spot and contract prices, demonstrating its dependence on the manner in which contract prices adjust to these shocks. We find that the persistence of these shocks is a function of structural parameters such as the fraction of trades carried out through contracts, the response of demand to price changes, and the costs of storage.

For simplicity, suppose that contracts are identical, thereby reducing the number of prices to two - the 'contract price' and the 'spot price'. The two-price system works as follows. A fraction α of world trade takes place through long-term contracts between producers and consumers, at price P^C. The remaining portion is traded on the spot market at price P^S.

The market is subject to demand shocks (ε_D) and supply shocks (ε_S), which are assumed to be independently and identically distributed with mean zero and variances σ_D^2 and σ_S^2, respectively. Let $\eta = \varepsilon_D - \varepsilon_S$ represent the net shock to the market. A contract is defined as an agreement to trade a specific quantity. The contract is signed at the beginning of the period, before shocks take place.

We do not allow contracts to be abrogated. Firms that are unable to make or take delivery on contracts must resort to the spot market to fulfill their contractual obligation. Hence, the spot market adjusts to absorb supply and demand shocks. As long as the trading parties are risk-neutral, the contract price will be equal to the expected spot price:

$$(1) \qquad P_t^C = E_{t-1} P_t^S$$

where t indexes periods and E_{t-1} denotes the expectation conditional on information available during period t - 1.

In this paper, we take the parameterization of the two-price system as given. Risk aversion is the motivation usually given for such a scheme. Risk aversion is not necessary, however; others have discussed a model in which the incentive to offer long-term contracts stems from the real effects of cash-flow variability on a firm's costs. Transactions costs may provide another justification. The resulting tradeoff between spot and contract trade involves, inter alia, the means and variances of the distribution of expected prices and the re lative ease of buyers' adjustment of inventories. These factors underlie the optimal value of α, which is assumed to be optimized and taken parametrically here.

Consider the case in which a negative supply shock (or positive demand shock) initially raises the spot price relative to the contract price. The presence of contracts implies that the spot market price is not the cost of a marginal unit, because a buyer could purchase the good at a lower contract price but would have to commit himself to that price for the duration of the contract. Once α is optimized, the relevant price for purchase decisions is thus

$$(2)\quad P_t = \alpha P_t^c + (1-\alpha)P_t^s.$$

Note that the marginal acquisition cost P_t differs from the average acquisition cost because of prices paid on existing contracts.

Total demand is the sum of consumption and speculative inventory demand. Price-taking speculators, who may also be producers or consumers, trade on the spot market in inventories in anticipation of changes in price, and are assumed to be risk-neutral. Let the objective of speculators over the period (t, t+1) be to

$$(3)\quad \max_{I_t}\ E_t\{(P_{t+1}^s - P_t^s)\, I_t - \frac{h}{2}\, I_t^{\,2}\},$$

where I represents the end-of-period stock level. Holding stocks is assumed to be costly - in fact, increasingly costly - in the size of the stock due to payments to factors fixed in the short run (e.g., storage facilities). Thus changes in price expectations cannot be fully acted upon instantaneously. We follow the literature in modeling such costs as quadratic, the simplest specification of 'diminishing returns'; these costs are indexed by the parameter h.

Maximizing (3) with respect to I_t yields the following demand function for stocks:

$$(4)\ I_t = h^{-1}(E_t P^s_{t+1} - P^s_t).$$

As with most other studies, the holdings of risk-neutral speculators are a function of the expected increase in price, taking into account the cost of adjusting stock levels. Inventory demand (stock change) is just

$$(5)\quad I_t - I_{t-1} = h^{-1}[(E_t\ P^s_{t+1} - E_{t-1}\ P^s_t) - (P^s_t - P^s_{t-1})].$$

Given the assumed contract-price setting behavior, spot and contract prices are equal in equilibrium. An interruption in contract supply ($\varepsilon_{St} < 0$) affects prices as follows. Given planned contract output of $\alpha\hat{Q}$, where a caret over a variable denotes its equilibrium value, there is excess demand at the prevailing contract price. The spot market, with output of $(1-\alpha)\hat{Q}$ plus a responsive addition of $Q^s(P^s_t)$, functions to absorb disturbances. That is, the spot price solves

$$(6)\ (1-\alpha)\ Q^D(P_t) + h^{-1}\ (E_t P^s_{t+1} - E_{t-1} P^s_t) - h^{-1}(P^s_t - P^s_{t-1}) + \varepsilon_{Dt}$$

$$= (1-\alpha)\ \hat{Q} + Q^s(P^s_t) + \varepsilon_{St}.$$

Under the simplifying assumptions of linear responses of supply and demand to price, we have

$$(7)\ Q^D(P_t) = A - f(\alpha\ P^c_t + (1-\alpha)\ P^s_t),\ \text{and}$$

$$(8)\ Q^s(P^s_t) = g\ P^s_t.$$

Hence equation (6) can be rewritten as

$$(9)\quad (1-\alpha)\ (A-f(\alpha\ P_t^c + (1-\alpha)\ P_t^s)) + \varepsilon_{Dt}$$

$$+ h^{-1}[E_t\ P_{t+1}^s - P_t^s - E_{t-1}P_t^s + P_{t-1}^s] = (1-\alpha)\hat{Q} + g\ P_t^s + \varepsilon_{St},$$

or

$$(10)\quad [g+f(1-\alpha)^2 + h^{-1}]\ P_t^s = (1-\alpha)\ (A-\hat{Q}) + \varepsilon_{Dt} - \varepsilon_{St}$$

$$-f\alpha(1-\alpha)\ P_t^c + h^{-1}[E_t P_{t+1}^s - E_{t-1}P_t^s + P_{t-1}^s].$$

If we define the long-run average price obtained when expectations are realized:

$$E_t P_{t+1} = E_{t-1} P_t = P_t = P_t^s = P_t^c$$

by $\hat{P}$, then it follows that

$$(11)\quad \hat{P} = (1-\alpha)\ (A-\hat{Q})\ /\ (g+f(1-\alpha)).$$

Let lower-case variables be defined in deviation form (i.e. $p_t = P_t - \hat{P}$). Using the definition of the contract price, if expectations are rational, we can solve the second-order in-homogeneous difference equation above by standard methods to yield

$$(12)\quad p_t^s = \psi\ p_{t-1}^s + \frac{\eta_t}{g+2h^{-1}+f(1-\alpha)-h^{-1}\psi},$$

where is the root within the unit circle of the quadratic equation:

$$h^{-1}\psi^2 - (g+2h^{-1}+ f(1-\alpha))\ \psi + h^{-1} = 0.$$

Even transitory shocks exhibit persistence effects on the spot price because of inventory behavior and the existence of contracts. Since $d\psi/d\alpha > 0$, the larger is the fraction of trades carried out under contracts, the greater is the persistence. That is, comparing this result with those of a one-price model ($\alpha=0$), we see that the persistence of transitory shocks is greater in the two-price regime.

EMPIRICAL RESULTS

We estimated equation (12) on monthly spot price data for Mideast Light-34, the most widely-traded crude oil, over the period]974 -]984. Because of the high frequency ofthe data, we allowed for first order serial correlation of the shocks. Our objective was to see if we could pick up the decline in the persistence parameter predicted by the model and industry folklore. Our estimated equation was:

$$(12') \quad p_t^s = \psi p_{t-1}^s + \delta + \varepsilon_t + \rho\varepsilon_{t-1}$$

Our OLS estimates are as follows (Standard errors in parentheses):

δ	ψ	ρ	SHIFT	$\bar{R}^2$	
.011	.955	.317	-.463	.88	(1)
(.177)	(.073)	(.116)	(.113)		
.057	.875	.437	-.016/month	.88	(2)
(.212)	(.075)	(.131)	(.008)		
-.053	.865	.441	-.012/month	.87	(3
(.218)	(.077)	(.131)	(.006)		

We attempted to pick up the decline in three different ways. Regression (1) allows a one-time shift downward in ψ in 1980. We find a dramatic decline in the persistence parameter, from .95 in the 1970s to .50 thereafter. Regressions (2) and (3) are variations on the theme. In (2) we let ψ decline monthly over the period 1980 - 1981; in (3) over the period 1980 - 1984. The results are similar.

CONCLUSION

In this paper, we have developed a simple, testable model of crude oil trading and price adjustment. Our empirical tests support the hypothesis that the market has become less rigid with the movement toward spot trading.

FOOTNOTES

1 The information in this paragraph comes from Arab Oil and Gas Directory (1984), which contains more details on the contracts.

2 Nordhaus (1980, p. 367) comments: "This argument does not rest on the quantitative importance of the spot market; rather, it treats the spot market as a thermometer for measuring the degree of tightness of world oil markets."

REFERENCES

Bohi, D.R. "What Causes Oil Price Shocks?" Resources for the Future Discussion Paper D-82S, Jan. 1983.

Fisher, F.M., P.H. Cootner, and M.N. Baily. "An Econometric Model of the World Copper Industry." Bell Journal of Economics 3, Autumn 1972.

Hubbard, R.G., and R.J. Weiner. "The Sub-trigger Crisis: An Economic Analysis of FLexible Stock Policies." Energy Economics 5, July 1983.

de Kuijper, M.A.M. "The Unraveling of Market Regimes in Theory and in Application to Copper, Aluminum, and Oil." Ph.D. Dissertation, Harvard University, 1983.

Nordhaus, W.D. "Oil and Economic Performance in Industrial Countries." BPEA 1980:2.

Verleger, P.K. Oil Markets in Turmoil. Cambridge: Ballinger, 1982.

TABLE 1:

INTERNATIONAL CRUDE OIL TRADE (million barrels per day)

	1973	1978	1979
TOTAL (excluding Communist bloc and intra-OECD)	34	34	34.5
MAJORS	25	16.9	14.5
of which resold	6.7	3.7	1.9
GOVERNMENT to GOVERNMENT	<1.0	3.9	6.0

Source: Jochen Mohnfeld "Structural Changes in World Crude Oil Trade," Intereconomics, Jan/Feb. 1980.

TABLE 2:
JAPANESE CRUDE OIL IMPORTS

Year: Quarter	Imports (mmb/d)	Spot Purchases (%)
1978	4.7	4.1
1979	4.8	7.8
1980	4.4	10.1
1981	4.0	5.6
1982	3.7	9.0
1983	3.6	17.9
1984:1	4.2	20.3
1984:2	3.7	20.2
1984:3	3.5	26.4
1984:4	3.3	25.9
1985:1	3.9	31.3

Note: Quarterly figures are medians of monthly data.

Source: MITI, Natural Resources and Energy Agency.

TABLE 3:
U.S. OIL IMPORTS (largest 31 refiners)

Year: Month	Imports (mmb/d)	Spot Purchases (%)
1979:4	5.5	2.6
1979:5	6.1	4.0
1979:6	5.7	12.3
1979:7	5.8	9.8
1979:8	5.7	7.2
1979:9	5.2	9.8
1979:10	5.8	14.0
1979:11	5.6	11.1
1979:12	5.3	11.8
1980:1	4.9	8.8
1980:2	4.8	12.6

Source: U.S.G.A.O. (1980)

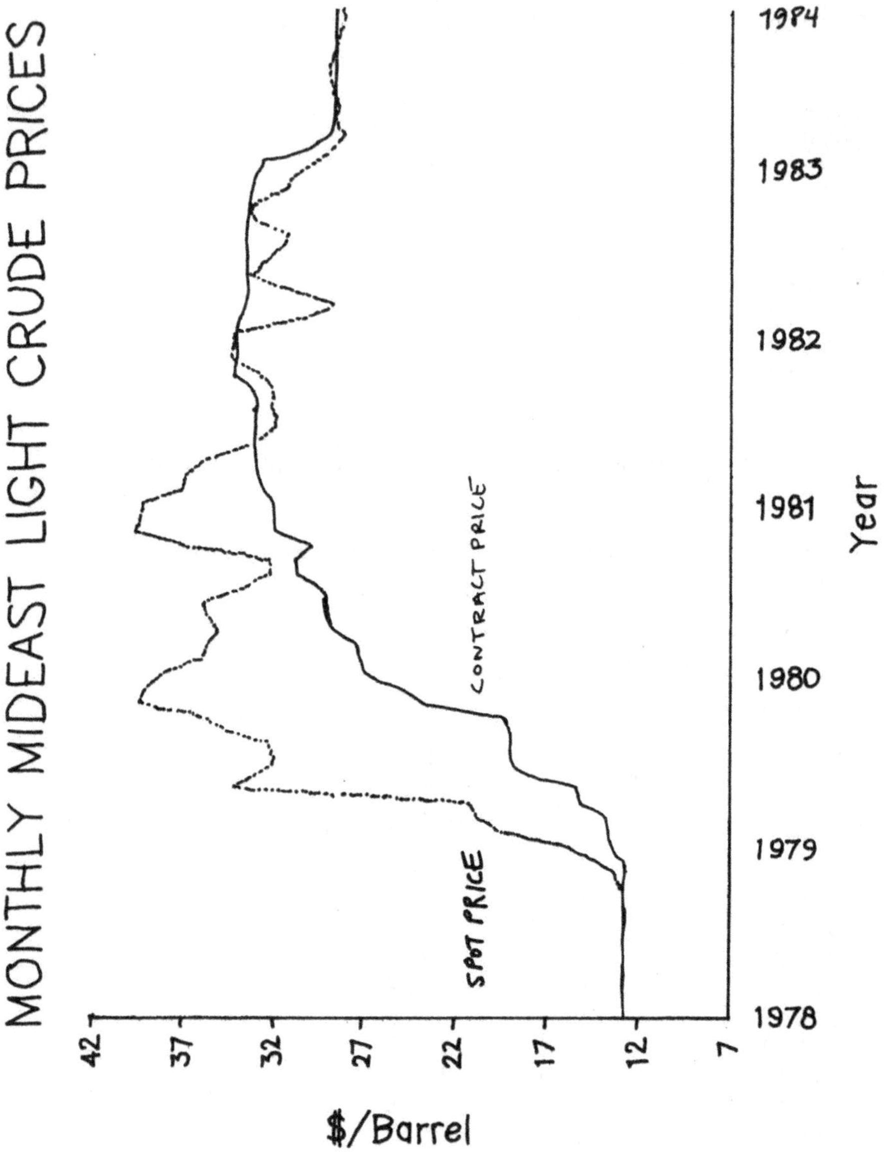
MONTHLY MIDEAST LIGHT CRUDE PRICES
$/Barrel
42
37
32
27
22
17
12
7
1978
1979
1980
1981
1982
1983
1984
Year
SPOT PRICE
CONTRACT PRICE

PART 3
NATURAL GAS MARKETS AND PRICES

17 The Evolution of Natural Gas Markets

Richard P. O'Neill, Energy Information Administration

INTRODUCTION

Gas markets in the United States are largely governed by regulations and laws developed over many years. Important historical events that still affect these markets include the conservation laws, Natural Gas Act of 1938, the Phillips decision in 1954, and the Natural Gas Policy Act of 1978. This paper examines this history, the adjustments made by the markets and regulatory bodies to Congressional legislation and Court decisions, and the possible future course of gas markets.

Traditionally, the natural gas markets have been heavily regulated largely due to the natural monopoly characteristics of the physical infrastructure of the market. To produce, move, or consume the first molecule of gas usually involves a great expense with the remaining molecules costing much less. Since natural gas markets are characterized by projects with high fixed costs and relatively low variable costs, a strong incentive exists for both buyers and sellers to enter stable long-term arrangements. This led to a regulatory certification procedure that inhibits short-term market response behavior. Most transactions take place under long-term contracts that are heavily influenced by regulation. Ironically, the Federal government was initially welcomed into the market as a regulator because it provided the order needed to ensure stability allowing recovery of large fixed cost investments and to protect customers from market power of the pipelines. This in turn made financing pipelines for new markets (e.g., the Northeast) much easier. Once the regulation was in place, however, it also became the scapegoat for any problem in market: blame regulation first.

With and without regulation, long-term contracts have traditionally been used both to guarantee recovery of large fixed cost investments and to prevent opportunism by the parties. Large fixed investments must be recovered from users, but partially because economic theory has not been able to present a definitive solution to the proper allocation of joint costs, there is considerable latitude in setting rates to allow companies to earn a fair rate-of-return. Consequently, the allocation of joint costs and sometimes not-so-joint costs is used to segment the market and price discriminate among users.

Whatever form of price discrimination is chosen, it is frequently justified as being the least damaging to economic efficiency. But in many cases, the rates are designed to meet local short-term market problems.

Historical Overview

The natural gas market traces its roots back to 1821 where the first natural gas well was put on production in Fredonia, New York. This well did not start a drilling boom because gas transportation over any distance was technologically infeasible.

The basic market and system of regulations that would eventually evolve to include natural gas were already being developed for manufactured gas. In 1816, Baltimore Gas Light was established to bring manufactured gas to the local market. By 1850, over 23 gas light companies were operating in the United States and by 1870, 46 cities had manufactured gas. By the late 1800's natural gas had been discovered in large enough quantities to generate attempts to build pipelines for transport. In 1891, a successful 120 mile pipeline was built from Indiana to Chicago. In the late 1800's, natural gas sold for under $.07 per thousand cubic feet (mcf) and manufactured gas sold in the range of $1.00 to $1.75 per mcf.

In 1889, the Courts decided that the rule of capture, used previously in questions of game animal property, applied to oil and gas. This later led to perverse incentives for over-production and to State efforts to control production.

From the early 1900's to late 1960's, the natural gas markets were in a state of short-run excess supply (that is, more gas available for production than customers able to buy it), and in a state of long-run excess demand (that is, more customers wanting gas than were hooked-up). From 1930 to 1972, consumption grew at a compound annual rate of 6.9 percent. In the late 1960's while the overall market continued to grow, some interstate pipelines became supply short and stopped hooking up new customers. From 1972 to 1983, consumption declined at a compound annual rate of 2.3 percent. In 1981, excess supply developed again and remains the situation today.

<u>Pre-Natural Gas Act</u>

At the beginning of this century, Pennsylvania and West Virginia were the leading producing States, and a small interstate natural gas market had come into existence in the Northeast and Midwest. But, a series of events soon created an enormous incentive to expand the market. From 1910 to 1930 massive natural gas discoveries including the Monroe, Hugoton, Panhandle and San Juan fields vastly expanded available supply and moved the centroid of reserves to the Southwest and the development of seemless welded pipe put this gas within reach of the industrial Midwest. In 1931, Natural Gas Pipeline built a successful line from Texas to Chicago. The principal stimulus for the building of these lines was the industrial user, large markets that could immediately switch from coal and start paying for the pipelines (see Marsten). From 1931 to 1938 the industrial market use grew and its market share increased from 50 to 62 percent. Residential and commercial markets were not as accessible due to distributor reluctance to abandon the manufactured-gas plant in the rate base due to the "used and useful" principle. Although their consumption grew, their market share fell from about 35 to 29 percent. By this time electricity had displaced gas in the lighting market.

In the late 1800's, a pure demand charge was typical for manufactured gas sales. In the early 1900's, natural gas was sold on a purely volumetric basis. Most gas was owned by the pipelines and not purchased at the wellhead. Industrial sales were often priced as a percent of retail sales, for example, 85 percent. Direct industrial sales were based on cost allocation procedures.

In a series of decisions, the Supreme Court made clear that the States could regulate both production to prevent waste and protect correlative rights, and sales to end-users. However, States could not regulate sales from interstate pipelines to local distributors. In 1935 a Federal Trade Commission (FTC) report stated that:

- there was waste by producers;
- wholesale rates were too high;
- pipelines were highly concentrated; and
- pipelines discriminated in purchasing and selling.

The stage was now set for Congress to act.

<u>Natural Gas Act</u>

The Natural Gas Act (NGA) of 1938 stated that:

- companies engaged in transportation or sale for resale in interstate commerce, that is, "natural gas companies," would be regulated by the Federal Power Commission (FPC);
- all rates must be just-and-reasonable and public;
- no undue preference or advantage could be granted or unreasonable differences in rates maintained;
- for increased rates, the burden of proof is on the pipeline;
- in order for the Commission to change existing rates, there must be a "finding" that rates were unjust or unreasonable;
- certificates would be required to construct or operate jurisdictional

facilities and to offer jurisdictional services;

- the Commission could direct facilities to be expanded or improved if found to be in the public interest; and
- no company could abandon facilities or services without Commission approval.

The NGA specifically omitted the authority for the FPC to mandate transportation or to regulate direct sales, local distribution or production.

Natural Gas Act to the Phillips Decision

From 1938 to 1954 (from passage of the NGA to the Phillips v. Wisconsin decision by the Supreme Court), natural gas production grew at the compound rate of 9 percent annually. The real wellhead price fell from 1938 to 1948, but from 1951 to 1954, rose at a rate of 9 percent annually. As late as 1947 over 17 percent of natural gas production was vented or flared, and manufactured gas production peaked. After the completion of pipelines to the Northeast starting in 1947, natural gas waste has declined and manufactured gas has been used primarily as a fuel to supplement natural gas during peak periods.

On the regulatory front, major changes were made in the approach toward allocation of costs. In the 1942 rate case for Hope Natural Gas, the Courts allowed FPC to retain volumetric rates, but recognized the difference in types of service allowing rate differentiation based on factors like size, load factor and delivery pressure. This decision eventually led to fixed-variable rate structures in the late 1940's, in which all fixed costs were allocated to demand charges based on peak usage.

Rate structures continued to evolve. In the 1952 Atlantic Seaboard rate case, the FPC decided to allocate half of the fixed costs to interruptible users through the commodity charge on the rationale that the costs were incurred for the benefit of all customers.

Congressional and Court decisions during this period were directed toward jurisdictional issues. In 1953, the Outer Continental Shelf (OCS) Act placed OCS gas firmly under FPC jurisdiction in the interstate market. In 1954, Congress passed the Hinshaw Amendment allowing portions of interstate pipelines that receive interstate gas, but operate solely in a given State, to be regulated by the State. Also, in 1954, the Supreme Court decided in Phillips v. Wisconsin that producers were natural gas companies engaged in sales for resale and so extended FPC regulation to include interstate wellhead sales.

Phillips to the Natural Gas Policy Act

From 1954 until 1978, the interstate natural gas market labored under the influence of the Phillips decision. Many (or most) regulatory decisions in this period were responses to problems arising from the decision. At first, the FPC attempted cost-of-service regulation for producers in a business that carried a strong risk component, large uncertainties, and thousands of participants. By 1960, with a backlog of 30,000 cases, the FPC switched to regulating all prices uniformly in an area--area rates.

Although wellhead price regulation was an administrative nightmare, from 1954 to 1972 it caused few market problems because real wellhead prices were essentially constant. Area rates set prices until 1974 when the FPC switched to national rates. In 1976, the FPC issued Opinion 770 which tripled existing price ceilings.

In the downstream market the FPC tailored regulation to fit the occasion. In 1958, the FPC allowed minimum commodity bills for partial requirements customers insulating pipelines from competition and indirectly establishing "guarantees" for wellhead contracts. In 1959, the FPC allowed Midwest Gas Transmission to "tilt" the Seaboard formula placing more costs in the demand charge. The effect was to lower prices to meet competition for interruptible customers from other fuels. Also in 1959, the FPC allowed United to put 75 percent of fixed costs into the commodity charge to suppress demand. In 1975, the FPC's right to determine ratemaking approaches was limited, when the Supreme Court ruled that it could not change rate designs without "close reasoning."

By the late 1960's, the interstate pipelines were not able to compete with intrastate purchasers on price, but the FPC could not or would not deal with the wellhead pricing problem directly. Instead, it set up a series of fringe market mechanisms to alleviate the worst problems. In 1970, the FPC (Order 402-A) allowed 60 day emergency sales without approval. In 1975, the FPC (Order 533) allowed producers to sell directly to feedstock users for up to 2 years. In 1978, Order 2 extended direct sales to other high priority users.

During this period, new intrastate markets in the Southwest grew and matured. In 1965, the Supreme Court prohibited commingling of interstate and intrastate gas virtually eliminating inter-market trade. After 1969, the buyers in the intrastate markets purchased virtually all the new onshore gas supplies available because they could pay more than FPC controlled rates. Initially, this imbalance was masked by the development of older fields already under interstate contracts and OCS reserves discovered and dedicated during the period. But by 1977, the market imbalance led to a simultaneous shortage on some interstate pipeline systems and a surplus in the largest (Texas) intrastate market. This chaos was the setting for the debate leading to Natural Gas Policy Act of 1978 (NGPA).

Natural Gas Policy Act

The NGPA significantly altered the structure of natural gas regulation in major ways:

- the Federal Energy Regulatory Commission (FERC) (successor to the FPC) was granted jurisdiction over the maximum price producers could receive for their gas in both inter- and intrastate markets. But the NGPA mandated the ceilings to be used and prescribed a phased decontrol of prices for most gas;
- it provided rules to allocate the costs of certain expensive gas to industrial users served by interstate pipelines;
- it allowed inter- and intrastate markets to interact in certain ways without coming under the jurisdiction of the NGA; and
- it removed the requirement of certification for most new gas in the interstate market.

NGPA to Partial Wellhead Decontrol

In 1979, as the ink dried on the NGPA the assumptions underlying the Act unraveled. The 1979 Iranian revolution sent oil prices soaring and destroyed the logic that went into the gas price ceilings that were designed to allow for a smooth convergence of oil and gas prices. In 1979, a small amount of gas was deregulated. The price for such gas rose to exceed $10 per Mcf for a brief but exciting period from 1979 through 1981. Incentive prices were proposed by FERC for gas from tight formations and 10,000 to 15,000 feet. In 1982, a severe recession hit and an excess supply of gas emerged. The understanding of this bubble was confused when the American Petroleum Institute (API) drilling statistics understated the unprecedented growth of drilling in each year from 1979 through 1982. Huge take-or-pay liabilities, in excess of $3.5 billion in 1983, rose from the reduced demand.

With the price of gas to consumers increasing in the face of a supply surplus, the rate structure of interstate pipelines underwent close scrutiny. In 1983, the _Seaboard_ and _United_ formulae became the subject of controversy because they forced commodity rates higher than variable costs when sales were threatened by competition. Natural Gas Pipeline was awarded modified fixed-variable (MFV) tariffs (in which all fixed costs except return on rate base are allocated to demand charges). At the same time, Columbia's application for MFV tariffs was denied forcefully. This confusion appears to have been resolved in the 1985 Texas Eastern rate case, where the modified fixed-variable tariff became the FERC's preferred rate structure.

In 1984, the FERC outlawed non-incurred cost in minimum commodity bills, thereby opening the market to more inter-transporter competition. Customers with more than one supplier have greater opportunities to purchase a lower cost supply mix, but service obligations were not adjusted to reflect this new reality and captive customers may face higher charges (see O'Neill, et al [1984b]).

In 1979, FERC allowed direct sales to replace fuel oil emergency sales continuing its special program approach started prior to the NPGA. In 1983, with high-priced wellhead contracts, mounting take-or-pay liabilities, and competition from oil and other sellers of natural gas, pipelines had trouble selling gas. To relieve this problem, FERC approved a series of special discount programs under the condition that it could be shown that all those affected received positive benefit from the program. Although these programs were heralded as new and innovative by many, they could also be considered as an extension of the special programs of the 1970's, designed to relieve immediate market problems with as little change to the basic regulatory structure as possible.

<u>Post-Partial Wellhead Decontrol</u>

January 1, 1985 came and went with little fanfare. On average the wellhead price did not change because the continuing excess supply of natural gas kept downward pressure on wellhead prices and an active spot-market continued to develop. Institutionally, over 50 percent of all wellhead price ceilings were removed, creating additional contract problems. In May 1985, the Court of Appeals terminated the special programs on the grounds they were discriminatory and FERC issued a sweeping proposed rulemaking that would fundamentally alter the market.

The current trend, since the excess supply developed in 1982, has been to more flexible shorter-term contracts with emerging spot-markets and possible futures markets. In the transmission segment, new tariff structures are emerging and unbundled service is becoming more important, allowing for more competition. Nevertheless, the concentration of sellers in wholesale markets is high enough to raise questions of market-disciplined competitive behavior. In this segment of the system, regulation and market forces are still out-of-balance. The distribution companies, facing diverse regulation by public utility commissions, must adjust to the new competitive forces while maintaining service obligations. In the end-use markets the role of new technologies, such as the heat pump and cogeneration equipment, will create increased competition.

Like most laws, court decisions and regulations, the NGPA was not the ideal economic solution for natural gas markets, but the NGPA started the market on a course to less regulation and more competition. FERC regulations have not been fully adjusted to the NGPA. Because it no longer has the authority, FERC is in the process of stepping back from regulation of new gas, curtailing its cradle-to-grave regulation and allowing more inter-market and inter-pipeline competition. Historically, after new laws and court decisions, FERC often has a difficult time in the process of adjusting.

Inertia that is inherently a part of regulation and is mandated, at the option of the pipelines, by the Natural Gas Act (NGA) often forces less than optimal adjustments and solutions. Some rate structures, that seemed to serve the market at the time, are 30 to 50 years old (for example, direct sales) and may need to be reexamined. Due to lack of transportation flexibility, pipeline customers must often engage in a non-optimal gas purchase strategy retaining higher priced or suboptimally packaged supplies to ensure some competition and continuation of multiple suppliers.

Because of the lead times, high fixed cost, and low variable costs of the natural gas business, long-term contracts will still be desirable. If gas is price regulated, shortages and surpluses could likely occur. If it is not price regulated, price swings could be expected to allocate temporary supply and demand imbalances.

REFERENCES

Energy Information Administration, 1984, Natural Gas Annual, 1983, Volume 1.

Marsten, P.M., 1985, "An Historical Perspective on Industrial Natural Gas Pricing," Public Utilities Fortnightly, July 11, 1985.

O'Neill, R.P., et al, 1984a, Competition and Other Current Issues in the Natural Gas Market, Energy Information Administration.

_______, 1984b, A Study of Contracts Between Interstate Pipeline and Their Customers, Energy Information Administration, July 1984.

Means, Robert C., Natural Gas Deregulation and Natural Gas Marketing (Swanson Energy Groups, January 28, 1985).

18 How Will Natural Gas Be Priced?

Arthur W. Wright, University of Connecticut and
MIT Center for Energy Policy Research

INTRODUCTION

The price of oil will likely continue to set the level of energy prices. Nevertheless, the pricing of natural gas will be significant for relative energy prices, which determine how efficiently the economy can adapt to changing oil prices. Adjustments by producers and users to swings in oil prices are driven by such "market" forces as geology, technologies, input prices, and the expected volatility of oil prices. But they also depend on policy constraints -- price ceilings, end-use restrictions, controls on market entry or exit, and of course the expected volatility of the policy constraints themselves.

A popular view holds that the U.S. natural gas industry is rapidly being deregulated. If so, the pricing of gas will soon cease to be constrained by policy. Unfortunately, this conclusion is premature.

True, wellhead prices are now effectively decontrolled

-- as much *de facto* as *de juris*, the result of a drop in demand in 1982 coupled with partial decontrol under the Natural Gas Policy Act of 1978 (NGPA). However, pipelining, end uses, and local distribution are still regulated. Even with wellhead decontrol, regulation-induced rigidities have plagued North American gas markets since 1982. Investment decisions have been delayed and the financial viability of many firms threatened for want of flexibility in the pricing of gas -- quite apart from the effects of declining gas prices *per se*.

That gas can be priced more flexibly in the long run is widely accepted. But how, and even whether, we can make the transition is the subject of controversy. Conceivably, most of the current regulatory restrictions will simply be swept away by a rising tide of market competition. But equally conceivable is that those same restrictions will prevent or distort the transition. If so, new natural gas legislation may be required if market competition is to prevail.

I. The Pricing of Natural Gas since 1982

Kenneth Lay of HNG/Internorth remarked recently that the U.S. gas industry is now in the fifth year of an 18-

month surplus. How could a surplus[1] exist even a year and a half, let alone five years? The proximate causes of the surplus were rising supply and falling demand. But the source of the sustained surplus -- as of the sustained shortage that preceded it -- is rigid legal and regulatory restrictions that prevent prices from adjusting to clear markets.

As detailed elsewhere,[2] these restrictions (which evolved over half a century of legislation, judicial interpretation, and regulation) amount to a set of highly-structured arrangements for determining who shall get which gas at what price. The purpose of these arrangements was primarily to appropriate economic rents at the wellhead and transfer them to certain end users, and secondarily to regulate interstate pipelines as natural monopolies. To accomplish this purpose, a pervasive regulatory apparatus (today, mainly at the Federal Energy Regulatory Commission, or FERC) was set up to administer prices, assign rights to reserves and pipeline capacity, and control entry, exit, and end uses.

This apparatus has six essential features:

(1) Wellhead price ceilings on all interstate or (since 1978) some interstate and intrastate gas.

(2) "Purchase-for-resale" (PFR) organization of trunk pipelining. PFR, under which pipelines buy, own, and resell gas to end users, makes pipelines both transporters and the predominant broker/traders of gas. They may -- but need not -- haul gas belonging to others.[3]

(3) "Roll-in" pricing, which requires pipelines to charge all customers the same weighted-average "purchase gas cost".

(4) FERC "certificates of public convenience and necessity" for both entry into and exit from pipeline activities.

(5) Cost-of-service, "non-discriminatory" pipeline transportation rates. Non-discriminatory pipeline rates are an obstacle to the adoption of efficient rate-setting schemes, such as "Ramsey" prices, in the presence of declining average costs.

(6) regulatory "service obligations" that extend beyond any private delivery agreements between pipelines and local distribution companies (LDCs). The service obligations, which confer upon the LDCs bundles of rights to gas reserves and pipeline capacity, reinforce the pipelines' economic and financial incentives to sign long-term supply contracts with producers.

The rigid institutions just described worked well enough so long as demand was not a binding constraint -- that is, while the U.S. gas industry was growing rapidly (1945-1965), and as binding wellhead price ceilings generated and sustained an interstate shortage (1965-1980). However, these same institutions were ill-suited to coping with the sharp drop in gas demand, beginning in late 1981, that made demand, not supply, the binding constraint. Ordinarily, falling demand would cause prices to fall; instead, gas prices rose. Subsequently they have slipped a bit, but not far enough to clear the market. Thus, where before regulators had to allocate a shortage, now they had to manage a surplus.

Gas prices rose in the midst of glut not because the laws of economics had failed, but because they were working -- given regulatory constraints. Field price escalations (both NGPA and contractual) and "regulatory-lag" rate increases each played a role at first. Pipeline load losses that raised average transportation rates proved more enduring. Most important, though, was the highly-structured apparatus, cited earlier, for "determining who shall get which gas at what price". This apparatus -- PFR, roll-in gas prices, certificated entry/exit, non-discriminatory pipeline rates, and service obligations -- simply could not let prices move and at the same time protect the various interests legally entitled to regulatory protection.

II. Making Gas Markets More Flexible

A combination of increasing demand and declining supply would "work off" the deliverability surplus. But it will take greater flexibility than now exists in natural gas markets to prevent the recurrence of a surplus, as conditions in oil and other energy markets change over time. Indeed, the likelihood of volatility in those markets puts an efficiency premium on increased flexibility in the trading of gas.

The key to flexible gas markets would be a well-organized, liquid spot market. Such a market would provide buyers and sellers with reliable, more accurate price information for longer-term as well as spot transactions. It would also support futures trading in gas, which would improve the allocation of the demand-driven risks that the industry now faces.

Spot trading in sufficient quantities to make the market liquid could not occur without assurance that the gas involved could be shipped. All parties, not just pipeline companies, would need convenient access, on predictable terms, to pipeline capacity.[4] Such access would in turn require unbundling the broker/trading from the transportation functions now combined under PFR, on at least a large proportion (if not all) of the pipelines' capacities. In return for this common-carrier obligation, of course, the pipelines should be relieved of comparable proportions of their current service obligations. Otherwise, third parties would not believe that their access rights could be enforced, even with costly proceedings or litigation.

We see, then, that it is simple to describe a more flexible set of arrangements for trading natural gas than we now have, and to sketch the changes required to bring it about. But getting there from here in real time seems much less simple.

III. Can We Get There from Here?

The road to more flexible North American gas markets is paved with good intentions. Industry speeches talk of a "new world" and "market responsiveness". FERC has proclaimed its intention to make gas markets "competitive". Even court opinions have invoked "competition".

Yet it remains to be seen whether we have made much progress down that road, or even whether we are on it. A number of encouraging signs, private and public, point to increased market flexibility. But we have also encountered obstacles to it. Not the least one is the evident ability of various actors to affect the transition politically or legally.

As ever in North American gas markets, the core issue is economic rents and their distribution. The usual amalgam of design and happenstance in setting economic policy has generated a complex set of claims and counter-claims. An important difference from the past is that the system now must deal with losses, not gains. These losses can be traced to the unexpected drop in gas demand in 1981-82, following frenzy of contracting activity spurred by passage of the NGPA.

The NGPA was designed as an instrument for phased decontrol. The phasing was intended to cushion the loss of rents by consumers as gas markets gradually cleared. Prices would rise as ceilings escalated but (more importantly) as pipelines rolled in above-market gas with below-market, price-controlled gas. Far from constituting "imprudent" or uneconomic behavior, paying above-market prices for some gas was the rational response to the constraints facing the pipelines -- including their regulatory obligations to LDCs.

Happenstance has thus far undercut the NGPA not once

but twice. First came the oil price spike of 1979-80, then the sharp decline in gas demand (brought on in part by falling oil prices) in 1981-82. The second event decontrolled wellhead prices, on average, sooner than everyone had expected.

The system could readily handle the "market-ordering problem" that issued from the oil price spike. It was more of the same, allocating a shortage. The surplus, however, posed new problems that the existing institutions for trading gas were not equipped to handle. With the sudden, unexpected disruption of contractual equilibrium, someone stood to lose a lot of money. Perhaps the key determinant of who lost how much would be the regulatory system.

With volumes down, LDCs and pipelines had rights to more gas than they could sell. But through "demand" charges and "take-or-pay" liabilities, they owed money on a good part of the surplus. Under the NGPA, the pipelines had bid higher-than-normal take-or-pay percentages (in the 90s instead of the 50s or 60s) for new gas supplies, in lieu of market prices that still exceeded the ceilings. They had also contracted for uncontrolled supplies at prices up to 4 and 5 times the NGPA ceilings; not all of these "supplemental" supplies were covered by safety-valve clauses (such as "market-outs") in case demand fell. Into the bargain, many actors (including gas producers counting on guaranteed "takes") had incurred heavy financial obligations in order to participate in the post-NGPA frenzy.

Pipelines, producers, LDCs and regulators had to turn to ad hoc measures to cope with the deliverability surplus. A few producers have accepted lower takes or prices in supply contracts. Several pipelines have invoked force majeure to break supply contracts[5] and are now in court over the matter. Seemingly more promising measures to maintain volumes were FERC-approved "blanket certificates" and "contract carriage" programs for third-party transportation, and so-called "special marketing programs" (SMPs). The SMPs were a package approach to the renegotiation of now uneconomic contracts, promising access to recaptured markets in return for suspension of price and take terms. Significantly, blanket certificates, contract carriage, and the SMPs all introduced elements of Ramsey price discrimination into a system in which demand was now binding and which clearly evidenced economies of scale and "network" externalities. The price reductions sought through these measures were aimed at the most price-sensitive customers. Less price-elastic demanders -- especially residential and commercial customers -- were excluded. Doubtless, the pipelines feared losing parts of these "captive" loads in the short term without receiving compensating reductions in their obligations to serve them in the long run.

For all their desirable price-competitive features, the ad hoc measures approved by the FERC have not succeeded in "working off" the surplus. For one thing, the FERC (fulfilling its statutory responsibility) had to restrict their scope to protect long-term rights to reserves and pipeline capacity, and to prevent "harmful" competition that would bail out one pipeline at the expense of another. Thus, the special programs amounted to introducing a little competition, piecemeal, into an administered allocation mechanism.

The blanket certificates and SMPs also proved vulnerable to legal attack. In May 1985, the U.S. Circuit Court of Appeals for the District of Columbia handed down two rulings (now known as MPC I and II) effectively banning both measures.[6] The opinions assert that they were "anti-competitive," but the context makes clear that the judges really meant "discriminatory" under the NGA, because the "captive" customers had been excluded. By our argument above, the judges' description (if not their language) was right. These decisions make one wonder whether gas markets can become more flexible under the NGA as it stands.

Shortly after MPC I and II, the FERC issued a "Notice of Proposed Rulemaking" (NOPR).[7] This sweeping proposal was meant to be viewed as a package that would systematically restructure the entire operation of U.S. natural gas markets.[8] The NOPR consists of four parts:

(1) Non-discriminatory, Blanket-Certificate Transportation of Gas: Pipelines choosing this option must provide access without discrimination. Their LDC customers could reduce their tariff volumes by 25 percent a year over four years.

(2) "Safe Harbor" for Take-or-Pay Liabilities: Pipelines choosing part (1) would be able to include in their rate bases a portion (not specified) of payments to buy out take-or-pay liabilities.

(3) Optional, Expedited Certification of Pipeline Services: Pipelines may qualify for simplified, accelerated certification of new services offered non-discriminatorily and at the pipelines' risk. Rates would be "volumetric" -- dependent on volumes supplied, with no "demand" charges or minimum bills allowed.

(4) Block-billing instead of Roll-In Pricing:

Price-controlled "old gas" would be segregated in Block 1 and reserved for firm customers (mainly LDCs) based on their 1982-84 purchases. The purchase costs of all other gas would go into Block 2. "Non-gas" costs of gas (as opposed to pipeline transportation) would go into Block 3, to be allocated between Blocks 1 and 2.

The NOPR has come under heavy attack from virtually every quarter, including state regulators and consumer groups. In a sense, this attests to the courageous, comprehensive nature of the proposal. Nevertheless, there are both political and legal doubts about its viability. There is already talk of withdrawing parts of the NOPR and trying again later. But that would vitiate the package nature of the rulemaking and run the risk of getting only piecemeal change -- or a quite different system later, say, under a different Commission.

The NOPR places the heaviest net burden on the pipelines. Block pricing would reverse the rent transfer effected by the NGPA, restoring rents on old gas to LDCs and their (mainly small) customers, and leave pipelines and producers to fight it out in order to make Block 2 gas price-competitive. Most pipelines would have to adopt option 1, non-discriminatory access to pipeline capacity, but the fates of their service obligations would be in the hands of the LDCs. In addition, as option 3 is now worded, "volumetric" rates might not cover pipelines' total costs under all market conditions.

It is not clear whether the FERC has the requisite authority to implement the NOPR (or a variant of it) by the autumn of 1985, when many of the *ad hoc* programs expire.[9] The matter is certain to end up in the courts, no matter how the final rulemaking is phrased. Recent experience with court decisions that have made economic policy is not reassuring. But trying to get Congress to rewrite the legislation governing the natural gas industry would entail its own set of risks. Most probably, the range of issues considered would be broader than that in the courts.

As of this writing, then, the probability that natural gas will be priced in competitive markets, much as other commodities are now, is positive but not certain. The possible outcomes range from business-as-usual to a completely free market, with the most probable outcomes as usual lying somewhere between.

NOTES

1 It is a surplus of "deliverability", not extraction or reserves. Producers would like to sell more gas than they can find buyers for, given current prices *and* the other

conditions of entry into markets. The flip side of surplus deliverability is a shortage of "takeability".

2 P. Carpenter, H. Jacoby and A. Wright, "Natural Gas Pipeline Regulation after Field Price Decontrol," MIT-EL - 83-013WP, Revised September 1983; also, P. Carpenter and A. Wright, "The Natural Gas Policy Drama: A Tragedy in Three Acts," MIT-EL-84-012WP, October 1984. The source legislation here was the Natural Gas Act of 1938 (NGA).

3 In fact, an interstate pipeline must obtain a special FERC certificate to transport gas for a third party. The original version of the NGA, initially part of the Public Utilities Holding Company Act of 1935, would have made interstate gas pipelines regulated common carriers. As passed in 1938, however, the NGA lacked the common carriage provision. Gas pipelines are the only major transportation firms not required to operate as "common carriers".

4 To take maximum advantage of the flexibility afforded by the liquid spot market, the terms of pipeline access should include Ramsey-like rates based on differential price elasticities of demand across customer classes, and of course peak-load pricing.

5 This unconventional legal argument places market forces in a class with war, pestilence and famine.

6 Maryland People's Counsel v. FERC 761 F. 2d 768, 780 (D.C. Circuit 1985).

7 50 Fed. Reg. 24130 (June 7, 1985). FERC Docket No. RM85-1-000, issued May 30, 1985. Technically, the NOPR grew out of two earlier "Notices of Inquiry", but it has since come to be viewed as FERC's response to MPC I and II.

8 Stephen F. Williams of the University of Colorado has dubbed the NOPR a "Proposed Sea-Change in Natural Gas Regulation" (working paper, August 6, 1985).

9 Williams concludes (ibid.) that it probably does have such authority -- provided the courts follow his legal reasoning.

19
The North American Gas Market: Key Developments and Observations

Benjamin Schlesinger, Benjamin Schlesinger and Associates

INTRODUCTION

The following is a summary assessment of the state of North American natural gas markets, with focus on developments in the U.S. and Canada. The assessment includes:

- Basic supply, demand, and price trends
- Structure and organization of the business
- The spot trading phenomenon
- Major changes underway in gas rules and regulations
- Emerging new commercial trading mechanisms
- Summary of over-riding issues in the business.

SUPPLY OVERVIEW

Since phased deregulation of natural gas prices was enacted as part of the Natural Gas Policy Act of 1978 (NGPA), U.S. gas reserves have remained roughly constant at about 200 trillion cubic feet (Tcf) as discoveries and upward adjustments have just equalled production. This contrasts with some 18-19 Tcf per year of current U.S. gas demand. Another 300-900 Tcf of gas is estimated to exist in the U.S. (including Alaska) and exotic sources of supply such as coal gas, advanced recovery technologies, etc. could conceivably double or triple this amount.

Beyond these volumes, significant reserves of gas are available in Canada and Mexico, which have 93 trillion cubic feet and 77 trillion cubic feet of proved reserves, respectively. For example, gas reserves in the Province of Alberta (62 trillion cubic feet) exceed those of Texas by more than 20 percent.

Canadian gas imports to the U.S. are not likely to rise far beyond their 6 percent share of the U.S. market, however, because the National Energy Board, despite recent reform, continues to require in effect that its gas be exported at higher-than-market prices. Sales of Mexican gas in the U.S. are almost totally prevented by Mexico's official export price of nearly double the prevailing U.S. market price.

DEMAND OVERVIEW

At first glance, overall gas demand in North America appears to have stalled out. U.S. gas sales have been generally static since the mid-1970s; Canadian gas consumption has been rising, although imperceptibly. Much of the 20 percent decline in U.S. gas demand since 1972 is permanent, that is, "built-out" gas markets for which substantial customer funds have been expended on conservation, efficiency gains or alternative fuels, especially electricity.

However, several distinct regional gas markets exist in the U.S. and Canada, some of which are rather under-saturated from a viewpoint of gas use. For example, the Appalachian mountains generally divide U.S. gas markets on an east-west basis: to the east of the Appalachians, gas provides only 15 percent of total primary energy use; to the west, gas is a third of primary energy. Some important submarkets are:

- The Eastern seaboard, where gas is a relatively minor fuel, as in many European countries. For example, gas constitutes only 9 percent of primary energy use in New England, whose pattern is dominated by imported oil. In northern New England and the Maritimes, natural gas use is virtually non-existent.

- The U.S. Southwest (e.g., Texas, Oklahoma, Louisiana, and Southern California), where natural gas is the dominant energy form, comprising 75 percent - 80 percent of the region's non-transportation energy use.

- "Rustbelt" (e.g., Illinois, Indiana, Ohio, Ontario, Michigan, Pennsylvania), where gas market penetration was historically excellent in both buildings and industry. Over the past decade, however, lower-cost coal and the economic slump have both severely, and to a large extent permanently, eroded gas sales in this region.

At the present time, a persistent surplus of annual gas producability (the "bubble") exceeding 3 Tcf per year, or about 15 percent over market requirements, exists in the U.S. and Canada together. This surplus is now severely depressing gas prices in both countries.

Three demand-side factors currently prevent any rapid resurgence of gas sales:

- World crude oil prices are still falling, thus inter-fuel competition between fuel oil and gas will remain severe, especially in industrial markets.

- Energy "experts" aside, a fear of future gas shortages continues to permeate gas markets. This deters many potential new large-volume gas customers from making economical capital investments for gas-using equipment. Many gas users vividly recall the gas curtailments of the 1970s, and they also point to the continued existence of such "gas demand constraints" as the Fuel Use Act, which bans new large gas-fired steam and electricity generating boilers in the U.S. This factor tends to tilt fuel preferences -- especially in growth situations -- toward coal and electricity, and away from natural gas.

- Few entities with a direct financial incentive are marketing gas at the retail level, hence gas marketing is generally not as aggressive as oil marketing. This point is developed in greater detail below.

Indeed, it may be said that, even with an improved economy, about 20 percent of 1972 gas sales have been permanently removed from, or "built out" of, gas markets. Total gas use will not, by itself, increase beyond current levels of 18-19 Tcf per year.

However, despite their current malaise, North American natural gas markets can grow in two ways:

- Sales of gas for traditional uses -- residential, commercial, industrial, electricity generation -- can grow in such non-gas re- regions as the eastern states/provinces.

- Sales of gas for non-traditional uses can be developed, such as:

  - Cogeneration in commercial buildings and industry, in which gas-powered machines produce saleable electricity, as well as heat, cooling, and hot water. California and Texas have led in development of gas-fired cogeneration markets.

  - Vehicular uses, including automobiles, trucks, buses, and marine applications. The Canadian government and several Canadian gas producers have taken the lead in developing this key potential market.

  - Select gas use, in which gas is used with coal or other fuels in a way that reduces air pollution/acid rain. Several dozen users in the U.S. have employed this technique.

Intensive market-building efforts will be required on the part of gas retailers (for the most part, regulated distribution utilities) in order to develop these kinds of gas markets successfully.

STRUCTURE OF THE GAS BUSINESS

The foregoing overview of the economics of North American gas markets -- including supply, demand, and price -- logically raises issues about how the gas business is structured and regulated, and how that structure and regulation are both now changing. Gas markets in North America have become bifurcated into two distinct submarkets, traditional versus direct sales, as follows:

The Traditional Market: Regulated "Chain" Sales

Both physically and in terms of its ownership, natural gas traditionally moves along a chain from producers, to pipelines, to gas utilities, and to non-switchable and switchable customers. Regulation of natural gas markets and participants is likewise fragmented:

- Drilling and production of natural gas falls generally within producing states' and provinces' jurisdictions.

- Interstate and inter-provincial transport of gas, as well as other services offered by pipelines, are federally regulated in both the U.S. and Canada.

- Gas utilities are regulated by the states/provinces.

- The use of gas in buildings and industries is regulated at all levels, e.g., for types of uses, local safety codes, etc.

This diverse regulatory control over gas markets has resulted from a variety of concerns (e.g., monopoly control, safety), and reflects a fundamental division among gas customers:

- Non-switchable users (especially the home heaters) generally control the political direction of gas regulation, since each small user also votes.

- Switchable users, however, generally control the economics of gas markets, since they may convert to their alternative fuel (usually residual oil) at will.

As a consequence of these divergent interests, in traditional gas markets, most participants in the industry agree that natural gas markets will always be regulated, and that the fragmented nature of that regulation will continue.

The Direct Sale Market: Semiregulated "Spot" Sales

The most significant structural change in U.S. gas markets has been the rapid increase in the direct sale market, including a burgeoning spot trade in natural gas on a nationwide basis. Initially a reaction to sinking oil prices in 1983, the U.S. direct sale market has ballooned to over 3 trillion cubic feet on an annual basis, as producers and pipelines compete with one another in "gas-on-gas" competition. In 1985, for example, gas customers will spend $12 to $15 billion in several thousand spot and longer term direct sale gas transactions.

The existence of a spot trade in gas has been fostered to a large extent by the Federal Energy Regulatory Commission's orders of June 1983, granting a blanket authorization for self-implementing transportation. This crucial permission has enabled commercial confidentiality and relative simplicity (at least from a regulatory standpoint), thus enabling the gas spot trade to flourish. Many states have picked up the FERC's lead and have also encouraged direct sale transactions.

For their part, an increasing number of gas pipelines and utilities are agreeing, without new rules, to "carry" direct sale and spot gas to keep up throughput as traditional markets decline. Often gas transport services are offered by pipelines in conjunction with renegotiated take-or-pay obligations to producers. In fact, the traditional chain sales described above now accounts for only slightly more than half of the U.S. gas market.

CHANGING FEDERAL REGULATION

In a major Notice of Proposed Rulemaking (NOPR), U.S. regulators recently proposed a major revision in the system to entice more interstate pipelines to transport gas for others; the states may follow suit where their utilities are concerned. The NOPR will increase direct/spot markets in several ways:

- First, the NOPR perpetuates the FERC's blanket authorization for self-implementing transportation, currently provided under Orders 319 and 234B.

- Second, the proposed rule would gradually release LDCs from "system supply" purchase obligations from their supplying pipelines, enabling the LDC to attempt to purchase as much of its requirement in the direct sale market as it sees fit.*

- Third, the NOPR eases the approval process at the federal level for construction of "utility by-passes," i.e., taps off interstate pipelines directly serving one or more industrial customers.

- Finally, the NOPR contains two major provisions that are designed to alleviate take-or-pay obligations on the part of interstate pipelines, thus tending to alleviate the most important single hurdle to the direct sale market -- i.e., the reluctance of many pipelines to displace their own gas sales with carriage of gas for others. The two provisions are (a) explicit take-or-pay renegotiation incentives and (b) revised rate design aimed at removing any possible market for high priced gas supplies (i.e., an implicit take-or-pay renegotiation incentive).

Hence, the NOPR acts to enhance direct sales and the spot gas market by increasing participation in it, and by extending its life. Consequently, U.S. gas spot trading will last as long as there are supply-demand imbalances, and the transportation capacity remains available to ship the gas to customers.

The key U.S. regulatory issues at this point are: How are the regulations changing at the state

*LDC = local distribution company

level, and what will they look like when they eventually settle out? The gas utility business will be affected by increased transportation services, both by potential reductions as customers seek to by-pass LDCs and connect directly with pipelines, and by potential increases, as the transportation business itself produces additional gas customers.

THE NEW MARKET MECHANISMS

The current increase in gas-on-gas competition, spot trading, and transportation activity taking place in U.S. gas markets is producing a set of trading structures not unlike those on the oil side of the business. Problems with the current ad hoc gas market mechanisms relate to the time-comsuming and individualized effort required to arrange for gas transportation for buyers other than existing long-standing contract customers.

In order to address these issues and smooth the process, several new mechanisms are evolving that will remain a part of the market indefinitely:

- Spot trading of gas in the U.S. currently involves over 1,000 individual transactions annually, and will stabilize as a feature of gas markets, given the likely continued encouragement of regulators at both the state and federal levels.

- Posted prices emerged on a pipeline-by-pipeline basis in 1983, and had expanded by 1985 to include trader-by-trader postings.

- Competitive transportation (i.e., pipelines competing with one another for carriage business along similar routes) is likely to be institutionalized late 1985 in the U.S., with approval of the NOPR by the Federal Energy Regulatory Commission, as described above.

- Clearinghouses that help buyers, sellers and brokers identify and facilitate transactions have evolved, although no single clearinghouse (i.e., a "winner" in the gas market information business) has emerged.

- Integrated gas marketers are successfully offering a variety of services to gas customers and producers, including transportation, resale, brokerage and storage. Various examples include Tenngasco, Yankee Resources, IESCO, Entrade, Northridge in Canada, and an increasing number of others. An increasing number of pipeline and utility companies have formed affiliates to market gas.

- Futures trading in natural gas is likely to commence early 1986.

Several of these new U.S. gas market mechanisms are described as follows:

Posted Pricing

Much as refiner postings of crude oil purchase prices, gas price postings reflect market net-back values, i.e., saleable "burner-tip" gas prices less transportation expenses. As pointed out above, many individual pipelines, gas marketing companies, and even some utilities who buy gas directly from producers, are posting purchase prices at this time. Of competitive necessity, price postings are good indicators of current gas market prices.

Were a shortage to occur, spot market prices would presumably rise above contract levels, and postings would likewise reverse to reflect "net-forward" prices. While this would be reasonable behavior to expect in a deregulated commodity market, some gas market analysts have expressed the concern that such a price "run-up" would attract the Congress to reimpose field price controls.

Postings will become increasingly important in the U.S. gas business because they provide the mechanism through which pipelines compete against each other for "hauling" customers on the basis of transportation margins.

Pipeline Space Competition

One of the constraints to more open natural gas markets has been the reluctance of many gas pipeline companies to offer gas transportation services. A major deterrant to pipelines has been their need to observe high take-or-pay provisions in their gas purchase contracts by continuing to sell (as opposed to transport) as much gas as possible. A more subtle problem has been the relative competitive positioning of the pipelines in each gas market.

In order to examine the latter factor, the chart in Figure 1 plots transport rates versus purchased gas costs for five hypothetical pipelines. Each axis reflects a separate area of business for the pipelines, as follows:

- Pipelines A and B can capitalize on the transportation business because of their relative advantage as carriers versus traders.

- Pipeline C, in the opposite situation because of its relatively low gas costs and high transport costs, is likely to prefer the traditional way of doing business: sales to contract customers versus carriage.

- Pipelines D and E have relative advantage in neither line of business, relative to the other line.

This paradigm has proven to be a useful guide to understanding the reluctance displayed by some pipeline companies, versus the vigor of others, in approaching the gas transportation business. Moreover, this analysis may also explains the extent to which some pipelines will in the future find it necessary to merge with others, as they seek to maintain competitiveness in a particular region or service through economies of scale.

Finally, this analysis is a moving target; the relative competitiveness of pipelines changes, sometimes subtly, with each rate case, as gas costs and transportation rates are modified.

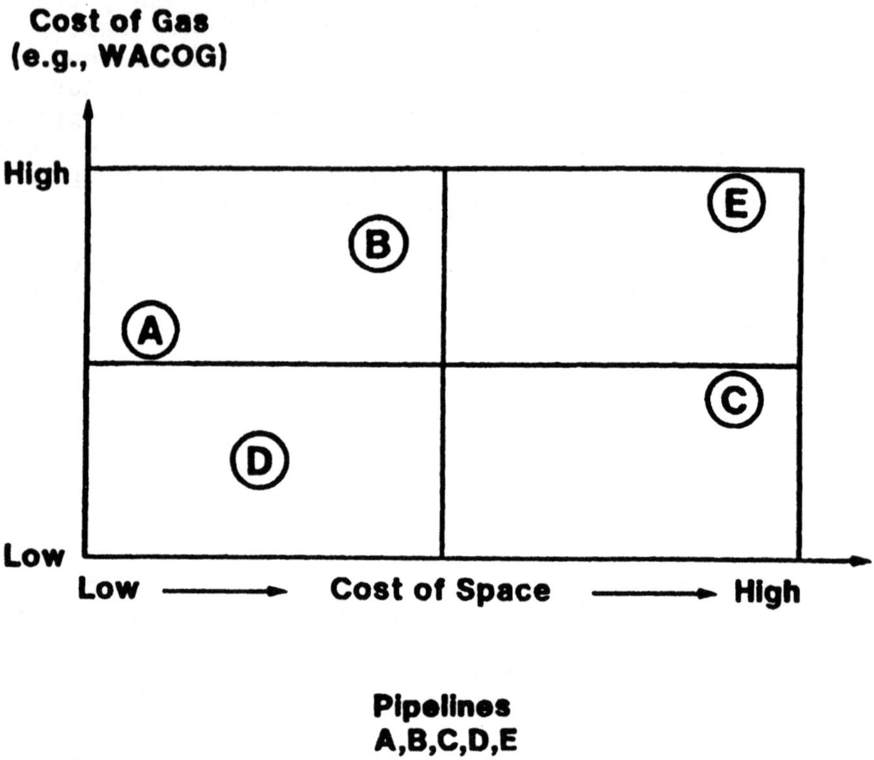

Figure 1
Pipeline Competition on a Basis of Gas Costs versus Space Costs

Gas Futures Trading

Trading of a natural gas futures contract is proposed to begin on the New York Mercantile Exchange in early 1986. Since the existence of an active spot market in natural gas is now well-established, e.g., especially in the Houston area, there is little doubt that a gas futures market will also succeed.

- Likely "hedgers" will include gas producers, industrial users and emerging marketers.

- Speculators will include gas marketers, brokers and traders, as well as the public.

An actively traded gas futures contract can work in conjunction with existing spot gas markets to enhance general confidence in the fluidity and flexibility of U.S. and Canadian gas markets.

CONCLUSIONS

Given the foregoing overview and assessment of North American gas markets, the following summarizes the market outlook in terms of several major unresolved issues confronting the gas business:

Marketing, Marketing, Marketing!

The gas industry's capacity to market gas lags way behind its capacity to produce, trade, and deliver gas.

Regulated LDCs currently retail some three fourths of the gas used in the U.S., with a similar percentage likely in Canada. But many utilities have precious little direct incentive to market effectively, e.g., some retain little or no marginal profit for marginal sales. Some are combination electric and gas utilities who prefer to add electricity sales for financial reasons.

Advertising is an effective means of marketing, particularly a mass-consumption product such as natural gas. Yet most gas retailers (LDCs) are barred from including tough, competitive advertising in their rate bases. Even in Louisiana, the second biggest gas-producing state in the U.S., a bill considered this year by the state legislature would prohibit LDCs from recovering advertising costs from ratepayers.

The result: natural gas just might be the most under-sold consumer product in widespread use in North America; consequently, current gas sales levels seriously understate the potential scope and reach of the market. Production suffers accordingly.

Perhaps the emerging independent gas marketing "segment" of the gas business will rise to fill the void, and eventually act to increase the size of retail gas markets in North America.

Market Research

Research into new ways to sell and use gas is practically non-existant in the United States. Despite the formation in the last decade of a Gas Research Institute, product research is literally off the agenda in the U.S., compared to the nation's other $100 billion industries.

Some of the new product developments the gas industry needs as soon as possible include:

- Automotive fuel switching and natural gas tankage systems designed for 1980s and 1990s vintage vehicles, not 1940s and 1950s, the level of today's available equipment.

- Safe, lightweight on-board vehicle and home-use compressors designed to fuel commuters' autos with natural gas overnight at home.

- Air quality control equipment, readily adaptable to existing coal-fired boilers, designed to optimize the select use of natural gas from both an efficiency (e.g., possibly through over-firing the coal with natural gas) and an environmental viewpoint, without scrubbers or precipitators.

- Simple, saleable cogenerators for use in commercial buildings retrofit situations, able to be tuned to local meteorological conditions.

- Low-cost room-heater retrofits designed for use in older buildings with oil heat, automatically kicking in the oil for peaking.

- Safe, low-cost combined compression and electronic metering systems for dispensing small quantities of natural gas, e.g., to automotive, marine, or other vehicles.

These and many other "demand-side" innovations need to be developed so that gas can compete in this and the next few decades with its major rivals: conservation, electricity, and fuel oil, in that order.

Refinancng the Utilities

The retail arm of the gas industry, its regulated gas distribution utilities, continues to be a favorite target of consumer groups and many politicians of all persuasions. The result is that many gas utilities are:

- Increasingly risk-averse, and unlikely to sell gas aggressively, to finance significant market expansion costs they will need, or otherwise to involve themselves creatively in gas marketing.

- Financially at the mercy of the political systems within which they operate, hence as a group are increasingly seen as risky long-term investments.

Regardless of who makes the sale of a new gas customer, the utility or an independent agent/broker, it is true that (a) the ratepayers will benefit by a broadened rate-base, and (b) the LDC will need to finance the costs of system expansion, reinforcement, and the like. Growth in gas markets is unlikely to be achieved if LDCs are unable to attract sufficient capital resources.

Organizing the Fourth Segment

The natural gas marketers, brokers, and traders represent a fourth segment of the gas industry, apart from producers, pipelines and utilities. They are engaging in a fundamentally different kind of business from the other three segments.

However, as long as the new gas brokerage and trading segment of the gas industry remains in its current immature stage of development, a void in gas marketing activities exists in the U.S. and particularly in Canada. Increasing self-regulation of trading and brokering concerns, and other signs of increasing stability and maturity, will enable individual players and consortia to take on the financial risks of market expansion.

Barring this move toward maturity, the independent gas marketers are not fulfilling their role in the marketplace.

No Law Should Prohibit Gas Use

To date, the U.S. has been unable to unshackle itself from its anti-gas laws, born of the conservation ethic. In fact, a variety of federal and state gas demand constraints continue to exist in U.S. law, deterring investment in use of gas by new and existing customers. Examples include the Fuel Use Act described above, Title II of the NGPA ("incremental pricing") which seeks to deter industrial gas use, and antiquated building codes and standards at the state and local levels. As long as these kinds of rules continue to exist, gas markets in the U.S. are held to artificially low sales levels.

Natural Gas and the Trade Deficit

Close to half the nation's balance of payments deficit this year will have been for its $56 billion imported oil bill. The U.S. currently imports over 5 million daily barrels of crude oil and products, and falling oil prices will cause this amount to rise as domestic production sags. At the same time, some one million daily barrels of U.S. oil use takes place in boilers that are equipped to burn natural gas. Consequently, if the U.S. were to adopt a vigorous policy aimed at reducing oil imports and vulnerability, an immediate and substantial increase in gas demand would be the result.

RECAP OF KEY POINTS

- Fixed-price gas purchase contracts are giving way to contracts with fluid, flexible pricing terms, increasingly linked to market indicators.

- A $12 - $15 billion per year direct sale gas market, including some 3 trillion cubic feet annually of spot trading in 1985, has quickly emerged in the U.S., and is here to stay.

- A new, fourth segment of the industry has emerged: natural gas marketing service companies.

- The industry's long-term supply orientation is yielding to a market-orientation; gas is deemed to be available, at a price.

- The search for crude oil that characterized exploration activities, while still a dominant consideration, is yielding to a search for <u>both</u> gas and oil.

- The rapid growth in gas demand which characterized pre-1970s gas markets has been reversed: natural gas markets will be demand-constrained for the foreseeable future.

The industry can only re-establish its sales levels, and develop new markets, through a coordinated program of vigorous market research, more aggressive marketing and advertising, and removal of all remaining gas use constraints. These efforts will require financing participation of all four industry segments -- producers, pipelines, distributors, and marketers.

20
Natural Gas in Western Europe: Major Expansion in Prospect

Peter R. Odell, Erasmus University, Rotterdam

Introduction

The natural gas industry as a significant element in the West European economy, dates from the discovery of the very large Groningen gas field in the Netherlands in 1959 and the first off-shore gas fields in the British sector of the North Sea in the mid-1960's. Unfortunately, even in that early period the potential role of gas was constrained by the monopolistic behaviour of the single producer of Groningen gas (a joint state/private enterprise venture involving the Dutch government on the one hand, and Shell and Esso on the other), and the monopsonistic control exercised by the UK's Gas Council over the development of Britain's offshore supplies.

Control over and/or regulation of the industry were intensifield after 1970 and have led to the under-development of Western Europe's gas resources in conditions in which two sets of factors would otherwise have ensured a much greater role for indigenous natural gas in the continent's energy economy, viz. first, the adverse changes for Europe since 1973 in the supply and price conditions of its oil imports; and second, the close proximity of production and potential production of gas in Western Europe to the centres of energy demand, so minimising the relatively high transport costs of moving gas to markets. (In this respect, as shown in Fig. 1, the geography of gas supply relative to that of energy demand in Western Europe is very much more favourable than in either the U.S. or the U.S.S.R. where, nevertheless, natural gas has become relatively more important).

In the Netherlands, the policy of pricing gas to the level of oligopolistically determined oil prices has led to the sales of constrained volumes of the country's very low-cost reserves so limiting the contribution of plentiful potential supplies of Dutch gas to the total energy requirements of both its own economy and those of neighbouring countries. As a result, the use of higher cost energy sources (notably coal and nuclear power which have not been subject to collusive pricing policies) have been stimulated, while much Dutch gas production potential has been shut in - especially the lowest cost gas from the Groningen field.

In the UK, market constraints also came to be important; initially, as a result of government pressures arising from concern for the impact on the coal industry of a greater use of gas in bulk energy markets; and somewhat later, because the Gas Council saw its objective as the achievement of a plateau level of sales at about $40x10^9$ m^3 per year (=c.4000 mcfd). These factors inhibited the willingness of both governments and the Council to accept the validity of the gas producers' claims for higher prices and so brought field development - and exploration - to a virtual halt. This negative development for British gas production was exacerbated by the government's 1971 refusal to allow producing companies to export their gas and by the Council's later decision to import gas from the Norwegian Frigg gield even though this was higher-cost than the potentially available additional U.K. supplies.

Both Dutch and British policies since the early 1970's have thus effectively inhibited the growth of the natural gas industry in Europe - and the contributions of the industries to the national economies. The costs of such policies have been justified in terms of the value of the gas that has been "saved" for future use, but this claim can only be justified with assumptions of future higher real prices in the energy market and of limited availabilities of additional gas resources. The joint probability of these assumptions being valid is low - and falling.

The impact of Dutch and British policies at the wider European level has been to create a perception of natural gas as a scarce, high value commodity; a perception which has led to much support elsewhere in Europe and by the E.E.C. for the curtailment of production and/or for limitations on the use of gas. As a result, equilibrium between supply and demand was achieved at a price well above the long-run supply price of the commodity; a situation which, in effect, created "jam-pot" conditions for potential exporters of gas to Western Europe - most notably the Soviet Union.

Meanwhile, however, Norway was able (as in the contract for its Frigg field gas with the British Gas Council) to take advantage of the way in which the natural gas market came to be perceived. It was able to offer gas from its large fields in a situation of perceived scarcity and, by playing off various prospective purchasers, was able to secure high oil related and oil indexed prices for the limited volumes it chose to produce. And thus continued the process, initiated by the Netherlands and the UK, of a limited development of the market.

The "Official" View of the Market - and its Implicatic

It is in the context of this policy-generated scarcity of gas and of regulated markets (in addition to the national controls, detailed above, there was also an E.E.C. regulation which inhibited the use of gas for power generation) that all official forecasts for indigenous natural gas' contribution to the Western European energy economy have been eminently pessimistic. This was clearly summed up in a 1982 special International Energy Agency study on gas in which the following conclusion was reached,

> "Good prospects exist for increasing production...but in practice this will depend not only on geology, technology and economics, but also on appropriate policy stances in the producing countries."[1]

The conclusion was reflected in the I.E.A.'s energy supplies' forecasts at that time for 1990.[2] These indicated a decline in indigenous gas production from 160 million tons oil equivalent (m.t.o.e.) in 1980 to 157 m.t.o.e. in 1990. The I.E.A.'s most recent set of forecasts[3] is even more pessimistic showing a 1990 indigenous production of only 150 m.t.o.e. and a year 2000 level of production of only 95 m.t.o.e. In other words, the I.E.A.'s forecasts of future Western European gas production simply appear to indicate acceptance of the idea that attitudes and policies towards the exploration for, and the exploitation of, the continent's gas resources can and will be maintained: and, in particular, that the Netherlands, Britain and Norway will continue to fail to respond to the supply opportunities offered by their considerable reserves (to be discussed below), and will be able to resist the now rapidly emerging much more competitive elements in the energy sector.

The history of regulation and control of the gas industry in Western Europe, as summarized above, certainly provides some justification for the I.E.A.'s extremely conservative view of the prospects for the future supply of indigenous natural gas. Since mid-1983, however, there have been developments in attitudes, policies and strategies in respect of the production of gas in Western Europe and its potential for meeting an increasing share of the continent's energy needs, viz.

i) There is growing embarrassment over the pre-emption of an increasing part of Western European gas markets by imports. Imports of gas have already almost doubled since 1980, as the result of take-or-pay contracts made with the Soviet Union and Algeria. Meanwhile, the production of indigenous gas has declined, in spite of the existence of an infrastructure capable of producing and distributing much larger volumes, a rapid build-up of proven reserves (see below), and the expectations of the governments of the producing countries in Western Europe that their production would have been greater. Commitments made by several Western European countries to take increased volumes of imports of natural gas in the coming decade now pose an even greater threat to indigenous production, unless the total market can be significantly expanded.

ii) This has led to an unwelcome and an increasingly acrimonious set of relationships between Western Europe gas importing countries and the continent's main producers. The latter are anxious to secure additional outlets for their gas, in order both to achieve the increased employment of resources by the industries which supply and service gas production, and to generate the revenues which the governments need - and on which, indeed, they had already reckoned prior to the weakening of the gas market. They now find that their objectives in this respect are being increasingly thwarted by competition from imported gas supplies.

iii) There is increasing recognition that the policy of pricing gas at or above premium oil products' prices or even electricity prices' equivalent, and of deliberately restricting the use of gas to high-value outlets is producing an uncompetitive energy pricing situation overall in Western Europe - compared with elsewhere in the world, most notably the U.S. where natural gas is viewed as a third-equal potential energy source, along with coal and oil, and is thus made available, as necessary and as appropriate, to low value energy markets, in competition with low-grade oil products, coal, and electricity.

These changes in attitudes towards natural gas markets are now producing moves towards the Western European equivalent of the U.S. recent deregulation of its gas industry. This development, with the consequent opening up of large markets in power generation and industrial steam-raising in competition with coal, fuel oil and nuclear power, provides the opportunity for the full exploitation of the large additional volumes of indigenous gas reserves which are already proven (see Table 1), and for the exploration and discovery of additional volumes of reserves which, to date, remain undiscovered as a result of the hitherto restrictionist policy.[4] Belated recognition by policy makers; <u>first</u>, that Western Europe is a gas-rich rather than a gas-poor region in terms of its reserves potential; and <u>second</u>, that it is not only economically justifiable, but also economically desirable, to find and produce these reserves quickly rather than slowly (while energy prices remain high) justify a hypothesis that the Western European gas industry is now at the beginning of a period of production expansion - a view which is markedly at variance with that of I.E.A., as indicated above. A 26% increase in the contribution of indigenous gas to Western

Europe's energy supply by 1990 and a 60% increase by 2000 seem possible. If so, then the prospective 240 m.t.o.e. of indigenous gas in the continent's energy supply in 2000 will be well ahead of the 160 m.t.o.e. which seems likely to be contributed in that year by indigenous coal.

Gas Reserves and Production Potential in Western Europe

The prospects for the expansion of the production of gas in Western Europe are already widely recognized by the oil industry - with an increasing number of highly optimistic statements on the opportunities for additional gas production from the companies most directly concerned in the exploration and exploitation processes. British Petroleum, for example, has described the 1980s as "the decade for gas expansion in Western Europe." AMOCO has indicated outstanding prospects for gas discovery and production; while Shell, which discovered the giant Troll field in the Norwegian part of the North Sea in 1979, has expressed the view that this provides an opportunity to move total European production to a level higher than the best achieved to date: a view which is shared by Mobil following a study in depth of the North Sea's remaining potential.[5] Table 1 shows the emerging situation on production, reserves, reserves development and production potential over the rest of the century in the countries of northwest Europe where most of the short and medium-term opportunities for an expanding indigenous gas industry are located. The relationship between currently proven plus probable reserves and 1984 production shows an R/P ratio of more than 40 years. This may be compared with a "necessary" minimum ratio of about 15 years and an R/P ratio of little more than 10 years in the United States with a current annual level of natural gas production which is almost four times higher than in Western Europe. This low R/P ratio in the U.S. necessitates additions to gas reserves in each and every year which are always large enough to replace all the gas which is used annually and it has to be done, moreover, in a country which has been intensively explored for its gas reserves over many decades.

By comparison, Western Europe has an easy supply prospect. Even after allowing for the depletion of proven reservoirs sufficient to match the planned production of indigenous gas over the second half of the 1980s (as shown in Table 1); and further assuming additional gas discoveries and field extensions which are modest, relative to both recent experience and the expenditure on exploration and field appraisal/development which is already committed, then the gas reserves which will be proven and probable in northwest Europe in 1990 will provide a reserves to production ratio which is higher than the current ratio of over 40 years. The ratio could, indeed, by then be in excess of 50 years and so make the region even more emphatically one of significantly under-utilized natural gas potential. The reserves situation by 1990 seems likely, in other words, to offer near certain prospects (viewed from the point of view of reserves availability) for major production expansion. The final column of Table 1 shows that annual production from these northwest European countries could be as much as $325 \times 10^9 m^3$. This is equal to almost 275 million tons oil equivalent: a production potential for natural gas from this part of Western Europe alone which exceeds the forecast above for a year 2000 production of indigenous gas of 240 m.t.o.e. from the whole of the continent.

Even if one allows for a (highly unlikely) run-down of natural gas production elsewhere in Western Europe (where gas has been produced for some decades already, and where, indeed, as will be shown later, there are plans for maintaining or even expanding production), a situation as forecast by I.E.A., of slow decline in the continent's gas output over the present decade followed by a strong decline in the 1990s implies such a serious failure on the part of the gas industries and governments' energy policy makers to secure the production and utilization of the gas reserves of north-west Europe as to be an eminently unbelievable proposition. The forces that are already at work to ensure that the production of natural gas in Western Europe gets back on to a growth curve undermine the validity of such a pessimistic view. These forces have already been presented in general terms but the following supply side developments in particular should be highlighted in order to show how opportunities for the expansion of the supply of natural gas are already well under way - and why they are likely to become stronger over the next year or so:

i) There will be an increase, rather than a decline, in production levels in the Netherlands as a consequence of the upward re-evaluation of existing reserves, the continuing discovery of new reserves, and the need by the government for the revenues it secures from gas production. It has, indeed, already been decided to maintain - and, if possible, to increase - the industrial use of gas; to sell more gas for power generation at least until 1987 and, in the absence of other markets, beyond that date; and to encourage the use of gas in combined heat and power installations, the development of which is being stimulated by government action. Meanwhile, some additional export markets for gas in neighboring countries have already been negotiated and others are under examination.

ii) There will be a more rapid than currently expected increase in production from Norway after the late 1980s. This will be the result of changed attitudes on production levels and prices in response to the market opportunities which are developing in Western Europe, in the context of a growing appreciation that the real value of gas left in the ground is not increasing (on the contrary, it is already declining quite rapidly and will continue to do so). Moreover, Norway will also need to export more gas in order to achieve the level of tax revenues the country requires and the level of offshore activities which are necessary to keep the resources available to the Norwegian offshore industry fully employed. Politically,

Norway will increase its efforts (which have so far been unsuccessful) to persuade gas-importing countries in Western Europe that Norwegian gas is preferable to Soviet gas. Indeed, a Norwegian/E.E.C. agreement on preferential treatment for additional gas from Norway seems highly likely by the early 1990s.

iii) There will be a significant expansion of British production as the result of the appreciation of the reserves of existing fields and the exploitation of new reserves, considerable volumes of which (over $1000x10^9m^3$) have already been found. Some production will eventually (before the end of the decade) be marketed directly by the producing companies themselves under revised legislation which will make this alternative to selling the gas to the B.G.C. more attractive. This includes the possibility of natural gas exports from the U.K. by one or more of the producing companies following a challenge to the validity of the current government ban on exports of gas to other member countries of the E.E.C. The potential for gas production from the relatively mature areas of the UK continental shelf (which still retain substantial prospects for exploration and development) is estimated as rising to some $50x10^9m^3$ per year by 2000. In addition there are good prospects for greatly increased levels of on-shore gas production and for offshore gas supplies from so far undeveloped parts of the continental shelf - such as the West Shetland basin.

iv) There are also prospects for additional output frm the other North Sea basin countries, viz. Denmark and West Germany, both of which are now belatedly pursuing intensified and more extensive gas exploration - and exploitation - policies. Expansion of their production will follow the expansion of the markets for gas.

v) Elsewhere in Western Europe there is a growing gas exploration effort in a wide variety of productive and potentially productive offshore basins (as illustrated in Fig. 2), and, increasingly, in reappraised onshore prospective regions (such as the Paris basin, the Pyrennees and in parts of the Alpine region). There is a near zero probability that all these efforts will be unsuccessful for if there were no chance of success then the exploration investments would not be made. With expected exploration successes, the currently generally low production levels in these countries (see Table 2) have a high probability of being modestly increased over the period to the end of the century.

Contrasts between the 'Official' and the Alternative Indigenous Gas Supply Prospects

The contrasting estimates of country by country volumes of natural gas production for 1990 and 2000 are set out in Table 2. The marked contrasts shown clearly demonstrate the unwillingness, or the inability, of the I.E.A. to take into account in its forecasts the opportunities for increased production offered by the rapidly evolving West European gas resource base (see Table 1). Except for the smallest producers (viz. Denmark, Ireland, Spain and Turkey, accounting in total for only about 5% of output), the I.E.A.'s forecasts of individual country's gas production in 2000 are not only lower than the forecast levels for 1990, in spite of expected major additions to reserves in the meantime, but they are also lower than the levels of production achieved in 1984 - even though production in 1984 was constrained by demand conditions. This forecast has been made in spite of a currently known availability of proven reserves which is more than adequate to sustain current levels of production well into the 21st century. And in the case of the three major producers (viz. the Netherlands, Norway and the UK), the I.E.A.'s forecasts of declining rates of production would, on extrapolation, bring production in those countries down to zero even before currently proven reserves are exhausted. Indeed, in the case of Norway, production would be near-zero before 10% of its reserves are depleted.

Given the motivation of the countries concerned to continue to produce gas - in order to serve national economic interests, if for no other reason - and the forecast of a continuing strong demand for natural gas in Western Europe (as shown by the I.E.A.'s own expectation that gas imports will increase from 45 to 137 m.t.o.e. between 1990 and 2000), the I.E.A.'s forecast of an imminent or a very near future decline in Western Europe's natural gas production and the impending demise of the industry soon after 2000, is, quite simply, inexplicable and unbelievable. Unless, of course, the Agency is forecasting that indigenous Western European gas production will be unable to compete in the marketplace against imports. If this is the cause of the pessimism, then it is worth noting the contrast with the I.E.A.'s view that West European deep mined coal will be able to compete so effectively against imports that indigenous coal output will increase. The latter depends on the I.E.A.'s expectation that energy prices in the 1990s will rise in real terms to levels higher than those of the early 1980s so indicating an expectation of energy shortage. Thus, the idea of market constraints on the relatively much lower-cost Western European gas industry is also an unlikely, if not an impossible, explanation for the organization's gas production forecasts. To put it bluntly, the I.E.A.'s indigenous gas supply forecasts appear to be based on irrational argument, and an inconsistent set of supply/demand relationships.

By contrast, the alternative forecast for an expansion of Western Europe's indigenous gas supply is related to the essential parameters of reserves' availability and national economic and political interests of the producing countries. The alternative forecast indicates, however, a level of production which is significantly less than the potential to produce (as defined by reserves and their producibility over time). It thus takes into account both nationally-determined constraints on production levels - particularly by Norway - and also an expectation that there will continue to be gas demand constraints in the short to medium term. These constraints are the consequence of high prices, conservation in residential use through technological developments, the impact of the recession on industrial use, and competition from external suppliers of natural gas. The combination of these factors is, indeed, so powerful that the increase in the production of indigenous gas over the next three to four years is likely to be slow. Thereafter, the constraints will gradually become less effective so that eventually the level of production will build up rapidly. This will apply particularly in the mid to late 1990s when the integrated Western European gas supply and transmission system will have been extended to all parts of the continent - including Scandinavia, the British Isles and the Iberian peninsula. (See Fig. 3 for the present network.) Lower real transmission costs and enhanced security of supply as results of the fully integrated network will then serve to stimulate gas use - and hence production from a still growing reserves' base. Natural seems likely to become Western Europe's most important source of indigenous energy very shortly after the turn of the century.

Competition From Imports of Natural Gas

In the meantime, however, the indigenous natural gas supply industry has to fight off increasingly virulent competition from imports. The I.E.A. clearly believes that the industry will not be successful in this respect as it forecasts that imports will increase almost four-fold from their present level by the year 2000 whilst indigenous production first stagnates and then declines. By 2000, according to the I.E.A., imports will contribute almost 60% of Western Europe's total gas supply. With an alternative view on the supply prospects for indigenous natural gas a much more modest increase in the volume of imports may be predicated. Over the period to 2000 imports seem likely to increase from just under 40 m.t.o.e. to 85 m.t.o.e. per annum. This implies a modest increase only in the share of imports in the total supply of Western Europe's gas, viz. from just over 20% in 1984 to about 26% in 2000.

The world is, of course, rich in discovered, but so far unexploited, gas and Western Europe has become something of a "jampot" for potential "supplying bees" from outside the continent for well over a decade. This condition has arisen, as indicated above, basically because the regulated high price of gas in Western Europe since the early 1970s provided a very profitable market for external suppliers. Two other factors have also been of importance; first, the size of Western Europe's energy market, and second, the geographical intensity of that demand. These factors create market conditions which are eminently suited to its being served by pipelined natural gas. In this respect the Western European energy market is a more interesting and suitable prospect for domination by natural gas than the energy markets of either the United States or the Soviet Union. The wide open spaces of both of those countries diminish the economic viability of natural gas in the generally distant markets. This contrast between Western Europe on the one hand, and the U.S.A. and the U.S.S.R. on the other, is shown in Fig. 1. Nevertheless, in spite of these relatively adverse geographical conditions in both the U.S. and the Soviet Union, gas use has expanded to fill about 30% of the energy markets in the two countries. By contrast natural gas in Western Europe has, to date, only achieved a little over half this degree of penetration of the energy market; a rough measure perhaps of the extent to which the gas industry in Western Europe has been restrained.

As demonstrated above in discussing individual country's policies, factors of nationalism have inhibited the speed of development of Western Europe's indigenous gas resources, compared with the level of development that would have been achieved under a continental-wide, unified politico-economic framework, akin to those of the U.S. and the U.S.S.R. In spite of the attractions of the market even imports of natural gas to Western Europe have been inhibited from some potential suppliers. The following factors have been important in this respect:

i). The large-scale contracts for imports that are required, to enable economies of scale in transportation to be achieved, necessitate the agreement of two or more of the potential importing countries - as, for example, with the plans, now on ice, to import additional supplies of L.N.G. from Algeria and Nigeria. This factor has also retarded the expansion of pipelined imports from the U.S.S.R. or, for example, in the unfulfilled plan to pipe gas via Finland to Sweden and on into other northern European countries.

ii). Large-scale imports require a commitment to a high level of capital costs, the investment of which create an inflexible delivery system involving possible political risks - as, for example, with the proposed natural gas line to Western Europe from Iran via Turkey and South East Europe.

iii). A commitment to a major scheme for the delivery of gas from a single supplier creates conditions in which the supplier can then exercise both economic and political pressures for changing the terms of agreements - as, for example, in the attempt by Algeria in 1982/3 to secure a higher price than that originally agreed for the gas through the Trans-Med pipeline to Italy.

iv). The high transport costs involved, both via long distance pipelines and, even more so, by L.N.G. tankers, imply a netback-value of the gas to the suppliers below that which they appear to expect (of, say, the energy equivalent value of crude oil exports). This means that agreements have been difficult to achieve, and/or that

> the gas, on delivery, is not available at a cost which enables it to be priced at a level which permits the expansion of the natural gas market. This is particularly true, as in the recent past, under conditions of stagnant or declining energy demand, and a plentiful supply of other sources of energy; notably of competing petroleum products which have become available at prices discounted from those on which the prices for gas have been determined.

The combination of the impact of these factors seems likely to continue to constrain the growth of natural gas imports to a rate which is well below that forecast by the I.E.A. over the rest of the century. This likelihood is enhanced in the context of the ability of the Western European gas producing countries to produce - competitively - much larger quantities of gas than the I.E.A.'s forecasts indicate. In this respect it is worthy of note that the I.E.A.'s 1983/84 forecast for gas imports in 1990 is 28.5% lower than its 1981/82 forecast for such imports.[6]

Nevertheless some new contracts for imports, to provide gas to Western Europe additional to that agreed under earlier contracts, have been made over the last few years. These include additional L.N.G. supplies from Algeria to France and Belgium (at prices now well above today's market prices so that the importers are negotiating reductions in the quantities involved); gas through the now completed Trans-Med pipeline from Algeria, via Tunisia, to Italy; and, most important of all, additional supplies (of up to 20 m.t.o.e.) of Soviet gas through the spare capacity in the pipelines to Western Europe which are already in operation (or in which additional capacity can be created, through the installation of new compressor stations on the lines). These agreements provide near certain additions to imports over the rest of the 1980s, as the contracts have generally been concluded on a take-or-pay basis. They will lead to a total of ca. 55 m.t.o.e. of imported gas by 1990.

6. The Impact of Competition from Imports

The ability and willingness of the potential exporters of more gas to Western Europe to sell this gas, if necessary, at a lower price than that which they originally thought they might get is an option open to them, given the low costs of gas production in the countries concerned. The phenomenon has already led to an expansion of the market for imports at the expense of some indigenous production - particularly exports from the Netherlands which are now running well below their anticipated levels.[7] Additional imports of gas by many Western European countries in the later part of the decade seem likely to intensify this difficulty for the Netherlands' planned level of exports. They also adversely affect Norway's production prospects as a result of that country's sluggish response to date to the challenge of the weakening energy market since 1981, and the potential over-supply of gas in Western Europe throughout the next ten years at least.

There is, moreover, an increasingly likely prospect that the countries exporting gas to Western Europe will, within the next few years, in order to make their exports more attractive, offer gas under conditions of price and deliverability which will make it competitive with imported coal, and thus well below the ex-refinery fuel oil equivalent price - to which gas for industrial use in Western Europe has generally been priced to date. Indeed, the first move in this direction has already been taken with the inclusion of a price-of-imported-coal component in the indexing calculations for pricing imports of Soviet gas to West Germany. Should this development escalate into a full-blooded attempt by gas sellers to compete with imported coal in Western Europe then the expansion of the gas market could be even faster than the alternative forecasts above suggest. Such a development would have the effect of increasing indigenous gas supplies to some extent (as some Western European producing countries responded to the challenge), and imported supplies to a much greater extent. This would produce, overall, a higher contribution of natural gas to Western European energy supplies than the 245 m.t.o.e. forecast above for 1990, and a total market for natural gas which is more than the forecast of 325 m.t.o.e. by 2000.

Though such a development would have some positive impact on the size of the total demand for energy, the greater effects would be on the markets for coal and oil products. Further substitution of oil and coal by gas would take place and the share of gas in the total energy market would be increased above the 26% forecast above for 2000. In this event the natural gas market in Western Europe by the end of the century would be moving closer to the characteristics of the gas markets in North America and the Soviet Union - with a considerable use of gas in bulk energy uses, in spite of the current E.E.C. and national directives to minimize gas use in power generation and industrial steam-raising. It is necessary to emphasize that this possible development in Western Europe is not resource-constrained. A combination of the full exploitation of indigenous resources (to provide an annual supply in excess of 240 m.t.o.e.) and a continental-wide integrated transmission system, plus the construction of expanded delivery systems for gas from outside the continent (whereby an annual deliverability of more than 150 m.t.o.e. would be possible) would place no strain on the ultimate availability of resources, nor on the funds necessary to enable the exploration, exploitation and transport investments to be made. This upside potential for natural gas over the next 15 years does, indeed, provide the element of greatest uncertainty in the future of Western Europe's energy supply possibilities.

Although oil prices are likely to remain the main determinant of the outlook for Western Europe's energy prices over the short and the medium-term, the continuing relative decline in the role of oil in total energy supplies will open up the possibility of "price leadership" moving elsewhere in the energy sector by the early to mid-1990s. Price competition between the suppliers (both indigenous and foreign) of the rapidly expanding volumes of natural gas, on the one hand, and the suppliers of imported coal, on the other hand, could by then have become acute - and so provide the "leadership" thereafter in the further evolution of the energy pricing situation. Oil prices would then, of course, have to become responsive to natural gas/imported coal prices competition.

Meanwhile, indigenous and imported supplies of natural gas, the prices of which are still closely related to oil prices, will be increasingly effectively marketed to out compete oil products - both fuel and gas oils. The present OPEC oil-related price for gas in

Western Europe gives, however, a general price level which is so far above the long-run supply price of natural gas for the volumes which are likely to be demanded that the declining real price for gas, which will emerge as a result of the falling oil price, seems unlikely to have an adverse impact on the evolution of the gas supply. Bulk gas for large users will become available relatively much more cheaply in order to keep markets moving ahead in the way required by the expanding supply. The large economic rents generated by low-cost gas production (relative to market values) will be squeezed, but this process will mainly reduce unit government revenues from gas production: a development which could well lead to an enhanced motivation for the governments concerned to seek to expand production levels in order to sustain total revenues from their natural gas industries.

7. Conclusions

The changes now under way in the gas industry in Western Europe are thus ones which are taking it away from the constrained, regulated and high price system of the 1970-83 period. Instead competitive forces are likely increasingly to dominate the prospects for the industry over the rest of the century. This change of structure is in the context of a growing appreciation that there are more than adequate reserves - both indigenous and imported - to sustain the long-term growth of gas markets at the expense of other sources of energy.

This predicated evolution of a competitive, expanding and declining real price gas market in Western Europe undermines the basis on which gas policies in Western Europe have been determined in recent years. The relevant issues in this respect are as follows:

i). It arouses skepticism over the validity of the central parameter in much European gas planning, viz. that there are relatively near future dangers (before 1995) over the adequacy of available resources to sustain existing, let alone increasing, levels of demands. The widely accepted - and much implemented - idea of a "gas depletion policy," with its implication of restraints on the level of gas production which might otherwise be achieved in the short-term, is related to this parameter.

ii). It raises doubt over the related implicit (or even the explicit) assumption lying behind the idea of gas production controls; viz. that gas saved for use over the long term has a value which exceeds its value in current and near-future additional use. This would be true only with unrealistic assumptions of a rising real price for the commodity and a constrained resource base which creates significant "user costs" in the short term. Neither of these have more than a low probability of being correct so that policies which emerge from them are unlikely to be appropriate.

On the supply side Western Europe is well-blessed with gas reserves and production potential (as shown in Tables 1 and 2) and it appears economically disadvantageous for the countries concerned to pursue policies which diminish the levels of production of its resources. One economic reason for restricting supply is related to the possible danger of a country becoming too dependent on the production of gas. This is not the case when the gas potential is viewed in the Western European context. The industry, even if doubled or tripled in size, would remain of limited importance relative to the country's economy as a whole. There is even less justification for the fear, often expressed, that gas used today, or in the near future, means less gas will be available for the mid to long-term future - so exposing our grandchildren to the danger of a scarcity of resources. The development of Western Europe's gas potential is, even after 20 years of production, still in its early stages. The geographical size and the emerging petro-geology complexity of the continent's potential gas-bearing regions - both onshore and offshore - indicate that many more decades of activity will be required before the totality of the resource base is properly known and evaluated. Equally lengthy periods of exploration/exploitation have been necessary in all other parts of the world where gas has become important - and, most notably, in the United States. The continuity of the search for, and the development of, gas resources depends, however, on incentives to the exploring and producing companies. The most effective incentive is a high positive cash-flow from the production of reservoirs that have been discovered and this, in turn, depends on the expansion of profitable markets for the commodity. In as far as markets are constrained and/or profits to the producers are otherwise too limited, then the exploration/exploitation efforts will atrophy - so that resources which exist will not be discovered and thus cannot be made available for use either for the short or the longer-term future. Depletion policies do not save gas for the future; they ensure that gas which could be used to meet future needs is never found and, in the meantime, they also diminish the positive effects on the economy that higher gas production rates could secure. This truth is slowly becoming known in Western Europe.

On the demand side gas policies in Western Europe have largely evolved in the belief that gas is a premium fuel to be used only in so-called premium markets. This is valid only in part; there are clearly uses for gas in which it commands a premium price. But these markets are limited. In the most important gas using countries - the United States and the Soviet Union - much gas goes into industrial steam raising and power generation. All other countries outside Western Europe with developing gas production potential use their gas in these non-premium markets. These markets are now becoming increasingly important in Western Europe[8] with the recognition that gas has to be flexibly priced to allow it to serve a range of potential markets in Western Europe. Thus, flexibility in gas pricing is now on the way to becoming the norm in Western Europe, while less and less is heard of the previously presented view that natural gas ought not to be burned "wastefully" in industrial boilers or in power stations. On the contrary, there is instead the beginning of a very positive attitude to such gas use - not only for economic, but also for environmental reasons. The latter development emerges from the recognition that the use of natural gas in power stations and for industrial steam raising provides a solution to the "acid rain" problem: a problem which has become one of rapidly increasing concern across the continent and in respect of which action is already required by many national governments and will soon be required by EEC regulations. The use of natural gas promises to be a lower-cost alternative for solving the problem than either the process of SO_2 removal from coal-fired power station stacks or the expansion of nuclear power. This is particularly the case when natural gas use for power generation opens up attractive economic potential for dispersed (rather than centralized) production of electricity, with wasteheat recovery achieved as a matter of course for industrial and/or residential and commercial use. Such combined heat and power production based on natural gas is, indeed, an increasingly important element in energy policy developments in many Western European countries. In this context maximising the use of natural gas is the preferred option by the increasingly important "Green" lobby: its support adds to the likelihood of expanding natural gas use in Western Europe.

Events since 1983 and the potential developments discussed above in the evolution of the natural gas markets in Western Europe over the coming years will make the future role of the gas industry very different from its role over the last 20 years. Controls on gas production and the regulation of its use and price are on their way out under the pressures of rapidly changing circumstances so that, as already in the United States and the Soviet Union, natural gas in Western Europe will eventually achieve rough parity, along with oil and coal, in providing the energy required for the region's continued development.

Notes

1. I.E.A., The Prospects for Gas to 2000, O.E.C.D., Paris, 1982, p.19.

2. I.E.A., Energy Policies and Programmes of the I.E.A. Countries, 1981 Review, O.E.C.D., Paris, 1982.

3. I.E.A., Energy Policies and Programmes of the I.E.A. Countries, 1983 Review, O.E.C.D., Paris, 1984.

4. As, for example, in the case of the U.K.'s potential reserves, as demonstrated in the recently published study by the UK Offshore Operators Association (U.K.O.O.A.), Potential Oil and Gas Production from the UK Offshore to the Year 2000 (London, September 1984). In this study which deliberately chose to work with conservative development potential parameters, the UK's gas production for the year 2000 is nevertheless shown to be significantly higher than the highest production level achieved to date.

5. M. Frisch (Mobil North Sea Ltd.), "The Supply Outlook for Gas from the North Sea", Petroleum Review, Vol.39, No.462, July 1985, pp.36-43.

6. See the I.E.A.'s 1981 and 1983 Annual Reviews; op. cit

7. Recently published West German trade statistics for 1984 show that its imports of Dutch gas decreased by 7.3% compared with 1983. By contrast West Germany's 1984 imports of Soviet gas were up by no less than 24% to provide about 35% of the country's total gas imports. The trade statistics indicate that the average unit price of imports from the Soviet Union was only a little more than two-thirds of the unit price of Dutch gas.

8. In 1984, for example, the Netherlands, Denmark and Italy decided to use (more) gas in power stations.

Table 1. Natural Gas in Northwest Europe: Production, Reserves and Potential (standard $m^3 x 10^9$)

Country/ Region	Production in 1962	1973	1984 est.	Cumulative Production to 1984	End-1984 Remaining Proven/Probable Reserves (1)	Reserves/ Production Ratio	Planned Average Ann.Prod. 85-90 (2)	Likely Remaining Reserves by 1990 (3)	R/P Ratio in 1990	Potential Peak Annual Prod. in 1990s (4)
Netherlands:										
Onshore	8	60	55	1015	1750 }	27 yrs	75	1550 }	27 yrs	102
Offshore	0	0	20	80	400 }			500 }		
W.Germany:										
Onshore	10	15	15	290	250 }	20 yrs	16	300 }	22 yrs	20
Offshore	0	0	0	0	25 }			50 }		
Denmark:										
Offshore	0	0	0.2	0.2	150	∞	2	200	100 yrs	10
Norway:										
North Sea	0	0	31	175	2500	81 yrs	40	at least 3000 }	minimum of	more than
North of 62°	0	0	0	0	substantial	∞		at least 1000 }	100 yrs	150
United Kingdom:										
South North Sea	0	25	27	425	650 }	40 yrs	45	450 }	45	45
Elsewhere on C.S.	0	0	16	65	1050 }			1450 }		
Onshore	0	0.2	0.2	3	50 }			150 }		
Ireland:										
Offshore	0	0	2	7	60	30 yrs	2	75	37	4
TOTALS	18	c.100	c.166	c.2060	at least 7000	over 40 yrs	c.180	at least 8725	at least 50 yrs	at least 325(5)

Notes:
(1) Based on Governments' and Companies' declarations of reserves
(2) Based on announced production schedules by governments and companies
(3) After allowing for production 1985-89 and for new additions to reserves in the meantime
(4) Assuming no artificial restraints on production (eg. policy restrictions), but allowing for technical restraints.
(5) This figure is less than individual countries' total because of temporal differences in peak production from country to country

Table 2 Forecasts of Natural Gas Production in Individual Western European Countries for 1990 and 2000 (in m.t.o.e.)

Country	1984 Production (estimated)	Forecasts for 1990		Forecasts for 2000	
		I.E.A.	This Study	I.E.A.	This Study
1. Major Producers					
Netherlands	55	50	65	24	70
Norway	34	26	30	4	55
United Kingdom	32	35	45	31	58
Sub-Total	111	111	140	59	183
2. Minor Producers in 1984					
Austria	1.5	1	2	1	2
Denmark	>1	2	4	2	8
Germany (West)	15	14	16	13	17
Greece	>1	>1	>1	>1	1
Ireland	2	1	2	2	5
Italy	12	10	12	10	12
Spain	>1	1	3	2	4
Turkey	>1	>1	1	>1	2
Sub-Total	32	30	41	31	51
3. Non I.E.A. member					
France	7	n.a.	8	n.a.	6
TOTAL WESTERN EUROPE	150	150*	190	95*	240

*) Includes 9 for France in 1990 and 5 for 2000.

Sources: -I.E.A. Energy Policies and Programmes of I.E.A. Countries, 1983 Review, O.E.C.D, Paris, 1984.
-This Study. Based on production potential from declared and expected proven/probable reserves, but with production limited by both supply side and demand (market) constraints.

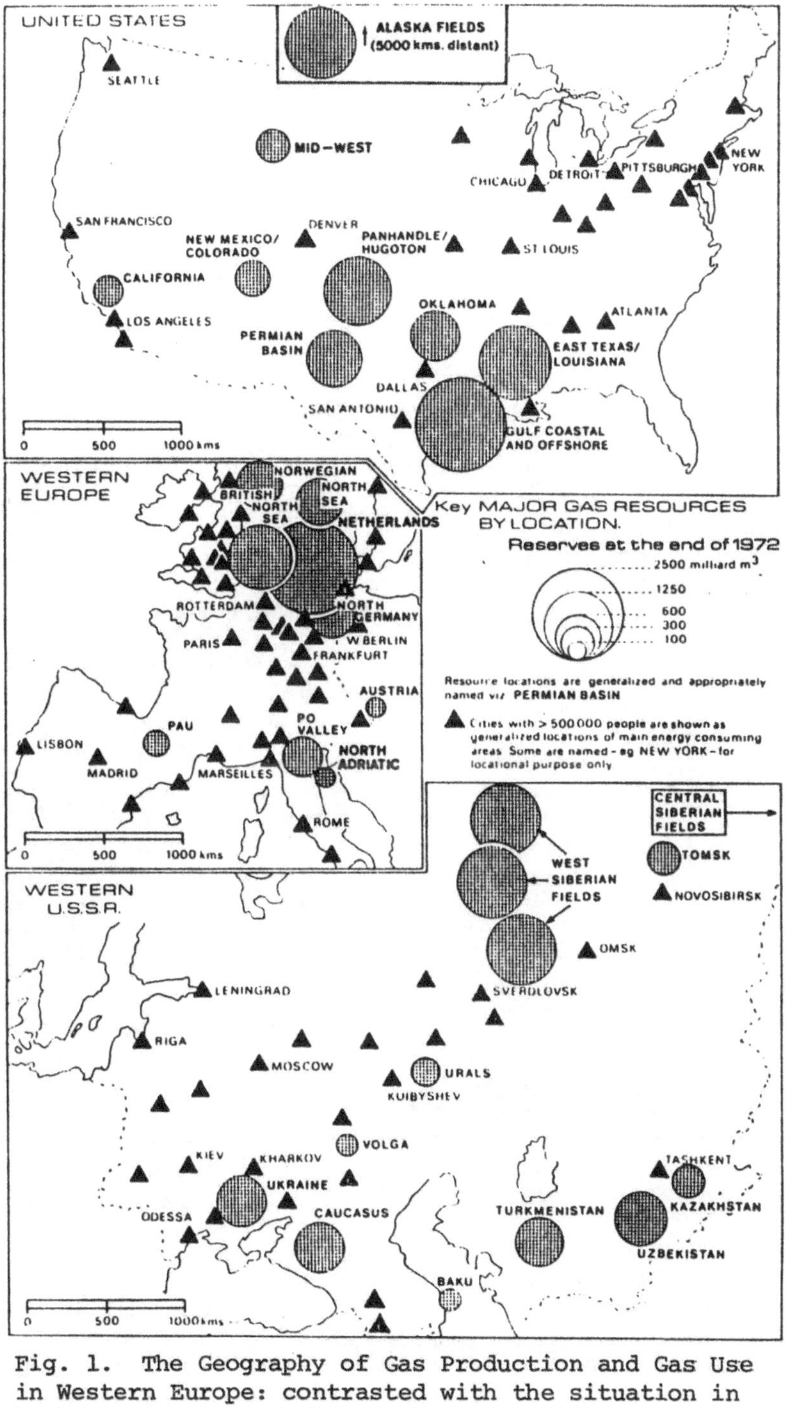

Fig. 1. The Geography of Gas Production and Gas Use in Western Europe: contrasted with the situation in both the U.S.A. and the U.S.S.R.

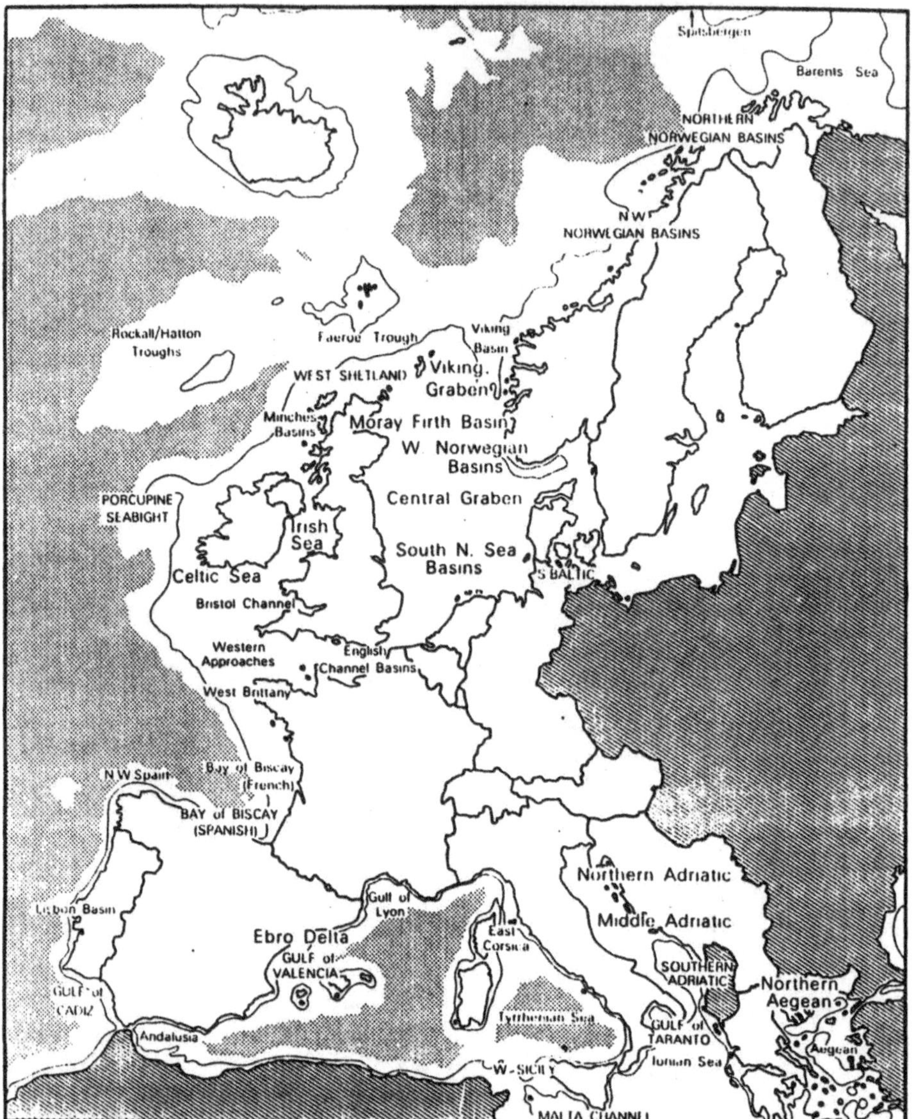

Irish Sea	Off-shore areas where oil and/or gas fields have been located and which are under active development
GULF of CADIZ	Off-shore areas where exploratory drilling has located oil and gas with prospects for field development
Viking Basin	Other off-shore areas with geological and/or geophysical indications of oil and gas

Non West-European countries

Sea areas deeper than 2000 metres

300 metre submarine contour

0 kms 500

©EGI 30/83

Fig. 2. Western Europe: Actual and Potential offshore Oil and Gas Basins.

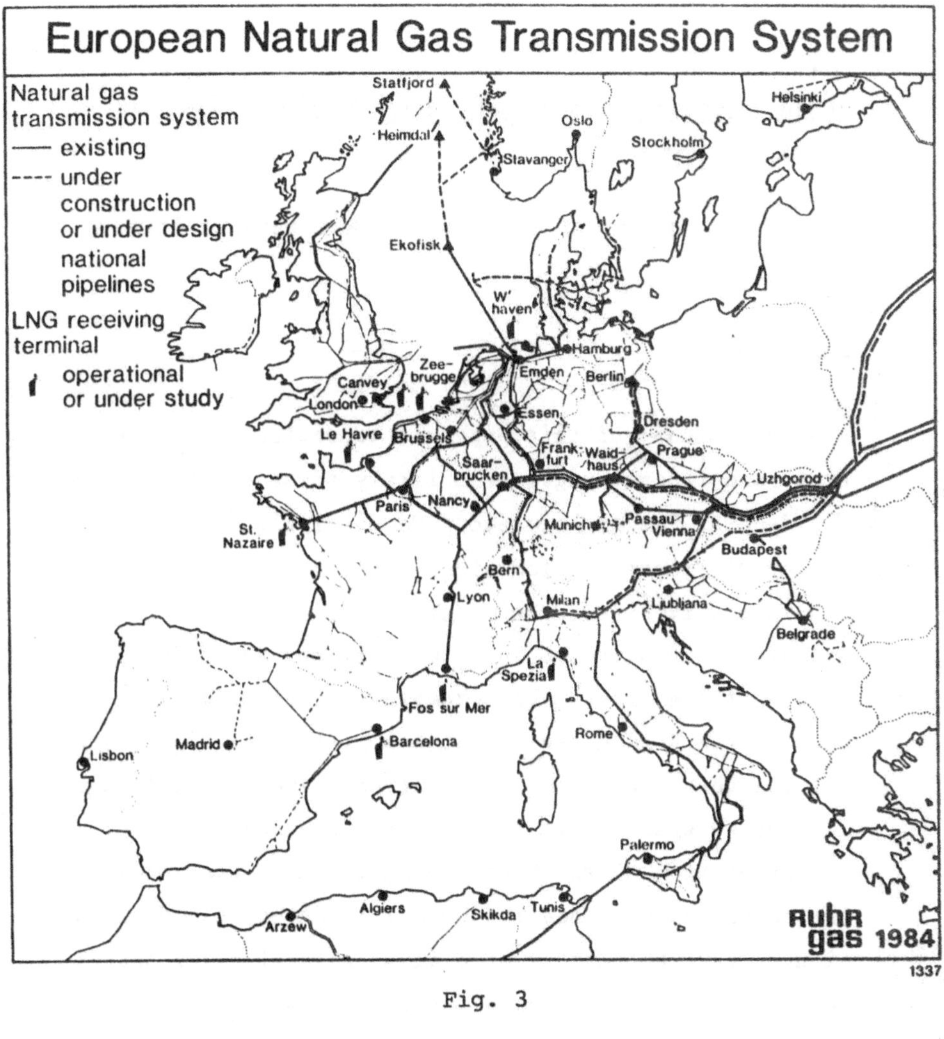
European Natural Gas Transmission System
Natural gas
transmission system
existing
under
construction
or under design
national
pipelines
LNG receiving
terminal
operational
or under study
Statfjord
Heimdal
Oslo
Stockholm
Helsinki
Stavanger
Ekofisk
W' haven
Hamburg
Emden
Berlin
Zee-brugge
Canvey
London
Essen
Dresden
Le Havre
Brussels
Frank-furt
Waid-haus
Prague
Saar-brucken
Uzhgorod
Paris
Nancy
St. Nazaire
Munich
Passau
Vienna
Budapest
Bern
Lyon
Milan
Ljubljana
Belgrade
La Spezia
Fos sur Mer
Barcelona
Rome
Madrid
Lisbon
Palermo
Algiers
Skikda
Tunis
Arzew
Ruhr gas 1984
1337

Fig. 3

21
The Interplay of State and Federal Issues in Natural Gas

R. Skip Horvath, Interstate Natural Gas Association of America

INTRODUCTION

The purpose of this paper is to outline the areas of state and federal regulation likely to be highlighted by the Federal Energy Regulatory Commission's (FERC) recent Notice of Proposed Rulemaking (NOPR). Many decades of regulatory experience have delineated some areas of federal and state jurisdiction, but the NOPR may shift the boundaries of those areas. For example, the block billing feature of the NOPR gives the states greater flexibility over pricing than they have under current federal regulations.

The relevant state issues for producing states are different from those of consuming states. Consuming states are concerned with how the NOPR will affect the distribution of gas, the matter of bypassing local distributors, and the security of future supply. Those concerns also affect producing states, which are additionally absorbed with ratable take laws, priority systems, and common purchaser laws. First, the issues facing producing states are examined, followed by those facing consuming states.[1/]

For the sake of brevity, I am assuming that the reader has a working familiarity with FERC's May 30, 1985, version of the NOPR.2/ For the purpose of this paper, we assume that the NOPR is implemented as is.

PRODUCING STATES

Regulatory commissions in major producing states have statutory responsibilities to regulate the production of natural gas so as to prevent waste and to protect the correlative rights of all owners. Some of the commissions' authority comes from state conservation laws, using a number of tools:

- Ratable take provisions and pro rata laws
- Common purchaser laws
- Priority systems

The purpose of each of these tools is to enable state commissions to fulfill their charters, and most producing states have had one or more such laws on their books for decades. Throughout this paper, "producing states" refers to the top five gas producing states (Texas, Louisiana, Oklahoma, New Mexico, and Kansas), which together produce about 86 percent of the natural gas produced in this country.3/ Table 1 at the end of the paper summarizes the above laws for each of these producing states.

Ratable Take and Pro Rata Provisions

Ratable or pro rata takes refer to the proportional cutback of production by producers.4/ The effect of such provisions is to limit takes to a fractional part of the total productive capacity of each well, regardless of price differences or other contract differences among the producers. The primary stated motivations behind prorating are preventing waste and protecting correlative rights within reservoirs.

While all of the producing states discussed here cite waste prevention as justification for ratable take laws, serious questions have been raised about the strength of the link between prorating and waste prevention.[5/] Prorating is more clearly provided for under correlative rights provisions.

Correlative rights laws are best explained by an example. Suppose producer A's well is physically located next to producer B's well in such a way that they both draw from the same gas reservoir. Without correlative rights provisions, producer A could theoretically draw gas at a rate which would drain the gas under producer B. Doing so would deprive producer B of the fair opportunity to recover the value of the gas beneath his surface acreage. Thus correlative rights laws are really a mechanism to provide market share to each producer in a reservoir.

Although the mechanics vary from state to state, prorating within a given reservoir occurs in the following manner:

- o Gas purchasers nominate the amounts of gas they plan to take from each pool (reservoir) for the next prorating period.
- o The responsible state body totals the gas required for each pool and assigns an "allowable" for each well in proportion, ratably, to the productive capacity of that well.
- o Wells are permitted over- and under-production for a specific period, after which time over-producing wells are generally shut in and under-producing wells lose their chance to make up the lost gas.

During times of excess production, the most important function of pro rata laws is to ensure that producers are equally affected by pipeline cutbacks in takes.

If block billing is implemented in a form approaching that described in the NOPR, the stage could be set for greater interaction of federal and state laws. Under block billing, gas will be grouped according to NGPA categories into two blocks: the average price of block 1 gas will generally be well below the current average price, while the price of block 2 gas will be well above the current average price. Unlike other features of the NOPR, the block billing scheme is required, not conditioned on pipeline acceptance of transportation access. There are two ways in which the block billing scheme intersects with pro rata and ratable take laws. The first involves takes between block 1 and block 2 gas, and the second concerns takes within block 2. Each is discussed in turn.

Pro Rata and Block 1 vs. Block 2 Gas. The size and price of block 1 gas make it important and marketable. Currently, gas which would be classified in block 1 comprises about 47 percent of annual takes.6/ Priced on average about $1/MMBtu below market-clearing levels, block 1 gas would appear highly attractive to customers who would bring tremendous pressure on pipelines to take delivery of as much block 1 gas as possible. For example, a distributor requests to take all of its allotted block 1 gas for firm customers, none of the pipeline's block 2 gas, and makes up the balance of its requirement with transportation contracts. State prorating provisions may require pipelines to take equal shares of block 1 and block 2 gas, thereby preventing pipelines from taking more block 1 than block 2.7/ Therefore, under ratable take provisions, pipelines may not be able to comply with such a distributor request. Thus pipelines will be pushed by powerful economic forces on one side to adjust their mix of takes, but prescribed by state laws on the other to take ratably.

Pro Rata within Block 2 Gas. In addition to the pressure caused by the price differences between their block 1 and 2 gas, pipelines must also deal with price disparities within block 2. Under the tremendous market pressures created under FERC's proposed rules, pipelines will have an incentive to increase their takes of any lower-priced block 2 gas and decrease their takes of any higher-priced block 2 gas in an attempt to minimize their costs. Again, state pro rata laws may baffle any such purchase pattern. In the long run, to the extent across-the-board renegotiations occur resulting in block 2 prices at parity with spot market gas prices, state ratable take provisions regarding block 2 gas could mesh with the incentives set up by the NOPR.

The Problem with the Block Pricing Mechanism. FERC expects market forces to cause individual prices of block 2 gas to be renegotiated downward to market-clearing levels. If that renegotiation were to happen, state pro rata requirements would yield a market-clearing average price. Unfortunately, because the prices of all block 2 gas on a pipeline system are averaged together, there is little incentive for producers of high-cost gas to agree to lower prices. The NOPR creates a "free rider" problem in which producers of expensive gas do not see the average price of block 2 gas fall by whatever price decrease they individually agree to.

In general, the smaller the volume a particular producer represents on a pipeline system relative to all the producers on that pipeline system, the smaller the change in the average block 2 price he will see as a result of renegotiating downward. In fact, for every dollar of downward renegotiation, an individual producer will see the average price of block 2 gas fall by an amount proportional to his share of the total block 2 take of that pipeline system. For example, if a producer represents 3 percent of a pipeline system's takes, a renegotiated downward drop of $1/MMBtu by that producer will result in a $0.03/MMBtu decrease in the average price of block 2 gas.

The "free rider" problem could be alleviated by breaking out block 2 gas into two subdivisions, one containing market responsive gas and the other containing high cost gas.8/ When a producer in the high-cost subdivision drops its price, its production will then go into the market-responsive block. Breaking out block 2 into subdivisions will put pressure on producers to renegotiate their non-market responsive gas. The breakout has the additional advantage of allowing current market-responsive block 2 gas to enter the market without waiting for the renegotiation of high-cost block 2 gas. Unfortunately, state pro rata laws may frustrate even this solution.

Outcome of Pro Rata Problem. There are many possible reactions to this conflict of market forces and state law, including:

- Federal preemption--The courts may determine that under federal preemption the pipelines are justified in attempting to adjust their gas mix.
- Including a price factor--The states may react by permitting purchasers to discriminate on the basis of price. (If one state relaxes its pro rata laws in such a manner, pressure may be put on remaining states to follow suit or lose revenue through a decreased market share.)
- Individual solutions--Because the enforcement of pro rata laws varies by state, unique solutions may be possible under certain circumstances.

At this time it is impossible to determine the resolution of the potential conflicting forces between market pressures set up by FERC's proposed rules and existing pro rata laws. LDCs are not likely to immediately exercise their NOPR option of cutting back contract demand by 25 percent because of the risk involved during a heating season and because they need time to assess the impact of such cutbacks on their long-term ability to get gas. Instead, LDCs may simply choose to take only block 1 gas, making up the balance of their gas requirements through transportation arrangements. Under such conditions, pipelines may not be able to comply with both market demands at one end and state pro rata laws at the other.

Common Purchaser Laws

The purpose of common purchaser statutes is to assure a nondiscriminatory market for all producers assigned an allowable within a reservoir.9/ Common purchaser laws generally address only the access of producers to purchasers, not the volume sold (the amount of gas is covered under the state pro rata laws). Producing states cite several reasons for common purchaser laws:

- To place shut-in gas on the market.
- To increase overall gas production in the state.
- To ensure that certain producers are kept whole for long-term interest of the state.
- To ensure that all producers are treated equally with regard to access.

State common purchaser laws may interact differently with the new federal regulations relative to the current ones. Under the open access to transportation provided by the NOPR, there should be few occasions, if any, where enforcement of common purchaser statutes would be needed.

Under the NOPR, new facilities can also be constructed for transportation on an expedited basis. But it is not clear who would pay for the facility. If the pipeline agrees to construct the facility under the optional expedited certificate, it must also agree to bear all the economic risks (recovery of costs) involved. Thus it is possible that a pipeline might find itself under pressure from a producing state to build a facility to connect a well to transport gas for a producer when the pipeline has little business justification to accept the risk.

Priority Systems

This regulatory device ranks sources of gas with respect to the order in which they must be taken for the prevention of waste. Oklahoma, for example, categorizes gas wells (in decreasing priority) as distressed wells, enhanced recovery wells, casinghead wells, and all other gas wells. Generally speaking, these systems emphasize the importance of conservation laws within a state, rather than correlative rights. Their principal intended effect is to ensure that gas which might otherwise be lost is produced.10/

Priority systems may interact with federal regulations under the NOPR because of the two-tiered billing scheme. To the extent that pipelines take old gas which also happens to be distressed gas or enhanced recovery gas or casinghead gas, the new federal policies will mesh with state priority systems. But much high priority gas will fall into block 2. Interstate pipelines representing roughly three-quarters of the total 1983 gas purchases have block 2 prices between \$3.25 and \$4.40/MMBtu, well above the recent spot prices of \$2.25 to \$2.40/MMBtu.11/ At current block 2 prices, pipelines required to take block 2 gas under state priority schemes would not find this gas marketable. While some pipelines have a larger share of priority gas than others, all pipelines will be caught by state requirements to take gas that a federal billing system has made unmarketable.

It is unclear how much interstate gas is affected by state priority systems. Of the top five producing states, three (Texas, Oklahoma, and New Mexico) have such laws. In Louisiana, which has no priority system, cases of distressed wells are handled informally.12/ In Louisiana at least, this informal procedure suggests that there is not a great quantity of "priority" gas. It is possible that priority schemes represent a potential conflict with proposed federal regulations.

CONSUMING STATES

The regulatory commissions of consuming states keep a watchful eye on burner tip prices and preserve an equitable allocation of natural gas. In practical terms, this charter translates to three policy areas (excluding safety) which intersect with those of the federal government:

- o Structuring LDC rates and service
- o Deciding the extent to which "bypass" is permitted
- o Ensuring availability of supply.

The state legislatures vary a great deal in the extent to which they have empowered their state commissions within each of the above policy areas. For example, some state legislatures task municipalities with LDC rate approval. These and other variations notwithstanding, the following discussion of the above three areas holds with respect to the policy implications of the NOPR and the states' authority to regulate gas within their borders.

Distribution Rates and Service

States have traditionally regulated the rates for all LDCs within their boundaries. State PUCs must simply ensure that the revenues generated from the various customer classes cover the total cost of service, including the cost of gas bought from interstate pipelines. Under the proposed rulemakings, states will have a new responsibility: the allocation of the two gas blocks. Although physically intermingled in the pipeline, the two blocks will be billed separately at the city-gate. The significance of this change in billing is that for the first time state PUCs will have to allocate gas which has been federally identified for firm customers. The NOPR specifies that the amount of block 1 gas dedicated to each LDC is to be based on historic volumes for firm customers. But once the gas reaches the city-gate, it is up to state regulators to determine the actual allocation of that gas. The states have the following options:

- roll block 1 and block 2 prices together,
- dedicate block 1 gas (with its lower price) to a specific customer class, or
- assign a mix of block 1 and block 2 gas to each specific customer class.

Each of these is examined in turn. A state might roll blocks 1 and 2 together in order to preserve the current average price to that state. For this strategy to work, two assumptions are necessary. First, the pipelines serving that state must not change their purchasing patterns. Second, the LDCs must buy the same amount and mix of block

1 and 2 gas as they do now. Many states may follow this strategy in the short term because the NOPR is to be implemented over a heating season, and because time will be needed for an assessment of the distributional and economic effects of block billing. As discussed earlier, ratable take laws may prevent pipelines from changing their purchased gas patterns. If ratable take laws are relaxed, demand by LDCs will permit higher takes of less expensive gas, resulting in a short run, lower average system price to be passed on to the consumers.13/

For political reasons, residential consumers are probably the only feasible customer class to which a PUC might dedicate block 1. While the actual price would vary by state, such an arrangement would guarantee residential consumers in each state the lowest gas price for as long as old gas continues to flow in sufficient quantity. All other customer classes will purchase any remaining block 1 gas, spot gas, or block 2 gas. During the transition months of the new rulemaking's implementation, nonresidential consumers will see relatively stable prices only to the extent that spot gas can be substituted for block 2 gas, or block 2 gas is immediately renegotiated downward to market-clearing levels.

As we have seen in the "free rider" discussion on ratable takes, however, far-reaching renegotiation by block 2 producers is unlikely in the short run, making block 2 gas unmarketable to nonresidential consumers. Industrial end users, for example, would almost surely not purchase block 2 gas, substituting one of the following actions instead:

- Obtain spot gas and arrange for transportation service through the appropriate pipeline and LDC.
- Switch to fuel oil.
- Attempt to bypass the LDC.

Industrial users (and electric utilities) without the above options must either pay a premium for the gas, institute capital changes to reduce their dependence on natural gas, or lower their level of operations. Because of the severity of these options, it is unlikely that states will dedicate block 1 to any one class in the short run. In the long run, the price of block 2 gas may well decline as market forces wear down producer resistance, at which point dedicating block 1 gas to one customer class may not be as disruptive.

A far more likely long-term strategy for state PUCs is to apportion block 1 and block 2 gas so that residential customers enjoy gas prices no higher than they now do while nonresidential customers are given as low a price as possible. (Note that completely rolling in blocks 1 and 2 is a special case of this more general apportioning.) Special allocation rules for industrial end users may be necessary if dealing with bypass, avoiding dependence on fuel oil, or avoiding manufacturing disruptions are important state goals. (For example, by allocating the blocks appropriately, bypass can be made either attractive or unattractive to industrial end users.) By keeping these apportioning rules flexible, state PUCs may monitor block 2 prices and respond to any changes in pipeline prices.

It is impossible to say at this time how states will respond in the long run to block billing. Because the dilemma of allocating federally earmarked gas has never confronted the states before, it is probable that each state will make every effort to analyze its unique circumstance before embracing a particular apportionment scheme. A partial list of the important factors affecting each state's circumstance follows:

- o the number of interstate pipelines with drop-off points in the state
- o the relative amounts of block 1 and 2 gas on each pipeline
- o the relative consumption patterns of the four customer classes (residential, commercial, industrial, and electric utility) and
- o the price of competitive fuels.

Bypass

"Bypass" refers to the act of existing end users directly hooking up to a pipeline instead of through a local distribution company.14/ The chief benefit to the end user is lower gas costs due to the avoidance of transportation charges which would otherwise be incurred from the local distribution company. The chief cost of bypass is the increase in fixed costs to the remaining customers on the distribution system.15/ While bypass is not a new issue, actual instances have been occasional because the economics of bypass has presented high hurdles to potential bypassers, and because the bypasser becomes vulnerable to supply fluctuations.

FERC's proposed rulemaking may increase the frequency of bypass because of the combination of block billing and open access to interstate transportation.16/ But increased instances of bypass will only occur under certain circumstances. If an LDC is unwilling or unable to transport at competitive prices, bypass becomes attractive when a user (or coalition of users) faces:

- o high gas prices,
- o a nearby interstate pipeline which has opened itself up to transportation to all requesting it, and

- o no capability to switch to a less expensive alternative fuel or insufficient capital to invest in the switching equipment.

State regulators have control over any high gas prices faced by industrial users through the rate making procedure. Regulators may approve of a rate structure for customers which presents industrial users with a gas price either just below or just above the switching level. Doing so means that some block 1 gas may need to be allocated to industrial end users to lower the average price these users face to near spot levels. Of course, the workability of this solution depends a great deal on the size of the old gas cushion. In cases where the cushion is small, there may not be enough block 1 gas both to influence the price to industrial producers and to satisfy any political requirements to keep residential prices low.

<u>Securing Availability of Supply</u>

In exchange for a franchise right to serve all the customers in a defined area, LDCs agree, among other things, to secure a gas supply. Under the NGA and the NGPA, LDCs signed contracts with their pipeline suppliers, thereby fulfilling the obligation to secure gas supply.

But under the NOPR, LDCs would have the right to cut their contract demand by up to 25 percent each year. LDCs would take this action to obtain lower-priced gas, but in doing so would be accepting more responsibility for securing supply. LDCs will be able to assure supply availability insofar as these transportation contracts are long term. To the extent that producers require a price premium to guarantee long term supply, however, LDCs have an economic incentive to sign short term contracts. When satisfying expectations of gas supply, state regulators will have the opportunity to assess the proper mix of short and long term transportation contracts and the prices paid during surplus and shortage.

CONCLUSION

The interplay between the new proposed federal regulations (the NOPR) and current state laws is both complex and important, affecting states which produce natural gas differently from those which predominantly consume it. In producing states, pro rata laws show perhaps the greatest potential to interact with the new federal regulations. These laws protect the correlative rights of producers by requiring proportional cutbacks in well takes by purchasers. The block pricing mechanism will put pressure on pipelines to take more block 1 gas than block 2, an incentive that butts the pipelines against the state pro rata laws. Similarly, state priority systems, which prevent waste by forbidding purchasers to reduce takes from certain classes of wells, may to a lesser extent also interact with the block billing system. Common purchaser laws, which now interact with the traditional regulation of construction of new facilities, may decrease in importance with open access to transportation. However, risks imposed under the optional expedited certificate provision of the new regulations could make it difficult for marginally economic wells to gain access to pipeline systems. Finally, the competitive forces set up by the NOPR might find producing states competing for market share through their prorating laws. One dimension of the competition might be to include price among the factors included in deciding allowables.

In consuming states, state regulators are likely to encourage a continuation of rolled-in pricing until the effect of separate pricing and availability of supply are studied. This cautionary approach is especially probable given that the new federal rulemaking will be implemented during a heating season. In addition, a policy of rolled-in pricing by the LDC in the short run is more likely to result in a smooth transition of the new regulations. In the long run, some states may choose to use the lower cost of the block 1 gas to structure the customer class rates so that specific state goals are promoted. For example, bypass can either be encouraged or discouraged by subsidizing the rates to industrial end users with block 1 gas. States may discourage LDCs from the immediate reductions in contract demand permitted under the proposed rulemaking. The uncertainty of future supply and the difficulty of finding pipeline capacity for spot gas transportation during the heating season may prompt a more studied reaction in consuming states.

The May 30 NOPR does not take into account the complexities introduced by state regulations and laws. The FERC Commissioners heard from state regulators on many of the above issues during the NOPR hearings in August. Perhaps FERC will accommodate these concerns in the final version of the rulemaking. If not, many of the benefits that FERC expects to obtain from the new regulations may be illusory.

Table 1. Summary Characteristics of Producing States

State	Sufficient Reason for Prorating	Common Purchaser Laws	Price	Basis of Prorating	Well Priority System
TX	To protect correlative rights, but limited to when demand is less than supply.	Yes	Price is not considered in establishing allowables, but TRC may deny allowable to producers who do not sell gas at a "reasonable price."	No discrimination within a field and no unjust discrimination between fields by pipeline system.	Casinghead gas; "special allowable;" high priority wells; non-prorated; prorated wells.
LA	To protect correlative rights.	Yes, but buyers can consider price.	Price is not among the items considered in establishing allowables.	Within a given reservoir.	None (done through informal channels when the need arises).
OK	To protect correlative rights.	Yes	Statute specifies that price not be among items considered in establishing allowables.	Within a given pool.	Hardship & distressed wells; enhanced recovery; casinghead; allocated, special allocated, and unallocated.
NM	Some indication of waste required before prorating, which then functions to protect correlative rights.	Yes, but limited.	Price is not among the items considered in establishing allowables, but may fit in with "other pertinent factors."	Within a given pool, but PUC has authority to prevent discrimination between pools (never used).	Wells damaged by shutin; casinghead; special categories. System not yet used.
KS	Some indication of waste required before prorating, which then functions to protect correlative rights.	None, but PUC believes it has the same power.	Price is not among the items considered in establishing allowables.	Within a given field.	Kansas statute does not provide for different treatment for casinghead gas.

NOTES

1. The views expressed in this paper represent those of the author, and do not necessarily reflect those of INGAA or its member companies. Excluded from discussion here are jurisdictional claims between a state and FERC. Normally these matters are settled by examining the facts of the case. Questions of jurisdiction are most likely to occur when the classification of a well, facility, or a pipeline has to be made.

2. Federal Energy Regulatory Commission, Notice of Proposed Rulemaking, "Regulation of Natural Gas Pipelines after Partial Wellhead Decontrol," Docket No. RM85-1-000 (Parts A-D), issued May 30, 1985.

3. American Gas Association, Gas Facts, 1982.

4. In this paper the more correct word "prorating" is used in place of the industry jargon, "prorationing." "Pro rata" and "ratable takes" and "prorating" all have the same general meaning, and are used interchangeably throughout the paper.

5. See McDonald, Stephen L., "Prorationing of Natural Gas Production in the Southwest: An Economic Analysis," proceedings from the conference on Natural Gas Prorationing and Ratable Take Legislation, at the University of Colorado, Boulder, School of Law, Natural Resources Law Center, June 26-28, 1985.

6. Based on calculations using data from EIA's Natural Gas Monthly, May 1985, published July 1985.

7. The pro rata issue is complicated by the fact that the states permit some discretion in producing a higher percentage of one gas category than another for a short period of time, as long as balance is achieved in a specified period.

8. During the NOPR hearings (see Transcripts of Oral Comments, FERC Oral Hearings, August 1-2, 1985), Chairman O'Connor indicated his belief that the NOPR did not prevent a pipeline from using its own authority and discretion to break out block 2 gas into subdivisions. However, the definition of "block 2" in the NOPR is unambiguous, and allows no flexibility in altering the composition of this block.

9. McDonald, p. 12.

10. Only Texas and Oklahoma have priority systems in place today. New Mexico has given priority to certain classes of wells, but the system has yet to be used. Other states deal with problem wells informally.

11. Block 2 prices from Foster Associates, Current Purchased Gas Costs of Interstate Pipeline Companies, Washington, D.C., July 31, 1985, Table 2a. Spot prices from the U.S. Gas Clearinghouse, "August Spot Market Price Survey," released August 9, 1985.

12. Telephone conversation with Patrick H. Martin, Professor of Law at Louisiana State University, formerly Commissioner of Louisiana's Conservation Commission, August 29, 1985.

13. Implicit in the scenario is that the short run elasticity of demand is low, so that a lower average system price will not result in increased gas demand in the short run. The long run elasticity is much higher than previously thought (witness the flatness of demand over the last several years), indicating that in the long run, demand will increase in response to a drop in price. However, in the long run block 1 gas will be depleted and have to be replaced by more expensive block 2 gas.

14. We are using "bypass" in a restricted sense here, in which a LDC customer or group of customers leave the distribution system and obtain their gas supplies from an interstate pipeline. More broadly construed, "bypass" could include a new customer arranging for his own gas supply without going through the LDC, or an existing customer leaving one LDC for another.

15. The actual costs and benefits are not quite so straightforward. It is possible, for example, for the increase in fixed costs to be partially offset by a reduction in the weighted average cost of gas (WACOG). Such a situation occurs when a customer purchasing expensive gas bypasses the system. By taking that expensive gas off the system, the bypass lowers the systems WACOG.

16. Note that <u>both</u> billing and open access are necessary for instances of bypass to increase. In areas served only by pipelines which have not opened themselves up to transportation, bypass is not difficult, but not impossible.

22
Can the Gas Industry Weather FERC's New Rules?

William F. Hederman, Jr., Interstate Natural Gas Association of America

"The future ain't what it used to be, but then, it never was."

Lee Hays
Weavers Reunion Concert
Carnegie Hall, 1980

The future of the natural gas industry looks much different after the Federal Energy Regulatory Commission (FERC) released its Notice of Proposed Rulemaking (NOPR, Docket No. RM85-1) on May 30, 1985 than it had prior to that time. I believe the Commission wants to play an activist role in the current natural gas industry transition in which the interstate pipeline business is shifting from a highly regulated and monopolistic structure to a much more competitive situation. The NOPR represents a bold initiative by FERC to direct this transition.

This paper provides a brief sketch of the regulatory policy framework proposed by the Commission in its NOPR. It also assesses the likely performance of the proposed policies with regard to the traditional regulatory goals of economic efficiency and equity. This paper was submitted prior to the issuance of a final rule by the Commission.

Commissioners have, however, indicated an intention to proceed along the lines described in the NOPR.1/

PROPOSED RULES

The Commission has proposed revolutionary changes in the regulatory system governing the interstate natural gas business. These rules address four subjects:

- New Billing Mechanism
- Open Access Transportation
- Take-or-Pay Buyouts
- Optional Expedited Certificates.

The Commission has emphasized that it views the integrity of the entire policy package as essential.

New Billing Mechanism

The Commission proposed that all pipelines operate under a new billing mechanism that would create two blocks of gas. "Old" gas would be in "Block 1." All other gas would be in a "Block 2" category. Other as-yet-unspecified costs in "Block 3" would be allocated between Blocks 1 and 2. The proposed mechanism would also allocate "old" gas on the basis of historic firm sales. Only this part of the NOPR is proposed for all pipelines, regardless of "transporter" status.

Open Access Transportation

Perhaps the most dramatic policy change would result from the proposal to require any pipeline that "elects" to transport gas for others to do so on a nondiscriminatory basis. I use the term "elect" even though the choice might be analogous to the choice you have when accosted some night and faced with the demand, "your money or your life." With one-third of flowing gas volumes now moved under transportation arrangements, do not expect to find many major pipelines electing out of the transport option. Through this proposed measure the Commission has aggressively interpreted its authority over the interstate pipeline industry and extended its reach significantly. The courts will have to decide if FERC has exceeded its authority. It also would allow pipeline customers to decrease unilaterally firm contract demand by as much as 25 percent per year.

Take-or-Pay Buyout

In recognition of the contract problems that some pipelines have with producer suppliers, the Commission also proposed a take-or-pay measure. This proposal was intended to provide relief from this serious contract problem through pre-approval of take-or-pay settlements at some as-yet-unspecified buy-out level (for pipelines electing the transport option). The Commission proposed a "safe harbor" provision for allowing recovery of acceptable level buyouts.

Optional Expedited Certificates

The Commission proposed special treatment for new pipeline services and facilities when a pipeline accepts full risk for the proposed venture. The special certificates would be available only to pipelines who have become transporters.

The Commission has made clear that it views its proposed package of policy changes as an integrated whole and that no part should be considered independently of the other.

REGULATORY GOALS

The Commission's proposed policies attempt to address the traditional goals of government intervention in markets through economic regulation. These goals are:

- o Efficiency
- o Equity.

Economic allocational efficiency is generally achieved through competition, but as Commissioner Stalon has noted, "competition...is not an end in itself."2/ Economic regulation can enhance efficiency when there is (1) insufficient competition, (2) significant externalities, or (3) other market distortions.

Equity is a more troublesome goal. First, it is difficult to define. Second, equity often conflicts with allocational efficiency. For instance, allocational efficiency alone would dictate decontrol of regulated old gas prices, but equity considerations have led policymakers to distribute the benefits of this gas in other ways.

In the context of the U.S. natural gas market, regulatory equity has generally emphasized two points. Regulators have sought to protect "captive customers," especially residential users, through cross-subsidy from interruptible customers (generally large industrial users). Regulators have also sought to maintain revenues sufficient to provide for the long term viability of the firms performing the business activities associated with supplying and moving natural gas to market.

Members of the FERC have mentioned other regulatory goals that generally relate to efficiency, equity, or both. These have included: assuring a risk and reward trade-off,3/ making competition constructive, and integrating natural gas into the nation's energy mix.4/

EVALUATION OF PROPOSED RULES

The Commission's proposal, if implemented, may not achieve acceptable levels of economic efficiency and equity. This should not detract from the Commission's accomplishment in quickly drafting a bold and comprehensive revision of natural gas regulation. It would be unreasonable to expect anyone to have crafted a comprehensive reformation of an institution as complex as the natural gas industry on the kind of crash schedule set by the Commission for the NOPR.

The Commission may revise its proposals to improve the likely performance of whatever policy is implemented. Rumors run rampant that the Commission is intent on sticking with its original proposal, but I believe that we should take seriously Chairman O'Connor's commitment to listen carefully to the many comments the Commission has received about its proposed rules.

The remainder of this section examines the specific policies and related policy objectives enunciated by the Commission.

Billing Mechanism

The proposed three block billing mechanism would apply to all pipelines. The proposal was frequently addressed in the Commission's August hearings, and most commentors did not support the mechanism as proposed.

The FERC's intent for this proposal is threefold. Consumers and producers would see clear, more accurate price signals (an efficiency goal). The advantage that some pipelines held through supplies of old gas would be eliminated so that competition would be fair and efficiency would be enhanced (both efficiency and equity goals). Economic rents from low cost, old gas would be preserved for pipelines' historic firm customers (an equity goal).

Examination of the specific policy steps proposed shows that serious problems are likely to hinder achievement of the goals unless major changes are incorporated. The proposed block billing may not improve the accuracy of price signals. Moreover, the billing proposal may not create a competition in which all participants have equal chances for success.

The first problem with the proposed block pricing is that if average prices are used by LDCs, no improvement in market signals will be achieved. The FERC responds that it can only create a situation where market signals could be transmitted accurately.

Other problems with the price signals relate to several features of the proposed billing procedure. The Block 2 gas is intended to reflect the marginal cost of natural gas production, but as proposed it would merely reflect the average price of all gas that is not low cost old gas ($3.48 per million Btu as of August 1985). Block 2 prices vary from \$2.87 to \$4.36 on individual pipelines, and would vary over a broader range for individual contracts. Moreover, the Block 2 idea appears to be based on a rather simplistic concept of marginal costs; there are long run and short run marginal costs for production and transmission.

Implicit in FERC's approach is an assumption that contract renegotiation will quickly lead to more uniform Block 2 prices. Unfortunately, however, the proposed block structure could hinder contract renegotiation.

In fact, the proposed Block 2 approach could lead new and high cost gas producers into a troubling situation very much like the "Prisoners' Dilemma" frequently cited in game theory. The Prisoners' Dilemma refers to a situation where each party would be better off if both parties chose one specific decision. However, because there are incentives for each party to make an alternate decision, both participants end up worse off.

The classic example (attributed to A. W. Tucker) is two prisoners who jointly committed a crime under interrogation. With no confessions, both go free for lack of evidence. The interrogators present the following rule: (1) if you confess that you both committed the crime, you can go free if your partner stays silent, (2) if he also confesses you each will serve a five year sentence, but (3) if you remain silent and your partner confesses, you hang. Rather than risk losing everything, each prisoner confesses and both prisoners get moderate sentences.

Consider the case where a pipeline buys Block 2 gas from two producers and its Block 2 gas has an average cost over \$3.00 and no sales are possible at that price. The pipeline will seek to renegotiate the problem contracts

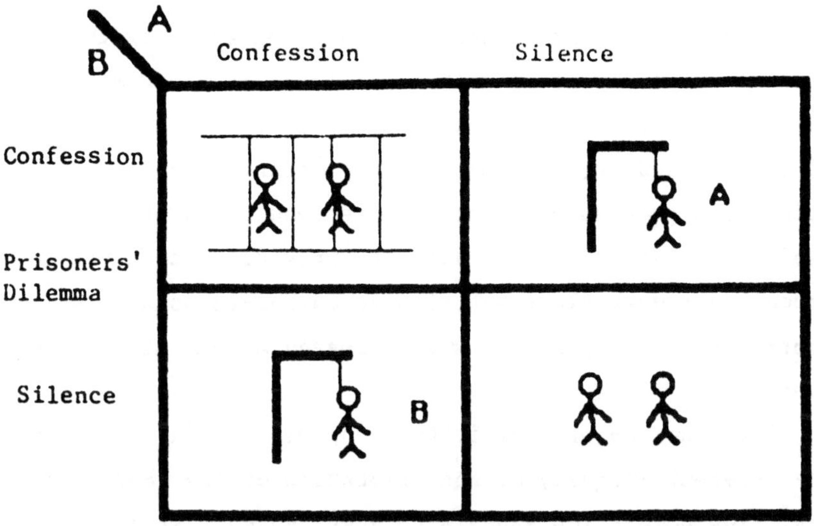

which cause the Block 2 gas to be unmarketable. However, the FERC billing proposal leaves the producers with the wrong incentives. Like the prisoners, the producers will choose the option with the least downside risk. By renegotiating, the producer faces the risk of losing everything. He loses the opportunity to sue the pipeline, and with the proposed Block 2 he cannot gain sales unless the other problem contract holder also renegotiates. Since each producer knows the other faces the risk of losing everything through renegotiation, each would realize he could not plan on the other party selecting that option. Thus, each producer refuses renegotiation, which leads to marketing problems for the producers and the pipeline.

The interrogators' strategy puts the prisoners behind bars, which was good for society. The FERC billing, however, traps the producers in a bind that does not serve the economy well. Of course, the real world of producer/pipeline contracts is more complicated than this example.

The way out of the bind will probably involve pipeline declarations of force majeure and protracted litigation.

There are ways to fix this problem. If the Commission insists on establishing something like its proposed new billing procedure, then segregating market responsive supplies from problem-contract supplies would represent a useful improvement. This approach provides incentives to encourage a workable transition to market-responsive supply contracts. Many parties have expressed agreement with this idea.

The other major flaw in the proposed billing scheme is the apparent inequity of the allocation of low cost, old gas. The Commission appears to have judged that any allocation of the gas price cushion would be arbitrary and therefore, decided to select an option based on historical firm gas sales. It is probably correct that the decision must be arbitrary in some ways, but the allocation selected is ill-advised in several ways that could cause serious market distortions.

One important distortion from the proposed Block 1 allocation is that all economic rents are assigned to consumers. I find it hard to review the NGPA without concluding that the Congressional intent was to use a share of the gas price cushion to subsidize some gas production. Another important distortion is the decision to base the shares of the cushion on historic sales; any historic period chosen arbitrarily assigns benefits to certain customers. For instance, through the proposed allocation scheme a plant that developed self-help supplies and arranged voluntary carriage during the specified period would be disadvantaged in gas costs relative to plants that remained on system supply during the period or who are served by distributors who had firm demand during the specified period. One pipeline mentioned the importance of its interruptible load, with many large customers buying gas for decades. The reason these customers should be denied access to low cost gas escapes me.

In addition, the block pricing proposal selectively leaves pipelines with the troublesome elements of wellhead price controls such as problem price escalation and take-or-pay clauses. At the same time, the proposal usurps the economic benefits of these same price controls for an arbitrary subset (firm consumers) of the natural gas market.

Take-or-Pay Relief

In another policy initiative aimed at focusing the gas industry on future challenges rather than problems from the past, the Commission proposed a "safe harbor" for take-or-pay buyouts. The intent exhibited by this proposal shows that the Commission correctly recognizes resolution of take-or-pay contract problems as an integral element of any regulatory reform.

Unfortunately, the buyout proposal is inadequate to the task of eliminating take-or-pay problems. First, take-or-pay buyout payments could only be collected inframarginally because of the Block Billing Mechanism. There are pipelines with serious take-or-pay problems that could not include buyout payments and keep gas prices at competitive levels. Where Block 2 prices exceed competitive levels, take-or-pay problems could be exacerbated.

In addition, the Commission proposed to use specified percentages as the guidelines for automatic passthrough of buyout costs. This approach would be ill-advised because as the industry's experience with price ceilings has amply demonstrated, we can expect specified policy figures to serve as the starting point for negotiations, not the end point. Pipelines have already reported losing ground in take-or-pay negotiations since the issuance of the NOPR.5/

Open Access Transportation/Optional Certificates

There has been a great deal of surprise voiced about the lack of controversy--especially from pipelines--concerning proposals for open access transportation.6/ The rapid growth of voluntary carriage--especially for distributors and end users, however, should have indicated how seriously pipelines view transportation as a major new business activity. One of the great ironies of the current flurry of transition policy decisions is that at the time the D.C. Circuit Court decided that Special Marketing Programs (SMPs) should stop because they discriminated against firm customers, SMPs were carrying more gas for firm than for interruptible customers.7/

Although the controversy about open access to the interstate gas transmission network may be less than many expected, several related transportation policy issues have arisen. Efficiency issues concern proposed rates and capacity allocation. Equity issues arise as well.

Contrary to FERC's other efforts to convey accurate price signals in the gas marketplace, it has proposed volumetric rates for transportation services that appear unlikely to achieve economically efficient outcomes. The

Commission seems to recognize this by mentioning curtailment rules.8/ One particular problem that may arise with the proposed nondiscriminatory system is that if a shipper arranges transport through a system bottleneck before others seek transport services, a pipeline would have no alternative but to allow the bottleneck to be tied up by the first transport customer. Even though subsequent shippers would make more efficient use of the pipeline, they would not be free to arrange the transportation they needed.

The NOPR discussion of rates is confusing. Cost-of-service is mentioned, but capacity allocation through rates is also proposed as a goal.9/ These are two different design principles unlikely to yield equivalent rates.

Many have interpreted the NOPR as providing for prorationing of capacity, but Chairman O'Connor has said that is not so.10/

Questions of fairness also arise concerning the rate proposals. For instance, given the great uncertainty introduced by the proposed rules, it is difficult to understand why the Commission feels justified in prohibiting downward revisions in volumetric estimates for the proposed rates.11/ Another issue that may arise has equity and efficiency aspects. That is, if pipeline LDC customers can reduce demand, should pipelines be free to compete for LDC customers through bypass?

Overall, the proposed rules represent an impressive accomplishment as a first cut attempt to develop a new regulatory framework for the natural gas industry. As proposed, however, the rules will not achieve the stated objectives. Hopefully, the Commission will recognize the limitations of its first proposal and revise it.

IMPLICATIONS FOR THE INDUSTRY

The proposed rules could cause serious problems for the natural gas industry. My concerns on this matter have been confirmed by investment analyst assessments of the NOPR.12/

There have been three dominant issues in the natural gas debate for some time:

- o Wellhead pricing
- o Transmission system access
- o Contracts problems.

With respect to wellhead pricing, the Commission has properly decided that its authority over old gas does not permit it to resolve the distortions caused by low cost old gas by decontrolling old gas prices. It has, instead, allocated the benefits in an attempt to minimize the market distortions caused by the regulated gas. This policy is likely to have an effect that I doubt the Commission intended. Once the Commission has assigned specific property rights to the low cost gas, the chances of old gas price decontrol will likely vanish. Few Congressmen from consuming states would assign greater weight to theoretical economic efficiency at the cost of their constituents' designated share of cheap gas.

The Commission has decided that open access is the best means to enhance competition in the gas industry. It takes an aggressive stand toward establishing open access; some would say that the Commission is exceeding its authority and attempting to mandate carriage.

The aggressiveness of the Commission in promoting open access carriage and removing long term commitments to pipelines by their customers is matched by a strong reticence to provide effective tools for resolving the contracts problem between pipelines and some of their producer suppliers.

The Commission's proposed rules would lead to stormy waters for the gas industry. Not all the producers, pipelines, or distributors could survive the resulting turmoil. Hopefully, the Commission's final rules will prove more navigable than their initial proposal.

Notes

1. See for instance, FERC Chairman O'Connor's response to questions from Congressman Philip Sharp, August 9, 1985.

2. Commissioner Charles Stalon, "Finding New Objectives for Natural Gas Pipeline Regulation," National Conference of Regulatory Attorneys, Hartford, May 13, 1985.

3. Chairman Raymond O'Connor, "Balancing Competition and Regulation in the Natural Gas Industry," Public Utilities Fortnightly, January 24, 1985.

4. Commissioner Charles Stalon, op. cit., May 13, 1985.

5. FERC, Docket No. RM85-1, hearings, August 1, 1985, statement by Dr. Kenneth Lay, Transcript at 126.

6. For instance, Merrill Lynch, Natural Gas Monthly, August 1985, p. 2.

7. INGAA, "Special Marketing Programs: Update 3," September 1985, p. 9.

8. See response of Chairman O'Connor to question 11 from Senator Wendell Ford, June 27, 1985 letter.

9. FERC, NOPR, pp. 8 and 34.

10. See response to question 1b, attachment to letter from Chairman O'Connor to Senator Don Nickles, July 19, 1985.

11. FERC, NOPR, p. 39.

12. For instance, see Paine Webber, "Natural Gas/FERC's Proposed Rulemaking," June 11, 1985; L. F. Rothschild, Unterberg, Towbin, "Natural Gas Pipelines: A Major Change in the Environment," June 12, 1985; Merrill Lynch, Natural Gas Monthly, "NOPR = Shortages?", July 1985.

23 Comment on Notice of Proposed Rule-Making Regulation of Natural Gas After Partial Wellhead Decontrol

Rodney T. Smith, Stratecon, Inc.

I. REVIEW OF POLICY OBJECTIVES EXPRESSED IN NOTICE OF PROPOSED RULE-MAKING

FERC has expressed a clear interest in the promulgation of regulations of interstate natural gas markets which secure the economic advantages of market competition and market allocation of natural gas, as expressed by Congress in its passage of the NGPA of 1978. This comment considers the logical and evidentiary basis behind FERC's contention that the proposed new rules promote efficient market allocations of natural gas by achieving the following three goals expressed in the Notice of Proposed Rule-Making (NOPR):

1. FERC's interest in "ensur(ing) that the natural gas markets are viably and sufficiently competitive so that consumers are provided (with) natural

gas at the lowest reasonable rates consistent with reliable, long-term service." (at p. 24131, emphasis added).

2. FERC's desire to establish appropriate levels of accountability and the allocation of risk (at p. 24135).

3. FERC's goal to "establish a long-term regulatory framework -- not to be a reaction to immediate circumstances." (at p. 24136).

Both economic theory and actual market developments suggest that the new rules outlined in Parts A-D may seriously jeopardize, rather than promote, the achievement of the above goals. In particular, the proposed rules threaten to cripple the economic function of voluntarily negotiated, long-term contracts. The resulting adverse consequences on financial arrangements for new investment will increase the long-term cost of natural gas to U.S. consumers and destroy the prudent allocation of risk within the natural gas industry.

II. AN ECONOMIC INTERPRETATION OF THE CURRENT "INDUSTRY PROBLEMS"

FERC's analysis incorrectly attributes the industry's current economic problems to the structure of contracts and current pricing of old and new gas by pipeline companies. Instead, the enumerated problems have resulted partly from natural economic benefits which consumers have received from deregulation of oil and natural gas prices, and partly from the fact that large disruptions in international petroleum markets have failed to materialize in the 1980s. The existing structure of contracts resulted from informed, prudent, though inherently risky business choices undertaken by pipeline companies and their customers in the late 1970s and early 1980s. Buyers who voluntarily entered into long-term contracts simply found that their price expectations were not validated by subsequent market events.

Economic theory provides a different viewpoint to the industry problems outlined in the NOPR. Given deregulation of natural gas and petroleum and the absence of a supply disruption in international petroleum markets, the following economic effects would inevitably occur in a well-functioning market and coincide with

FERC's statement of "The Problem in a Nutshell" (at p. 24155):

1. "Many interstate pipelines have contracted for more gas supply than can be marketed at the prices set forth in those contracts."

2. With falling petroleum prices, the demand for natural gas would be diminished, thereby resulting in an apparent surplus where "the market could not absorb (the additional supply from deregulation) at prevailing prices."

3. With demand by existing customers being less than anticipated, "(p)ipelines...(will seek) alternative markets as well...(as) new customers."

4. "Purchasers of natural gas, seeing the availability of supplies in the field...(will seek) to purchase gas in the field and receive it instead of the supplies which the pipeline has obtained under...long-term contracts."

FERC's analysis views these market events, in contrast, as evidence that long-term contracts interfere with the market allocation of natural gas. Their position neglects the economic incentives for parties to renegotiate their contracts when subsequent economic events render existing contractual terms economically inefficient. In theory, it is in the mutual interest of buyers and sellers to release buyers from contractual obligations to purchase more natural gas than they demand at prevalent spot prices, provided that buyers pay sellers a sufficiently large side payment. The side payment must be at least as large as the difference between the contract price and spot price plus the costs incurred in selling the portion of the released quantities which it is profitable to resell on the spot market, plus the foregone profit that would have been earned under the contract on the released quantities which it is not profitable to resell on the current spot market. In fact, contractual renegotiations have been prevalent throughout the industry.

III. THE ECONOMICS OF CONTRACTING AND PROPOSED FERC RULES PARTS A AND B

The discussion found in the NOPR neglects the role of long-term contracts in the rational, economic development of natural gas reserves and transportation of natural gas to customers. Rather than inhibit, long-term contracting is essential in facilitating the economic efficiencies associated with the market allocation of natural gas. Many elements of the proposed rules in Part A and B interfere with long-term contracts performing their natural economic functions.

A. The Law and Economics of Long-Term Contracts

In comparison to petroleum, for example, natural gas is less flexible in its transportation opportunities once investment in production and transportation facilities is in place. Therefore, long-term contracts are important tools in locating future demand for the gas produced and transported by investment. For example, it is well-known in the investment banking literature that a project with assured demand can offer a lower return than another project with unassured demand to obtain capital from financial markets. In effect, long-term contracts communicate the presence of prospective consumer demand to potential suppliers, rather than "phantom" demand estimates from planning models which have no economic obligation to back up their statement of future demand with financial resources.

Given the ex post immobility of capital once in place, long-term contracts also limit the potential opportunism which buyer and seller may engage in if trade was organized solely on the basis of spot market transactions. For example, a natural gas producer invests in a field on the expectation that pipelines will transport their natural gas to final consumers. A pipeline invests in transportation facilities, in turn, on the expectation that producers will ship natural gas on their pipeline. After investment is in place and immobile, producers may attempt to "squeeze" pipelines by offering a price which solely reflects operating costs, and offer no return on the pipeline's capital investment. In turn, pipelines may attempt to "squeeze" producers by offering them a price for their gas which solely reflects their operating costs and offer them no return on their capital investment. Pricing rules specified in long-term contracts before investment is undertaken can control these problems. Long-term contracting is the market solution to these economic problems and enables investment and exchange to proceed.

Contract law recognizes these economic advantages. Provided that neither party negotiated under duress, fraud, or incompetence, the law will enforce contracts, even if subsequent economic events make a contract less valuable than a party anticipated when it entered into the agreement. As shown by the law and economics literature, such legal rules facilitate efficient market exchange, because it protects the economic function of contracts. If parties were released from their obligations simply because their expectations were not satisfied, then long-term contracts would not provide their information role in revealing firm future demand, not prevent ex post opportunism. For example, a buyer will state a larger future demand, reflecting solely future conditions of high demand, if he can be released from contractual obligations if future conditions of low demand are realized. A seller could use the pretext of unanticipated conditions as a ploy to extract quasi-rents from the other contracting party.

Contract law, of course, does allow contracts to be overturned in special circumstances, even if contracts were negotiated without duress, fraud, or incompetence. The circumstances involve commercial impracticality, but are limited to severe situations where an <u>unforeseeable</u> market event occurs which jeopardizes the <u>existence</u> of a contracting party, rather than simply the mere profitability of the contract to that party. The realization of losses from assumed risks is not sufficient to overturn a contract, because the law recognizes that contracts are tools by which parties allocate risk among themselves. Provided that competition prevails, voluntary negotiation will result in the efficient allocation of risk among contracting parties.

B. <u>FERC Rules: Part A and B</u>

Both parts may seriously jeopardize the role of contracts in facilitating market exchange in natural gas. The rules explicitly allow the unilateral abrogation of some contracts and provide incentives for other contracts to be abrogated.

Part A orchestrates explicit contract abrogation by allowing customers to modify their existing service agreements, at the rate of 25 percent per year. According to FERC, (at p. 24132):

> "This would enable such customers to choose more freely among a portfolio of service options offered by pipelines."

This reasoning is suspect because, under contract renegotiation, customers already can choose among alternative services and pipelines. Part A merely allows customers who signed contracts to do so without the normal legal obligation of honoring one's contracts or purchase release via standard procedures of renegotiation.

Part B provides the framework for contract abrogation between pipelines and natural gas producers. On its surface, Part B may seem to facilitate renegotiation because it establishes a "rebuttable presumption of prudence for certain limited and circumscribed payments." However, Part B continues (at p. 24132):

> "This presumption would be available only to pipelines willing to offer non-discriminatory access to transportation service; this in turn gives rise to an option for firm sales customers to reduce their contract demand."

Given the expressed intent of FERC to overturn long-term contracts which were voluntarily negotiated between the contracting parties, this link between Parts A and B raises the real possibility that pipelines can claim a regulatory *force majeure* to abrogate their contracts with natural gas producers. After all, Part A allows their customers to abrogate their contracts, and Part B establishes the "rebuttable presumption of prudence" only if pipelines allow customers to so abrogate those contracts.

FERC instructs readers of the NOPR to analyze each part of the proposed rules in conjunction with each other (at p. 24140). Examining Parts A and B in conjunction with each other, it is clear that FERC's proposal enables pipeline customers to abrograte their contracts at the ultimate expense of natural gas producers. After all, Part A enables customers to scaleback their contract demand and demand charges, minimum bills, etc. in proportionate amounts to each other. Nothing in the proposed rules prevents the "logic" of pipelines "passing on" these contractual adjustments to natural gas producers.

IV. PIPELINE PRICING AND PROPOSED RULE D

The proposed billing mechanism for old gas supplies limits the flexibility of pipeline decisions in an effort to solve a presumed allocation problem under existing regulation. In its analysis of current industry problems, NOPR states (at p. 24133):

> "Pipelines have sought alternative markets as well and sought out new customers. But the existing customers of the pipelines have been concerned that so-called 'off-system' sales would effectively transfer to the new customers a portion of the

> economic rent associated with the
> old, price-controlled gas."

The three-block pricing rule described in Part D is designed to prevent pipeline's from cross-subsizing new sales from the rents of old gas.

The block-pricing proposal attempts to solve a problem not obviously present in economic theory, nor well documented in fact. Like any profit-maximizing firm, pipelines have no economic incentive to cross-subsidize customers. Furthermore, unless forced by pipeline regulation, pipeline companies also have no incentive to pass on the rent from price-controlled gas to their customers. Pricing reflects marginal, not average cost, and demand conditions represented by the prices of close substitutes. Therefore, any rents from old gas would be captured by pipelines in their profit margins, not by consumers as lower prices.

Binding pipeline regulation, which requires average cost pricing, would change the situation. However, market evidence questions the relevance of that regulation in this context. First, pipeline margins have increased with the rents from price-controlled gas during the late 1970s and early 1980s, as predicted by the viewpoint expressed in the preceding paragraph. Second, retail prices of natural gas have closely followed the price of a close substitute, residual fuel oil, during the same time period. Therefore, field price controls did not prevent prices paid by consumers from following the path which would be expected to have occurred in an unregulated marketplace. In sum, there is no strong evidence in support of an important corrolary of FERC's theory of cross-subsidization.

The proposed block-pricing will achieve two results. First, and within the context of the rent transfers under existing law, the block-pricing scheme will transfer rents from pipelines to customers who receive rights to old gas under the proposed rule in Part D. From FERC's viewpoint of economic efficiency, of course, this rent transfer would be viewed as neutral.

The second effect does not portend well for the market allocation of natural gas. Neglected in FERC's discussion, the establishment of rights to rents from old gas will create inflexibility in the allocation of gas. Nothing in the proposed rules makes the rights to old gas <u>transferable</u>. Given the "permanency" of old gas, this means that if a customer's demand for natural gas should change in the future, he must relinquish his right to old gas if he wishes to reduce his consumption of old gas. In effect, consumption decisions of old gas will reflect the controlled price, not the market price of gas. The block-pricing proposal actually establishes subsidization of gas use, not abolishes it as intended by FERC. As demands by different customers change in the future, gas will not be re-allocated to its highest-valued use.

V. CONCLUSION: THE PROPOSED RULES EXTEND REGULATION, DO NOT FACILITATE A FREE MARKET

While FERC intended to devise new rules which will facilitate the transition to the "new economic realities" of unregulated, competitive natural gas markets, economic analysis suggest that the opposite outcome will occur. The fundamental problem is that FERC did not correctly analyze the economic role and consequences of long-term contracting. If the proposed rules are adopted, FERC will place a "regulatory cloud" over all future contracting activity in natural gas markets.

As discussed in Section II above, the "industry problems" resulted from natural economic consequences of petroleum and natural gas decontrol, and the fact that market events did not validate price expectations of buyers who had voluntarily entered into long-term contracts. Many of the contracts under review were negotiated after the passage of the EPCA of 1976 and the NGPA of 1978, which respectively announced the scheduled deregulation of petroleum and natural gas. Therefore, the "new economic realities" which require adjustment are, ironically, not the type of unforeseeable circumstances which normal contract law would entertain as reasons for overturning contracts on the basis of "impracticality." FERC desires to achieve with regulation that which would not occur under the Uniform Commercial Code.

In many ways, the regulations outlined in Parts A and B are properly viewed as government interference in market pricing. By its intent to determine a percentage of prudence for buy-outs of contracts (as described at pp. 24147-49), FERC implicitly would place price regulation on the "market for renegotiation." Nothing in economic theory, or common commercial practices, supports the implied contention that an unregulated market requires regulation of pricing under, or renegotiation of, long-term contracts.

With the precedence established by its proposed rules, FERC will not achieve the goals summarized in Section I above. First, by burdening the enforceability of long-term contracts, FERC will not provide the proper legal framework required for an economic marketplace to be competitive and provide consumers with natural gas at the "lowest reasonable rates consistent with reliable, long-term service. Instead, the "spot market bias" inherent in FERC's analysis and rulemaking will limit natural, contractual solutions to significant economic problems associated with the long-term planning, financing and construction of natural gas production and distribution facilities. While "contract relief" will be provided for the existing cohort of contracts, future negotiations will include "price premia" to compensate both parties for the increased "expropriation risk" created by FERC adopting similar rules in the future. Smaller investment, higher contract and future spot prices will occur than would have been the case if long-term contracting had not been limited by regulatory action. Pipeline companies will number among the long-term losers, as there will be economic incentives for natural gas customers to "vertically-integrate" with producers through equity arrangements.

Second, by imposing its own standards about who shall bear risk, FERC interferes with the market allocation of risk and accountability for actions. Without the implied buyer commitments communicated through long-term contracting, because future regulatory action may relieve them of that responsibility, fewer participants in the marketplace will become accountable for their "forecasts" of future market conditions. By its attempt to "centralize" the responsibility for forecasting, FERC has denied the import market function of using "decentralized planning" for the creating and transmission of information about future opportunities of production, consumption and trade.

Finally, in the guise of providing a reasonable legal framework for an unregulated market, FERC has reacted to "immediate circumstances." If price expectations of buyers in the late 1970s had been validated by market events in the 1980s, then the impetus for "adjustments" in contractual requirements would have been absent. In such a situation, Parts A-C of the proposed rules would never have been drafted. Instead, FERC has been drawn into the renegotiation process, without recognizing how its proposed actions will "destabilize" the legal structure required for the efficient operation of an unregulated marketplace in natural gas.

24
Natural Gas: An Expanded Role for the Future

Jeffrey A. Strausser, HNG Internorth

For those of us who watch the energy markets, the past ten years have made us witness to many changes. Some were good; many were not so good. We have seen OPEC as a near invincible united force and as thirteen quarreling siblings. Oil and gas have been both scarce and bountiful over a period just long enough to change one's mind. Nuclear power--heralded as the energy resource to take us through the 80's and beyond--has faded away after over $100 billion was spent on its development.

Although we have seen the effects and felt the shocks resulting from our energy markets being taken on a wild roller coaster ride, the United States, in the winter of 1985, is no closer to formulating a strategy for stabilizing the energy sector than it was a decade ago. Our own memory should tell us this period of apparent calm will someday give way to new, and I suspect, harsh realities of the world energy markets. The numbers aren't in yet for 1985, but 1984 marked the first rise in energy consumption, measured on a per capita basis, since 1978--the year the United States displayed its most ravenous appetite for energy. The present hiatus from energy turmoil has led to waning conservation efforts. Thus, wherever we are going in the energy realm, we are going to get there faster.

Someone studying this period years from now, will surely be perplexed by what appears as reckless inaction. After all, it is undeniable that so goes the energy market, so goes the economy, so goes.... Our friend of the future will take note that we were forever reacting to short term movements in the energy markets. As a result, we always kept ourselves vulnerable to the frequent short run changes characteristic of the market. It will be apparent by then that many of our contemporary counterproductive laws and practices had roots in knee jerk reactions to short run aberrations. If our student is persistent and does not throw up his hands in utter amazement and walk away, he will find our energy nonpolicy appeared to be constructed on the following conceptual foundation.

1. Coal and nuclear energy must assume the role as primary resources as they are the only energy resources the United States has in abundance.
2. The marketplace will determine the proper energy mix.

3. We will have to expose our environment to the risk of increased pollution in order to secure energy supply.
4. The problems of the mid-70's associated with our dependence on foreign oil will never recur.

It is difficult to talk about each premise separately because they are all interrelated. And, with a convolution of logic, they can be made to support one another. It is this intertwined reinforcing relationship that makes it difficult to adequately expose and judge each statement on a stand alone basis.

I am sure it is safe to say that an energy resource must be present in abundance if it is to be awarded the lead role. Abundance implies stability and assures favorable economics. However, abundance cannot be the sole criterion. Nuclear energy is abundant but I feel it is not necessary to discuss the problems associated with our nuclear power program. The remaining diehards need only to talk to planners and executives of the utility industry that are the proud owners of white elephants in the form of nuclear power facilities in various stages of nonconstruction.

Coal, projected to be the workhorse of electric utilities and heavy industry, also appears to be abundant. This is, however, according to past coal reserves reports. Now many are beginning to question the numbers set forth in some of these estimates. Coal, along with nuclear energy, will impose a price on our environment.

Some, although it is not really clear how much, environmental quality will have to be sacrificed. The destruction will be in direct proportion to usage. How much pollution we citizens and our children will be willing to accept for coal fired energy has not yet been ascertained. But sacrifice we must, as pollution appears to be the debt of energy stability.

This of course presupposes a greatly expanded role for coal and nuclear power. However, if this happens, our country will have overlooked it's most abundant, efficient and environmentally suitable energy resource--natural gas. Table 1 depicts annual growth rates in consumption by fuel in the United States. The projections are composite in nature, based on several studies.

Table 1. Projected Annual Growth Rate of Consumption of Various Energy Resources

Resource	1985-1990	1990-1995	1995-2000
Oil	+0.9%	+2.4%	-1.6%
Gas	+1.1%	-0.8%	-0.3%
Coal	+1.6%	+2.7%	+4.0%
Nuclear	+9.2%	+1.9%	+1.0%

Source: Composite

The reason for the nongrowth in gas consumption is somewhat difficult to discern. I suppose there may be some political or special interest groups working to curtail its usage. However, I believe the reason, for the most part, is rooted in misconception. Many of our citizenry, even a great deal of whom that have been deemed knowledgeable enough to hold positions of responsibility in business and government, speak of natural gas and oil as one inseparable resource. Since we are running out of domestic oil (geological studies pretty well demonstrate this), we must be running out of natural gas as well. An entry level petroleum engineering course will show that natural gas exists over a much wider range of temperature and pressure conditions than oil. It is for this reason natural gas is many times more plentiful than oil.

The misconception is further exacerbated by, of all people, energy forecasters. These forecasters, or more correctly, extrapolationists, utilize a mathematical rather than a geological approach to the treatment of quantifying gas reserves. This approach is simplistic and understates gas reserves. Yet this approach is widely used for the following reasons:

1. Most forecasters have no geological or petroleum engineering expertise so they are limited to extrapolation techniques.
2. It is fast because it lends itself to computer utilization.
3. The results look impressive and the premises and assumptions get lost in the mathematics.

Groups such as the United States Geological Survey use a volumetric estimation procedure to estimate reserves. This is a much more sophisticated approach than the extrapolation method. In this type of analysis, the volumes of potential gas-bearing reservoir rock are estimated by adding up estimates of individual traps and trap sizes. Techniques such as play analysis and field number and size approaches are used to construct an area wide volume estimate based on a variety of existing geological data. Yield factors (gas volumes/rock volumes) are then calculated by selecting appropriate analogs from producing areas and adjusting the yields to account for geochemical factors such as the thermal history of the source rocks. The analysts then multiply the volume by the yield estimates by their assessments of the probabilities that traps actually exist and that an actual accumulation of gas has occurred.

The United States Geological Survey and the Potential Gas Committee, both of which employed a volumetric approach, peg remaining recoverable reserves to be somewhere in the neighborhood of 700-800 TCF. My own work in the area, taking a similar approach, yields about 600 TCF remaining. All these estimates are predictably higher than those made by extrapolation methods. The past cannot be used to indicate the future.

The extrapolationists failed to predict the discovery of the Tuscaloosa Trend, the Overthrust Belt and Mobile Bay. The United States Geological Survey and the Potential Gas Committee had identified these areas prior to discovery. Extrapolationists will continue to miss new plays because there is nothing in past production data to indicate their presence. We have really only recently begun looking for gas reserves below depths of 15,000 feet. There is no question that tremendous reserves potential exists at these deeper depths. New technology and improved prices will allow for their development. This same technology and economics will allow us to go back into old fields and recover additional gas reserves.

The extrapolationists, many of whom are closely listened to by government and industry leaders, point to the decline in proved gas reserves, or more correctly the decline in new reserves additions, to show our gas resource base is well into depletion. However, in actuality, the declining reserves additions are an efficient industry finding enough reserves to sustain market demand. We do not expect, and indeed consider it poor practice for business to carry excessive inventories, why should the gas industry be different?

Figure 1 depicts the annual anticipated supply available to the United States through the year 2000. Notice the shortfall from conventional supply, that is, reserves which can be produced economically at present prices and technology, is met over time by imports and non-conventional resources. The non-conventional reserves become conventional as time goes on.

Figure 1. Anticipated Annual Available Deliverability of Natural Gas

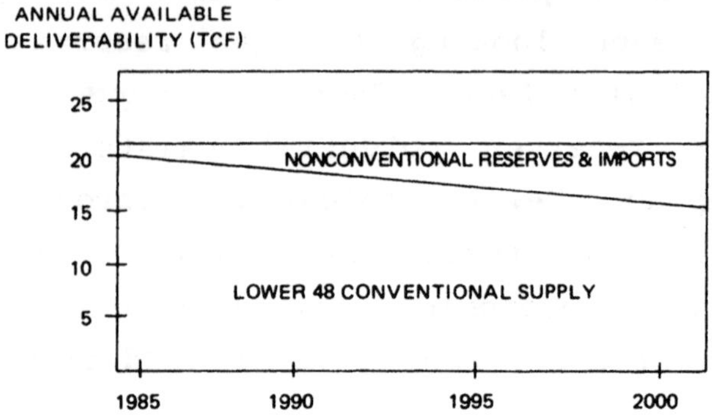

SOURCE: COMPOSITE

The United States has a natural gas reserves base that can meet a 20-22 TCF annual demand through this time period. This is above our current 17.5 TCF annual demand.

Table 2 depicts a projection of gas demand by sector in the United States through the year 2000. These are composite projections from several different studies.

Table 2. Natural Gas Demand by Economic Sector (Quadrillion BTU)

Sector	1985	1990	1995	2000
Residential	4.6	4.5	4.2	4.0
Commercial	2.5	2.7	2.7	2.7
Industrial	7.0	7.4	7.5	7.8
Electric Utility	3.0	3.5	3.0	2.6
Transportation	0.5	0.5	0.5	0.5
Total	17.6	18.6	17.9	17.6

Source: Composite

Table 2 tells an interesting story. First, projected demand is less than the possible sustained production. This is not to say there will be a "gas bubble" or excess supply, but rather that industry is capable of producing more but has no incentive to do so. Gas consumption by the electric utilities to generate power reaches 3.5 Quads within five years. However, it declines over the next ten years even though electricity usage continues to rise. By the year 2000, the electric utility industry will be using natural gas mainly to service peak loads.

Table 3 projects the predominant share of the electric utility generation growth will be in coal fired capacity.

Table 3. Projection of Consumption of Various Energy Resources by Electric Utilities (Quadrillion BTU)

Resource	1985	1990	1995	2000
Oil	1.5	1.9	2.1	2.2
Gas	3.1	3.5	2.9	2.6
Coal	14.6	16.3	20.0	22.7
Nuclear	4.0	6.1	6.7	6.9
Hydro	3.7	3.8	3.8	3.9
Total	26.9	31.6	35.5	38.3

Source: Composite

This is, in part, a result of misconceptions concerning the availability of natural gas and counterproductive laws such as the Fuel Use Act.

I will say more about the Fuel Use Act later. It exemplifies an overreaction to a short run phenomenon. However, the huge cost of constructing a coal fired electric power facility (requires about three times the capital expenditure as a similar size gas fired facility) and the deleterious effects on the environment such as acid rain should make one pause to consider increased electricity generation through approaches utilizing natural gas.

Table 4 is a composite projection showing energy consumption in the industrial sector.

Table 4. Projection of Consumption of Various Energy Resources by the Industrial Sector (Quadrillion BTU)

Resource	1985	1990	1995	2000
Oil	8.0	9.3	9.7	10.1
Gas	6.9	7.3	7.5	7.8
Coal	2.6	3.9	4.4	5.3
Electricity	2.9	3.5	4.1	4.6
Other	3.0	3.0	3.0	3.0
Total	23.4	27.0	28.7	30.8

Source: Composite

Notice the steady increase in oil consumption by this sector from present on into the future. Also, note the more than doubling of coal use and steadily increasing electricity consumption (mainly coal fired as we have already seen). Gas's growth is at a much slower rate. If these projections reflect future reality, and I believe they do, it becomes clear we are setting the stage for difficult times. The United States will forego its environment and increase its dependence on foreign oil. The concerns of the 70's and early 80's seem to be forgotten.

Let's just look at what we are going to do to ourselves with oil imports. U.S. energy use will probably increase from the current 75 Quads per year to about 85 Quads by 1990. Our domestic oil consumption will probably be in the 16 MMBO/D range. Our domestic production will have fallen to around 10 MMBO/D. Figure 2 graphically shows our predicament.

Figure 2. Production of U.S. Oil Demand Versus Domestic Oil Production

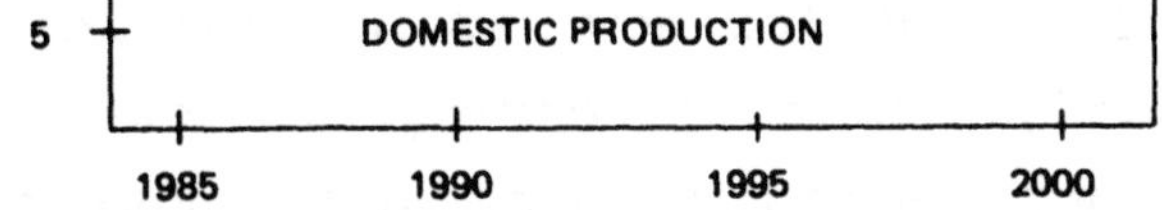

SOURCE: COMPOSITE

The United States will continue and, for the most part, has always taken all the domestic oil production available. This situation is unlike the natural gas market. The continental United States oil production peaked in the early 1970's and has been on the decline ever since. Since there are no major market constraints, one concludes our oil supply is in its autumn years. Actually, many projections show the Lower 48 as being one of the oil poor nations of the world within 10-15 years. Obviously, the shortfalls will have to be supplied by OPEC and others. We can expect crude oil prices to rise as OPEC production increases. Reality has shown their price discipline is weak whenever total OPEC production falls below 20 MMBO/D. In the 20-25 MMBO/D range, prices firm with inflation. When it reaches 25 MMBO/D, which should be in the early 1990's, crude oil prices will exceed the inflation rate and the next major energy shock will be ushered in.

It appears we are unwaveringly headed for a brick wall. Increased natural gas usage can soften, and possibly prevent, the impact. The supply is there. The natural gas industry is ready to provide some solutions. However, the country, at least for now, is not turning a deaf, but certainly a hard of hearing ear toward them.

The once staid natural gas industry after being battered and buffeted by mergers, bubbles and intense competition has been transformed into an efficient market sensitive entity. Costs have been reduced and the industry has shown innovation in solving problems.

An example of the gas industry's attempt to better utilize it's abundant resource and get us off the energy treadmill is cogeneration.

Cogeneration is the simultaneous production of electricity and process steam from a single fuel source. Natural gas is the most frequently used fuel in cogeneration systems. It is preferred because of abundant supply, mechanical efficiency and environmental considerations.

The gas fired cogeneration system will make industrials and utilities more efficient in their energy usage. Energy efficiencies for most electrical power generating plants are 35-50% for steam systems and 40% for gas turbine designed with waste heat recovery systems. Cogeneration of electric power yields conversions around 75%. The efficiencies translate into energy savings which makes the conversion to natural gas fired co-generation financially sound.

On a large national scale, cogeneration has the potential to back out as much as 1,000 MBO/D of oil equivalent just in the electric power generation sector alone. It could hike U.S. gas use by about 1 TCF annually by the year 2000. This would slash overall import bills, mitigate some of our environmental problems and provide energy savings to industrials and utilities.

Cogeneration is even applicable in the residential and commercial sector. These groups which are faced with rising utility bills will be able to enjoy the same energy efficiencies from cogeneration as heavy industry and utilities. The market for cogeneration in the commercial sector could be as large as that identified for the industrial sector.

I believe it is clear that the availability of natural gas and the renewed gas industry can play a lead role in stabilizing our markets. It is imperative that we begin clearing needless obstructions and misconceptions as they will only become more difficult to clear away as time goes on. We have reacted rather than acted on the problem of energy stability. Decisions made in haste or under misconception by well intentioned people are hindering progress. An example is the passage of the Fuel Use Act.

The prohibition on the construction of new gas fired large industrial facilities and electric utility plants, as mandated by the Fuel Use Act (FUA) of 1978 is hindering our electric utility sector and industrials from attaining cost efficiencies and higher environmental standards.

The generation of electricity via new gas fired technology would require only a portion of the capital expenditures as a similarly sized coal fired unit while producing virtually no sulfur dioxide or particulate matter.

I believe I have shown where we are, where we are going and where we should be going. The planning and development to stabilize our energy consumption market will require a commitment of a long term nature. The marketplace, in its present form, cannot be left to determine the proper energy mix for the future. Our past meddling has made certain mechanisms in the market inoperable. We, therefore will continue having difficulty distinguishing between short term and long term trends and indicators.

An energy plan based on misconception will surely lead us into trouble. The time is now to direct our efforts into developing our abundant and most efficient energy resource--natural gas. The United States must not let our dependence on foreign oil grow. We have previewed the consequences of this course of action. We also must not trade the environment of future generations for the utilization of an energy resource.

REFERENCES

American Gas Association. 1984. "Projected Economic and Environmental Impacts of Retaining the Fuel Use Act Through the Year 2000". Energy Analysis.

Ashby, Anne B., Paul D. Holtberg and Thomas J. Woods. 1984. "1984 GRI Baseline Projection of U.S. Energy Supply and Demand, 1983-2010". Gas Research Insights.

Bupp, I. C. 1985. "U.S. Natural Gas After Deregulation". Cambridge Energy Forum.

Cook, James. 1985. "Nuclear Follies". Forbes. Volume 135 No. 3, 82-100.

Energy Information Administration. 1984 Synopsis of the Annual Energy Review and Outlook 1983.

Gibbons, John H. 1985. U.S. Natural Gas Availability. Office of Technology Assessment.

Hendricks, Thomas A. 1975. "Estimating Resources of Crude Oil and Natural Gas in Inadequately Explored Areas". Methods of Estimating the Volume of Undiscovered Oil and Gas Resources. 19-22.

Strausser, Jeffrey A. 1985. "Energy Forecasts: Where Are They Taking Us?" IAEE Newsletter.

Weeks, Lewis G. 1975. "Potential Petroleum Resources-Classification, Estimation and Status". Methods of Estimating the Volume of Undiscovered Oil and Gas Reserves. 31-49.

25
Coal and Electric Utilities Market Assessment Outlook

C. Hoff Stauffer, Jr., ICF, Inc.

INTRODUCTION

Recent events have again confirmed that the fortunes of the U.S. coal industry are closely linked to the domestic electric utility industry. Opportunities for synfuels, exports and industrial consumption have waned in the face of falling oil prices, surplus gas and reduced economic growth. Electric utilities have dominated most of the recent swings in the coal markets and future coal-fired generation will be critical to regional coal production, excess mining productive capacity and coal prices. This report, therefore, focuses on the utility industry and the uncertainties affecting it. First, the near-term outlook will be discussed in which new nuclear plants and moderate growth in electricity sales will limit coal consumption. The long-term growth is then discussed in which oil and gas prices and electricity growth rates will determine the characteristics of long-term growth potential for coal.

THE NEAR-TERM

Coal Consumption Will Not Grow Significantly

- Between 1985 and 1990 increases in nuclear generation, Canadian imports and cogeneration will limit growth in coal consumption and decrease oil and gas consumption.

    - Over 39 gigawatts of new nuclear capacity are added by 1990. This is equivalent to over 100 million tons of coal consumption per year.

    - Canadian electricity imports and cogeneration will increase by over 30% displacing 30 million tons of potential annual coal demand.

- Low oil/gas prices and gas-fired cogeneration will prevent coal from serving near-term growth in industrial energy consumption.

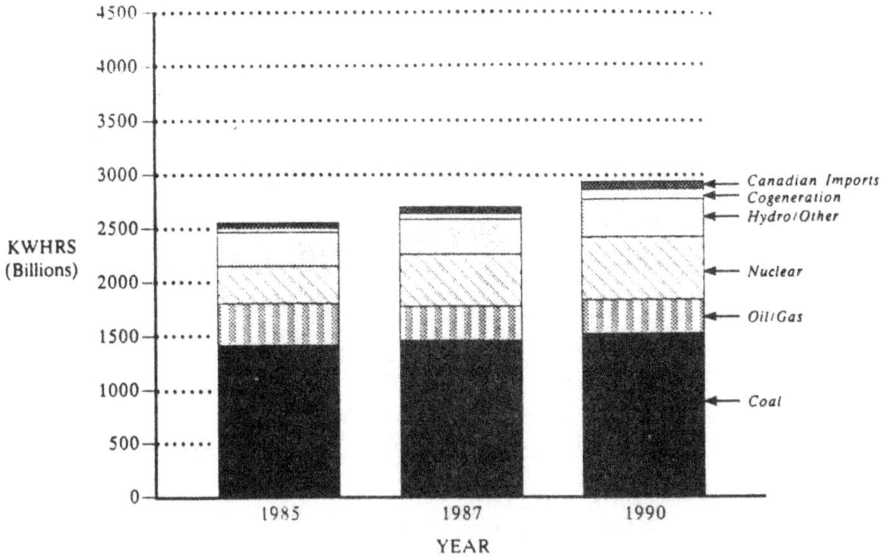

Figure 1. National Electric Utility Consumption by Fuel Type

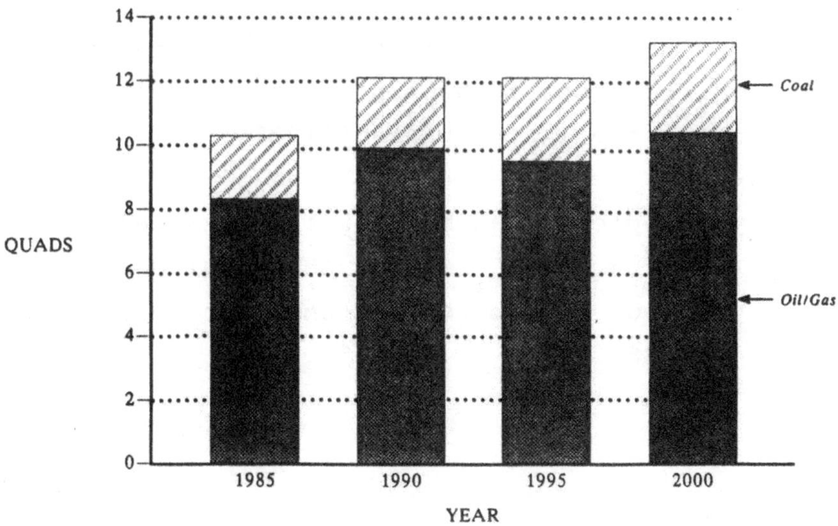

Figure 2. Industrial Fossil Fuel Consumption

THE NEAR-TERM (Continued)

Stock Adjustments Have Greatly Restricted Coal Shipments In 1985

- o In 1985 consumption will increase in both the West and East over 1984 levels. Shipments, however, will decline across the nation as a whole but regionally will increase in the West and decrease in the East.

Change from 1984 to 1985	East	West
Consumption	+23	+25
Stock Swing	-43	-8
Shipments	-20	+17

- o Coal shipments have declined in the East due to stock drawdowns.

- o Shipments will rebound in the East when the stock adjustment is over, beginning in the latter part of 1985.

- o Shipments can be expected to accelerate again in 1987 due to stock build-ups prior to a potential UMWA strike in 1988.

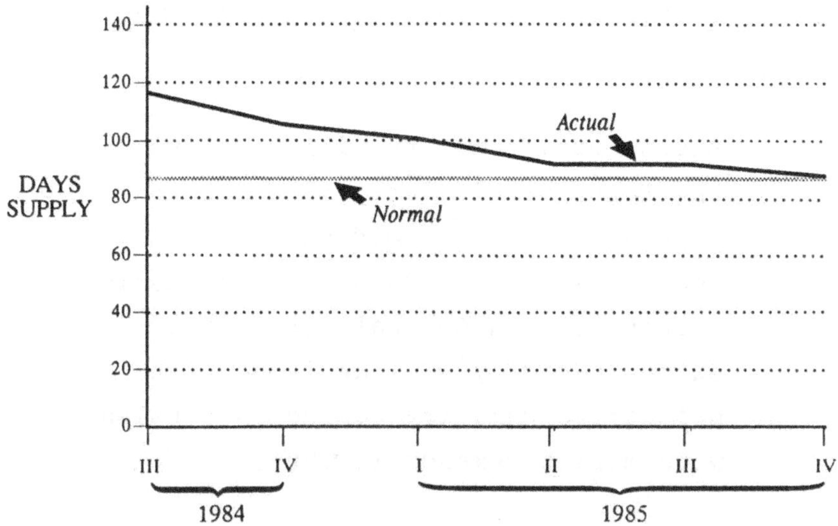

Figure 3. Comparison of Actual and Normal Electric Utility Day's Supply of Stocks

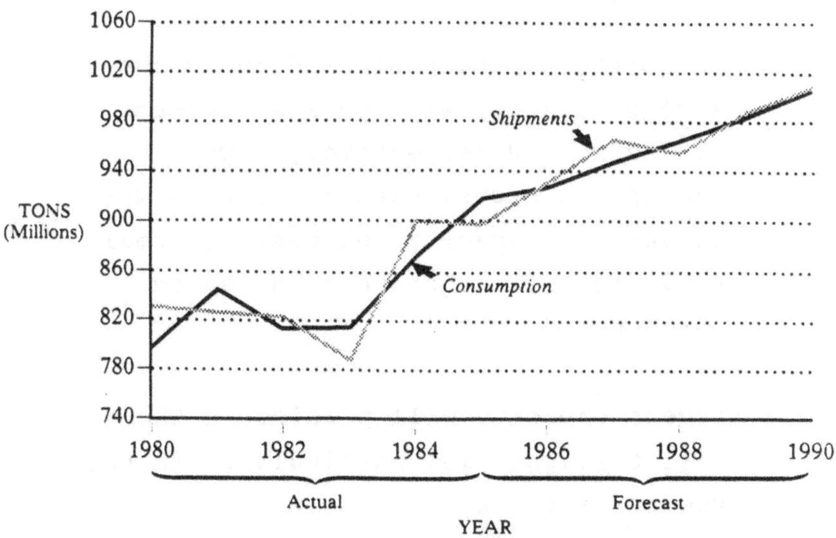

Figure 4. National Coal Consumption and Shipments 1980 Through 1990

THE NEAR-TERM (Continued)

By 1990, Excess Coal Productive Capacity Will Disappear In The East, Remain In The West

- Excess coal capacity will be higher in the East, particularly in Northern Appalachia and the Midwest, in 1985, because stock drawdowns are depressing shipments. In Central Appalachia, excess capacity will decrease with productive capacity coming into balance with market demands in 1986.

- In the West, excess coal capacity will be lower in 1985 as a result of increased consumption and only modest stock drawdowns.

- In Northern Appalachia and the Midwest excess capacity will persist through 1987 and 1988 respectively. The decline in excess capacity occurs more because of capacity decreases (normal retirements) rather than increased shipments.

- Excess capacity will persist in the West through 1990, particularly in the Powder River Basin.

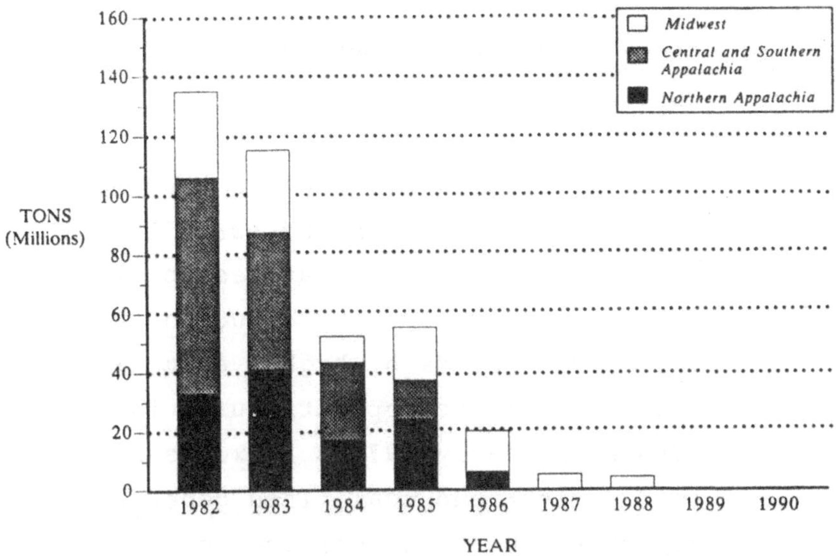

Figure 5. Excess Productive Capacity East of the Mississippi

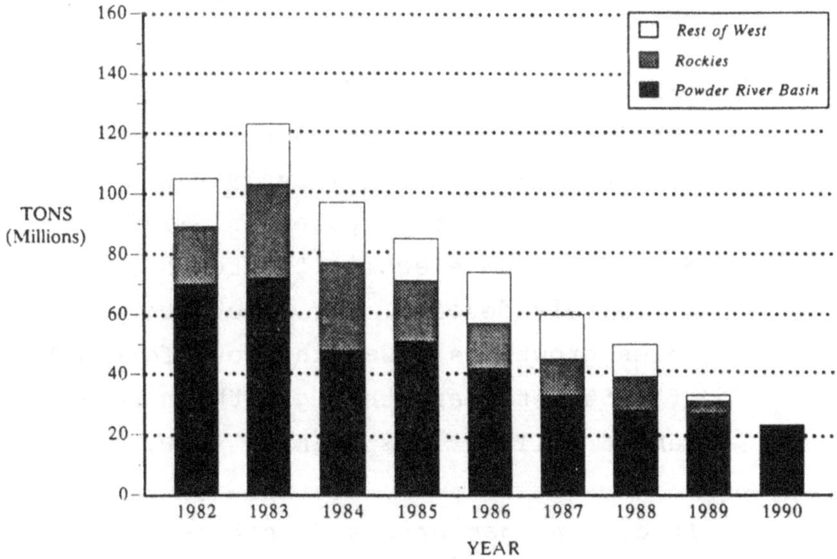

Figure 6. Excess Productive Capacity West of the Mississippi

THE LONGER TERM

Electric Utility Fuel Consumption In The 1990's Reflects Current Excess Generation

- Electric utility oil and gas consumption will increase in the early 1990's as electricity growth catches up with current excess capacity. Much of this "excess" consists of higher cost oil- and gas-fired powerplants built in the 1960's and early 1970's. Excess base-load nuclear and coal-fired generation capacity, built in anticipation of growth in demand that did not occur, reduced utility oil/gas consumption in the 1980's.

- The potential exists for electric utility coal consumption to increase substantially in the late 1990's. The realization of this potential will depend on how electricity growth rates ultimately develop. If electricity sales growth is lower than our forecast of 2.5% per year, then growth in coal demand will be less than we show.

- If oil and gas prices do not increase in the early 1990's, new gas-fired combined cycle generation capacity could displace new coal-fired capacity.

THE LONGER TERM

<u>Electric Utilities Will Remain The Dominant Consumer And Account For Most Of The Growth</u>.

- The other major potential growth sector for coal is in large industrial boilers, but this potential is inhibited by lower oil/gas prices and cogeneration.

- There is some moderate potential for growth in steam exports in the mid-to-late 1990's going to Europe and the Pacific Rim.

- We foresee no long-term growth in the metallurgical sector.

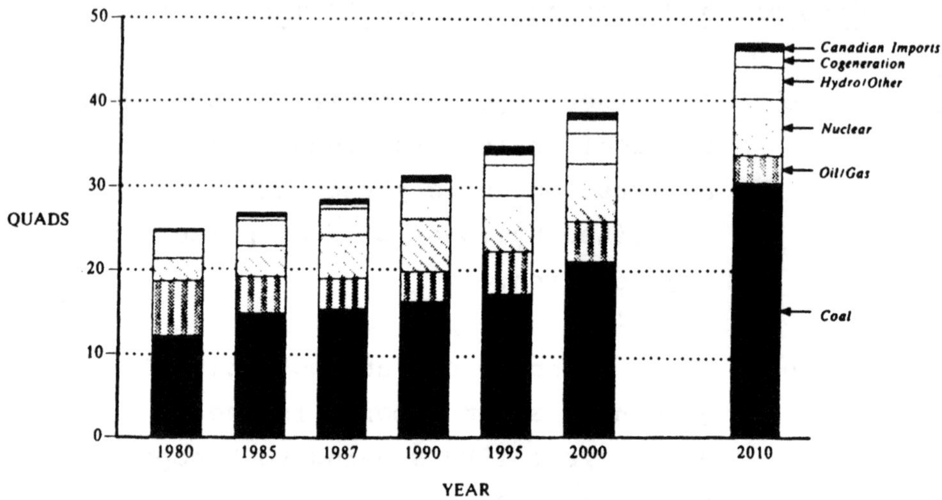

Figure 7. Long-Term Electric Utility Consumption by Fuel Type

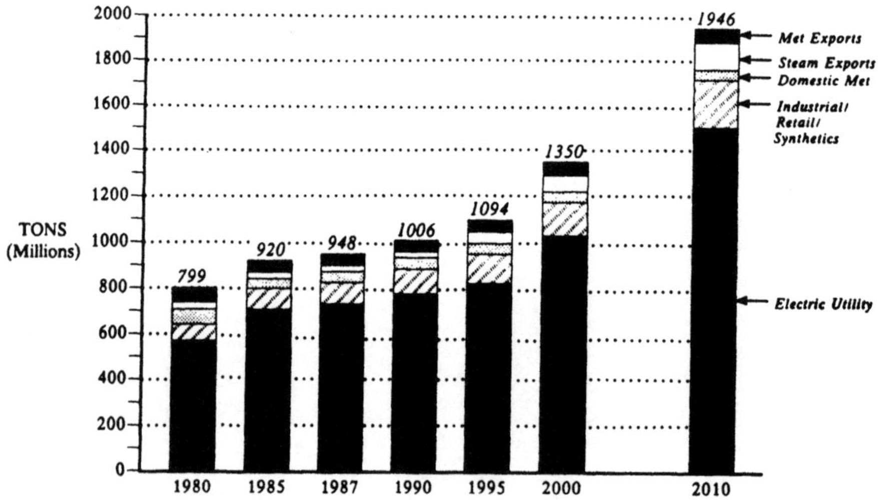

Figure 8. National Coal Consumption By Sector

THE LONGER TERM (Continued)

The Growth In Coal Production Will Not Be Spread Evenly Across Producing Regions

- Through 1995, there will be essentially no growth in the higher sulfur producing regions: Northern Appalachia and the Midwest. This market outlook results from increased nuclear generation, Canadian power imports, tall stacks regulations and, after 1990, an assumed acid rain mitigation program. After 1995, there will be growth in these high sulfur regions to serve new powerplants.

- Growth in coal consumption will be greater in the West than the East through 1995 because economic and electricity growth rates are higher in the West and substantial nuclear capacity is coming on-line in the East.

- The growth will be concentrated in four regions:

  - Central Appalachia will grow to meet new demand. Between 1990 and 1995 it will also grow as a result

THE LONGER TERM (Continued)

of the assumed tall stack regulations by 1990 and acid rain mitigation legislation between 1990 and 1995.

-- The Powder River Basin will grow to serve new powerplants generally in the area between the Mississippi and the Rockies, except for the portions of the West South Central served by local lignites.

-- Gulf lignite will grow moderately through 2000, primarily in Texas. Growth, however, will be limited by cogeneration and low oil and gas prices.

-- The Rockies will grow to serve local utility markets and the industrial sector throughout the West. It will also grow to serve Midwestern high sulfur powerplants shifting to lower sulfur coals as a result of tall stacks regulations and the assumed acid rain mitigation program.

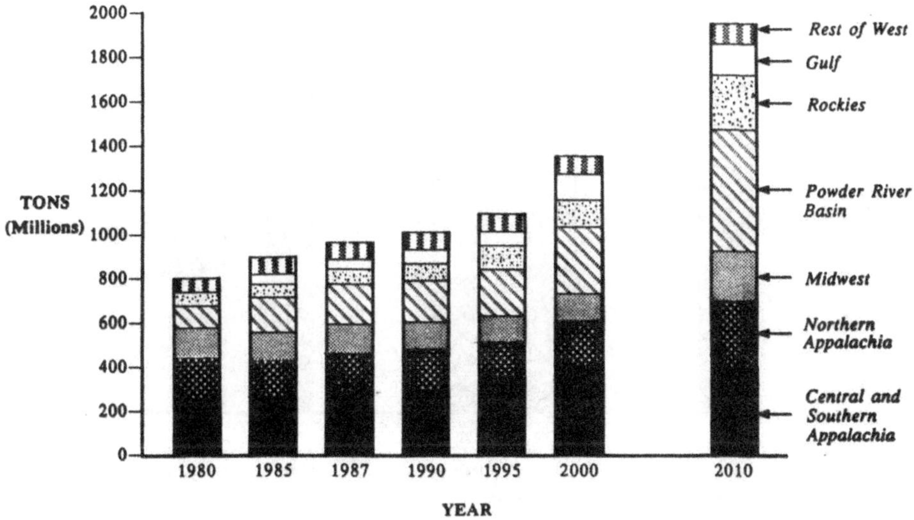

Figure 9. Regional Coal Production 1980 Through 2010

We Believe Acid Rain Legislation Will Be Enacted

o The impacts will depend on the type of legislation passed. Figure 10 shows the impacts of a program assuming:

-- an 8 million ton reduction from existing plants,

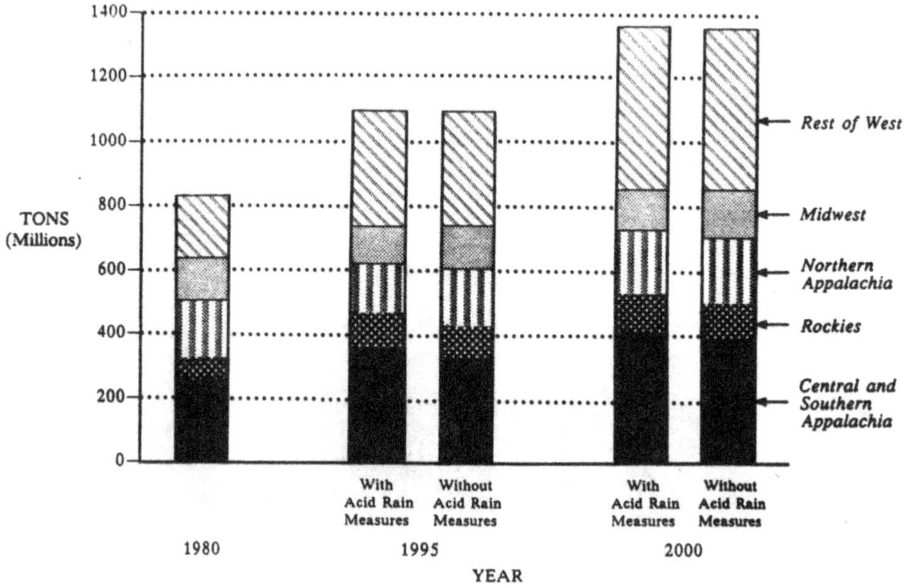

Figure 10. Effect of Assumed Acid Rain Legislation On Regional Coal Production

THE LONGER TERM (Continued)

-- limited local coal protection scrubbers installed on 28 GW of capacity currently burning high sulfur coals,

-- reductions in the 31 states east of and bordering the Mississippi River,

-- compliance by 1995 (some "phased-in" reductions before 1995 could be required).

o The effect of such legislation would be:

-- to limit production in the high-sulfur regions of the Midwest and Northern Appalachia to approximately 1980 levels, until after 1995,

-- to stimulate further production in Central Appalachia and the Rockies.

26
The Role of U.S. Coal in the International Coal Market

Manfred G. Raschke, Dun & Bradstreet

THE ROLE OF U.S. COAL IN THE INTERNATIONAL COAL MARKET

INTRODUCTION

Three theses will be briefly argued here:

(1) The United States will continue to be only a marginal or swing supplier in the international steam coal market.

(2) U.S. coal exports will continue to be dominated by metallurgical coals until the end of this century and possibly beyond.

(3) Coal imports to the United States will continue to be insignificant in volume in the coming decade; imports of no more than five million tons are probable by the early 1990's.

U.S. STEAM COAL EXPORTS

The new Golden Age for coal which was heralded by professional forecasters, industry leaders, and government officials in the late 1970's and early 1980's has come --and gone. It is illuminating to briefly look back at why all the forecasts and projections went wrong. The Arab oil embargo of late 1973 and early 1974, which artificially constricted world oil supplies and quadrupled prices, set off a frantic search for substitute energy supplies in both industrialized and developing countries. In view of the environmental, technical and financial obstacles being encountered in the mid 1970's by nuclear power programs in the United States and Western Europe, coal appeared to be the only near-term alternative energy source. Plans were made for the massive substitution of steam coal for oil and natural gas in the industrial and electric utility sectors in all of the nations of Western Europe and the Far East. Corresponding plans to build new mines and export-related intrastructure were made in Australia, South Africa, Canada, and Colombia.

In 1980-1982 the long awaited "take-off" for coal appeared to have arrived. Steam coal exports from the United States, after averaging less than 15 million tons per year in the 1970's and constituting only 20 to 25 percent of total U.S. coal exports, suddenly doubled in 1980 and then almost doubled again in 1981 to 45 million tons. In 1982 the decline began and, by 1984, only 23.8 million tons were exported.

The key event which precipitated this rush to buy U.S. steam coal was the collapse of Polish coal exports due to the impact of the Solidarity Movement. Other more or less simultaneous events contributed. The invasion of Iran by Iraq culminated a two-year period of growing instability in the Persian Gulf that had begun with the overthrow of the Shah and had led to a steady rise in oil prices. In Australia, labor unrest raised fears that exports from that country might not meet expectations. The European, Japanese and South Korean cement industries began to convert to coal and Japanese steel companies converted their blast furnaces to all-coke operation.

The result of the confluence of these events was a sudden apparent upsurge in demand which led to the same psychological response as could be observed during the oil crises of 1973-74 and 1978-80. In both cases, the supply of petroleum products exceeded the volumes needed for immediate consumption, but the market reacted by rapidly raising the levels of stocks held by consumers and intermediate traders. Thus also with coal, the demand levels perceived by the market in 1980-1982 considerably exceeded actual consumption levels in those years.

The stockpiling of coal which occurred in 1981 greatly exceeded what was needed for immediate short-term consumption. The motives for such stockpiling were in part speculative and in part a reflex response conditioned by earlier fears of oil shortages. The result of this wave of panic buying was an enormous build-up in European coal stockpiles. The signals perceived by the market -- the escalation of prices and the long lines of bulk carriers waiting outside the world's major coal ports -- were misinterpreted as an indication of a long awaited coal boom.

In 1983 reality returned. There will be no rapid escalation in overseas coal consumption and those increases in demand that do occur will be primarily met by other suppliers. The conversion of the Far East cement industry to coal and the switch to all-coke operation in blast furnaces were one time affairs and not part of a rapidly accelerating trend toward greater coal consumption.

Steam coal supply will continue to exceed demand throughout the 1980's and 1990's. In Western Europe, where the United States has an advantage, at least in terms of proximity to market, compared to Australia and Canada, overseas imports of steam coal are expected to increase only 2.5 to 3.0 percent per year between now and 1995. The entire increase, about 25 to 30 million metric tons, could be met by the El Cerrejon Mine in Colombia. In the Far East, however, where U.S. steam coal is at a distinct transportation disadvantage, the demand for steam coal imports can be expected to grow at about 10 percent per year until 1995. Most of this increase will be met by mines in Australia, Western Canada, South Africa, the Peoples' Republic of China and Indonesia. In total, therefore, by 1995 we can anticipate that the volume of internationally traded steam coal will increase about 75 to 90 million metric tons per year from present levels.

To determine the exporters who will be most successful in capturing the largest portion of this market, one can compare each of the exporters to certain criteria which may be regarded as important for success in the international market. These criteria are:

*Low delivered costs,

*Good quality coal,

*The producer's partnership in a joint mining venture with an importer or consumer of coal,

*The producer's international business orientation and commitment to penetrating the market,

*The producer's reliability as a supplier, and

*Political pressure exerted by the producing country on consumers.

In general, these criteria are applicable to both the steam and the metallurgical coal trade, although in the case of the latter, one should consider the possession of unique quality coals as on a par in importance with delivered cost. In periods of market crisis or rapid increases in demand, such as in 1981-1982, considerations of cost may be displaced by the reliability factor. This may include everything from the dependability of the labor force and the political stability of the producing country on the one hand, to the size of the coal reserve base on the other.

Based on the criteria listed above, the most

successful exporters will be South Africa, Colombia and Poland. This is a low-cost group of suppliers with which the United States basically cannot compete.

There is a second group of supplier nations that will be less competitive than the first: Australia, the Peoples' Republic of China, and Canada. In this second group, costs cover a very broad spectrum. Some of the best mines are competitive with South Africa in the Far East but not in Europe; but some of the new projects appear to have costs above what current market prices can sustain. Furthermore, the appreciation of either the Australian or the Canadian dollar could well render some additional projects uneconomic.

If we compare our estimate of incremental internationally traded steam coal demand with incremental production capacity being developed to meet that demand, the excess capacity situation becomes clear. By 1995 export capacity in Colombia will be at least 25 million metric tons per year. This is very conservative given that Carbocol/Intercor's (an Exxon subsidiary) El Cerrejon project alone will have that capacity. There is, in addition, the Prodeco mine in the central zone of El Cerrejon, which is already exporting, and the recently announced 5 million ton per year mine in the La Loma coalfield which is being developed by Greenley Energy and Siderurgica de Medellin. Nor is Colombia the only South American coal exporter on the horizon. In Venezuela, one state-owned mine, known as the Zulia project, and one private mine, known as Fila Maestra, are under consideration for development by 1990. In addition, Brazil and Argentina are marketing steam coal internationally. In both cases, although press reports indicate that some sales have been made, it seems unlikely, both because of rising domestic demand and because of poor quality steam coal, that any sustained export effort is credible. Thus, to be conservative, we can assume that total incremental export capacity in South America will be 25 million metric tons per year.

In Western Europe, I am assuming no incremental export capacity in either Poland or the United Kingdom. Other European coal producers do not play a significant role in the international steam coal trade.

South Africa in the Phase IV-A export allocations made in 1982 projected steam coal exports of 70 million metric tons (more than double the anticipated 1985 exports) by 1990. Soft market conditions and problems with the financing and construction of the incremental Richard's Bay rail line capacity now make 70 million tons per year by 1995 appear more realistic. Thus, we have an incremental capacity of 35 million tons per year in South Africa. By 1995 we may be seeing the beginning phases of new projects in Botswana, Swaziland or Malagasy, but I have not counted any of these for purposes of this calculation.

For Australia I have assumed a further increase of 30 million metric tons per year of steam coal export capacity. This is less than half of what is planned and announced for 1995, but again, I think one must be conservative.

In Canada, there is little prospect of any new steam coal export capacity being built in British Columbia and Alberta in the foreseeable future. Thus, with steam coal produced by new metallurgical coal mines and expansions of existing mines that are already underway, we can add 3 million metric tons per year by 1990.

In the Far East, I am assuming that the projects being developed on Kalimantan in Indonesia -- and I understand that Arco will be shipping coal from its new mine by early 1986 -- will meet rapidly rising domestic demand. Export-oriented steam coal projects in Siberia and the Peoples' Republic of China are good for another 5 million metric tons per year. Again, this is only a fraction of the announced intention.

When you add up these admittedly rough calculations, you get about 100 million metric tons per year by 1995. This non-U.S. capacity is targeted at the 75 to 90 million metric tons of incremental demand which I mentioned above. Thus, for U.S. producers to participate in this growing market to any substantial degree will be difficult. U.S. producers can point with pride to the improvement they have made in productivity in Central and Southern Appalachia in the past three years. But high F.O.B. port prices are not the only problems U.S. exporters have to contend with. The United States, due to the questionable practices of a few exporters in 1981 and 1982, has developed a reputation for poor quality control. There is also considerable concern overseas about high U.S. rail rates, but this is also in large part self-inflicted bad publicity.

As a forecast for steam coal exports from the United States, we get an increase of approximately 14 to 18 million tons per year by 1995. On top of the 24 million tons exported in 1984, that gives us about 38 to 42 million tons per year by 1995.

Can anything occur to alter this rather dismal forecast? Quite a lot. If compelled to choose between sharply higher oil prices or supply disruptions in one of the other major exporters, I would at present be inclined to favor the latter probability. South Africa immediately comes to mind. It would require that sustained racial unrest actually lead to a serious reduction of coal production or the sabotage of the Richard's Bay rail line. Such events are not impossible in the current climate of racial tension but it should be recognized that just as Poland recovered market share after 1980-1981 and Iran in the oil markets after the events of 1978-79, there are not likely to be occurrences in South Africa that would remove that nation's coal from the international market permanently.

U.S. METALLURGICAL COAL EXPORTS

Metallurgical coal exports will continue to exceed steam coal exports from the United States through the remainder of this century.

In late 1984 while I was a consultant at Temple Barker and Sloane, I completed a steel mill-by-steel mill analysis of coke blends at primary iron and steel facilities throughout the world. The Soviet Union and Eastern Europe were excluded. However, in Eastern Europe we did include Yugoslavia and Romania. In the Far East we included both North Korea and the Peoples' Republic of China. The historic data was drawn from 1981, 1982 and 1983; the projections were for 1985 and 1990.

In the preparation of this world metallurgical coal overview we assessed a considerable number of factors that have a significant impact on world steel demand and on metallurgical coal demand. We considered the following macro trends in our analysis:

*The rate of real economic growth in nations with primary steel production capacity,

*Regional changes in steel intensity,

*A geographic realignment of world steel production.

In addition, we examined the impact of several other less significant factors:

*Technological changes in steelmaking that will change the pig iron/raw steel ratio,

*Technological changes that will alter the coke rate

*Technological changes that will alter the coke blend.

Total pig iron production for the countries included in this study was 394 million metric tons in 1979, 321 million metric tons in 1982 and is projected to be 357 million in 1985 and 371 million metric tons in 1990. In 1985 total met coal demand in these same countries was projected to be 330 million metric tons and in 1990 it is 340 million metric tons. In 1985, 139 million metric tons is internationally traded and in 1990, 154 million tons is expected to be internationally traded.

The shifts in the geographic concentration of pig iron production are expected to continue throughout the 1980's and 1990's. Steel production is gradually moving geographically closer to the emerging markets in the newly industrialized nations. This is a reflection of the fact that steel intensity, defined as tons of apparent steel consumption per million (constant) GNP, has been in decline in the United States since the mid 1960's and in Japan and Western Europe since 1973.

Europe and the Far East will continue to be the major markets for internationally traded met coal -- despite the growth projected in pig iron production in Latin America, South Asia, and Africa. Europe and the Far East are projected to account for 85 percent of the demand for internationally traded met coal in 1985 and 84 percent in 1990. New sales opportunities for all grades of met coal are expected to arise both from the construction of new integrated steel capacity (e.g., in South Korea, Taiwan, Romania, and Yugoslavia) and from significant declines in the domestic production of these coals in major European coal-producing countries, such as France, the United Kingdom, and West Germany.

The analysis which we performed of changes in coking technology on a company-by-company basis indicates that, in general, coke blends can be expected to change in the next decade to emphasize a greater use of high volatility coals with weak coking properties. But one can foresee no technological shift within the next decade that will cause a fundamental change from current coke blends. The primary commercialized technologies that will result in the greater use of high-volatility coals are coal preheating, coke dry quenching, and coal briquetting. Lower international met coal prices, the market's perception of excess met coal supplies, and a smaller differential in the prices of steam and met coal than at some periods in the 1970's may combine with the financial limitations on many steel companies to curtail investments in these technologies.

Thus, although high volatility coal demand will grow faster than total met coal demand, the frequent reliance on local sources for this type of coal is expected to produce something quite close to the following aggregate blend for internationally traded met coal in the early 1990's: 22.6 percent low volatility, 51.2 percent medium volatility and 26.2 percent high volatility. Therefore, although premium grade U.S. low volatility coals will continue to suffer intense competition from higher ash products available in Canada and Australia, U.S. medium volatility coals and high volatility, high fluidity, coals should do well in the international market.

This results in a forecast of 50 to 55 million tons of met coal exports in 1995. Total exports are thus projected to be between 85 and 97 million tons in 1995.

COAL IMPORTS

Discussion about coal imports into the U.S. East and Gulf Coasts has attracted a great deal of attention in the past year. I propose here to give this topic all of the attention that I think it merits -- two minutes.

Until about 18 months ago, coal imports attracted no particular attention. The United States has always imported some coal. Historically the peak years have been 1974 with 5.7 million tons imported, 1978, with 8.3 million and 1979, with 6.1 million tons. Most of this, however, was imported as coke; actual steam coal imports reached a peak of just under 3.0 million tons in 1978. In the past four years, steam coal imports have not topped 1.5 million tons per year. Most of this coal comes from South Africa and is imported under a contract for 800,000 tons per year to Gulf Power. This contract began in 1976 and will expire in 1987.

In 1984, 1,286,000 tons of steam coal were imported. About 0.2 percent of total consumption. However, the purchase of test cargos of Colombian coal by Florida Power, followed by a short-term contract with Carbocol by the same utility, as well as offers of Colombian coal to a dozen other coastal utilities, has sparked a political cause celebre. The introduction of a bill by Nick Rahall (Democrat, West Virginia) in the

House calling for an $8.00 per ton import levy was followed by a number of forecasts projecting rapid increases in coal imports. A Department of Commerce study put the potential for imports by 1990 at 17.7 million tons. D.R.I. projected imports of 6.5 million tons by 1995 and Forrest Hill & Associates put imports at 10 million tons by 1990.

Although recent imports have come from Australia, Canada, Poland, South Africa and Colombia, only the latter is a serious threat. When one considers coal specifications, the ability to receive coal by water, and existing contracts, the size of the market available to imports shrinks dramatically. Furthermore, one must keep in mind political considerations and the innate conservatism of utility fuel/purchasing practices. Utilities which have tidewater access at one or more of their plants can be expected to welcome small volumes of low cost imported coal as a very convenient pressure point on domestic coal prices and rail rates. However, I am inclined to believe Exxon, that North America is the target market for no more than 3 million tons per year of El Cerrejon coal by 1990.

Total coal imports by 1990 will not therefore exceed 5 million tons and may well be only 3 million tons. As for the import levy on coal, it is a waste of valuable Congressional time and is potentially an embarrassment to those who support it.

27
Prospects for the French Power Sector Through the Year 2000

Bernard Montfort, Electricité de France

SUMMARY

Increasing the role of electricity and adopting strong overall energy conservation policies are sometimes presented as inconsistent objectives. This does not have to be so, depending on the resource base of the country concerned and subject to appropriate planning mechanisms. In the case of France, growth prospects over the period 1984-2000 call for a reduction in energy intensity at about 1.5 % per annum, and, at the same time, for an increase in electricity intensity at about 1 % per annum.

Electricity is thus expected to continue to increase its share of the French energy market and help achieve an appropriate national energy balance with a reduced reliance on oil. This is on account of its economic advantage over alternative energy sources in a large number of uses, the relative predictability of its tariffs in an otherwise uncertain energy picture, and its low level of dependence on imported goods.

The share of electricity as a proportion of total energy use in France has increased from 23 percent in 1973 to 35 percent in 1984. It could be expected to increase further and to reach 50 percent before the year 2000. In the year 2000, nuclear energy is expected to represent about 80 percent of electricity generation, and thus meet about 40 percent of total energy consumption.

INTRODUCTION

This paper focuses primarily on the role that electricity can play in helping to achieve an appropriate energy balance in France. Some of its qualitative conclusions would however be relevant in other countries with similar characteristics.

The paper assumes that the nuclear fuel cycle and safety problems will continue to be satisfactorily resolved, and that they will not impose severe constraints on the growth of otherwise economically justified nuclear energy. Breeder reactors are not considered because the concern here is on the broad patterns of energy supply and demand, whereas the impact of such facilities on the energy supply situation could be expected to be substantial only towards the beginning of the next century. For similar reasons, the so-called renewable energy sources are not discussed either.

1. RE-OPTIMIZATION OF ELECTRICITY GENERATION MIX

1.1 Base load operation and optimum generating plant mix

The economic advantage of nuclear electricity as a base load is quite clear in the French situation. This is illustrated in the first column of table 1 which shows the generation costs for nuclear and coal plants to be commissioned in 1992, assuming base load operation throughout the plant life time and an opportunity cost of capital of 9 percent in real terms.

Table 1. Generation costs per kWh, depending on plant factor (French centimes of january 1, 1984)

Type of plant	Hours of use per year		
	6,200*	3,200	1,600
Nuclear	22.8	38.8	70.7
Coal without desulphurization	32.6	42.7	64.5
with desulphurization	35.0	47.1	73.2
Oil without desulphurization	72.8	81.5	100.0
with desulphurization	75.2	85.9	108.7

* Base load.

In order to determine the appropriate share of nuclear generation in the demand diagram over base load operation, generation costs for various plant factors should be considered. Table 1 summarizes such data. The break-even plant factor when substituting nuclear for coal is below 2,000 hours of plant use, while oil is virtually eliminated, with the exception of gas turbines for peaking purposes.

Foreign exchange considerations further reinforce the economic advantages of nuclear as a least-cost means of meeting the electric load, since its foreign exchange component is below that of coal and oil.

There is also a decided advantage from the point of view of reliability of primary energy supply, made possible by the relatively low cost of building up a stock of nuclear fuel. The French policy on this point is to maintain a stock of uranium representing three years of use of this fuel. This is equivalent, in cost, to a stock of oil representing only three months of use.

1.2 Outlook to the year 2000

With regard to future installed capacity and generation balances, the paper considers two scenarios (see para 2.2 for the underlying assumptions). The target scenario calls for a total national electricity consumption of 370 TWh in 1990 and 510 TWh in the year 2000. The low scenario envisages the levels of 350 TWh and 450 TWh in the same years. Excluding possible exports, the outlook for nuclear development is then as shown in Table 2. It can be seen that the proportion of electricity met by nuclear is similar in both scenarios, reaching almost 80 percent in the year 2000.

Table 2. Projected evolution of nuclear output
(Excluding exports)

Scenario	1984	1990	2000
Target scenario			
Installed capacity (GW)	33	56	81
Nuclear generation (TWh)	177	280	409
Total generation (TWh)	282	370	510
Nuclear share (%)	63	76	80
Low Scenario			
Installed capacity (GW)	33	56	65
Nuclear generation (TWh)	177	268	350
Total generation (TWh)	282	350	450
Nuclear share (%)	63	77	76

2. SUBSTITUTION OF ELECTRICITY FOR OTHER ENERGY SOURCES

2.1 Advantages of electricity

2.1.1 To the extent the power supply generation mix has been reoptimized to tap the most attractive primary energy sources, electricity has an overall economic advantage in a number of end-uses for which it can be utilized more efficiently and more conveniently at the point of consumption, particularly in space heating and in industry. In the latter sector, the traditional role of electricity in providing motive power and lighting is expected to account for only a fraction of the increase in electricity use between now and the end of this century. The balance is expected to come primarily from the adoption of new heating processes. While heating uses have so far, by and large, been fueled by oil, coal and gas, a wide variety of new processes (some already proven) are emerging, by which electricity can be put to work more efficiently, particularly on account of the possibility of reducing energy waste by transmission of electrical heat only to the areas where, and at the specific times when, heating is required. Also, the non-energy production costs, including labor and plant maintenance costs, may be reduced and the working conditions upgraded. Furthermore, the ability to control temperature within precise limits may improve the quality of the products.

2.1.2 In a number of countries, substitution of electricity may be beneficial from the point of view of macroeconomic considerations. Again subject to proper optimization of the generation mix, electricity may indeed rely to a lesser degree on imported goods than other energy sources and help cope with foreign exchange constraints (para 1.1).

2.1.3 Electricity may also have a decided advantage from the point of view of reliability of primary energy supply in those countries which must rely one imported energy due to a lack of indigenous resources. For one thing, some degree of substitution between primary energies may be effected quickly in the event of a disruption in supplies, to the extent that the generation mix presents flexibility. Also, those countries which have built a nuclear generating capacity benefit from the relatively low cost of building up a stock of nuclear fuel, as already mentioned in para 1.1.

2.1.4 Assuming an adequate regulation based on cost-related pricing policies, a further advantage of electricity is the relative predictability of its tariffs in an otherwise uncertain energy picture. Tariff predictability is indeed an important point considered by consumers since they need to plan their own investments with as reliable data as possible. This is not to say that electricity prices are predictable within narrow limits since economic uncertainties tend to affect all segments of the economy. However, the reliability and flexibility of primary energy supply referred to in paras 2.1.2 and 2.1.3 do provide a shock absorber capability : the sector can partially offset adverse changes in primary energy prices by appropriate substitution and it may also be more protected than some of its competitors against shifts in foreign exchange rates.

2.2 Electricity substitution for other energy sources to meet end-use demand

The considerations set out above indicate that electricity is becoming increasingly competitive from a national point of view. Its cost is attractive, with the exception of supply during peak periods (see under "pricing policy"). It does not rely to any substantial degree on imported goods and, in particular, oil is being virtually eliminated as a source of primary energy in the French electric sector. Consequently, the foreign exchange component of power supplies is small. Because of these advantages, comparison of electricity with other energy sources -from the point of view of national efficiency- suggests that the former can usefully substitute for the latter in a large spectrum of uses, both in the industrial and residential sectors.

As far as industry is concerned, the principal avenues to be followed in order to promote an efficient use of electricity are :

(1) to accelerate the development of continuous uses based on already proven technologies, such as heating by conduction or induction, drying processes using heat pumps, mechanical vapor recompression, etc ;
(2) to promote off-peak or "summer" dual-energy uses (for steam processes for example), which should benefit from the low level of investment required, and which should be attractive in such sectors as mechanical industries, agro-industries, textiles, paper, etc ;
(3) to prepare for the advent of future technologies, particularly thermal plasmas.

In the residential sector and offices building, one can mention in particular dual-energy heat-pumps for heating -including in individual houses- as well as for some air-conditioning, and water-heating, particularly during summer periods.

As already indicated in Table 2, two load-growth scenarios have been considered. They differ by the GNP growth assumptions made as well as by the degree of success in achieving substitution of electricity. The low scenario -- 350 TWh in 1990, 450 TWh in the year 2000 -- is based on a GNP growth at an average annual rate of 1.5 percent until 1990 and 2.5 percent during the period 1990-2000 ; it includes some degree of substitution taking place spontaneously, based on the evolving relative costs of competing energy sources and on the convenience of use of electricity in a number of applications. The target scenario -- 370 TWh in 1990, 510 TWh in the year 2000 -- is based on a GNP growth at 2 percent per annum until 1990 and 3.5 percent per annum during the period 1990-2000 ; it assumes a more active approach, including information and commercial programs to promote the use of electricity. The resulting increases in consumption, by 20 TWh in 1990 and 60 TWh in the year 2000, are estimates of what can be anticipated on a realistic basis after taking into account the inevitable inertia on the part of the consumers. They can be broken down between industry, residential and offices as shown in Table 3.

Table 3. Electricity substitution in France (TWh)

Scenarios	1990	2000
Low scenario	350	450
Additional consumption		
Industry	12	26
Residential	5	19
Offices	3	15
Target scenario	370	510

2.3 Evolution of the energy market share met by nuclear

The share of total energy needs met by nuclear can be described by a combination of two ratios, obtained by relating nuclear to electricity on the one hand and electricity to total energy on the other. The opening section of this paper covered the first element. The second element is illustrated in Table 4, where all energy amounts have been converted into tons of equivalent oil (TOE).

Table 4. Shares of energy market met by nuclear/electricity

	1984		1990		2000	
	MTOE	%	MTOE	%	MTOE	%
High scenario						
Nuclear electricity	41	23	62	33	91	42
Total electricity	63	35	82	44	113	53
Total energy	179	100	188	100	215	100
Low scenario						
Nuclear electricity	41	23	59	32	78	43
Total electricity	63	35	78	43	100	56
Total energy	179	100	176	100	180	100

2.3 Impact of electricity substitution on pattern

Nuclear energy would be the main source which would be mobilized to meet additional electricity consumption. For example, the 20 TWh difference in 1990 in electricity use between the low and high scenarios would be met mostly by nuclear (70 percent) and coal (30 percent), while the incremental quantity of oil involved would be negligible. Based on reasonable assumptions on the amounts of fuel imports which would thus be avoided, it is estimated that the foreign exchange savings in the year 1990 alone would be about 7 billion francs of 1982, assuming unchanged fuel prices. The 60 TWh difference in the year 2000 would be met to an even larger extent by nuclear, with correspondingly higher foreign exchange savings. Similar data can be established on specific uses. For example, Table 5 shows the percentages of nuclear, coal and oil generation which would be needed to meet an incremental consumption in selected uses :

Table 5. Generation mix to meet incremental consumption (%) (N = Nuclear, C = Coal, O = Oil)

	1984			2000		
	N	C	O	N	C	O
Industrial						
Vapor Recompression	20	75	5	100	-	-
Residential						
Electric Heating	10	70	20	80	20	-
Heat Pump with Oil Back-up	10	80	10	90	10	-
Water Heating	25	65	10	100	-	-

It is then possible to estimate the primary energy shifts and foreign exchange savings associated with the substitution of electricity. While resistance furnaces and heating by conduction or induction are expected to be responsible for about 13 TWh, or one half of additional electricity use in industry by the year 2000, other economically justified processes should not be overlooked, even though of a more modest scope.

For example, mechanical vapor recompression is an efficient process, utilized in particular for concentration of milk products. This process consists of recompressing vapors of the product to be concentrated by means of an electric motor, and feeding them back at higher temperature and pressure as a heat source in the condensor. Thus, only one heat exchanger is needed in the installation, enabling a high efficiency performance where 1 kWh can replace approximately 10 Kcal of alternative energy. It is expected that electricity use in this area could be increased from 1 TWh in the low scenario to 2 TWh in the high scenario in the year 2000. As will be seen from Table 5, this increment of 1 TWh would be met basically by nuclear generation.

Another example is that of dual-energy heat-pumps in existing housing with oil or propane furnaces. Electricity use in individual and collective dual-energy heat-pump installations could be increased altogether from 12 TWh in the low scenario to 18 TWh in the high scenario in the year 2000. About 90 percent of this increment would be met by nuclear.

3. PRICING POLICY AND COMMERCIAL MEASURES

In order to lead consumers towards energy consumption patterns in line with the national interest, one needs both an appropriate pricing policy and a commercial approach. These points are considered below.

3.1 Pricing policy

Load management can be tackled by a combination of pricing mechanisms, physical controls and commercial measures. As is well known, France has historically adopted mainly the first of these approaches, although it is now also relying to some extent on physical control programs through telecontrol facilities and is stepping up its commercial efforts.

France has followed for the past 25 years a policy of basing its electricity pricing system on long-term marginal costs. With the exception of the imbalance caused by the 1974 oil crisis, this has so far worked well. In spite of the difficulties currently experienced in terms of sluggish economic outlook and temporary generation capacity overinvestment, EDF intends to continue applying the same principles, taking into account the new features of the supply-demand situation. A comprehensive pricing study was conducted in the late 70s and early 80s, and its recommendations have been, by and large, implemented.

One of the principal characteristics of the new system is a marked widening in the range of marginal costs during the year. This is due to a combination of two factors : on the supply side, a massive commissioning of nuclear facilities is taking place, while on the demand side there is a continued deterioration of the annual load factor, mainly because residential consumption is growing faster than industrial consumption. At the same time, there is a considerable improvement in the daily load factor. In line with the principle of providing consumers with pricing signals based on long-term costs, it has been recommended to introduce the new cost structures reflecting long-term marginal costs.

It has also appeared desirable to adjust the degree of detail of the tariff system to the capability of consumers to understand and react, and to the corresponding metering costs. Consumer bills are basically dependent on their subscribed demand and on their energy use during various time periods. Also the use of optional tariffs has been reinforced : more options are offered to the clients, the latter becoming more involved in the selection of the tariff option best adapted to their own needs. Three families of tariffs are now offered : green, yellow and blue, depending on consumers' subscribed demand. The green tariff applies to about 20,000 consumers above 250 kVA, and is an improved version of its predecessor. The yellow tariff applies to about 200,000 consumers with a subscribed demand comprised between 36 kVA and 250 kVA, and is a simplified version of the former green tariff. The blue tariff applies to about 23 million low voltage consumers below 36 kVA and is kept as simple as its predecessor.

In addition, "peak day withdrawal" optional tariffs are being introduced to reflect the evolving costs of peak supplies. The latter have changed considerably because of the improvements in the daily load factor on the one hand and the increase in sensitivity of the load to temperature changes on the other. The peak period now covers a large number of hours per day during a small number of days during the year. These peak-days do, however, occur at unforseeable dates. The peak day withdrawal options -offered to small as well as large consumers- therefore aim at dealing with this situation. They include a peak-period consisting of 18 hours on 22 days which are selected by the producer in real time, based on the operational difficulties of all kinds which may be encountered (low temperature of course, but also possibly unscheduled outages and low hydro inflows). The energy prices vary even more widely than with the standard tariffs, as evidenced in Tables 6, which show some of the tariffs proposed to customers below 36 kVA :

Table 6. Tariffs for subscribed demand below 36 kVA
(Excerpt for 12 kVA only)
(Effective February 15, 1985)

	Basic Tariff	Time-of-day Tariff	Peak-day Withdrawal
Fixed charge (francs)	1148.40	1583.04	694.80
Energy charges (c/kWh)			
Peak hours/days	50.70	50.70	295.00
Off-peak	50.70	29.00	32.45

The "peak-day withdrawal" tariffs are particularly suitable for providing an incentive for developing dual-energy systems : for example, space-heating where an oil furnace already exists. Coupled with high oil costs, these tariffs provide stronger incentives for the combined use of electricity and oil : the bulk of needs being supplied by low cost electricity while limited amounts of oil are used during a small number of hours per year when electricity is costly. The resulting operational savings can be large enough to pay for the installation of appropriate equipment.

3.2 Commercial aspects

An appropriate program of commercial measures is necessary because of the fact that consumers' subjective decision-making criteria may differ from the objective national efficiency criteria. A number of difficulties are encountered :

(1) Both industrial and residential consumers tend to behave more like imitators than innovators and are reluctant to switch to electricity if it involves a new process. It is therefore necessary to implement credible pilot programmes in order to establish the feasibility of the new processes.

(2) There is a general scarcity of investment capital which may lead consumers to adopt very stringent investment criteria, implying rates or return higher than the social rate of discount of 9 percent in real terms.

Financial mechanisms must be established to ensure that consumers receive appropriate financial assistance to help promote energy decisions --concerning uses as well as conservation -- in line with the national energy policy.

(3) Consumers are not well informed about the relative costs of the various energy sources available to them.

(4) The perceived risks of power curtailments may hinder the development of electricity.

(5) It should finally be added that there is in some quarters a view that electricity should generally not be transformed into heating energy --except for specific efficient uses -- on the grounds that this is wasteful in terms of primary energy consumption. In this respect it is necessary to emphasize that the relevant evaluation criterion should not concern primary energy alone. It should rather be the net overall effect in economic terms, i.e. combining volume and price effects in one integrated evaluation.

28
Exporting Blue Gold: Who Will Absorb the Forecast Risk?

Mitchell P. Rothman, Ontario Hydro

As the Chief Economist of Ontario Hydro, I am responsible both for forecasts of the Ontario economy and of our electricity sales. We are a government-owned electrical utility, supplying almost all of the Province of Ontario. We have installed capacity of about 25,000 megawatts to serve a peak load that last year reached about 19,500 megawatts. Last year we were the largest corporation in Canada, ranked by total assets.

Our current generation mix is about one-third each from hydraulic, nuclear and conventional thermal (coal-fired) resources. By the end of this decade we expect over half of our power supply to be nuclear, with only 10 percent coal-fired.

We are building a ten billion dollar four-unit nuclear station scheduled to come into service between 1988 and 1992. Despite external critics, who question its usefulness, Ontario Hydro believes that by the year 2000 we will need it plus some additional sources of electricity. Without too much exaggeration, I can say that this belief is related directly to my forecast of electricity sales.

So my company is betting billions of dollars on my economic and electricity sales forecasts. But why should my senior management believe my forecasts?

FORECAST UNCERTAINTY

In fact, I don't expect or want them to "believe" any one forecast - including mine - in the sense that they act as if it is the only possible outcome. Forecasts are much too uncertain for that.

In my forecasts, I emphasize that uncertainty. I tell management that my preferred long-term forecast only represents the center of the most-likely range. One reason they should use my forecasts, then, is that I don't claim certainty: rather I give them some of the information they need to cope with an uncertain future.

How wide is the band of uncertainty, what makes it broader or narrower, how useful is the forecast for planning, and what planning options do we have?

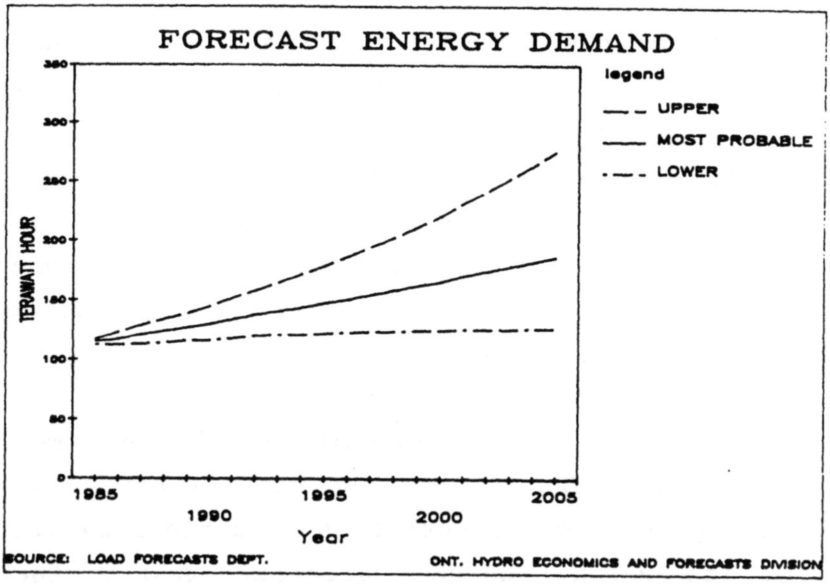

Chart 1. Demand Forecast With 60% Probability Bands

Chart 1 quantifies the uncertainty: it shows a 60 percent confidence interval for the Ontario Hydro 15-year forecast. Relative to the system, the most-likely forecast has total load just above the planned capacity. But there is a 20 percent probability that we will not need any of the new capacity we are building. There is also a 20 percent chance that we will need a system about twice as large as planned.

This probability calculation assumes that the future is about as predictable as the past was, and that the the forecast is about as accurate. I think that these assumptions do not overstate the amount of uncertainty.

One contributor to uncertainty is the length of the forecast horizon. We have good information on how much electricity we will sell tomorrow because we know how much we sold today. Since the stock of electricity-using capital equipment changes only slowly over time, today's sales tell us very much about tomorrow's. Over periods up to two years, we can use time-series techniques to produce the lowest variance forecasts.

But the longer-term picture is much more confusing. The size of the capital stock, its energy-using characteristics, and the intensity of its use all become variable. Add to that the greater uncertainty in long-term forecasts of economic activity, and it is clear that long-term electricity sales forecasts are highly uncertain.

How can such an uncertain forecast be useful to an electrical utility? Ontario Hydro's planning horizon is from fifteen to forty years. Can the message that we may need no, one, or half a dozen new nuclear stations help the planners design a system?

I think that message is not only useful, it is essential. I will tell you why after looking at the sources of the uncertainty.

SOURCES OF FORECAST UNCERTAINTY

Uncertainty in long-term load forecasting can be broken into uncertainty about two apparently simple questions: how fast the economy will grow, and how fast demand for electricity will grow relative to total economic activity.

Recently, Bill Hogan (1984) showed that there has been no unexplained break in the pattern of energy and electricity use. The observed decrease in energy intensity of output is simply a response to the changes in relative prices of energy. Electricity intensity has not fallen as much as energy intensity because of its lower rate of price increase.

Hogan's analysis implies that the uncertainty is about relative prices of electricity and of energy, not about autonomous conservation. Autonomous conservation does not exist. The only relevant questions for conservation are whether relative electricity prices will change, and how much of the adjustment to previous price changes is already done.

The question can be put as whether the income elasticity of electricity demand will be above or below one. Chart 2 tracks electricity and energy intensity of the Canadian economy.

Total energy intensity fell from 1974 to 1976, then levelled off until 1980. The large drop in total energy intensity after 1980 followed both the second OPEC price shock and, more importantly, controls that allowed higher Canadian oil prices. Electricity intensity has increased steadily, because real electricity prices in Canada did not increase as fast as fossil fuel prices.

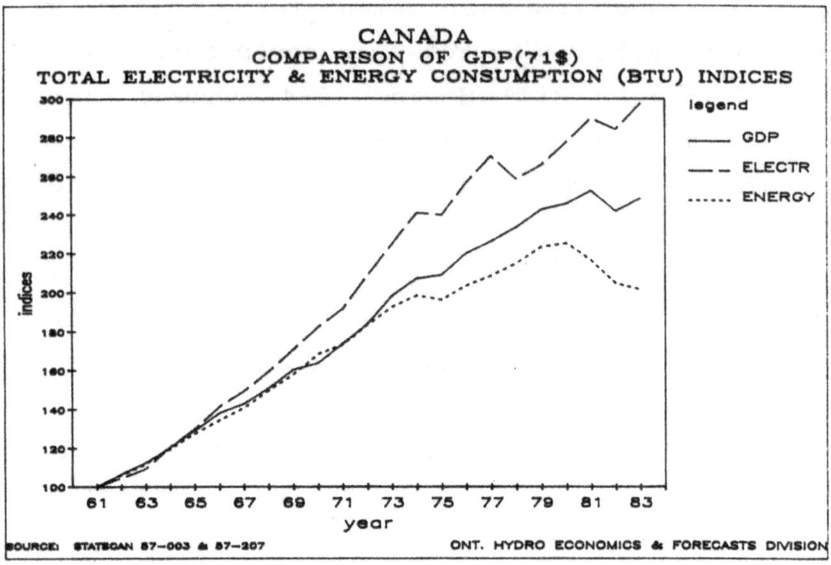

Chart 2. Electricity & Energy Consumption to GDP

A plot of the observed income elasticity of electricity sales would show extreme volatility, but not much trend, and an average value above one. In Ontario the pattern is similar--energy intensity has been falling, but electricity demand has been rising both in absolute terms and relative to the economy as a whole.

Since historical values of income elasticity demand are all above one, the forecaster who puts it less than one must be heroic. The differences are significant. Chart 3 shows electricity demand for Ontario Hydro under several assumed values of income elasticity, taking the economic forecast as correct. By

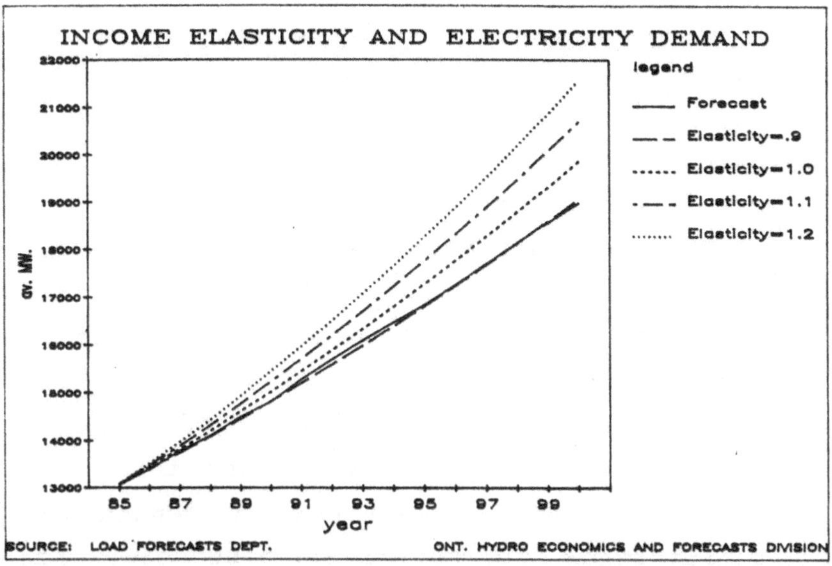

Chart 3. Income Elasticity & Electricity Demand

the year 2000, electricity demand with an elasticity of 1.0 is about 2000 megawatts higher than with an elasticity of 0.9. The difference is about the annual output of our four-unit Pickering-"A" Nuclear Generating Station.

The value of the long-run income elasticity has been debated widely elsewhere. I do not want to enter that debate. But I do want to cast it in the appropriate terms. Following Bill Hogan, I think that the answer comes from analysis of the effects of the relative prices of energy and of electricity, along with analysis of the effects of other structural changes.

ONTARIO HYDRO FORECAST

Ontario Hydro's forecasts that electricity sales will grow more slowly than the provincial economy over the next twenty years. Economic growth is forecast to average 2.8 percent, with electricity demand growth at 2.5 percent.

This forecast attracts criticism from both sides. The environmentalists say our prices are too high and we have grossly underestimated conservation, even under the existing price structure. Econometric forecasters think the forecast is too low, because they think that income elasticity of electricity demand will not fall below one, especially since electricity prices are forecast to rise slower than those of competing fuels. They conclude that we have overestimated conservation.

However, conservation alone does not drive the forecast. The three basic factors reducing the forecast are the remaining effect of the real electricity price increases in the 1970's, demographics, and the effect of a changing industrial structure on energy use.

Large energy and electricity price rises were delayed until the late 1970s in Canada. Given the long time it takes to replace the capital stock, we have still not felt the full effect of these relative price increases. Demographic factors strongly influence growth in demand for electricity in the residential and commercial sectors. Since both population and number of households will be growing more slowly than the economy in the 1990s, the demographics will help keep electricity demand growth rates low.

Finally, the most energy-intensive industries in Ontario are metal mining, smelting and refining, forest products, chemicals, and nonmetallic minerals products. These resource-based industries are highly vulnerable to competition from emerging third-world exporters. Our forecast assumes that they will diminish in importance for Ontario, and their replacements will not be as energy intensive.

To summarize, Ontario electricity demand is forecast to grow somewhat more slowly than economic activity, even though relative prices will favor electricity over fossil fuels. However, I do not assume autonomous improvements in energy efficiency, but rather the effects of previous price increases, demographics, and industrial structure.

DEALING WITH UNCERTAINTY

But the planners need more than a central forecast and a "confidence" interval. They want to test their plans against several possible future states of the world. So we produce alternative scenarios which are, in effect, completely specified alternative forecasts. Each scenario is assigned a subjective probability as the center of a range of similar possible outcomes.

I have just described two ways to quantify future uncertainties, each essentially suited to different uses in the planning process. The probability bands presume ignorance of the future, so we must assume that it will be like the past. Scenarios depend on certain central assumptions that produce the described future.

These two approaches are used by different groups in the Corporation in different ways.

The finance group uses the probability ranges to perform Monte Carlo simulations. We estimated probability distributions as an extension of the methodology we used to produce the uncertainty bands. Then they asked for joint distributions to account for the interdependence among the variables. The problem is that the distribution of the real rate of interest in Canada for every year up to 2000 is hard enough to estimate with confidence; it is worse to have to estimate its joint distribution with, say, the rate of inflation in those years. We must be careful not to treat the resulting simulation results as precise, even if they are presented to five decimal places.

The generation planners use the scenarios rather than the ranges. They need completely worked out sets of consistent numbers to evaluate the impact of possible system additions. The scenarios, as complete forecasts, already contain the information on the joint results for interdependent variables.

These allow complete system and financial analysis of alternative plans under each scenario.

I am a little uncomfortable with the heavy reliance that planners are putting on what I recognize are risky forecasts. But I am very happy about two things: first, they are paying attention, and second, we have successfully communicated that there is uncertainty.

WHO TAKES THE RISK?

One result of this focus on uncertainty is that the Corporation is becoming more ready to incur costs to guard against the risk of incorrect forecasts. It buys insurance against technological risk by diversifying its sources of generation; now it knows it has to get some kind of insurance against forecast risk.

Previously, Ontario Hydro's public ownership encouraged it to weigh undercapacity risk more heavily than overcapacity, because it could consider total social costs. Private utilities assume more risk if they have overcapacity, since a regulatory commission could refuse to allow the "insurance" facilities into the rate base, while the customers suffer most shortage costs.

Recently, as the overcapacity costs have dominated, the public has become more critical of the earlier decisions. So have we in Ontario Hydro. Because we are paying the price now of ignoring some risks in the past, we are more ready to pay something now to avoid similar costs in the future.

But insurance does not come cheap. Insurance in the usual sense is available only if a number of entities face a similar but independent risk. That is not the case for utilities. If economic growth or recession makes one utility short or long on capacity, its neighbors will probably have the same problem.

In fact, many North American utilities have come to realize how much risk they face. One reaction is to try to shift the risk to someone else. The candidates are the utility's customers, its suppliers, maybe some neighboring utilities, or the taxpayers in the utility's service area. If none of these will pick up the risk, then it must wind up back on the utility's owners or its bondholders.

The risk always used to fall on the customers. They bear most of the undercapacity risk, since they would have to cut back their business or household activity if there were not enough electricity. They can also bear the overcapacity risk if the regulatory commissions allow the resulting facilities go into the rate base. However, the commissions have become increasingly reluctant to do that.

The suppliers have typically not been willing to assume much risk, even when - as in technological areas - they are really responsible for it. They will in any case not take on more risk for free. Most likely, the price of the contracts would go up in compensation.

Similarly, taxpayers have not been good candidates. Governments have become even more reluctant than they ever were to bail out utilities. It is much more likely to get a balky regulatory commission to allow some facilities into the rate base than it is to get a government to pick up some of their cost. That leaves the neighbouring utilities.

Neighboring utilities can help some. For example, Ontario and the adjacent U.S. utilities have peak demands in different seasons. However, seasonal interchanges cannot help with the capacity problem because they are not firm.

Some U.S. utilities could try to shift undercapacity risk to Canada. British Columbia, Manitoba and Quebec could build more hydraulic generation facilities for export. Can the U.S. utilities get Canadian utilities to absorb some of the risk for them?

My answer is no. The Canadian utilities know all about the risk of negotiating long-term electricity sales contracts without proper regard for alternative futures. Right now, for example, Quebec is buying electricity from Newfoundland at under one cent a Kwh, and that price is guaranteed for another 40 years. No one will be signing contracts like that again.

So if we are to get much help on the undercapacity risk from our neighbours, it will generally have to be in the form of long-term firm exports.

Our own discussions with our Canadian neighbors indicate that they will not be willing to assume much of the forecast risk if they sell us power from new hydraulic generation sites.

However, they may well want some share of the price risk. Because Newfoundland did not want to do that, they lost out on some substantial profits from their hydraulic power resources.

CONCLUSION

If the utilities cannot lay off risks on each other, and cannot readily buy insurance, then they must try to manage the risk. That means we must look for options that are less risky in themselves, and that can be reversed more easily if we are wrong.

Such options are likely to make power more expensive than we could get if we knew the future with certainty. That additional expense is a cost imposed by the risk.

I do not mean that we should abandon all plans for large-scale centralized generation facilities. The system is too big and the costs of smaller generation too high for that. What I do mean is that we must carefully explore all the options available to us, including demand-management programs and smaller-scale generation, before we commit ourselves to new, large projects. We should plan to use some smaller options to reduce our risk-adjusted costs, even if they are more expensive than large-scale.

Flexibility costs money. In an inherently risky situation, utilities must pay the price and buy as much flexibility as their own situation warrants, after careful analysis of the risks and the options available.

REFERENCES

Government of Canada, Department of Energy, Mines & Resources, Electric Power in Canada 1984

Government of Canada, Statistics Canada, Quarterly Report on Energy Supply-Demand in Canada, Various years

Hogan, William W., "Patterns of Energy Use," John F. Kennedy School of Goernment, Harvard University, May, 1984

National Energy Board of Canada, Canadian Energy Supply & Demand 1983-2005, 1984

29
Deregulate the Electric Industry

John R. Siegel, Atomic Industrial Forum

The nation is headed for a serious electric supply crisis. Why? Because the demand for electricity is rapidly increasing while rate regulatory disincentives continue to exist regarding investment in major new facilities. The solution: deregulate the bulk power sales market for all new generating facilities irrespective of whether they are large or small scale.

FAILED REGULATION OF THE ELECTRIC INDUSTRY IN THE RECENT PAST HAS RAISED THE ISSUE OF ELECTRIC SUPPLY PROBLEMS

Quite recently, some regulators have begun to shift towards market policies which <u>seek</u> to encourage more cost effective electric production. This has come about in part due to a realization that current utility strategies may not, in the long run, be in the ratepayer's or the nation's best interest. These strategies are the result of the failure of rate regulation in the recent

The views presented are solely those of the author.

period of high inflation, poor economic growth, and rising fuel costs, and a resultant diminishing of utility financial health.

A few examples of the current environment:

- o Utilities discuss commitments to combustion turbines to meet electric demand, citing not lead-time constraints, but "regulatory uncertainty".

- o Last July, FERC (Federal Energy Regulatory Commission) denied the New State Power Authority a construction license to build a 1000 MWe pumped storage unit in Prattsville, N.Y. The application was filed in 1977.

- o The ongoing permitting and financing process for the Seabrook plant would give Lewis Carroll reason to pause.

- o PURPA (the Public Utility Regulatory Policy Act of 1978) is being abused:

  (Some) utilities encourage, and (some) regulators applaud, the addition of alternative or "least cost" energy sources which are neither least cost nor reliable; for example, wind sources with the "potential"[1] to produce electricity at 10-15¢/Kwhr...double to triple the price of oil; sources dubbed "the juiciest tax shelters in the land" by Forbes magazine;

- FERC is deluged with hundreds of "PURPA" based cogeneration facility applications, most of which are modified jet engines, using as fuels those "dwindling natural resources" which PURPA was designed to save;[2]

- Cogenerators petition to sell utilities electricity at avoided costs and buy it back at industrial rates;

- A regulatory commission disallows inclusion in the rate base of a completed coal plant on the premise that it is not "used and useful"...while simultaneously requiring the utility to contract with small producers for power at "avoided costs" higher than the life cycle costs of the coal plant.

You can count on one hand the number of firm commitments for base load power plants in the United States since 1978. Of necessity, electric utilities have adopted a "capital aversion strategy" which is predicated more on maintaining financial health and less on providing a reliable and cost effective supply of electricity.

This strategy is the by-product of the existing regulatory process. The electric supply sector--unlike the supply sectors of the gas and oil industry--continues to operate under price controls. The same inefficiences which exist in any regulated business with excessive government intrusion are now hamstringing the United States electric supply sector.

Investment decisions are made with the knowledge that risks will be borne primarily by the stockholder, while benefits flow to the consumer. No wonder the current utility behavior. It is quite predictable, given this uneven playing field.

Unfortunately, the consumer--as always--will soon pick up the tab for the inefficiencies of the current system. In effect, the electric sector is painstakingly acting out the final phase of the "energy crisis."

Demand is rapidly outrunning supply. If current trends continue, by the end of 1985 demand will up about 12% since 1982. Supply, only 5%. And only 7% additional supply is under construction.

A shortage is inevitable. The only question is when. Industry and DOE say the early 1990s. On a scenario which reflects the changed economy and electricity's improved price competitiveness

...the late 1980s. In either case, it is already too late to respond in a cost-effective manner, given the lead times for base load construction.

The implications: electric reliability problems will become wide-spread by 1990; marginal prices will rise as inefficient capacity is thrown on line; and the use of oil and gas to produce electricity will go from 3 MBD (million barrels per day, oil equivalent) today to 8-9 MBD by 1990, putting pressure on oil and gas prices and raising oil imports.

THE HIGH GROWTH SCENARIO

High electric growth in the 1980s is based on improved economic growth and electricity's dramatically improved price competitiveness.[3] Sustained economic growth averaging 3.5-4% per year, versus the 2.2% of the 1973-1982 period, is predicated on:

- The success of the Administration's economic policy--A long term program focused on controlling inflation through consistent monetary policies and reducing tax and regulatory burdens, thus encouraging incentives to invest in new capital stock

- Stable or falling energy prices--Driven by falling oil prices in the 1980s, versus the 170% run-up in real retail energy prices in the 1970s

- Increased productivity and real income growth --The result of a declining rate of increase in the labor force in the 1980s, in marked contrast to the 1970s, increased capital investment and low inflation.

According to conventional wisdom, 3.5-4% sustained economic growth correlates into 3.5-4% electric growth. But owing to electricity's improved price position, it is probable that <u>the electric growth-to-GNP ratio is turning up:</u>

- Electric penetration into oil and natural gas markets ("cross" price elasticity effects), due to the much greater run-up in oil and gas prices has offset any reduced electric demand due to "own" price elasticity effects. As a result, electricity continues to increase its energy market share, from 27% in 1973 to 35% in 1984 (Exhibits 1 and 2).

- The relationship of electric growth to GNP appears to be a nonlinear function of the magnitude of GNP...increasing with increasing levels of GNP. This has been the case over the last 30 years and reflects increasing capital spending, a precursor of increased productivity, and personal income gains. Upturns in the ratio of load growth to GNP appear to lag capital spending trends by about 2 years, which, in turn, lag economic upturns by 12-18 months.

EXHIBIT 1

ELECTRICITY'S SHARE OF THE ENERGY MARKET HAS INCREASED SIGNIFICANTLY

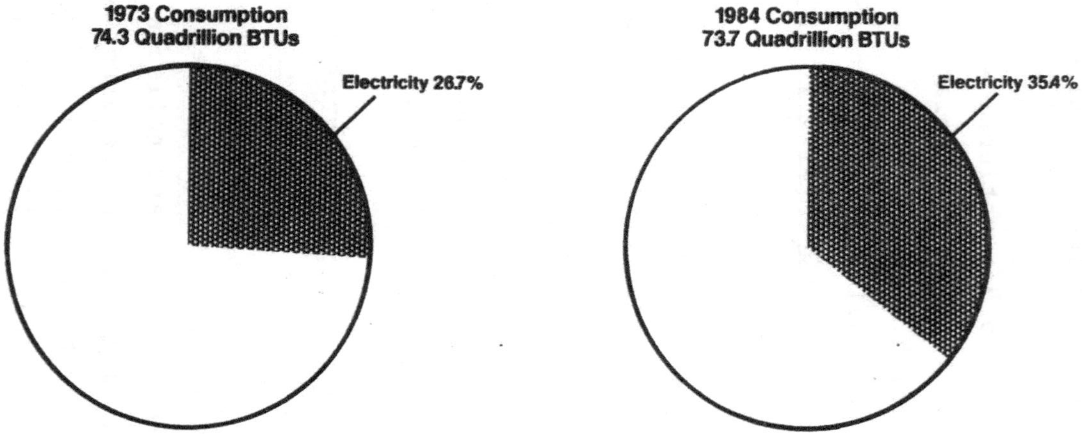

Source: DOE/EIA Monthly Energy Review, March 1985

EXHIBIT 2

RECENT RELATIVE PRICE CHANGES OF THE PRIMARY ENERGY COMMODITIES HAVE ENHANCED ELECTRICITY'S MARKET ATTRACTIVENESS

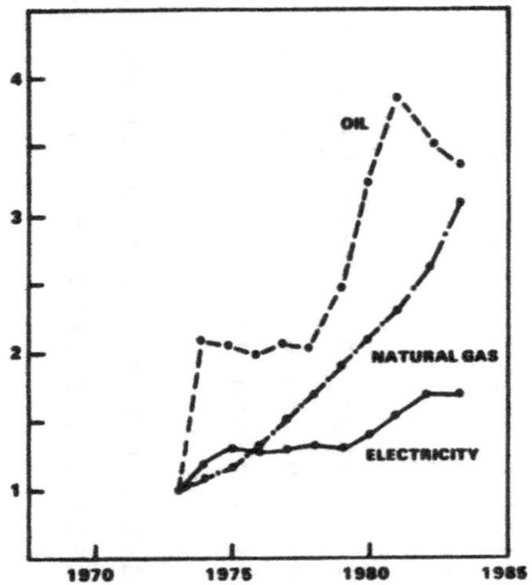

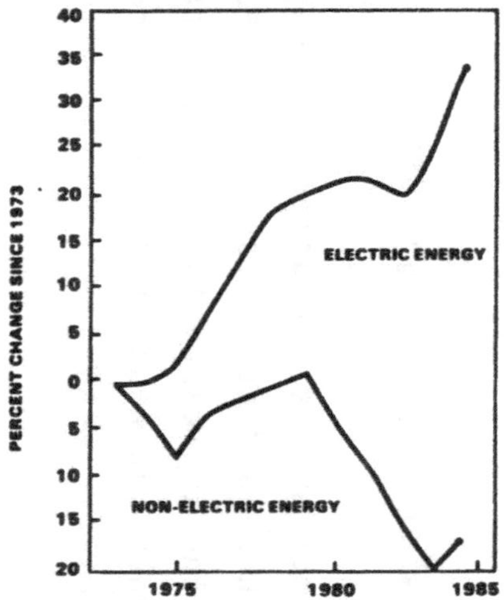

NATURAL GAS — PRICE IS AVERAGE OF RESIDENTIAL HEATING GAS
OIL — PRICE IS AVERAGE OF HOME HEATING OIL
ELECTRICITY — PRICE IS AVERAGE OF RESIDENTIAL, COMMERCIAL AND INDUSTRIAL CHARGE

SOURCE: DOE, *MONTHLY ENERGY REVIEW*

- Real electric prices could decline throughout the 1980s--at about a 1.5% annual rate--owing to continued stable fuel prices, increased use of nuclear and coal fuel, and declining unit production costs as reserve margins decline from 41% in 1982 to 20% later in the decade.

THE RECENT DATA SHOULD FOCUS THE ELECTRIC DEBATE

Reviewing 1983 through 1985:

- The economy has rebounded strongly. Real GNP has increased about 13% since 1982. Capital spending increased 14% in 1984, the biggest one-year increase in 28 years, and continued strongly in 1985.

- Retail energy prices are off about 12% since 1982, led by falling oil and natural gas prices.

- Electric output and peak load increases are exceeding expectations. Each has increased about 12% since 1982.

This data should serve to focus recent arguments on future electric prices and demand:

- The "low-growthers" have been proven wrong--A number of individuals predicting electric growth rates for the 1980s in the 0-2% range have clearly missed the mark. Exhibit 3 presents actuals versus several mid-1982 estimates.

EXHIBIT 3

COMPARISON OF PROJECTED GROWTH IN ELECTRIC OUTPUT

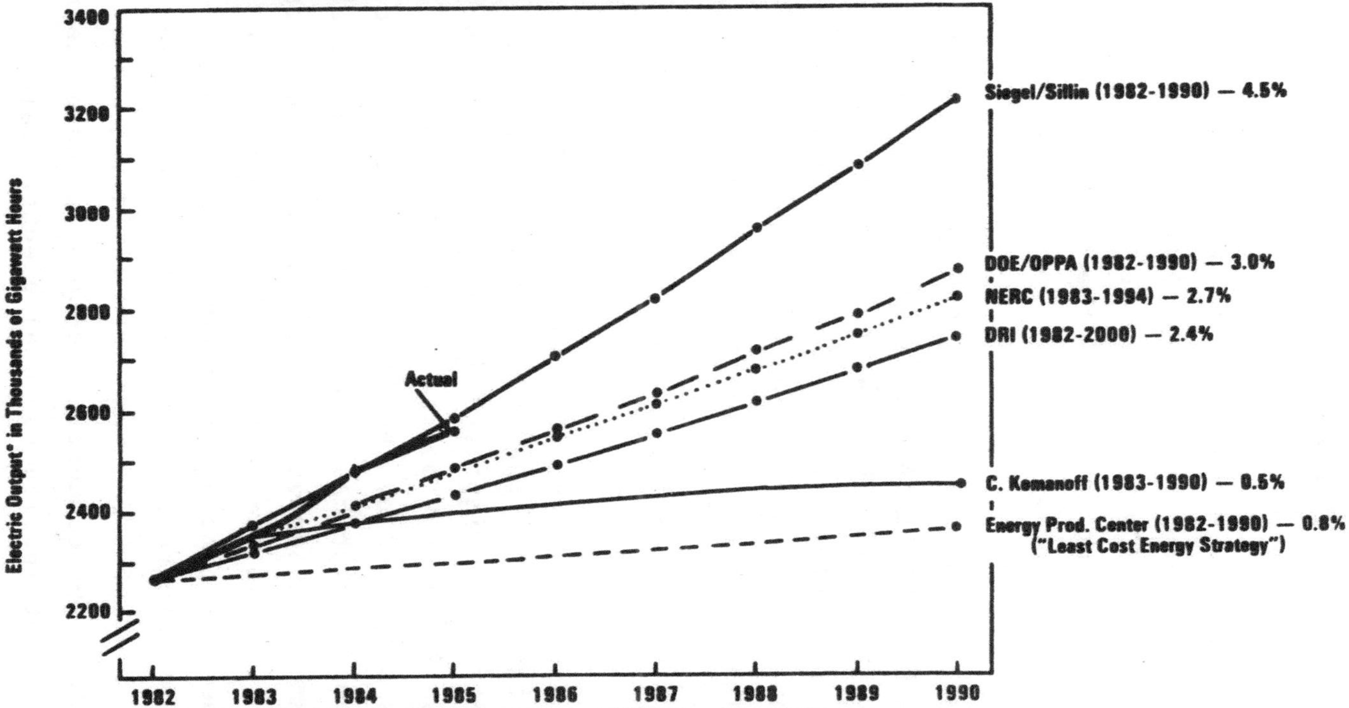

*Electric Output: Total electricity made available for consumption; per EEI "Total Source," Quarterly Report.

NOTE: Due to difficulties in identifying the first forecast year of each projection, and the fact that some projections are changed on an annual basis, 1982 was assumed to be the base year. Exceptions: NERC and C. Komanoff, whose base year was determined to be 1983; 1985 point is an estimate and assumes 3% growth. Sources: Energy productivity center estimate taken from "Eight Great Energy Myths," R.W. Sant and D.W. Bakke, 1981 (Note: 0.8% not a "forecast," but a discussion of a possible outcome if "technology applied on a basis of economic self interest"); C. Komanoff, from Nucleonics Week, 10/84.

- <u>Real electric prices are falling</u>--Prices at the national level are off 2% since 1982 (Exhibit 4), in spite of the "expensive" plant now entering service. This falling price trend should accelerate in the late 1980s as less and less plant is put into service.[4] The great "fly-up" in electric prices is rapidly going the way of the natural gas fly-up rhetoric.

- <u>A strong correlation between electric growth and GNP continues to exist</u>--The electric output to GNP (EO/GNP) ratio has averaged 0.85 the past five years. This correlation continues despite the fact that the impact of higher personal income and accelerating capital investment are only beginning to be felt in the electric sector.

In addition, the electric content of GNP should increase as the cross elasticity effects of electricity's improved price competitiveness increase its energy market share. This hypothesis is supported by the dramatic upturn in electric demand which has occurred in the residential and commercial sectors. Over the past five years, demand in these two sectors is running at about 1.5 times the rate of GNP growth. This trend should contribute to a rise in the overall electric content of GNP as the more rapidly growing residential and commercial sectors increase their relative contribution to total electric sales. Since 1979, this has increased from 54% to 61%.

EXHIBIT 4

SINCE 1982, REAL ELECTRIC PRICES HAVE BEEN FALLING

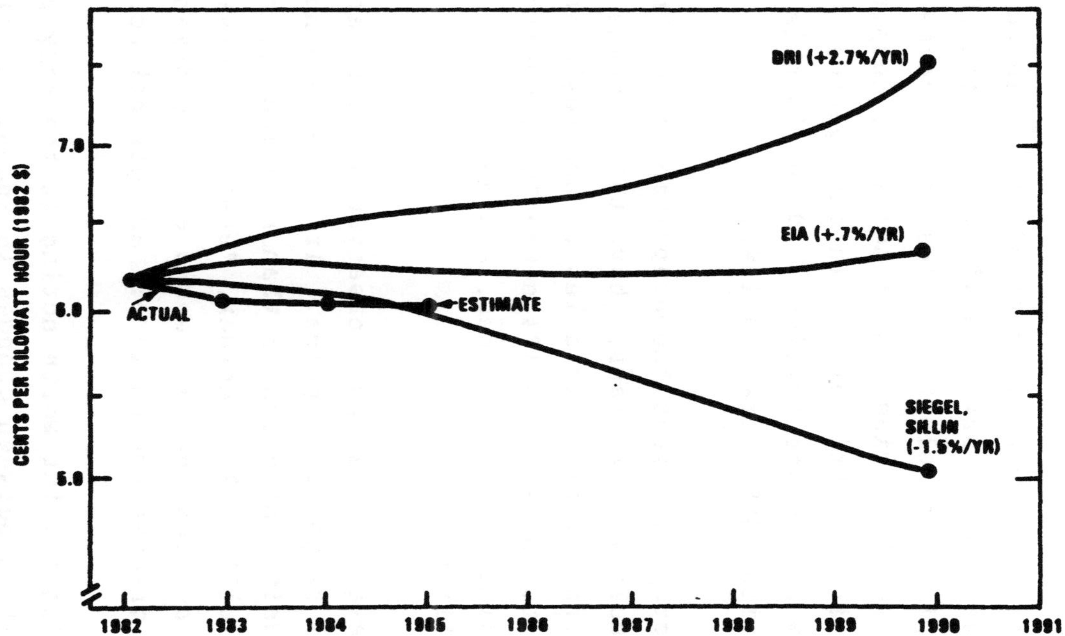

SOURCES: J. SIEGEL AND J. SILLIN, "CHANGES IN THE REAL PRICE OF ELECTRICITY: IMPLICATIONS FOR HIGHER GROWTH", *PUBLIC UTILITIES FORTNIGHTLY*, SEPTEMBER 15, 1983. EIA (ENERGY INFORMATION AGENCY) AND DRI (DATA RESOURCES, INC.) PROJECTIONS, TAKEN FROM DOE'S JUNE 1983, *THE FUTURE OF ELECTRIC POWER IN AMERICA*.

This suggests a question for advocates who laud conservation to hold down electric demand. Specifically, when one cites:

o This "energy efficient" office building or that "energy saving device," have the advocate explain why electric sales to the commercial sector have risen 26% since 1979, despite rising electric prices in this period, and now prices are falling. (Note: in this same period, GNP increased 13%.)

o Energy efficient "home appliances" or "home insulation programs," have the advocate explain why electric sales to the residential sector have risen 17% since 1979, despite rising electric prices, and now prices are falling.

The answer is that conservation is by and large a response to price. If prices are not rising significantly faster than real income, conservation will fail. Further, "energy conservation" has translated into increased electric demand due to the greater run-up in oil and gas prices.

A final point worth noting is the very poor correlation between changes in industrial electric sales and GNP since 1979. This would appear to be largely due to little or no change in industrial production since the electric content of industrial production has been steady. This sluggish industrial production appears to be largely a function of the U.S. dollar which appreciated roughly 60% on a trade weighted basis between 1979 and early 1985. The recent decline in the dollar should contribute to a strengthening industrial sector in 1986.

ELECTRIC RELIABILITY WILL BECOME AN ISSUE BY 1990

On a high growth scenario, national reserve margins shrink to 20% by 1990 (Exhibit 5). Reliability problems will manifest in some regions before 1990. The Northeast is one of these regions.

Significant commitments to central station technology are needed today (Exhibit 6). Commitments in the range of 30 to 40 GWe per year. This is not occurring.

Finally, alternative energy sources can not fill this gap. The total supply of alternatives ranges between 30 and 60 GWe by the year 2000, depending on electric price assumptions. This is 1-2 years supply on the high growth scenario.

POLICY RECOMMENDATIONS: DEREGULATE THE SUPPLY OF NEW SOURCES OF ELECTRICITY

Congress should enact legislation which deregulates the supply of new sources of electricity. That is, legislation which allows any entity--utility or non--to construct and operate any size electric plant and to wholesale the plant output

EXHIBIT 5

WITH A 4 TO 5% GROWTH SCENARIO, RESERVE MARGINS FALL BELOW 20% BETWEEN 1988 AND 1990

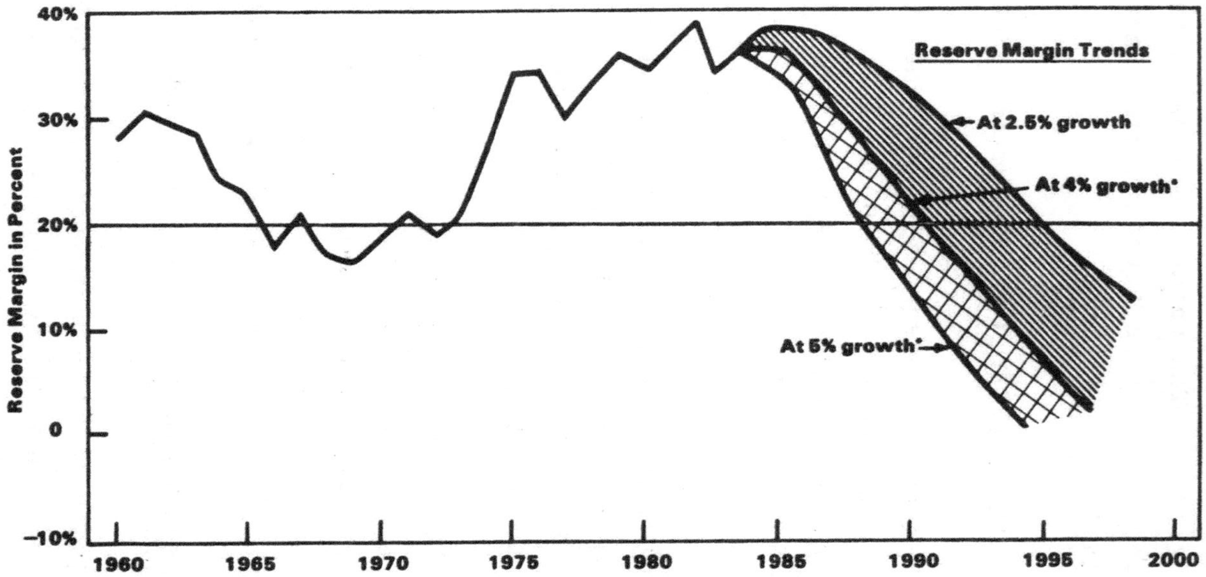

*Assumed: Peak load annual increase of 4% and 5% through 1990, and respectively, 3% and 4% to 2000.

NOTE: Historically, a national reserve margin of approximately 20% has been identified as that which is consistent with reliable electric service. For some regions a reserve margin as low as 15% and as high as 25% may be more appropriate, reflecting regional grid capabilities and peaking phenomena.

Source: Available Resources, 7/84 National Electric Reliability Council "Electric Power Supply and Demand"

EXHIBIT 6

POWER PLANT ORDERING TRENDS AND PROJECTIONS*

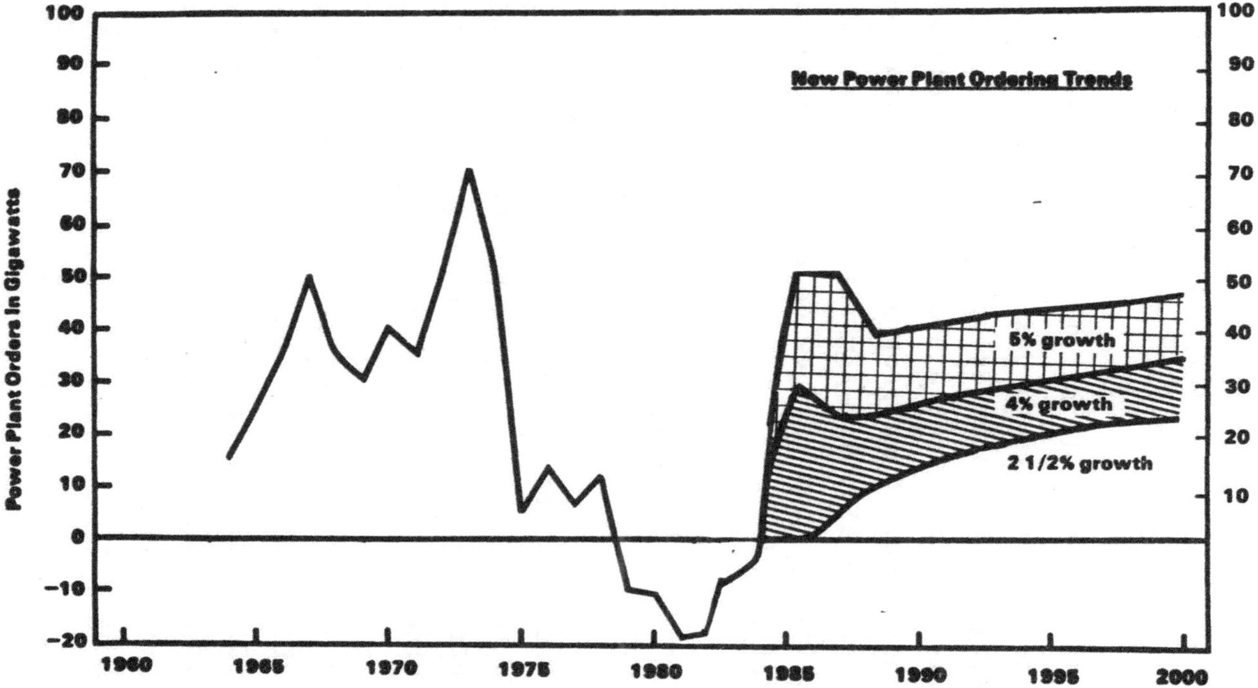

*Projections of plant orders assume an 8 year licensing and construction lead time and maintenance of a 20% capacity reserve margin; growth is annual peak load increase; 4% assumed to decrease to 3% after 1990; 5% assumed to decrease to 4% after 1990.

at whatever price the market will bear. Specifically, the price for electricity generated by new capacity should not be subject to any pricing formula. And new capacity to be defined to include coal, nuclear and all other centralized, as well as decentralized options.

This concept is similar to the recent price de-control of oil and gas supply; and more narrowly, PURPA clauses opening the electric supply sector to certain qualifying facilities and entities. This proposal takes PURPA one step further, by allowing <u>any</u> entity to market the electricity from <u>any</u> new generation source at market rates.

Deregulation of the electric supply sector would:

- o Result in true competition among the various alternatives, stimulating innovation and efficiency, thus encouraging least cost electric supply options.

- o Provide benefits to suppliers commensurate with risks taken, thus enhancing management efficiency in the construction and operation of new plants; specifically, investors could earn higher rates of return in exchange for increased risk of capital intensive options.

- o Encourage non-utilities to invest in the electric sector, thus bringing new capital, management, and engineering resources into the electric sector.

- o Increase system reliability as base load generation would be encouraged.

As the electric industry restructures to take advantage of free market opportunities, some rate commissions would be forced to change policies which are not only anti-utility, but anti-central station technology. Further, the risk of 20-20 political/regulatory hindsight would be eliminated to the extent "3rd party" electric supplies would be protected by the legal process and "take and pay contracts."

This anti-central station bias underscores what is perhaps the greatest irony of PURPA's implementation...that to a large measure, marginally priced supply options are backing out future base load generation additions. Thus, the process is institutionalizing higher electric prices.

Finally,renewables should be put on the same tax status as central station technologies. Windmills and other so-called renewable supply options can presently avail themselves of large tax breaks. Without these tax subsidies, little commercial investment in renewables would occur. These tax subsidies should be eliminated.

Returning to the question of reliability, if a market exists for electricity, and if a competitor is allowed to compete in this market and earn a fair return on his investment, there will be no shortage of private interests bidding to provide the service. And if the service is provided with conventional base load technology--that which the United States has used for the past 100 years--the reliability of service will be far better than the hodge-podge of supply options that current trends portend: windmills with capacity factors of 15%, cogeneration supply which may wane if the core business (e.g., petrochemical refining) declines, or Canadian supplies which could be withdrawn in the early 1990s to meet Canada's own requirements at the exact time the United States will be in short supply.

References

1. "Windmills Close the Gap," Energy Daily, February 19, 1985.

2. Per Table 5.4 in Creating Abundance: America's Least Cost Energy Strategy (by R. Sant, D. Bakke, and R. Naill, McGraw Hill, 1984) 75% of the planned co-generation capacity additions in the 1980s would use natural gas.

3. Siegel, John R. and John O. Sillin, "Rethinking Utility Strategy under Conditions of High Growth," Public Utilities Fortnightly, September 13, 1984.

4. The Energy Information Agency, in its 1/85 Annual Energy Outlook, now projects falling real electric prices over the next ten years.

30
Planning to Meet Future Electricity Demand: A Look at the Economics of the Nuclear and Coal Option

John H. Crowley, Mark A. Bernstein,
United Engineers & Constructors Inc.

INTRODUCTION

In the next few years, some electric utilities will begin planning for capacity expansion to either replace electric generating units being retired and/or to meet increasing demand. When evaluating new or replacement generation requirements, these utilities will take into consideration a number of key factors; including the long-term need for power, the fuel mix of the current generation capacity, the relative financial position of the utility and the total generation cost of the capacity to be added. This paper addresses the latter consideration.

Current base load power generation is dependent primarily on nuclear and coal energy sources. Technical feasibility and economic factors should dictate that these two technologies will be chosen for baseload power in the short term with most planners leaning toward the fossil alternative. This paper focuses on these alternatives and will evaluate historical trends in costs, and expectations for the future of these technologies.

Two basic methods for evaluating capital and generation costs are econometric analyses and engineering-economic analyses. (An econometric analysis is presented in another paper in this session and will not be addressed here.) The engineering-economic approach to cost estimating which will be introduced here allows for detailed comparisons between different plants, between common systems and components in each plant, and between site, and geographic location features.

The paper is divided into three main sections. The first includes an explanation of data bases developed by the Advanced Engineering Department (AED) of United Engineers including the DOE sponsored Economic Data Base which includes capital, fuel and operating and maintenance costs for 13 different types of nuclear and coal-fired units. The second section provides a historical view of the changes in costs in nuclear and coal plants, followed by an evaluation of current costs. The final section discusses the future of coal and nuclear power, highlighting the major factors that will impact power plant costs in the future.

DATA BASE BACKGROUND

The Economic Data Base developed over the years by AED provides current, representative power plant, technical and cost information for use in evaluating and monitoring U.S. civilian nuclear and coal power generating facilities, and further provides a consistent means of evaluating the nuclear options and alternatives. This data base was first developed by United for AEC in 1968 and has been updated annually since then. United is currently working on Phase VIII (1985) and is contracted for updates through Phase IX (1986).

The data base contains historic capital, fuel, and operating and maintenance costs for different types of nuclear stations, and comparison coal-fired power generating stations. Each cost estimate is based upon a detailed technical model which includes system design descriptions for over 400 systems, a detailed equipment list containing over 1,250 mini-specifications and up to 10,000 lines of commodity, material and equipment quantities, labor hours and costs. The technical models are based on actual power plant designs and over 50 years of power plant design and construction experience.

Costs are given in constant (inflation-free) dollars of the date of the estimate. The engineering-economic data base estimating approach allows for credible cost comparisons because all components of "bottom-line" amounts in the different estimates are readily identified and compared through a uniform accounting system. For example, base construction costs are presented as equipment, labor, and site material costs in a uniform code-of-accounts. Each system, component or commodity that is common to two or more of the technical data models has the same account identifier in every data model.

All estimates are point estimates that generally represent the median of an actual or projected range of cost estimates for each data model for the update year. Yearly variations in the availability and quality of power plant technical and cost data tend to obscure actual year to year cost changes.

Consequently, the series of point estimates generated during the seven updates are considered to be more representative of cost trends than of point-to-point variations.

The data models selected for the most recent update were the PWR: Median Experience (PWR:ME/1139MWe); PWR: Best Experience (PWR:BE); Large Scale Prototype Breeder (LSPB/1320 MWe), and the High Sulfur Coal Plant (HS5/486 MWe).

Nuclear/Coal Cost Trends

In 1978, the year of the Phase I Update, the cost for electricity was estimated to be significantly less for a nuclear power plant than for a coal-fired power plant of comparable capacity. However, when the Phase V Update (1982) was issued, the estimated cost of electricity from large nuclear and coal-fired power plants were almost the same. Today, median to high cost experience light water reactor power plants are not competitive with coal-fired power plants. On the other hand, it appears that current best to median cost experience nuclear power plants could be competitive with coal-fired power plants if some government and industry actions are taken to encourage resumption of their deployment.

A significant factor contributing to the decrease in economic advantage for nuclear power plants was their large and continuing capital cost increases between 1978 and 1984 compared with the smaller capital cost increases for coal-fired power plants, even accounting for increases of coal plants due to increasing pollution control. The rapid rise in nuclear power plant capital costs was due in part to large increases in the amount of craft, engineering and field service manhours and to a lesser extent to increases in the quantities of commodities and equipment. These increases along with large increases in time related costs such as mounting interest on funds used during construction, the ability to generate funds needed for construction, licensing delays, and long construction times, have had profound effects on a utility's decision regarding the type of generating station to be constructed.

Figure 1 shows a history of costs of 1000 MWe nuclear power plants, starting from original WASH reports in 1967 through phase VI of the energy economic data base. These are for reactors beginning commercial operation from 1972 to 1995. While physical plant cost has escalated well above inflation, the time-related costs have grown even faster. This is primarily due to lengthening construction schedules caused by changing regulation and increasing intervention. Some of this is also attributable to increasing interest rates over this time period.

Of the physical plant costs, the craft labor and engineering portion has been the primary cost-driver as seen in figure 2. The material costs have remained stable while the labor costs have almost doubled.

A comparison to the high sulfur coal plant shows that the best experience plants can be competitive to coal plants at this level. Certainly the time-related costs will add more to the costs of the nuclear plants, but this shows that if those costs can be reduced (by shorter lead times, regulatory reform, lower interest rates) nuclear generation may be competitive.

FIGURE 1

PLANT INVESTMENT COST ESTIMATES FOR A SINGLE 1000 MWe U.S. NUCLEAR PLANT

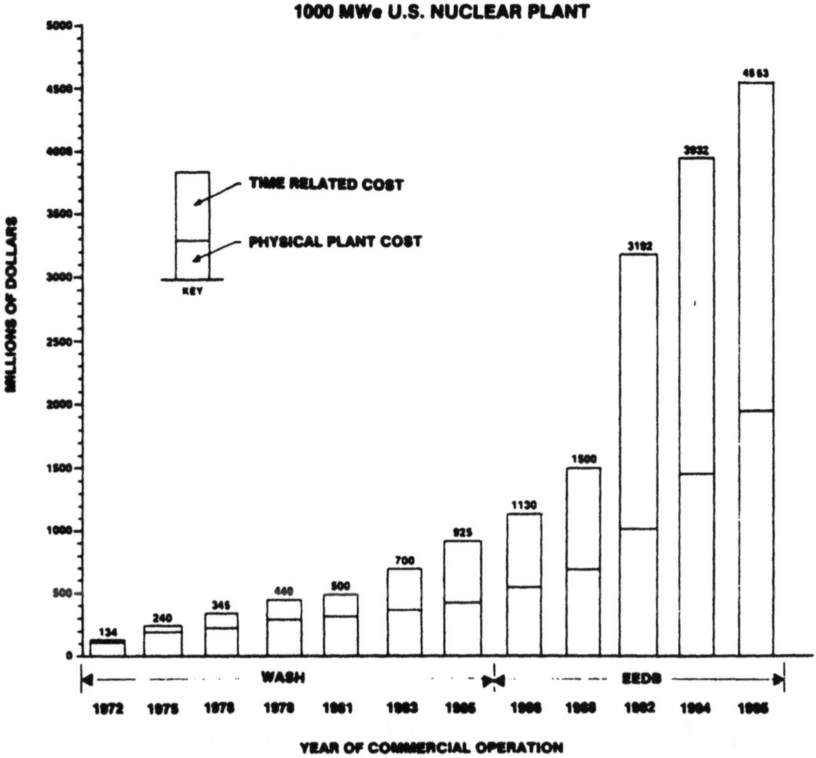

Figure 2 also shows the relatively smaller increase in construction costs for coal-fired plants. The explanation for this can be found in figure 3. Labor related costs have not escalated in the same manner as nuclear plants, and therefore costs have remained more stable. Coal plants have also not faced similar increases in time related costs.

FIGURE 2

ENERGY ECONOMIC DATA BASE (EEDB) PROGRAM
COMPARISON OF PHASE I (1978), PHASE VI (1983) AND PHASE VII (1984)
PWR AND HS 5 BASE CONSTRUCTION COSTS

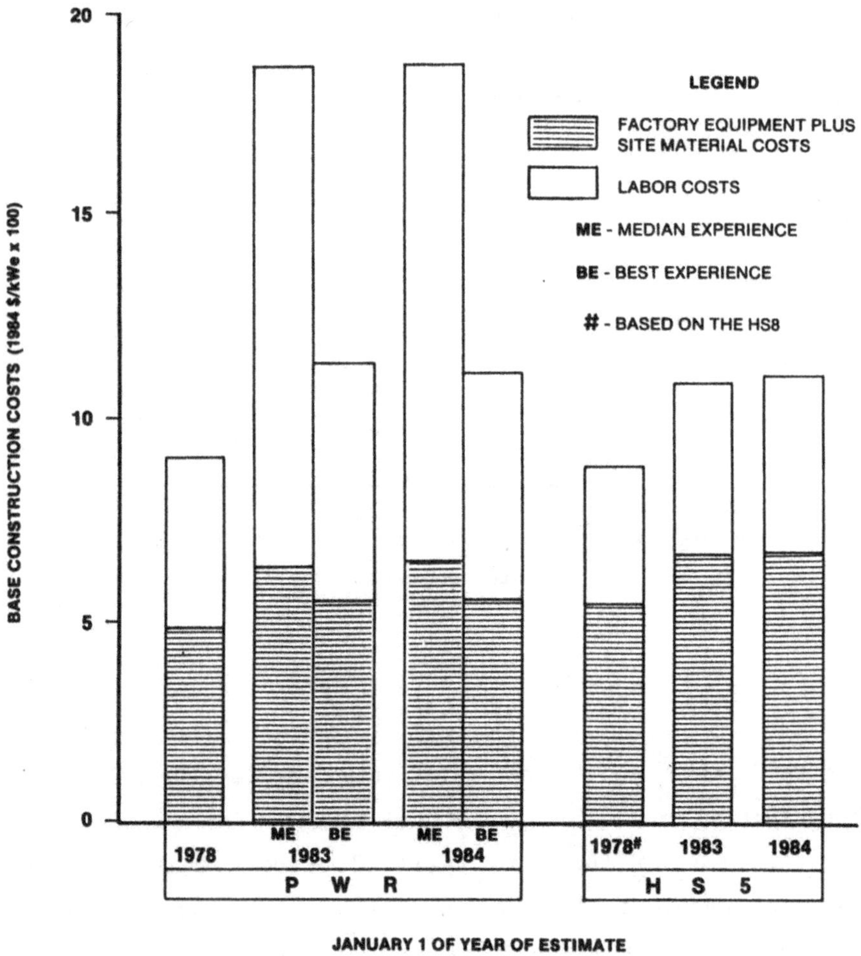

FIGURE 3
ENERGY ECONOMIC DATA BASE (EEDB) PROGRAM
COMPARISON OF PHASE I (1978), PHASE VI (1983) AND PHASE VII (1984)
PWR AND HS 5 LABOR COST

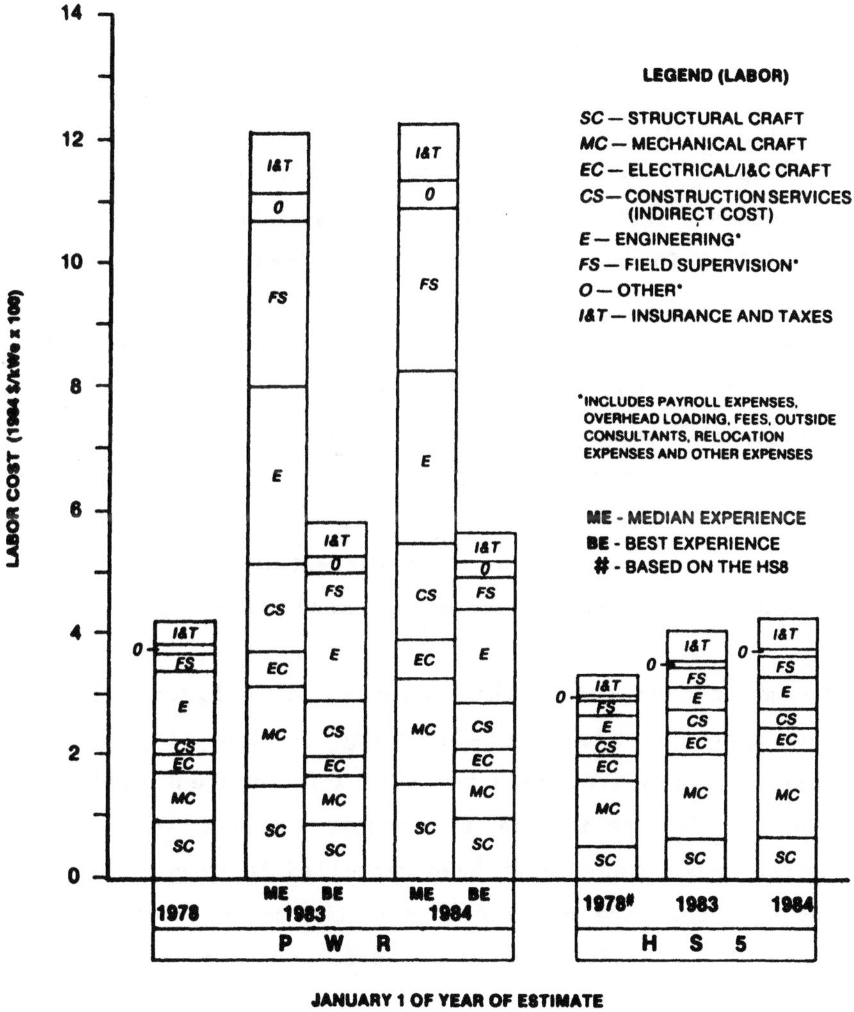

For nuclear plants, it has been increases in engineering, field supervision, and contruction services costs which have been the primary drivers of the labor portion (Figure 3). The first two-engineering and field service-are due primarily to changing regulations causing the need for changes in designs, increasingly complex analyses and rigorous quality assurance programs (this is over and above normal inflation for these services).

Construction services are impacted by labor productivity, made up of worker competence, rework (caused by design changes and interferences) and delays (caused by extended schedules, inspections, insufficient lead times).

Overall though, the driving force of costs for nuclear power plants have been the time-related costs. Figure 4 depicts the percent of total costs that are made up of time related, indirect (contingency and professional services) and direct costs. So while all the costs have increased to some extent, the percentage that AFUDC contributes to total costs have increased dramatically.

One might have gotten the impression from figures 2 and 3 that there has been a slackening of cost increases in nuclear plants from 1983 to 1984. This apparent stabilization may in reality be a phantom, because some of the "worst" case plants have been cancelled in this time frame, and therefore are not included in the calculations for the Phase VII update. Therefore some cost escalation has probably occurred in this time frame, but has not been captured in this latest update.

FIGURE 4

SHIFTS IN DISTRIBUTION OF U.S. NUCLEAR POWER PLANT TOTAL INVESTMENT COST COMPONENTS

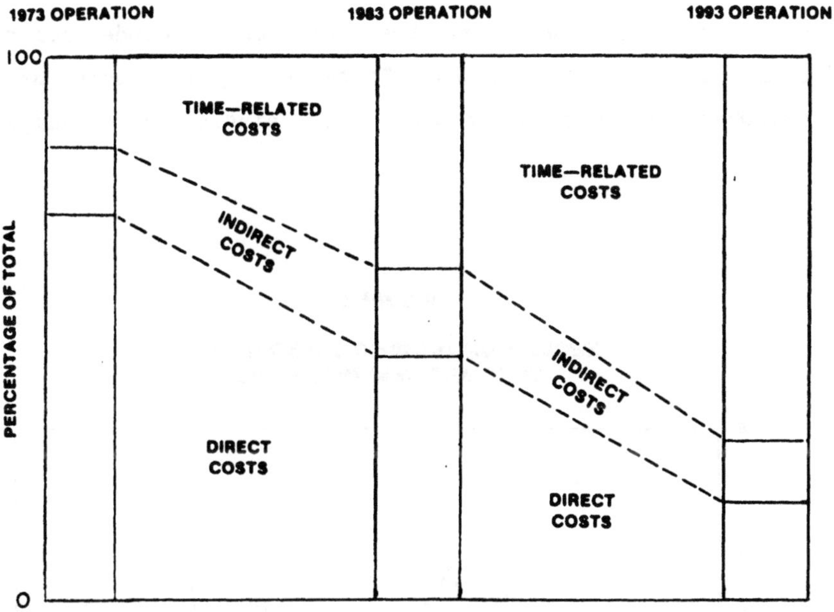

Variations in Power Plant Costs

Estimating the construction cost of power plants is becoming increasingly difficult. The variation in costs between plants has become wider over the last decade, forced by site-related differences, wage rates, design differences, and construction management. These factors bring into question the use of a single point estimate to evaluate construction costs.

Figure 5 shows the estimated construction costs (1985 $/kw including AFUDC) for individual units currently under construction. The variation in costs is obvious, and the variation is becoming wider for plants expected to begin commercial operation after 1988. There are a number of observations that can be made. First, a number of plants due to go on line in the next two years are first units of a two-unit plant, and therefore may include costs common to both facilities. Therefore these costs are somewhat higher than if they were single units only.

FIGURE 5

NUCLEAR UNITS UNDER CONSTRUCTION
CONSTANT $/KW INCL. AFUDC

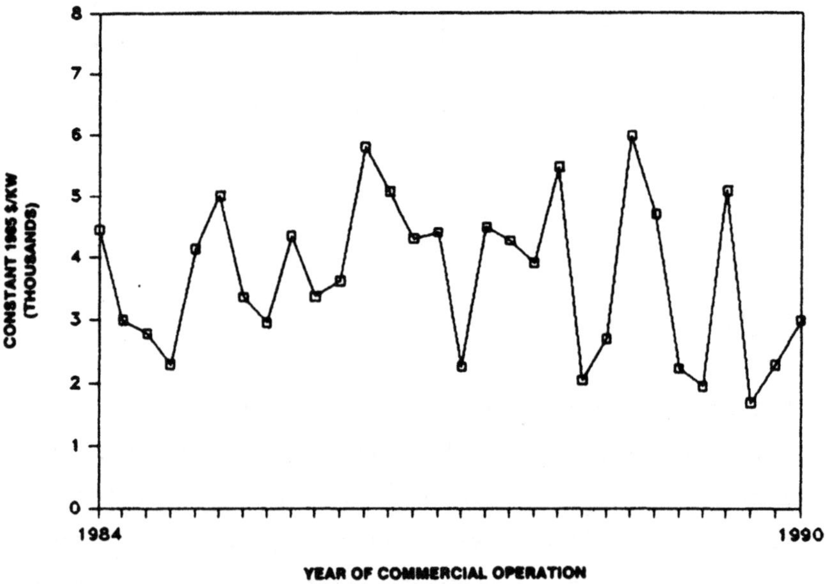

Second, while there appears to be no escalation in costs, this is not necessarily the case. These are estimates published in December 1984, and if the past has any relationship to the future, the plants due for commercial operation in the late 1980's are probably underestimated.* Unexpected costs will lead to higher construction costs, and as the plant nears completion, the costs tend to get higher, and more accurate. These plant estimates are likely to increase in costs, and some escalation in costs may become apparent. This under-estimation may be some of the cause for the wider variation in costs in the later plants, since some of the estimates may be worse than others. We do not expect the variations to disappear completely though.

Figure 6 shows construction costs per kw (mixed $) for some coal-fired plants that went on line between 1981-1984.** These are representative of future plants because only plants built with scrubbers are included here. At first glance it appears that some variation exists, and that there has been an increase in costs over time. The differences and increases are probably caused more by plant and site related characteristics, than by time related factors. For instance the first four plants are either units built on existing sites (therefore utilizing common facilities already built) or units with scrubbers, which meet new source performance standards (NSPS) less stringent than the 1979 requirements; thereby holding down the costs.

*Data from FERC Form 254

**Data from FERC Form 1 and telephone conversations

FIGURE 6

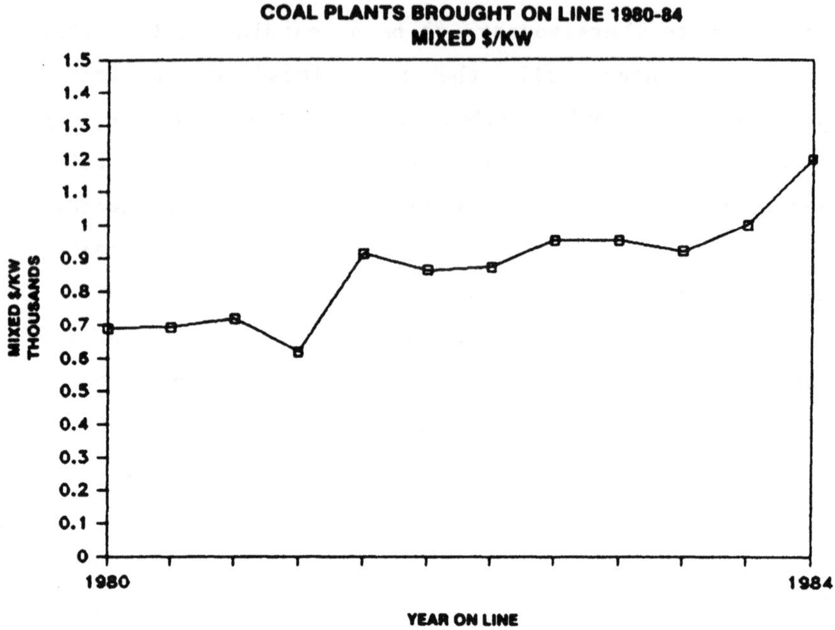

The remaining plants show consistency on overall construction costs (except for the last plant), though there are individual differences between the plants, and costs are distributed differently.

This brings us back to the original question about whether it is fair to compare the costs of two plants, especially when these are used to evaluate management "prudency." The reasons that nuclear plant costs differ by as much as $4000/kw is more complex than just management ability to build the plant (though management differences certainly make up some of the differences). Detailed analysis of the many factors which impact costs is the only way to fairly evaluate the differences. Engineering-economic analysis, incorporated with a data base can be used to estimate the impact on costs that were due to site-specific characteristics, design differences, labor rates etc. Aggregate analyses may not be able to pick out the subtle differences among the plants.

Future Expectations

There are a number of factors that will impact on costs of coal and nuclear in the short and long-run. One major factor, which will impact greatly both technologies, but in different ways, is regulatory change. Nuclear power plants will be affected by regulatory reform in the licensing process while fossil-fired plant costs will be impacted by acid rain control legislation.

Regulatory reform proposals are being directed towards streamlining the licensing process for nuclear power plants. Much of the cost increases in nuclear costs (in AFUDC and others) are brought on by the long construction times which are caused in part by a lengthy and unpredictable licensing process. Other proposals include reformatting the Price-Anderson Act and the restructuring of regulatory guides related to the design and construction of nuclear plants.

Future acid rain control legislation, impacting the type and extent of pollution control will be the overall determining factor with respect to increasing capital costs for coal plants. There is also possible pollution legislation being introduced concerning not only SO_2, NO_x and particulate emissions, but also CO_2 emissions and their implications to the "Greenhouse effect" on our global environment. If any legislation passes it will be a major force driving up the costs of coal-fired generating plants.

Other factors, such as technological change and waste disposal solutions (for both nuclear and coal) will have some impact on costs, but not to the immediate extreme that regulatory changes may have.

Regardless of the technologies chosen, there are a number of key factors that need to be addressed to make it economically feasible to build any new base load generation. These factors are:

- Need for a less capital intensive plant, most likely smaller or modular in design
- A shorter construction schedule
- Adaptable to automation and robotics
- Flexible expansion to follow load growth
- Minimize site-related design

The first factor needs some technological innovation, but is possible in the near term. A shorter construction schedule would come about as a result of smaller and modular units, and also from regulatory changes, especially for nuclear plants.

As technology for robotics advance, the power industry needs to take advantage, to reduce operating costs for all types of units.

Modular units would provide flexible expansion; the ability to expand plants quickly and inexpensively to allow for following low load growth patterns. This would provide for less capital extensive expansion programs, and would help in expediting the licensing and regulatory processes.

A more consistent design is needed so that learning can take place from one plant to the next. Characteristics related to the site should be minimized, so that plants can be built with similar designs, and a learning curve can be carried through.

These factors, among others, will be the key to the future of electricity generation. Expected costs, even in the near term, are difficult to predict because of the changing regulatory climate, and variable demand expectations.

This will force delays in planning new generation by electric utilities, and while there is no cause for concern in the immediate future, new demands and retiring plants may cause the need for new capacity. Research for developing a technology which is relatively inexpensive, and re-building the regulatory system so it does not dramatically increase costs, will be important for long term planning in the electric generation industry.

31
The Current Economics of Coal and Nuclear Power in the United States

Louis J. Perl, National Economic Research Associates

INTRODUCTION

The purpose of this paper is to analyze the current economics of coal and nuclear plants as sources of base load electric generation in the United States. To this end we estimate the levelized cost of electricity from hypothetical plants coming on-line in 1985 in each of 10 regions of the United States. In the analysis we will address two questions:

1. Which of these alternatives—coal or nuclear—is likely to provide electricity at lowest cost in each region?

2. What is the effect of size and boiler type (subcritical and supercritical) on cost for coal fired plants?

This analysis differs from most traditional analyses of power plant economics in one key respect. Most utility analyses of generating costs are based on engineering studies in which detailed assessments of plant design and informed judgement are used to estimate construction costs and operating performance. In this study we have relied, instead, on statistical analyses of historic data to derive the capital costs, operating costs, and measures of operating performance for hypothetical generating plants. The analysis provides a useful exploration of the strengths and weaknesses of this statistical approach to deriving key cost relationships.

The remainder of the paper is divided into two subsections. In the first of these we discuss the methodology used in this study to estimate the cost of electricity from coal and nuclear plants. In the second the empirical results of the analysis are summarized.

METHODOLOGY

In this analysis we have projected the levelized cost of electricity from a series of hypothetical coal and nuclear plants which are assumed to start operating in 1985 and to continue operating over a 30-year lifetime.

To determine levelized costs we first calculate the annual cost of electricity to consumers in each year of plant life. To do this, we estimate the cost of constructing each plant and then, using a utility financial accounting model, derive annual capital-related costs. These include the cost of amortizing the initial investment, any post-commercial capital additions, interest on debt, a return on equity, and all income and property taxes. For nuclear plants they also include the ultimate cost of decommissioning the project. In addition, we estimate annual fuel costs, non-fuel operating and maintenance expenses and annual electric output assuming that the plant is operated whenever available (base load operation). We then calculate the discounted present value of these annual costs and solve for an annual charge which is constant in 1985 dollars and yields revenues with the same present value. This is the levelized real cost of electricity. (In nominal dollars the levelized real cost rises at the rate of inflation over the life of the plant.)

The levelized charge provides a useful index of the lifetime economics of these options. The option with the lowest levelized cost minimizes the discounted present value of costs for any specified level of generation. Of course, as with any calculation involving discounting, the levelized cost is sensitive to the discount rate used. The discount rate used here is the after-tax cost of money to the utility building the plant. The use of this rate assures that the option with the lowest levelized cost can be used to minimize the cost to consumers regardless of their actual discount rates. This is because the after-tax cost of money is the rate at which utilities borrow and lend funds on behalf of their consumers. Consequently, by altering the timing of its charges (by changing the depreciation schedule, for example) a utility (or utility regulator) can always assure that the option which yields the lowest levelized cost when evaluated at the after-tax cost of money also yields the lowest cost at any other discount rate.

In estimating many components of cost we have relied on the statistical analysis of historic data. Such analyses were used to estimate construction costs, annual O&M costs and the maximum achievable capacity factor for both coal and nuclear units. They were also used to estimate post-commercial capital additions for nuclear plants and to estimate annual heat rate for coal units. In deriving each of these components of cost and performance, we relied on data for a sample of plants built or under construction in the United States from 1965 to 1985. Based on these data, multiple regression analysis was used to estimate a series of equations relating cost and performance to various plant characteristics. These regression equations, which are summarized in Table 1 for nuclear plants and in Table 2 for coal plants, also enable us to identify any systematic trends over time and any systematic regional variations in cost and performance.

Let's examine these equations in somewhat more detail. For nuclear plants Table 1 contains equations for initial construction

Table 1. **Parameters of Regressions Relating Components of Nuclear Cost to Plant Characteristics, Region, and Time**

Nuclear Capital Cost ($/kW)				
Variable Name	Reg Coef	t-Stat		
Constant	7.751	149.519		
Rock	-0.152	2.642		
Cooling Tower	0.068	1.322		
Northeast	0.219	3.344	Adj R Sq	0.7915
Single Unit BWR	0.202	2.462	No of Obs	59
Utility is Constructor	-0.256	4.275	F-Stat	32.463
Ln of Wage Index	0.371	2.421		
Subsequent	-0.419	8.368		

	Post Commercial Capital Additions		O&M Expense ($/kW)			
Variable Name	Reg Coef	t-Stat	Reg Coef	t-Stat		
Constant	4.502	2.732	5.063	8.692		
Ln No.Units	-0.392	2.117	-0.416	7.560	Capital Additions:	
Ln Unit Size	-0.646	2.412	-0.471	5.235	Adj R Sq	0.2590
1/Plant Age	1.275	4.014	--	--	No of Obs	380
Ln Plant Age	--	--	0.087	2.299	F-Stat	7.310
Ln Wage Ind.	1.096	1.722	0.626	3.373		
Northeast	0.213	1.210	0.226	4.371		
South	-0.051	0.201	0.184	2.445	Expensed O&M:	
Saltwater	0.220	1.520	0.140	3.236	Adj R Sq	0.7001
Operating Year:					No of Obs	445
1971	0.166	0.219	0.057	0.301	F-Stat	50.368
1972	0.125	0.188	0.146	0.820		
1973	0.556	0.921	0.441	2.639		
1974	1.031	1.724	0.617	3.787		
1975	1.123	1.971	0.614	3.801		
1976	1.285	2.273	0.865	5.444		
1977	1.855	3.256	0.991	6.227		
1978	1.791	3.197	1.100	6.910		
1979	1.857	3.281	1.227	7.600		
1980	2.502	4.409	1.422	8.673		
1981	2.703	4.765	1.553	9.403		
1982	2.536	4.493	1.610	9.712		
1983	2.881	5.023	1.782	10.486		
1984	3.266	5.649	1.972	11.490		

Capacity Factor (%)	BWR		PWR			
Variable	Reg Coef	t-Stat	Reg Coef	t-Stat		
Constant	60.97	38.98	78.76	24.58	BWR:	
1/Age,Yrs 1-5	-10.75	2.92	-8.27	2.94	Adj R Sq	0.1199
Ln(Age-10), Yrs 11-20	-9.55	3.99	-8.86	4.54	No of Obs	252
Size(Ner DER)	--	--	-0.02	3.66	F-Stat	9.547
Salt*Ln(Age)	-5.44	3.50	-3.66	4.43	PWR:	
New England	11.52	3.52	8.48	3.18	Adj R Sq	0.1288
BW Boiler	--	--	-5.54	2.57	No of Obs	445
					F-Stat	11.940

cost, non-fuel O&M cost, post-commercial capital additions and capacity factor. Separate capacity factor equations were estimated for Boiling Water (BWR) and Pressurized Water (PWR) Reactors. For capital and O&M costs, the dependent variable in these equations is the natural log of cost per kilowatt in constant 1984 dollars.

For capital costs, these estimates are based on data for 59 units which started construction in 1972 or later. (We also examined data for units built earlier, but the later data were used because costs for units built after 1971 are markedly higher than those built earlier and there also appeared to be a marked shift in cost determinants after 1971.) Of the 59 units in the sample 18 are completed and most of the rest are scheduled for completion between 1985 to 1987. Since for uncompleted units the costs are estimated rather than actual, the cost data on which this regression is based could still be revised upward when the units are finally completed.

For nuclear O&M costs, post-commercial capital additions and capacity factors, the equations are based on the actual costs and performance of units operating in the United States from 1967 to 1984. In these equations data on individual operating years have been pooled so that individual plants are represented by as few as one and as many as 18 observations.

In Tables 2A and 2B we present equations for forecasting capital costs, O&M costs, equivalent availabilities and heat rates for coal-fired units. With respect to capital costs there are separate equations for plant, scrubber and particulate costs. For O&M we present separate plant and scrubber equations and for heat rate and equivalent availability there are separate equations for sub-and supercritical units. The equivalent availability equations were used to forecast the maximum capacity factor for coal units when operated in a base load mode. Based on data

Table 2a. Parameters of Regressions Relating Components of Coal Plant Cost to Plant Characteristics,Region,and Time

Plant Capital Cost ($/kW)

Variable Name	Reg.Coef	t-Stat
Constant	4.398	14.42
First Unit	0.293	9.73
Lagged First	0.139	4.08
Low Sulfur	0.079	2.50
Log of Size	-0.208	6.41
Log of Wage	0.567	3.98
Operation Date	0.040	11.08
Supercritical	0.850	1.49
Supercrit.*Size	0.126	1.42
Outdoor	-0.066	2.08
Cooling Tower	0.059	1.88
A-E 1	0.136	2.95
A-E 2	0.232	4.38
Util 1	0.080	0.91
Util 2	0.383	3.74
Mountain Pacific	-0.853	1.26
Mount Pac Trend	0.012	1.40
Southwest	-2.222	1.22
Southwest Trend	0.027	1.18
Northeast	-1.869	2.17
Northeast Trend	0.028	2.28
Adj R Sq	0.69	
No of Obs	295.00	
F-Stat	31.178	

Scrubber Capital Cost ($/kW)

Variable Name	Reg.Coef	t-Stat
Constant	4.175	13.60
Subsequent Unit	-0.209	1.77
Lime/Limestone	-0.340	2.82
Percent Sulfur	0.016	4.71
Pre-1978 On-Line	0.599	5.43
Adj R Sq	0.4999	
No of Obs	65	
F-Stat	16.995	

Particulate Capital Cost ($/kW)

Variable Name	Reg.Coef
Constant	5.634
Ln of Size	-0.200
Ln of Wage	0.500
Percent Sulfur	-0.066
Partic.Emiss.Lim.	-5.095

Plant O&M Cost ($/kW)

Variable Name	Reg.Coef	t-Stat
Constant	6.500	4.62
Ln No. Units	-0.092	2.34
Ln Unit Size	-1.893	3.92
Ln Size,Squared	0.173	4.14
Ln Plant Age	0.340	5.28
1/Plant Age	0.330	1.97
Time	0.029	5.77
Ln Wage	0.888	3.10
Northeast	0.138	2.76
South	0.055	0.84
West	0.232	4.02
Scrubber	0.568	5.22
Adj R Sq	0.4429	
No of Obs	661	
F-Stat	48.694	

Scrubber O&M Cost(mills/kWh)

Variable Name	Reg.Coef	t-Stat
Constant	0.165	0.07
Lime/Limestone	-2.497	2.46
Percent Removal	0.110	3.13
Lb.Sulfur Removed	0.292	1.14
Adj R Sq	0.2990	
No of Obs	63	
F-Stat	9.814	

Table 2b. Regression Parameters Relating Equivalent Availability and Heat Rate to Plant Characteristics, Region, and Time

	Equivalent Availability				Heat Rate			
	Supercritical		Subcritical		Supercritical		Subcritical	
Variable	Coef	t-Stat	Coef	t-Stat	Coef	t-stat	Coef	t-stat
Constant	133.74	6.56	176.19	19.37	5049.13	3.59	5988.87	4.08
Vintage 1	2.58	0.74	-4.33	3.24	155.82	1.94	303.63	6.95
Vintage 2	9.19	2.58	--	--	431.98	5.44	--	--
Vintage 3	13.78	3.10	--	--	230.80	2.48	442.31	6.96
Vintage 4	19.21	3.48	-2.56	1.24	73.36	0.59	795.81	9.25
1/Age	-4.99	0.76	-20.20	4.67	247.44	1.87	278.46	1.84
Ln Age	-1.93	0.70	-7.38	4.41	257.73	5.22	208.88	3.99
1/Size	--	--	--	--	482899	5.80	402141	6.30
Ln Size	-11.16	3.45	-12.61	10.29	1307.31	7.18	1240.12	6.12
Ln Heat	--	--	--	--	--	--	-649.96	4.76
Ln Sulfur	--	--	-1.18	2.14	--	--	--	--
Bal. Draft	1.20	0.67	3.06	3.68	--	--	--	--
Cyclone	-7.41	3.75	-4.59	4.28	219.12	5.18	130.18	3.38
Boil Mfg:A	5.47	3.38	-2.75	2.99	-81.43	2.06	80.81	2.36
B	-2.40	1.30	-10.41	7.52	120.32	3.02	300.20	5.34
C	-1.45	0.37	-5.33	3.36	-11.15	0.14	116.16	1.77
Turb Mfg:A	--	--	--	--	36.27	1.11	78.54	2.80
B	--	--	--	--	--	--	-31.24	0.44
A/E : A	-5.61	2.44	-2.08	1.56	262.33	2.82	26.01	0.50
B	--	--	-4.66	3.64	--	--	-33.34	-0.65
Utility: A	-2.70	1.36	0.55	0.41	218.50	5.30	95.05	1.89
B	11.06	3.53	3.86	2.21	-699.72	11.69	-282.06	4.29
C	11.05	5.42	0.13	0.09	-340.93	6.86	-52.23	1.00
D	2.75	0.82	-3.41	2.97	-447.23	5.63	-106.70	2.47
E	--	--	-14.35	10.16	--	--	-56.62	1.02
Other	--	--	1.00	0.86	241.45	4.28	42.44	1.12
Post-1974	-5.54	2.97	-5.52	5.92	--	--	--	--
Equiv Avail	--	--	--	--	-4.02	4.60	-6.28	6.96
Ln Out.Fac	--	--	--	--	-1249.4	9.42	-895.78	9.68
Adj R Sq	0.1309		0.3023		0.5748		0.3323	
No of Obs	742		1756		691		1679	
F-Stat	7.202		39.025		45.410		35.801	

for nuclear plants and supercritical coal units (both of which are generally based loaded) we estimated the maximum achievable capacity factor to equal 93% of the equivalent availability.

The equation for plant capital cost is based on data for 295 coal units built from 1965 to 1983. In addition to the plant capital cost we made use of two other equations in estimating capital costs for coal units. The first of these relates scrubber costs to plant characteristics and was estimated using data on scubbers constructed from 1970 to 1981. The second equation relates particulate cost to plant characteristics and the sulfur content of the fuel burned and was estimated based on a study of particulate costs done for EPRI by Stearns Rogers. We have used this engineering equation in estimating particulate cost because particulate standards have risen markedly in the last few years and this is expected to increase particulate costs in ways which could not be predicted from historic data.

Operating and maintenance costs for coal plants were estimated based on data for a sample of 62 plants operating from 1965 to 1983. A separate scrubber O&M cost equation is also presented. These costs have been estimated separately because only 3 percent of the observations in the O&M cost sample had scrubbers and, hence, these data did not provide a reliable estimate of the effect of scrubber characteristics on scrubber cost. The O&M cost estimates are based on data published by DOE on the O&M cost of scrubber plants but this estimate is adjusted downward to conform to the observed difference in O&M cost between plants with and without scrubbers.

For equivalent availability and heat rate, the equations are estimated on data for units operating from 1960 to 1981. In addition to the variables of primary interest in this study these equations also suggest some significant differences in unit performance among turbine and boiler manufacturers, A/E's and utilities. These differences are presented in Tables 2A and 2B, but the better or worse than average performers are not identified by name since this is not relevant to this study.

To forecast cost and performance from these equations we established a set of hypothetical plant characteristics which define the units analysed in terms of the inputs to these equations. We examined both single and two-unit nuclear plants assuming a unit size of 1000 megawatts. In other respects the units were a composite of units currently under construction in the U.S. This composite consisted of a sample in which 70 percent of the units were PWR's and the rest BWR's; 61 percent of the units were assumed to be built on rock and the rest on soil sites and 60 percent were assumed to be built with cooling towers. For conservatism none of the units were assumed to be built by an experienced utility operating as its own constructor. (Since the estimated costs for such plants is currently 23 percent below those for other units in the sample, excluding such units may exaggerate somewhat the average cost of nuclear units.) With the exception of projected wages, which were based on the SMSA nearest the plant site, the same composite characteristics were used in each region.

For coal plants we considered two plant types—the first consisting two 400 megawatt subcritical units and the second consisting of two 700 megawatt supercritical units. These were assumed to be balanced draft, non-cyclone fired units for which performance reflects a weighted average for all turbine and boiler manufacturers and A/E's supplying utilities over the past 20 years. (As with nuclear plants, the coal units were assumed to have been designed and constructed by an A/E and not by the utility operating on its own). The plants were fully indoor,

Table 3. Wage Indices Used In Evaluating Coal and Nuclear Construction Costs

Region	City	Nuclear	Coal
Northeast	Albany,NY	0.919	0.917
Southeast	Atlanta,GA	0.822	0.826
Great Lakes	Columbus,OH	0.990	0.979
North Central	St.Louis,MO	1.014	0.982
Northern Plains	Omaha,NE	0.948	0.938
South Central	Dallas,TX	0.826	0.835
Mountain	Salt Lake City,UT	0.918	0.907
Southwest	Phoenix,AZ	1.050	1.002
Pacific	Fresno,CA	1.246	1.163
Northwest	Portland,OR	1.188	1.088

Note: Reflects the ratio of construction wages in the SMSA nearest the site to the national average. For coal the index is the average journeyman wage as reported by BLS. For nuclear it is a weighted average of specific construction trades important in nuclear construction as reported by R.S Means,Co.

60 percent had cooling towers and all were built with scrubber and particulate systems adequate to meet current environmental requirements. As with nuclear plants, construction wages were based on the SMSA nearest the hypothetical plant site. The sites used for coal and nuclear plants in each region and the wages at each site are summarized in Table 3.

The determination of levelized costs also requires us to estimate fuel costs. For the coal plants we estimated coal costs using a linear programming model which simulates coal prices in each of 22 regions of the U.S. by balancing supply and demand for coal. Sequential runs of this model were used to derive coal prices over the projected thirty year lives of these plants. In each region this model projects coal prices by sulfur and heat content. We selected coals in each region which would minimize total levelized costs. The delivered coal prices and characteristics for each of the 10 regions analyzed in this study are summarized in Table 4.

Table 4. Price and Characteristics of Coal Used by Region

Region	Delivered Price 1984$/Ton	Heat Content	Sulfur Content	Assumed Price Escalation
Northeast	$55.68	12064	2.13%	1.01%
Southeast	50.90	11945	1.46	0.90
Great Lakes	49.46	12113	2.14	0.93
North Central	31.70	9920	3.30	0.83
Northern Plains	28.86	8752	0.35	0.00
South Central	20.16	6517	0.80	1.41
Mountain	24.39	8986	0.36	0.00
Southwest	28.98	9936	0.53	1.81
Pacific	43.09	9936	1.25	1.01
Northwest	27.12	8100	0.68	1.13

With respect to nuclear fuel prices we used a model developed by NERA to forecast future uranium oxide prices. This model forecasts future prices of this fuel by balancing expected U.S. supplies and demands. For the other components of nuclear fuel--conversion, enrichment, fabrication and waste disposal--we used estimates developed by NUS in a study for the electric industry. The assumed prices for each of the components of nuclear fuel are summarized in Table 5. This table also indicates the estimated characteristics of fuel—specific power, burnup, and enrichment--which are needed to assess nuclear fuel costs on a mills per kilowatt hour basis.

Table 5. Nuclear Fuel Assumptions

	Unit	Price $1984 /unit	Real Escalation
Uranium Oxide	lb	$22.95	2%
Conversion	kg	8.89	0
Enrichment	swu	195.53	0
Fuel Fabrication	kg	213.31	0
Waste Disposal	kg	337.74	0
Characteristics:			
Enrichment	Percent	3.75	
Burnup	MWD/MTt	40000	
Specific Power	MW/MTt	37	

Using the equations summarized in Tables 1 and 2, the plant characteristics summarized above and in Table 3 and the fuel characteristics described in Tables 4 and 5, we estimated the levelized cost of electricity for hypothetical coal and nuclear plants in each of 10 regions of the U.S. Where the equations suggested historic trends in costs (coal capital and O&M costs, nuclear O&M costs and post-commercial capital additions), we assumed the level of costs prevailing in the last year of the analysis would prevail throughout the lives of our hypothetical plants. Thus, coal capital and O&M costs were based on the level prevailing in 1983 and nuclear O&M and capital additions on the level prevailing in 1984. While we did not extrapolate historic trends in cost, operating costs were not assumed constant over plant life. As indicated by the equations, constant dollar O&M cost increases with plant age. In addition, O&M costs and capital additions were assumed to rise with inflation over time. Moreover, as indicated in Tables 3 and 4, U_3O_8 and coal prices were assumed to escalate at 1 to 2 percent above inflation to take into account depletion effects.

In order to estimate annual capital-related revenue requirements, we made use of a utility financial accounting model. Given an estimate of direct construction costs this model estimates the book value of the capital cost as of the time the plant comes on line, and calculates the annual revenues needed to amortize the plant, pay interest on debt, a return to investors, all applicable taxes and nuclear decommissioning expense. With respect to coal plants, for which we do not have a direct estimate of post-commercial capital additions, these were assumed to be 0.5 percent of initial construction costs annually (in constant dollars). The nuclear plant was assumed to require 10 years to construct (from 1975 to 1985) and the coal plant was assumed to take 7

Table 6. Key Financial Assumptions

	Share	Rates: Under Construction Coal	Rates: Under Construction Nuclear	Rates: After 1985
Cost of Money:				
Debt	50%	13.36%	12.13%	10.81%
Preferred Equity	12	12.36	11.31	10.16
Common Equity	38	14.58	13.83	12.93
Inflation Rate		6.59	6.43	5.66
Tax Rate		-----------48---------		

years. The assumed cost of debt and equity capital during the construction period and over the remaining life of these plants is summarized in Table 6. The historic costs of money used in this analysis reflect those typical of a utility with a double-A debt rating. Future debt rates are based on projections of double-A utility debt rates currently being made by DRI. Future equity rates assume the same premium over debt rates as has prevailed historically.

RESULTS BY REGION

Levelized electricity costs for coal and and nuclear plants in each of 10 regions of the U.S. are summarized in Table 7.

Table 7. Levelized Cost of Electricity from Nuclear and Coal Plants

Region	Nuclear	Coal Sub-Critical	Coal Super-Critical	Nuclear Cost Advantage (Disadvantage) Sub-Critical	Nuclear Cost Advantage (Disadvantage) Super-Critical
	--------------(cents per kwh)-----------				
Northeast	6.34	5.72	5.37	-0.62	-0.97
Southeast	5.17	4.60	4.35	-0.57	-0.82
Great Lakes	5.44	4.68	4.42	-0.76	-1.02
North Central	5.50	4.21	3.94	-1.29	-1.56
Northern Plains	5.35	4.04	3.82	-1.31	-1.52
South Central	5.18	4.25	3.96	-0.93	-1.21
Mountain	5.28	4.03	3.83	-1.25	-1.44
Southwest	5.58	4.67	4.44	-0.90	-1.13
Pacific	5.99	5.43	5.12	-0.56	-0.87
Northwest	5.87	4.92	4.64	-0.95	-1.23

As is clear from this table, the projected cost of electricity from the coal plants is lower that that from nuclear plants in every region. In the Eastern half of the country and in California the disparity is relatively small. In these regions the coal nuclear disparity is about 6-7 mills per kilowatt hour when compared to subcritical coal and 8 to 10 mills when compared to supercritical plants. This is a 10-15 percent cost disparity and, given the uncertainties underlying the differences in these costs, could be eliminated or reversed by plausible changes in cost assumptions. This is important because most of the nuclear plants built or under construction in the U.S. are located in these regions. The disparities are somewhat larger in the rest of the country. Differences of 9-12 mills are observed in the South Central, Southwest and Northwest regions which are somewhat nearer to low cost coal supplies. Still larger differences (13-18 mills) are observed in the North Central, Northern Plains and Mountain regions which have abundant reserves of low cost, low sulfur coal.

While this comparison is not very favorable to nuclear power, it may actually understate the current economic disadvantages of this option. First, the comparisons described above assume a two-unit nuclear plant. But because of the high capital costs involved, many utilities have found it difficult to construct two-unit nuclear plants and the second units of numerous plants have been cancelled or deferred. Levelized costs are nearly 25 percent higher for a single unit nuclear project than for a two-unit plant.

Second, in forecasting levelized costs we have not extrapolated the historic trends in operating costs for either coal or nuclear units. If these trends were to continue, levelized costs would be higher for both coal and nuclear plants, but the effect would be much greater for nuclear than for coal. Over the past decade, the average annual increase in nuclear oparating costs has been about 20 percent per year and obviously even a modest continuation of this trend would substantially worsen the economics of nuclear power.

Third, under current utility accounting conventions the costs of nuclear power are particularly high in the early years of operation. Even where their levelized costs are the same, with no change in accounting conventions the cost of electricity from coal would be less than that from nuclear power for about the first 12 years of operation. While the high front end cost of nuclear power could be eliminated by the use of more realistic accounting conventions, without such changes this option is likely to prove particularly unpopular with consumers.

While this comparison clearly suggests that nuclear plants are less economic than coal in the U.S., this was clearly not always the case. In Table 8 we make a retrospective comparison between coal and nuclear power based on data available in each

Table 8. Historic Analysis of the Levelized Cost of Electricty from Nuclear and Coal Plants

		Coal		Nuclear Cost Advantage (Disadvantage)	
Year	Nuclear	Sub-Critical	Super-Critical	Sub-Critical	Super-Critical
	(1984 cents per kwh)				
1973	1.62	2.19	2.22	0.57	0.60
1974	1.76	2.89	2.92	1.14	1.16
1975	2.25	3.32	3.23	1.08	0.98
1976	2.54	3.35	3.17	0.80	0.62
1977	2.55	3.42	3.24	0.87	0.69
1978	2.92	3.61	3.41	0.69	0.49
1979	3.01	3.85	3.63	0.84	0.62
1980	3.20	3.94	3.72	0.75	0.52
1981	3.46	4.08	3.84	0.62	0.38
1982	4.30	4.45	4.17	0.15	-0.12
1983	5.60	4.67	4.37	-0.94	-1.23

year from 1973 to the present. As is clear from these data, through 1982 nuclear appeared to have a cost advantage over coal. The gradual erosion of the nuclear cost advantage over this period reflects three factors. First, regulatory changes have dramatically increased nuclear construction and O&M costs, which nearly tripled in the decade from 1973 to 1983. Second, after 1980 interest rates rose markedly in the U.S. These rising rates have nearly doubled the levelized capital costs of nuclear plants and contributed substantially to the erosion of the nuclear cost advantage. Finally, the operating performance of nuclear plants in the U.S. has not lived up to expectations. Whereas early projections of nuclear capacity factors were 70 percent or more, large plants, which predominate among plants now under construction, have generally achieved capacity factors of only 60 percent. Given the high fixed costs of nuclear power, these relatively low capacity factors have also contributed to the erosion of the projected nuclear advantage.

SCALE AND ECONOMICS FOR COAL PLANTS

Given the relative economics of coal and nuclear plants, it seems probable that U.S. utilities will rely primarily on coal plants in meeting future generating needs. It is therefore useful to explore the relative economics of alternative coal plants in more detail. Of particular interest is the choice of unit size and the choice between sub- and supercritical units. In Table 9 we summarize the levelized costs of electicity from subcritical and supercritical coal plants in unit sizes ranging from 200 to 1000 megawatts. This analysis is based upon plants located in the Great Lakes region, but results would generally be similar in other regions.

The results appear to suggest somewhat lower costs for supercritical than for subcritical in all size ranges. For subcritical

Table 9. Levelized Generating Cost for Coal Plants by Size and Type

	Capital Cost	O&M Cost	Capacity Factor	Heat Rate	Levelized Total Cost
	----($/kw)----		(%)	(Btu/kWh)	(mills/kWh)
Subcritical					
200 MW	1284	13.66	74.2	10535	46.85
400 MW	1135	14.08	66.1	10437	46.83
600 MW	1058	15.43	61.4	10651	47.82
800 MW	1007	17.01	58.0	10879	48.93
1000 MW	969	18.70	55.4	11087	50.06
Supercritical					
200 MW	1471	13.66	79.3	9803	46.41
400 MW	1210	14.08	72.1	9512	44.18
600 MW	1082	15.43	67.9	9669	44.04
800 MW	1001	17.01	64.9	9871	44.38
1000 MW	944	18.70	62.6	10065	44.88

plants, costs appear to decline with size only up to 400 megawatts and rise with size thereafter. Consequently, the 400 megawatt units constitute the least cost alternative. For supercritical plants, costs fall as size increases from 400 to approximately 600 megawatts and rise with size from 800 to 1000 megawatts. Consequently, for supercritical plants, units in the 600 to 800 megawatt size range probably constitute the lowest cost option.

What is the source of the very limited scale economics observed in this study? They reflect several offsetting influences. There do appear to be considerable economies of scale in constructing coal-fired units. But the statistical analysis of operating data also suggests some diseconomies of scale in operating these plants. As size increases, both unit availabilities and heat rates appear to deteriorate. Moreover, large units also appear to have higher O&M cost per kilowatt than smaller units. At least for subcritical units, the operating diseconomies appear to offset set the economies of scale in construction. And, even for supercritical units, where economies of scale in construction are relatively large, the operating diseconomies offset the construction economies at sizes in excess of 800 megawatts.

We should also note that while supercritical coal units appear more economic than subcritical units in this study, they have some disadvantages which are not fully reflected in the analysis. Because these units take a relatively long time to come to full power and only run efficiently at or near their maximum output, they are only suitable for baseload operation. Subcritical units can be used either in a base load or cycling mode. The operational advantages of subcritical plants may more than offset the relatively small economic disadvantage observed in this study.

SOME CAVEATS

These empirical analyses of costs for coal and nuclear units illustrate both the strengths and the weaknesses of this statistical approach to evaluating power plant economics. The key advantage of this approach is that it relies on actual experience rather than design parameters in forecasting cost. And, as these results indicate, there can be marked differences between the actual cost and performance of plants and their design specification. This has proven to be particularly true for nuclear construction and O&M costs and, to a lesser extent, for coal heat rates and equivalent availabilities.

On the other hand it is also clear that this approach does not solve all of the problems of evaluating power plant economics. As a perusal of the equations in Tables 1 and 2 indicates, the standard errors of estimates from the regression equations are generally quite large. Consequently, the estimates of cost and performance are associated with substantial uncertainty. And in many cases the difference in projected cost between the various options is often very small. For example, the difference in projected cost between the most economic sub- and supercritical units is less than 7.0 percent. Consequently, it is difficult to draw firm conclusions from these analyses. Of course, the same uncertainties are also implicit in engineering analyses of costs, but the reliance on historic data makes the problem more apparent.

An even more serious problem is raised by the apparent trends in cost and performance over time. Both coal and nuclear plants, have exhibited marked increases in both capital and operating cost over time. These trends make it very difficult to predict the future. If the trends are assumed to continue, the cost of nuclear power will prove to be markedly higher and coal power somewhat higher than projected here. But, since the historic trends in cost appear to be primarily related to regulatory change, there is no reliable basis for assuming that they will continue. It is equally likely that they will stop or even reverse. A better understanding of the factors which have driven up cost in the past and a better mechanism for predicting these changes in the future is needed before we can have reliable analyses of power plant economics.

32
Avoided Cost Pricing: New Ideas for a New Era

Michael A. Einhorn, Rutgers University

I. INTRODUCTION

In 1980, the Federal Energy Regulatory Commission (FERC) issued regulations under Section 210 of the Public Utility Regulatory Policies Act of 1978 (PURPA) which required public utilities to purchase any power made available by cogenerators and small power producers (called "qualifying facilities" or QF's). In general, state regulatory commissions were required to set rates for new QF's at avoided costs, which were defined as the "incremental costs to an electric utility of electric energy or capacity or both which, but for the purchase from the qualifying facility or qualifying facilities, such utility would generate itself or purchase from another source." (45 FR 12233, Feb. 25, 1980)

In this ruling, the commission implicitly established a pricing rule which is analogous to first-best marginal cost pricing. If the power company's prices to its ultimate customers are first-best as well and if its resulting rate of return is neither too high nor too low, this avoided cost pricing rule is appropriate. However, if the resulting rate of return under first-best prices is unsuitable, prices must be adjusted to bring the rate of return into line. Under these circumstances, avoided cost pricing might no longer be desirable. Other first-best or second-best strategies must then be implemented.

Two major court cases have considered the appropriateness of FERC's avoided cost regulations. In 1982, the District of Columbia Court of Appeals vacated FERC's avoided cost pricing rule; it argued that FERC failed to consider sufficiently the relevant consumer welfare and public interest provisions of Section 210. _American Electric Power Service Corporation_, _et_. _al_. v. _Federal Energy Regulatory Commission_. 675 F. 2d 1226. However, in 1983 the Supreme Court overruled the lower court's ruling; Justice Marshall ruled that although consumer prices might not be minimized under avoided cost pricing, avoided cost rates can still be in the public interest since they provide a maximum incentive for more efficient energy generation. _American Paper Institute_, _Inc_. v. _American Electric Power Service Corporation_, et. al.; _Federal Energy Regulatory Commission_ v. _American Electric Power Service Corporation_, et. al. 51 LW 4547. Neither court explicitly considered the problem of excessive or insufficient utility rates of return and economically appropriate ways of dealing with it.

This paper reviews several issues in designing appropriate prices for the purchase of QF power under regulatory constraint. Section 2 reviews the FERC regulations. Section 3 discusses economically optimal ways to ensure to the utility a sufficient rate of return; Section 4 discusses some second-best price adjustments. Section 5 concludes the paper.

II. FERC REGULATIONS UNDER SECTION 210

In 1978, President Carter signed into law PURPA as one of five pieces of legislation included in his National Energy Act. Section 210 of PURPA authorized FERC to prescribe, and revise from time to time, rules designed to encourage small power production and cogeneration by non-utility owners as well as the sale of any excess electricity generated back to the utility. Electric companies are obligated to purchase such power and also to sell to the QF any electricity that it may need.

Over the next two years, FERC issued regulations under its mandate. The Code of Federal Regulations, Title 18, Chapter 1, Part 292 contains these regulations. Section 292.303 of Subpart C specifies that "each electric utility shall purchase, in accordance with Section 292.304, any energy and capacity which is made available from a qualifying facility ..."

18 CFR 292.303(a). Sections 292.203-206 of Subpart B specify the maximum size, fuel use, ownership requirements, and operating and efficiency standards for defining eligible QF's. In Section 292.304, paragraph (a) specifies that rates must be "_just and reasonable_ to the electric _consumer_ of the electric utility and in the _public interest_" (emphasis mine) and that rates must not "discriminate against qualifying cogeneration and small power production facilities." 18 CFR 292.304(a). Paragraph b(2) specifies that setting rates at avoided costs (considering certain complications) can satisfy the rules of 292.304(a); paragraph b(4) continues to say that rates for the purchase of electricity from new capacity shall be in accordance with paragraph b(2). 18 CFR 292.304(b) In other words, new QF's must be paid avoided costs; the implication is that such pricing is just and reasonable to the ultimate customer and in the public interest.

There are two noteworthy items which are missing in Section 210. First, FERC provides no formula by which regulatory commissions must calculate avoided costs. Second, there is no mention anywhere of the utility's financial well-being. In specific, we never hear of what modifications are appropriate should the utility's rate of return under first-best pricing prove deficient.

III. FIRST-BEST STRATEGIES

Pricing utility purchases of QF power at avoided cost is analogous to marginal cost pricing. By setting avoided cost prices, the utility signals to the QF how much money can be saved if one less kilowatt-hour is generated in a utility-owned power plant. The QF will sell to the utility only electricity which can be generated at avoided cost or lower; consequently, the QF's less costly means of generation displace the utility's more costly methods. A more efficient means of generating power is then ensured.

Figure 1 illustrates the determination of a QF's supply of power to the utility following the implementation of avoided cost pricing; the QF's supply curve is of course its marginal cost of generation locus. Q_0 represents the level of total sales; ABC represents the QF's level of profits from the sale of power to the utility.

In a first-best world, utilities can sell power at marginal cost and purchase QF power at avoided cost. The difficulty with this ideal theoretical approach resides in the fact that first-best marginal cost pricing in no way ensures to the utility a level of operating income that is sufficient to cover a reasonable rate of return on its rate base. When operating income is deficient under first-best pricing, various strategies are possible on both ultimate

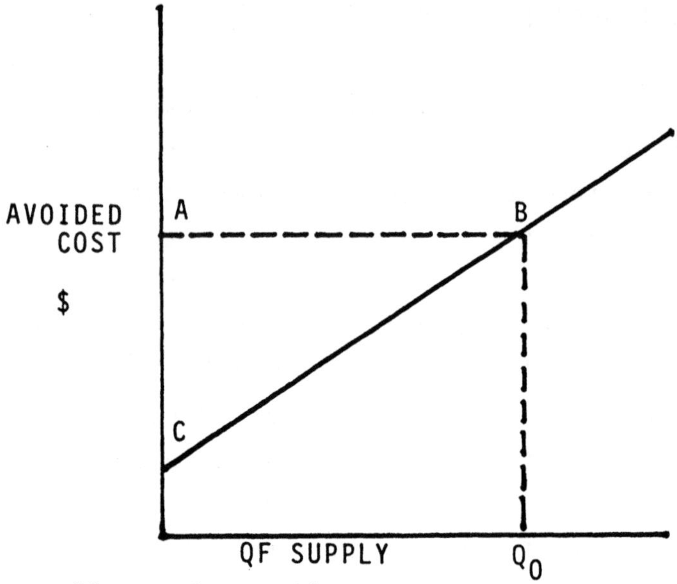

Figure 1. Utility Purchases of QF Power

customer and QF prices.

The first-best strategy would be to continue to price QF sales to the utility at avoided cost but return some of the surplus ABC to the utility. An approach that is frequently used in wholesale power pricing is to split the savings, in our case between the avoided cost and the QF's marginal cost of generation. With this strategy, we guarantee to the QF a profit above its marginal cost on each kilowatt-hour that it sells. If QF marginal costs are defined to include capacity costs and if risk aversion is not too serious a concern, just as much QF power will result under "split savings" pricing as under full avoided cost pricing.

FERC considered but rejected implementing a "split savings" approach for QF power; it felt that such an approach would require QF's to appear in regulatory hearings to determine their costs of generation. FERC felt that this regulatory burden would act as a deterrent to QF's coming on line; rather, FERC explicitly exempted QF's from many of the regulatory provisions of the Federal Power Act and the Public Utility Holding Company Act. In the Circuit Court case which vacated FERC's avoided cost rule, Justice Wilkey upheld FERC's aversion to split savings; splitting the savings would have veered toward "the public utility style rate setting that Congress wanted to avoid." 675 F. 2d 1232.

Granting that FERC's desire to avoid subjecting QF's to regulatory hearings is a reasonable one, we still can identify two alternative strategies which can split the savings without dragging QF's into regulatory hearings. First, part of the profits from QF sales can be subjected to a profits tax; the proceeds of this tax could then be credited to the utility's taxes. This would have the same net effect as would splitting the savings; however, the QF would be subject to no more regulation than is required under a corporate income tax. Indeed, most QF's must pay these taxes now.

A second strategy is based upon Demsetz's (1968) franchise bidding approach to regulation. I shall assume temporarily that the only differences among QF's result from different generation capacities and costs of generation. (In fact, QF's can differ among one another by items such as reliability, delivery voltage, number of years of availability, and need for standby power.) Presuming that this is the case, we may prescribe the following process to secure the optimal level of QF power and a simultaneous sharing of the savings. First, each existing or prospective QF must submit a closed bid which specifies the amount of electricity to be sold and the price per kilowatt-hour. While receiving bids, the utility and the commission determine a suitable measure of avoided cost. The utility must then buy power from all QF's that have submitted bids below its own avoided costs. If QF's bid at or near long-run marginal cost, we see that the utility would purchase only electricity with a marginal cost of generation below avoided cost. However, instead of pricing power at avoided cost AC, we price it at P = (1 - f)AC + f BIDPRICE. f lies between 0 and 1. This approach is perfectly analogous to a profits tax or splitting the savings.

Things would become somewhat more complicated once we allow for QF differences in reliability, voltage level, contract length, and other factors which affect cost. Each bid that the utility receives must specify these relevant cost factors. For each bid, it is then necessary to calculate a specific avoided cost, since avoided costs certainly depend on items like reliability and contract length.

While complex, this process would not require any more utility work than what is now necessary to determine avoided cost prices. In fact, commissions and utilities should consider all of the factors we have mentioned whenever they estimate avoided costs. The argument could be made that a bidding procedure would place an additional burden upon the QF's to determine their generation costs when estimating their bid prices. However, it is difficult to imagine that any QF would decide to set up operations without having a reasonably firm idea of its generation costs. All our process does is require the QF's to pass the information over to the regulatory commission.

Of course, it is not necessary that any savings split that is implemented -- via profits taxes or bidding -- be 50/50; a healthy profit should be ensured to the QF's to maintain their incentives. It may not then be possible to return to the utility a large enough share to secure a reasonable rate of return; in this case, we should then implement second-best strategies on ultimate customer prices also.

IV. SECOND-BEST STRATEGIES

If it is not possible to implement any of the first-best strategies which have been described, then second-best price adjustments are necessary on both the ultimate customer and the QF prices. The simplest second-best alternative would be to lower QF prices and raise customer prices according to a modified Ramsey rule (for the classic discussion of Ramsey rules as they relate to public utility pricing, see Baumol and Bradford 1970):

$$\frac{(P_i - C_i)}{P_i} = \frac{k}{e_i} = \frac{(P_j - C_j)}{P_j} = \frac{k}{e_j} \qquad (1)$$

where:

P_i = price of electricity to customers
P_j = price of electricity from QF's
C_i = marginal cost of supplying customer power
C_j = avoided cost of utility-generated power
e_i = elasticity of demand for electricity
e_j = elasticity of QF supply of electricity
k = constant; k is less than zero

Modifications for marginal and avoided costs which differ by time of use and customer class are desirable if the resulting increase in social surplus is greater than the additional metering costs. Further improvements in social surplus can also be obtained with nonuniform pricing (see Goldman, Leland, and Sibley 1977), such as inverted block pricing on the QF side and declining block rates on the ultimate customer side. Two-part tariffs are a commonly used simpler variant of nonuniform prices; for discussions of two-part tariff pricing as it relates to public utility ratemaking, see Ng and Weisser 1974, Faulhaber and Panzar 1977, and Schmalensee 1981.

If first-best pricing produces a deficient level of operating income, then consumer prices should be increased and QF prices should be decreased relative to their first-best levels. If QF prices are instead kept at avoided cost, then consumer prices must be increased yet more. Furthermore, the total level of social surplus would be lower if only consumer prices were adjusted to bring utility revenues into line. Accordingly, downward reduction of QF prices would then appear to be justified under the "just and reasonable" and "in the public interest" provisions of Section 292.304(a).

In the Circuit Court case, FERC argued that any passed-on benefits to the electric consumer would result in insignificant rate reductions. Justice Wilkey ruled that FERC had not sufficiently demonstrated this; "it is possible that if cogeneration becomes substantial, a rate uniformly set at the statutory ceiling may be quite costly to electric consumers." 675 F. 2d 1232. The Court then suggested the idea of fixing prices as a set percentage of avoided cost; it did not specify how this percentage was to be determined. Of course, Ramsey rules come to mind here.

The Supreme Court overruled the Circuit Court on this matter. Justice Marshall rejected the respondents' claim that "just and reasonable" requires that purchase rates be set "at the lowest possible reasonable rate consistent with the maintenance of adequate service in the public interest" (Atlantic Refining Company v. Public Service Commission of New York, 360 U.S. 378, 388, quoting the original version of the Natural Gas Act):

> "The commission recognized that the full avoided cost rule would not directly provide any rate savings to electric utility consumers, but deemed it more important that the rule could 'provide a significant incentive for a high growth rate' of cogeneration and small power production and that these rate-payers and the nation as a whole will benefit from the decreased reliance on scarce fossil fuels, such as oil and gas, and the more efficient use of energy." 51 LW 4547, 4550.

Moreover, the Court also argued that determining an appropriate rate below avoided cost would be "extremely difficult, if not impossible" due to the vast amount of alternative technology that was available.

We should now reconsider FERC's desire to provide the maximum incentive for a higher growth rate of alternative technologies. In the late 1970's, our nation's concern with fuel shortages and energy conservation may have led to an overemphasis on policies ostensibly designed to reduce fuel usage. While reducing our energy usage is desirable in some sense, we must not do this at all costs or regardless of all consequences. Furthermore, the course of future oil prices looks much different now than it did in the late 1970's. One particular consequence that FERC's maximum incentive strategy seems to ignore is the additional burden that consumers and society must carry when QF's are allowed full avoided costs instead of a more suitable first- or second-best alternative.

Regarding Justice Marshall's contention that estimating an appropriate rate below avoided cost would be difficult, such a determination may indeed have been impossible in the early years of Section 210. However, now that a few years' worth of data can be gathered, we might now be able to estimate reasonable elasticities of QF-supplied power.

V. CONCLUSION

The FERC regulations enacted in 1980 are not etched in stone; Section 210 specifically states that FERC may from time to time revise these regulations. The appropriate time to revise and the suitable course to take depend on what we learn from our nation's experience with QF power. Where we go from here depends on how much and how well we learn.

REFERENCES

Baumol, W.J., and D. Bradford. 1970. "Optimal Departures from Marginal Cost Pricing." American Economic Review: 265-83.

Demsetz, H. 1968. "Why Regulate Utilities?" Journal of Law and Economics: 55-65.

Faulhaber, G.R., and J.C. Panzar. 1977. "Optimal Two-Part Tariffs with Self-Selection." Bell Telephone Laboratories Economics Discussion Paper #74.

Goldman, M.B., H.E. Leland, and D.S. Sibley. 1977. "Optimal Nonuniform Prices." Bell Telephone Laboratories Economics Discussion Paper #100.

Ng, Y.K., and M. Weisser. 1974. "Optimal Pricing with a Budget Constraint -- The Case of the Two-Part Tariff." Review of Economic Studies: 337-45.

Ramsey, F. 1927. "A Contribution to the Theory of Taxation." Economic Journal: 47-61.

Schmalensee, R. 1981. "Monopolistic Two-Part Pricing Arrangements." Bell Journal of Economics: 445-66.

33
Impact of Lower and Falling Oil Prices on Emerging Power Generation Technologies

Fereidoon P. Sioshansi,
Southern California Edison Company

INTRODUCTION

One of the lesser known effects of sharply rising oil prices in the 1970s was the impetus provided to a myriad of new and exotic electric power generation technologies. Higher oil prices made many new technologies cost-competitive with conventional means of electricity production. This, coupled with expectations of rising oil prices, meant that it would simply be a matter of time before many small-scale, emerging technologies would become commercially viable.

The views presented and conclusions reached in this paper are solely those of the author and do not necessarily represent the official views of the Southern California Edison Company.

Several other factors, including lower electricity demand growth rates and difficulties financing large, central power plants, added to the attraction of the small, modular, short lead-time technologies. At the same time, proponents of renewable energy resources were highly successful in promoting the virtues of the "soft-energy-path." Enthusiastic federal R&D support, and generous financial incentives were also responsible for the prevailing euphoria in the late 1970s and early 1980s.

Conditions have changed rather dramatically since 1980. The world-wide oil glut has resulted in lower, not higher, oil prices, a situation which is expected to continue through the end of the decade. Cost and penetration projections for new power generation technologies have turned out to be overly optimistic and, in some cases, off the mark. Many of the financial incentives for new technologies have expired or been reduced and the federal government has drastically reduced and changed its R&D priorities. The net effect of these developments is that the cost competitiveness hurdle dates for many new energy technologies have been postponed from the decade of 1980s to 1990s and beyond.

DOOM AND GLOOM

Prior to 1973, with abundant and inexpensive energy supplies, many utilities, including those in California, were heavily dependent on oil- and gas-fired generation to satisfy their customers' electrical needs.

With the 1973 Arab oil embargo and the subsequent passage of the Fuel Use Act, the industry was encouraged to reduce its dependence on oil and gas at almost any cost. President Carter's National Energy Policy stated that "...the quest for energy independence should be looked upon as the moral equivalent of war."

The Iranian revolution and Iran-Iraq war of 1979-80 resulted in a panic which saw spot prices for oil exceeding $42 dollars in 1980. The ensuing crisis mentality resulted in near unanimous consensus among energy analysts that oil prices would continue to rise, as exemplified by the projections shown in Figure 1.

At the same time, falling electrical demand growth rates, and increasing uncertainty about future growth patterns was making it more difficult to justify the need for large, central power plants (Figure 2). The high cost of capital and high inflation rates during the late 1970s made it extremely difficult to finance long lead-time, capital-intensive projects.

As a result of these developments electric utilities were going through a period unprecedented for an industry accustomed to rapid and steady growth and financial stability. The industry's response to these developments was to cut back on capital investments and concentrate on reduced oil and gas consumption (Alm & Dreyfus, 1982).

THE DAWN OF A NEW ERA

It was in the midst of this period of great uncertainty and high cost of capital that utilities across the country began to re-evaluate their future energy resource options (Sioshansi, 1984). Several factors were improving the attractiveness of the so-called renewable and alternative energy resources:

First, renewable and alternative resources (R/As) tend to be small, modular, and have short construction lead-times which means that they can be financed and constructed in small

Figure 1. 1980 Projections of Oil Prices

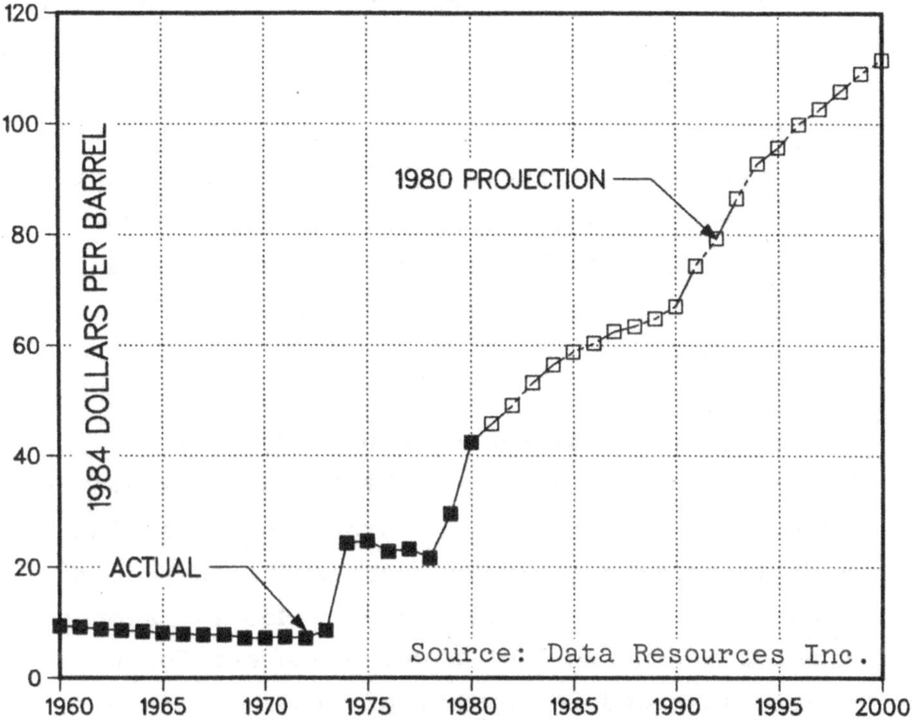

Figure 2. Electric Sales Growth Forecasts

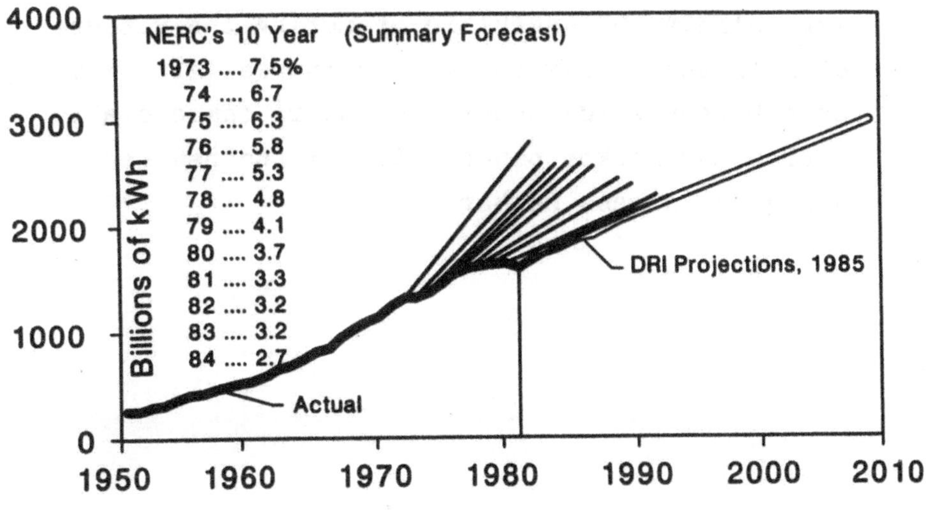

increments and on short notice. These features enable utilities to better match their uncertain future capacity needs and reduce their financial requirements.

Second, the federal government, particularly the Department of Energy (DOE)--highly enthusiastic about the future prospects of R/As--was spending millions of dollars on research and development (R&D) during the late 1970s (Figure 3).

Third, the passage of Public Utility Regulatory Policies Act of 1978, better known as PURPA, and availability of other generous financial incentives including accelerated depreciation and energy tax credits provided yet another impetus to independent power producers for rapid development and deployment of R/As.

Fourth, proponents of the "soft energy path" were highly successful in promoting the virtues of R/As and overly optimistic (unrealistic may be a better word) about the future commercialization and market penetration of the new technologies in mass numbers.

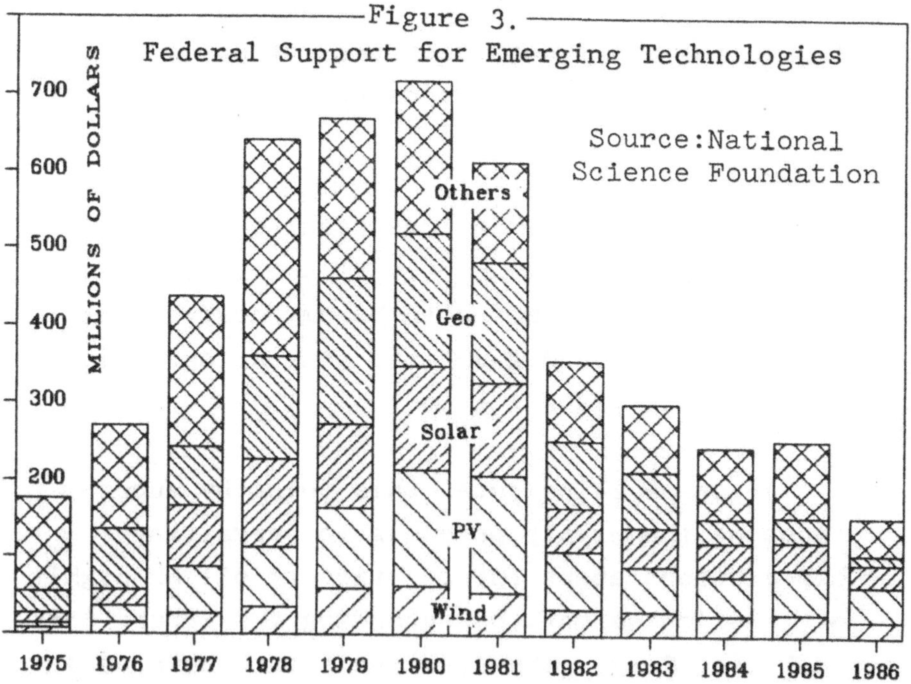
Figure 3.
Federal Support for Emerging Technologies
Source: National Science Foundation
MILLIONS OF DOLLARS
700
600
500
400
300
200
Others
Geo
Solar
PV
Wind
1975
1976
1977
1978
1979
1980
1981
1982
1983
1984
1985
1986

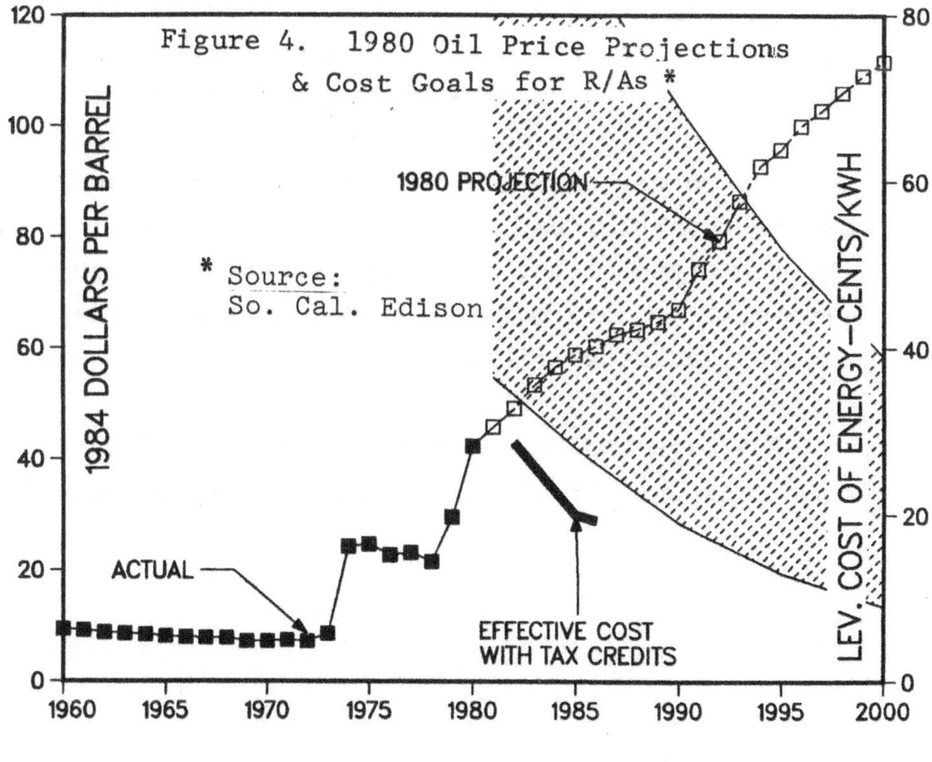
Figure 4. 1980 Oil Price Projections & Cost Goals for R/As *
* Source: So. Cal. Edison
1984 DOLLARS PER BARREL
LEV. COST OF ENERGY–CENTS/KWH
1980 PROJECTION
ACTUAL
EFFECTIVE COST WITH TAX CREDITS
0
20
40
60
80
100
120
1960
1965
1970
1975
1980
1985
1990
1995
2000

Most important, of course, was the underlying belief and expectation that price of oil would continue to rise substantially in the 1980s.

Combined, these factors resulted in a self-fulfilling prophecy wherein virtually any new technology was expected to become cost-competitive with oil- and gas-fired generation during the 1980s or 1990s.

Figure 4 illustrates this point by superimposing the highly pessimistic prevailing expectations about future price of oil on highly optimistic assumptions regarding the future cost goals for R/As. The cost goals are shown as a band representing an envelope covering the full spectrum of new and evolving technologies. The upper end of the envelope represents the more exotic and less developed technologies and the lower band representing the more developed and mature technologies. The solid line parallel to the lower end of the band represents the effective cost of more mature technologies with tax credits and other financial incentives.

The expected rapid drop in cost of energy from R/As was attributed to anticipated technological advancements resulting from R&D in new technologies and expectations that large-scale commercialization and mass production would further reduce the costs. Given these assumptions, it was simply a question of time before any new technology would become cost-competitive.

RENEWABLE AND ALTERNATIVES COME OF AGE

Supported by PURPA, renewable and alternative energy resources were catapulted into the mainstream of utility generation options by the expectations of higher oil prices. Taking full advantage of tax incentives and other provisions of PURPA, independent power producers created a new industry overnight. Wind parks and cogeneration projects were taking shape, particularly in California, Texas, Florida, and several New England states.

Utilities, by and large, were and continue to be supportive of these developments since these projects have the effect of reducing the utilities' own financial requirements. The State of California, supported by its two major utilities accounts for a disproportionate percentage of the total R/A installed capacity in the U.S.

GOLD AT THE END OF THE RAINBOW

There has been several dramatic developments since 1980 which have drastically changed the future prospects of R/As. The most significant turnaround being the unexpected drop in oil prices which has been experienced since 1980. As shown in Figure 5, successive projections of future oil prices have been scaled down to what amounts to a falling curve in real terms for the remainder of the 1980s, slowly rising in the 1990s, but not reaching its all-time high of over $42 per barrel until the turn of the century. This represents a dramatic change from the prevailing expectations of the late 1970s.

The significance of this turnaround cannot be overstated for three reasons. First, since the price of oil is often used as a yardstick against which all other energy prices are measured, falling oil prices have the effect of lowering the price of alternative fuels such as natural gas. Second, since the price of oil directly impacts the "avoided cost" of energy--for most utilities oil-fired combustion turbines--lower oil prices translates into lower avoided costs, hence making R/As less attractive to investors. Third, with lower oil prices,

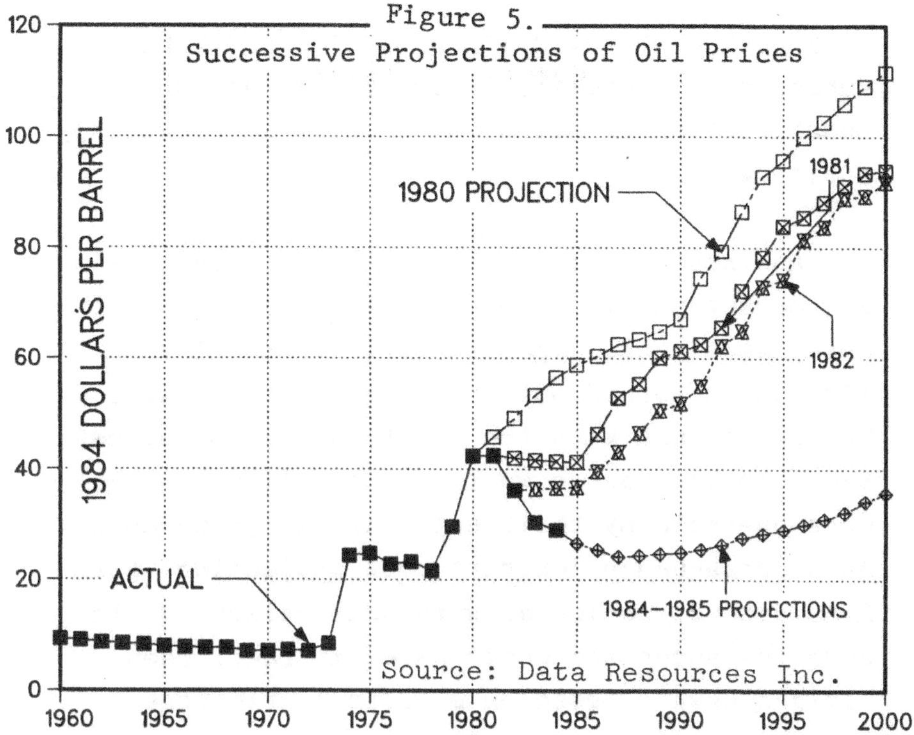
Figure 5.
Successive Projections of Oil Prices
1984 DOLLARS PER BARREL
1980 PROJECTION
1981
1982
ACTUAL
1984–1985 PROJECTIONS
Source: Data Resources Inc.
0
20
40
60
80
100
120
1960
1965
1970
1975
1980
1985
1990
1995
2000

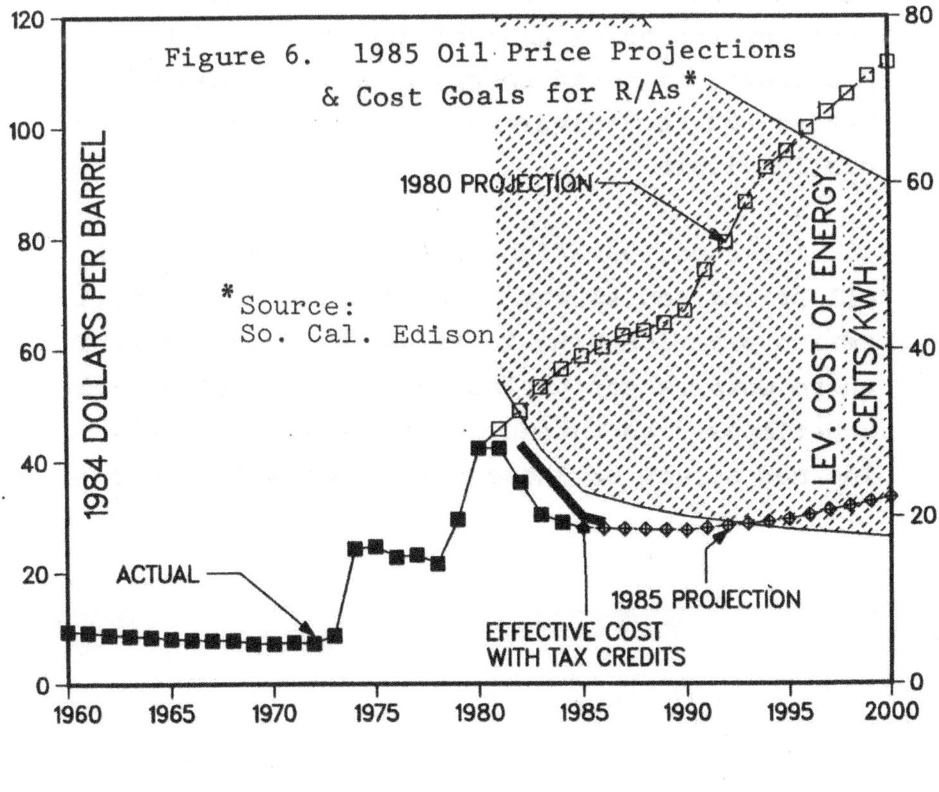
Figure 6. 1985 Oil Price Projections
& Cost Goals for R/As*
1984 DOLLARS PER BARREL
LEV. COST OF ENERGY CENTS/KWH
1980 PROJECTION
*Source:
So. Cal. Edison
ACTUAL
1985 PROJECTION
EFFECTIVE COST
WITH TAX CREDITS
0
20
40
60
80
100
120
1960
1965
1970
1975
1980
1985
1990
1995
2000

many of the cogeneration projects involving enhanced oil recovery in California and Gulf Coast states are not as attractive as previously anticipated.

Another important factor is that cost goals and market penetration projections for R/As which were considered realistic in the late 1970s have turned out to be highly optimistic. The experience with the first generation of new technologies has shown that most--if not all--were oversold by their enthusiastic proponents. As a consequence, current cost projections for R/As are not as low as were once believed. In some instances the costs have, in fact, been revised upward based on more realistic recent projections. Additionally, the performance of some new technologies indicates that additional R&D and/or improved energy storage is needed before the technology may be considered commercially viable.

The combined effect of substantially lower oil prices and slower than expected commercialization pace for R/As is illustrated in Figure 6, where more recent projections of oil prices are superimposed on current cost projection goals. The net effect of these developments is clear:

technologies that were expected to become cost-competitive with oil during the 1980s and early 1990s--based on 1980 oil price projections--will not become costcompetitive until the 1990s or beyond--based on today's oil prices. Some of the more exotic, less-developed technologies, are not expected to become economically feasible until the turn of the century with the current oil price projections.

To make matters worse, the Department of Energy has reduced its R&D budget substantially since 1980 and has shifted its emphasis away from many R/As, particularly for technologies in demonstration and commercialization phases. (Figure 3). This is unfortunate because many technologies have not evolved to a point where the private sector could take over the demonstration activities which must precede commercial-scale applications.

Furthermore, expiration of some of the financial incentives, notably accelerated depreciation and energy tax credits, has the effect of increasing the cost and risks of investment in new technologies. Collectively, these developments represent a reversal of trends and expectations from the prevailing conditions of the late 1970s. This reversal does not necessarily suggest an end for R/As; what it does suggest is a re-evaluation of priorities and a more selective strategy for the future (Allen, 1985).

SELECTIVE R/A STRATEGY

As the preceding discussion suggests, what is needed today is a critical re-evaluation of objectives and priorities relative to R/As and a more selective R&D strategy for the future. The strategy of the decade of the 1970s was appropriate given the crisis mentality which prevailed during that tumultuous period of uncertainty and rapid change (Sioshansi, 1985). What is needed now, in view of today's market realities, is a more flexible strategy which is selective in four ways:

First, the industry must adjust its priorities with respect to R/As in a way which recognizes their cost competitiveness, timeliness, and potential contributions to system-specific needs. This suggests that technologies which are most likely to pass the hurdle of cost-competitiveness in the near to medium term should receive top priority in R&D funding. Technologies with longer-term potential must receive additional funding support from DOE and the federal government before they can be pursued by the private sector.

Second, because many R/As, notably solar- and wind-driven technologies, are intermittent and unreliable in nature, the need for energy storage has assumed increased significance and should receive immediate and increased attention.

Third, the most important lesson of the past 15 years is that one should not rely too heavily on any single forecast, no matter how strong the consensus. As a corollary to this, one should plan for the future with flexibility by maintaining many options and allowing for timely, mid-course corrections. This approach favors modular, short lead-time technologies and a more balanced mix of energy resources.

Finally, the current oil glut and falling price of oil may be short-lived and should not make us complacent. By contrast, we should take advantage of this breathing period to prepare for the next energy crisis by pursuing an aggressive and diversified R&D effort.

REFERENCES

Alm, A. L. and D. A. Dreyfus, 1982. Utilities in Crisis: A Problem in Governance, Aspen Institute for Humanistic Studies, New York.

Allen, H. P., 1985. "Public/Private Partnership in Developing Renewable Energy," Keynote address at the Renewable Energy Technologies Symposium, Anaheim, CA, June 4, 1985.

Sioshansi, F. P., 1984. "The Outlook for the Electric Utility Industry: Evolving Trends and Opportunities," in The Energy Industries in Transition 1985-2000, Weyant, J. P. and D. B. Sheffield, Eds., Proceedings of the Sixth Annual North American Meeting, San Francisco, November 5-7, 1985, International Association of Energy Economists.

_______________, 1985. "Alternatives/Renewable Sources of Power as Energy Solutions," presentation to New York Society of Security Analysts, New York, June 1985.

34
World Economic Outlook

Howard Howe, Wharton Econometric Forecasting Associates

INTRODUCTION

The growth differential between Europe and the United States is narrowing, but not because Europe is picking up. A widening trade deficit is the major factor behind a projected U.S. slowdown to under 3 percent growth this year. Complemented by a continuing decline in U.S. interest rates, the ongoing trade leakage is contributing to a U.S. outlook characterized by low but steady growth rather than a sharp downturn in 1986. The U.S. current account deficit continues to widen. Last year's deficit of $102 billion was over double the 1983 level. The correspondingly large capital inflows have kept the dollar strong. Although it has generally weakened since mid-March, the dollar remains approximately equal to its end-1984 level. On a trade-weighted basis, the dollar has strengthened by 53 percent since the end of 1980.

MAJOR ISSUES AND RISKS

With the rapid growth of the U.S. economy in 1983 and 1984, the "two deficits"--the U.S. federal deficit and the U.S. current account deficit--illustrate the economic imbalances associated with the global recovery.

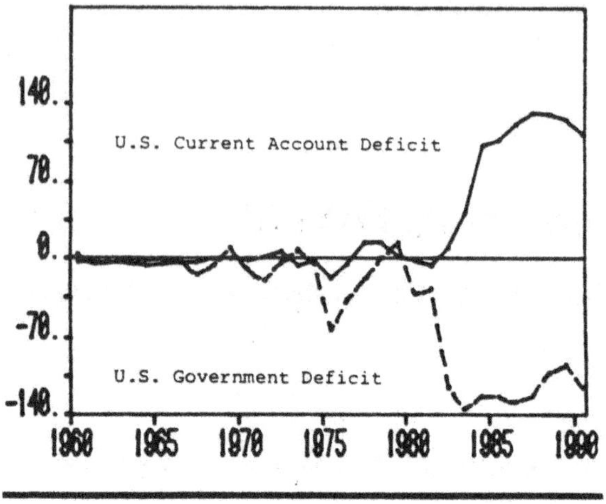

Figure 1.1
The Two Deficits of the United States
(Billions of dollars)

Strong U.S. economic growth and the high dollar led to a large merchandise trade deficit, whose mirror image is strong foreign capital inflows. Domestic capital formation has not been crowded out, since the foreign source of funds has increased so dramatically. But the merchandise trade deficit is putting unprecedented pressure on the U.S. manufacturing sector.

To demonstrate the relative sizes of the two deficits, Figure 1.1 shows one use of funds--the total government deficit (federal deficit less the state and local surplus)--and the source of funds that has increased most in response to the increased federal deficit--net capital inflows from abroad, that is, the negative of the current account deficit. Historically, these two deficits have been relatively small. But in 1983 and 1984, the current account deficit amounted to 23 and 56 percent, respectively, of the federal budget deficit.

The large current account deficit acts as an export-led stimulus for the rest of the world. However, the accompanying large capital outflows keep pressure on foreign monetary authorities lest their currencies again start to depreciate against the dollar. What does this trend mean for the international economy? The international system is adjusting to U.S. fiscal policy at much higher levels of gross deficits than previously. As a result, the international economy is subject to a number of risks ranging from interest rate runups, a rapid dollar depreciation triggered by a loss of confidence, a procyclical fiscal contraction in the United States, a protectionist showdown, or a structural change away from U.S. industrial activity brought on by the protracted trade deficit.

Shape of the Next Economic Cycle

The prolonged large U.S. trade deficit brings its own set of risk factors. If the U.S. downturn is deeper than projected, the economy will tend to stay weak longer because a shaky net-export position cannot be corrected rapidly through relative prices. In many ways this is uncharted territory for the U.S. private sector; an extended period of slow growth could have negative repercussions on investment. Moreover, protectionist pressures are building.

Japan's "Closed" Markets

Concern over Japan's merchandise trade surplus with the United States is increasing. The U.S. press and Congress have become more aware of qualitative restrictions in the Japanese market as a result of discussions over access of U.S. exports to the Japanese telecommunications sector. With abundant illustrations of "unfairness" in marketing structure, inspection procedures, and other non-tariff barriers, the U.S. public and Congress are increasingly willing to consider measures limiting Japanese access to U.S. markets.

For some time, protectionism arising from the pressures of high European unemployment has been considered as a risk to continued world economic growth. The risk of protectionism is increasing as the focus broadens to include Japan's import practices and the inability of Japanese policymakers to lessen the dependency on export-led growth.

A Soft Landing for the Dollar

While the dollar is expected to continue to weaken, its decline will not be rapid enough to undo the gains in price competitiveness enjoyed by foreign producers. Continued depreciation is likely over the remainder of the year, but the high level reached by early March implies that the average effective dollar exchange rate will still have appreciated on average for this year. Although the path is not likely to be smooth, steady depreciation through 1990 is projected.

The main reasons behind the soft-landing path for the dollar are the continued growth differential between the United States and Europe and continued high savings in Japan relative to domestic loan demand. Nevertheless, the possibility of a sharp depreciation of the dollar remains a significant risk in the forecast.

Export Prices and the Dollar

How deeply will the expected decline in the dollar cut into European and Japanese export volumes to the United States? While the dollar appreciated 43 percent on average between 1980 and 1984, the unit value of U.S. imports of manufactured goods declined only 10 percent. Estimating that production costs rose 15 percent over that period, we are left with a "wedge" of 18 percent between the selling price and production costs that can be interpreted as an increase in producers' profit margins.

Now that foreign producers have penetrated U.S. markets, adopted specific model designs, and established distribution and service networks, will they insist on maintaining existing profit margins at the expense of market share? Probably not.

We assume that exporters in the industrial countries will hold back local-currency export prices to help lessen the impact of the dollar's 4 percent and 8 percent depreciations expected in 1986 and 1987. This imperfect-pass-through assumption is the reason why world price indexes of manufactured goods increase as little as 6 and 9 percent in 1986 and 1987 and world export volumes of the same goods grow as much as 4 percent in the same years.

Oil Prices To Remain Weak

A continuing increase in non-OPEC crude oil production and slow growth in world oil demand will keep real oil prices declining for several more years. The movement of nominal-dollar oil prices is likely to be more irregular. After two years of price weakness, the decline in the dollar and economic expansion will lead to a pickup in consumption and a rise in nominal-dollar oil prices in 1988. Real oil prices are expected to stabilize at the end of the decade, and real oil price growth is expected from that point forward.

The Debt Crisis Revisited

The declining interest rate profile for 1985 and 1986 reduces the risk of a Latin American default. Uncertainty on rescheduling plans now runs high for Brazil and, to a certain extent, Argentina. In Brazil, targets agreed on with the IMF were not met, and negotiations on a new program have yet to produce a new set of targets. In Argentina, the signing of a new agreement with the IMF will pave the way for new debt negotiations, but creditors are unlikely to make major concessions before the government's ambitious monetary reform is seen to be on track.

Contractionary domestic policies induced by the debt crisis have severely hurt the developing countries. The ability of the debtor countries to continue indefinitely in such a low-growth mode is still a significant risk factor. The LDCs have little room to maneuver, and a renewed run-up in interest rates, a sharper-than-expected deceleration of world growth in 1985-86, or a further decline in oil prices could trigger a renewed crisis.

OUTLOOK FOR THE INDUSTRIAL COUNTRIES

What kind of economic forecast do these factors imply? Even with the aforementioned risks, the best-current-information outlook is for continued--albeit slower--growth this year and in 1986. Inflation is expected to remain close to current levels through the remainder of the decade.

All major economies except the United Kingdom and France are expected to grow more slowly this year than in 1984. The deceleration from 4 1/2 percent to under 3 percent this year, however, is largely a result of the U.S. slowdown. European growth will differ little from its 1984 rate. With the resolution of the miners' strike, U.K. growth will pick up from 1.6 percent last year to 3.6 percent in 1985. OECD growth will remain below 3 percent this year and next.

The diverse movements of the major European countries add up to growth just below 2 1/2 percent this year, only slightly above 1984. Although a decided improvement over the 1.3 percent growth registered for 1983, this performance reflects the combined effects of tight policy and structural rigidities that still plague the European economies.

The slackening activity is initiated by slower U.S. growth and compounded by deterioration in Europe's competitive position because of the already visible decline in the dollar. The Japanese economy will also slow as external stimulus diminishes and domestic expansion fails to take up the slack. Japan's growth will slow to about 3 percent in 1986.

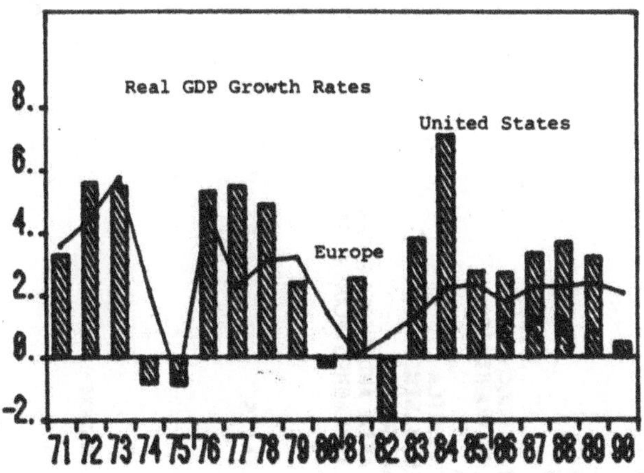

Figure 1.2
The U.S. and European Business Cycles

TABLE 1.1 WORLD FORECAST SUMMARY

	1983	1984	1985	1986	1987
	REAL GDP (PERCENT CHANGE)				
WORLD	2.2	4.0	2.9	2.8	3.2
OECD	2.4	4.6	2.8	2.4	2.9
UNITED STATES	3.8	7.1	2.8	2.7	3.3
CANADA	2.8	4.7	3.5	3.1	2.7
JAPAN	3.0	5.7	4.0	3.1	3.3
EUROPE	1.3	2.2	2.4	1.8	2.3
GERMANY	1.0	2.6	2.3	1.9	2.3
FRANCE	.7	1.3	1.4	1.6	2.3
ITALY	-.4	2.6	2.3	2.1	3.0
UNITED KINGDOM	3.2	1.6	3.6	1.0	2.1
DEVELOPING COUNTRIES	-.1	2.8	2.8	3.9	4.1
AFRICA	-.5	1.0	2.7	2.7	3.0
LATIN AMERICA	-3.4	2.7	2.4	3.5	4.2
PACIFIC BASIN	5.7	5.9	5.9	6.4	6.5
ARABIAN GULF	-2.6	-.7	-1.5	2.9	3.6
OTHER ASIA AND MIDDLE EAST	4.5	4.6	3.8	4.2	2.6
CENTRALLY PLANNED ECONOMIES	3.4	3.1	3.1	3.2	3.3
	PRIVATE CONSUMPTION DEFLATORS (PERCENT CHANGE)				
OECD	5.7	5.1	4.9	4.8	4.7
UNITED STATES	3.7	3.2	3.2	4.0	4.6
CANADA	5.8	4.1	4.7	5.1	4.5
JAPAN	1.6	2.0	2.8	2.9	3.3
EUROPE	8.3	7.6	6.5	5.7	5.1
GERMANY	2.9	2.6	2.5	2.1	2.0
FRANCE	9.5	7.1	5.5	4.8	4.3
ITALY	15.2	11.1	9.0	7.5	7.7
UNITED KINGDOM	5.4	5.1	6.3	5.5	4.4
	UNEMPLOYMENT RATES (PERCENT OF LABOR FORCE)				
OECD	9.5	9.1	9.1	9.2	9.3
UNITED STATES	9.6	7.5	7.4	7.5	7.4
JAPAN	2.6	2.7	2.7	2.8	3.0
EUROPE	11.2	11.7	12.0	12.2	12.3
GERMANY	8.0	8.0	8.0	8.0	7.9
FRANCE	8.4	9.8	10.5	10.8	10.9
UNITED KINGDOM	13.1	13.2	13.2	13.5	13.8

TABLE 1.1 CONT'D.

	SELECTED COMMODITY DOLLAR EXPORT PRICES (PERCENT CHANGE)				
WHEAT	.0	-3.1	-1.7	-1.8	-3.0
OTHER CEREALS	-3.5	-12.7	-4.8	-8.1	-5.5
COFFEE, TEA, COCOA	7.1	15.0	-3.5	5.0	6.5
MINERALS EXCEPT FUELS	-6.6	-3.1	-7.0	-2.0	10.0
SAUDIA ARABIA AVERAGE EXPORT PRICE OF CRUDE PETROLEUM ($/BARREL)	29.31	28.47	27.82	27.50	27.50
PERCENT CHANGE PER YEAR	-12.4	-2.9	-2.3	-1.2	.0
	SHORT-TERM INTEREST RATES (PERCENT)				
EURODOLLAR RATE	9.6	10.8	8.1	6.8	7.5
LONDON INTERBANK RATE	9.6	10.8	8.0	6.7	7.4
UNITED STATES	8.9	10.2	7.6	6.5	7.1
JAPAN	6.4	6.1	6.2	5.9	6.0
GERMANY	5.4	5.5	5.0	4.2	4.1
FRANCE	12.5	11.7	10.4	8.8	8.4
UNITED KINGDOM	9.6	9.3	10.3	9.5	8.4
	EFFECTIVE EXCHANGE RATES (MERM WEIGHTS, PERCENT CHANGE)				
UNITED STATES	5.9	7.9	6.6	-4.2	-8.3
JAPAN	10.0	5.7	.7	3.7	3.3
GERMANY	2.4	-2.7	-.8	6.3	8.2
FRANCE	-8.7	-6.1	.0	4.4	6.0
UNITED KINGDOM	-8.0	-5.4	-6.1	3.0	2.0
	WORLD TRADE (PERCENT CHANGE)				
VOLUMES(EXPORTS), TOTAL	2.2	9.3	5.8	4.4	3.9
PRIMARY COMMODITIES (NON-FUEL)	.3	10.1	6.7	6.1	4.9
FUELS	.0	.7	1.0	2.9	2.6
MANUFACTURED GOODS	3.9	10.5	6.9	4.7	4.2
PRICES (EXPORT DEFLATORS, DOLLARS), TOTAL	-4.5	-2.8	-2.3	4.3	7.8
PRIMARY COMMODITIES (NON-FUEL)	-.3	-2.7	-4.0	2.2	6.4
FUELS	-10.8	-.4	-3.4	-1.7	2.3
MANUFACTURED GOODS	-3.6	-2.7	-1.3	6.5	9.4

Steady but unremarkable growth is projected for the remainder of the decade. The pace of European growth will be barely enough to stabilize unemployment rates. Growth is projected to average no more than 2.3 percent, well below the 3 percent range that might dent unemployment rates.

IMPLICATIONS FOR THE REGIONAL ECONOMIES

Continued Slowdown in the Middle East

While most industrialized and non-oil developing countries achieved strong economic recovery during 1984, the year brought little relief to the depressed economies of the Middle East and North Africa. Oil markets remained soft, budgets were cut further, imports continued to fall, and major development projects continued to be cancelled or postponed. Given the current situation in international oil markets, there is little hope for a turnaround before 1987.

The six member-states of the Gulf Cooperation Council (Saudi Arabia, Kuwait, the United Arab Emirates, Oman, Bahrain and Qatar) experienced a decline of 2 percent in non-oil GDP last year; their nominal merchandise imports dropped by 2.8 percent, following a 7 percent decline in 1983. Nonetheless, the group's current account continued in deficit and is projected to remain so through 1988. The short-term growth prospects of the GCC states are not much brighter. Non-oil economic activity in the region is expected to remain stagnant this year and next, followed by 2 to 3 percent growth in 1987 and 1988.

An Improved Outlook for Latin America

Latin America experienced an uneven and still insufficient recovery in 1984, the first positive growth since 1981. The strength of the recovery exceeded official expectations in the two largest economies, Brazil and Mexico, as well as in Colombia. Venezuela, on the other hand, suffered a 1.7 percent decline in real GDP, and Chile experienced a slowdown in the second half of the year after achieving a 6 percent annual growth rate in the first half. Regional GDP growth of 2.6 percent was a welcome development, but not enough to compensate for the declines in the two previous years.

Renewed efforts to control inflation in some countries will prevent faster regional growth this year. The recovery is expected to continue in Brazil and Mexico, although at a slower pace. Chile and Colombia appear headed for lower growth, owing to the implementation of new stabilization measures, while the shift to drastic stabilization policies is expected to result in a 5.6 percent contraction of real GDP in Argentina. Venezuela, on the other hand, is expected to begin to recover from a six-year-long recession.

Mexico and its creditor banks formally signed the first part of the public-sector debt rescheduling, passing a milestone toward a solution of the country's debt problem. However, it may take longer for Argentina and Brazil to negotiate similar arrangements, necessitating more forbearance on the part of creditor banks.

"Miracle Growth" Temporarily Revisited in Asia

Developing countries in the Pacific last year rode the wave of the global economic recovery and posted growth rates reminiscent of the "miracle" years of the 1960s and 1970s. A surge in exports--primarily to the United States--fueled Taiwan's double-digit growth and led to buoyant expansions in South Korea and Singapore. The Hong Kong economy benefited from strong sales to China and the United States, and from the more stable political environment following the Sino-British agreement last fall.

Except for the Philippines, commodity-exporting Asia also experienced an upturn in growth. However, budget deficits and balance-of-payments constraints held growth rates in these countries--Indonesia, Malaysia, and Thailand--significantly below those achieved by the Asian NICs.

This year, owing to the slowdown in U.S. import growth from its explosive 27 percent in 1984, Asian export performance has weakened. In South Korea, for example, the loss of export momentum was the primary factor behind the (annualized) 4 percent growth realized in the first quarter. Other NICs in the Pacific are also experiencing some deceleration in export and GDP growth. Commodity exporters have felt the pinch of soft export prices and thinner markets for light manufactured products. For the region as a whole, structural problems and internal and external budget constraints, together with the export deceleration, will hold growth below 6 percent in 1985.

Rapid Growth in the People's Republic of China

Economic performance in the People's Republic of China last year surpassed even the most optimistic projections. Spurred by accelerated economic reforms, industrial production rose by 14 percent. A record grain harvest and healthy sideline production led to equally impressive gains in agriculture.

Concern has mounted, however, that the economy may be overheating as a result of urban reforms. Wharton's projections for China call for strong growth over the forecast period, with brief growth pauses likely as China struggles to adjust to ongoing reforms and eliminate energy and transportation bottlenecks. Capital inflows will more than offset a gradual deterioration in the current account balance, and the external payments position should remain relatively strong.

Continued Recovery in Eastern Europe But Poor Results for the Soviet Union

Despite continued economic recovery in Eastern Europe last year, Soviet economic performance was relatively poor. This pattern can be expected for the next few years, although there is a chance that the Soviet Union could achieve slightly better results under its new leadership.

Overall economic growth in the Soviet Union suffered from poor performance in agriculture. With only modest improvements in other sectors, total output showed the second lowest increase in the postwar period (the lowest being in 1979). It is unlikely that Soviet growth rates will increase sharply over the next few years, even under the new leadership.

East European economic growth in the second half of the 1980s will necessitate a surge in investment and increased imports of capital goods and intermediate goods from the West. During the economic crisis of the early 1980s, East European authorities emphasized consumption relative to net investment in order to minimize social unrest. But if these countries are to retain growth momentum after the recovery period and become competitive in exporting to Western markets, they must modernize their economies. Eastern Europe is likely to turn once again to the West for technology and equipment to help achieve this objective. The forecast embodies a shift by East European countries to faster growth of imports from the West at the end of the 1980s, accompanied by moderate increases in hard-currency indebtedness.

Some Improvement in the African Picture

The major sub-Saharan economies are moving into a cyclical recovery. The recovery is weak, and it remains to be seen whether it can be sustained, especially if the industrial countries slip into a more pronounced growth pause than foreseen here. There is little doubt, however, that almost all large African countries will experience growth this year, the first in several years for many.

The near-term forecast for South Africa is now more pessimistic. Little growth can be anticipated this year in light of the fiscal tightening initiated at the end of March. Racial tensions are exacerbating an already weak economic situation. While the current policy package is expected to reduce inflation, the long-term outlook for South Africa remains pessimistic.

For Nigeria, 1985 will be a year of growth despite austerity and import cuts. In the Francophone countries of West Africa, the relative strength of tropical beverage crops and favorable terms of trade are contributing to growth. Economic activity in the Ivory Coast is expected to increase this year, despite a sharp drop in real public-sector spending. In Zimbabwe, inflation remains high; however, the agricultural sector has performed much better than expected.

CONCLUSION

The prognosis for the remainder of the decade is world growth in the 3 percent range. This is a problematic outlook in that it implies continued high unemployment in both the developed and developing economies and ongoing difficulties for the debtor LDCs in meeting their external financing requirements. Continued retrenchment on the part of policymakers is another important component of this outlook. The added uncertainty attached to the "two deficits" problem is making policymakers in the major industrial countries skeptical about implementing positive growth policies with either fiscal or monetary tools.

There is a good deal of discomfort attached to an outlook embodying protracted large gross positions such as the "two deficits." But, without dramatic breaks in key assumptions, we are left with a baseline outlook built on only small adjustments to current policy positions. The major sources of vulnerability emphasized at the beginning of this outlook point out the usefulness of a set of alternative scenarios describing the "adjustment" process. Alternatives addressing dollar depreciation, lower oil prices, reduction in the U.S. budget deficit, and international policy coordination can help the planner understand the range of economic outcomes and the potential variation in his own business activity. With ongoing economic imbalances very much in the cards for the world economy, scenario analysis takes on added importance in the planning function.

35
1985 GRI Baseline Projection of U.S. Energy Supply and Demand: 1984–2010

Paul Holtberg, Gas Research Institute

INTRODUCTION

This paper summarizes the 1985 GRI Baseline Projection of U.S. Energy Supply and Demand, which has been adopted for the current planning cycle by the Gas Research Institute (GRI).

This is a particularly difficult time to discuss the outlook for energy markets. There is considerable uncertainty among energy analysts concerning future energy markets. For example, uncertainty exists concerning energy prices, the future role of electric utilities, and the changing nature of the industrial sector. In deference to this uncertainty, this paper focuses on the major issues and uncertainties that have arisen out of the GRI analysis.

MAJOR ASSUMPTIONS

The refiner's acquisition cost of crude oil is assumed to decline in real terms through 1987. Starting in 1988, the real price is assumed to gradually rise, reaching $26.00 per barrel (in 1984 dollars) by 1990.

It is assumed that as a result of low oil prices, domestic production will decline and imports to the United States will rise. Global exploration and development will slow, and production will be reconcentrated in the Middle East. As a result, one or more oil price spikes are assumed to occur after 1990. In lieu of fixing specific dates for the price spikes, a 4 percent per year real price increase is assumed from 1990 to 2010. This results in a real price of $38.50 per barrel in 2000 and $57.00 per barrel in 2010, both in 1984 dollars.

The average real Gross National Product (GNP) growth is assumed to be 3.2 percent per year between 1984 and 1990 and 2,4 percent per year between 1990 and 2010. Overall, between 1984 and 2010, GNP is assumed to grow at 2.6 percent per year.

PRIMARY ENERGY CONSUMPTION

Total primary energy, shown in table 1, grows at a rate of 1.1 percent per year or at 45 percent of the GNP growth rate. The energy-to-GNP ratio is projected to fall from 47,700 British thermal units (Btu) per 1972 dollar in 1984 to 32,600 in 2010.

Table 1. U.S. Primary Energy Consumption (quadrillion Btu)

	Actual 1984	1990	2000	2010
Petroleum	31.1	32.3	34.6	35.7
Gas[a]	17.9	18.3	18.7	16.5
(Total gas fuels)[b]	(18.0)	(18.4)	(19.0)	(17.3)
Coal	17.2	19.6	24.9	30.9
Nuclear	3.6	6.4	6.5	5.7
Hydro	3.7	4.0	4.0	4.0
Renewables	4.3	5.1	6.7	9.4
Total	77.8	85.7	95.4	102.2

[a]Excludes synthetic gas from petroleum and coal.

[b]Total gas fuels includes 0.1, 0.3 and 0.8 quadrillion Btu of synthetic gas from petroleum and coal in 1990, 2000 and 2010, respectively.

Petroleum consumption is projected to grow at only 0.5 percent per year or at less than half of the rate of growth in total energy demand. Most of the growth in petroleum consumption is projected to occur in the industrial sector. About 40 percent of this growth is for feedstock purposes.

Despite the relatively slow growth in petroleum demand, declining domestic production results in a significant increase in imports. Domestic oil production is projected to fall from 10.3 million barrels per day in 1984 to 7.8 million barrels per day in 2010. Therefore, despite slow growth in demand, oil imports are projected to increase from 4.8 million barrels per day to 9.2 million barrels per day in 2010.

Primary gas consumption increases from 17.9 quadrillion Btu in 1984 to 18.7 quads in 2000 or at the average rate of 0.3 percent per year.

Without the inclusion of gas supplies likely to be available from expected technology advances, gas demand is projected to decline after 2000. Using an alternative supply slate that assumes advanced technologies for the production of gas from tight formations and other unconventional sources, a demand level of about 19 quadrillion Btu could be sustained through the year 2010.

Over the entire projection, coal has an economic advantage over oil and gas in industrial applications. Although its use is constrained by physical and regulatory limitations, coal progressively gains in its share of new demand over the projection timeframe.

RESIDENTIAL SECTOR

Table 2 presents the projection of residential sector energy demand.

Total residential energy demand is projected to increase at only 0.2 percent per year between 1984 and 2010. The slow rate of growth reflects an expectation of continued strong energy conservation and a reduced projection of new home construction.

Table 2. Residential Sector Delivered Energy Consumption (quadrillion Btu)

	Estimated[a] 1984	1990	2000	2010
Petroleum	1.5	1.5	1.1	1.0
Gas	4.5	4.3	3.9	3.6
Coal	0.1	0.1	0.1	0.1
Electricity	2.7	3.0	3.4	3.6
Renewables	0.9	1.0	1.4	2.0
Total	9.7	9.9	9.9	10.3

[a]Historical EIA statistics for 1984 do not disaggregate data for the residential and commercial sectors.

The share of new single-family homes using gas for space heating is projected to increase from 42 percent in 1984 to 46 percent in 1995. After 1995 this share gradually falls to 44 percent by 2010.

The total number of gas-heated housing units increases from 44.5 million in 1984 to 57 million in 2010. However, the increasing number of units is not great enough to offset the impacts of conservation and the increased efficiency of new appliances. Gas demand in the sector gradually decreases after 1990.

The projected growth in total residential energy consumption occurs in electricity and renewable energy, which offset declines in petroleum and gas.

COMMERCIAL SECTOR

The projection of commercial sector energy demand is shown in table 3.

During the balance of the 1980s and into the 1990s, the rate of economic growth in the commercial sector is still expected to be greater than that of the general economy. Commercial square footage is expected to grow at 3.3 percent per year through the year 1995, compared with GNP growth of 2.9 percent per year. After 1995, commercial square footage and the general economy both grow at slightly greater than 2.0 percent per year.

Table 3. Commercial Sector Delivered Energy Consumption (quadrillion Btu)

	Estimated[a] 1984	1990	2000	2010
Petroleum	0.9	1.0	0.8	0.7
Gas	2.4	2.8	3.7	4.5
Coal	0.1	0.1	0.1	0.1
Electricity	2.2	2.6	3.0	3.4
(Cogenerated elec.[b])	c	c	(0.3)	(0.6)
Renewables	0.1	0.1	0.4	0.8
Total	5.7	6.6	8.0	9.5

[a]Historical EIA statistics for 1983 do not disaggregate data for the residential and commercial sectors.

[b]Energy consumed to produce cogenerated electricity is included in the totals for gas.

[c]Less than 0.05 quadrillion Btu.

High growth in lodging, health care, and restaurants, which have significant requirements for water heating, space heating and cooking, along with the increased requirement for space cooling, emphasize the potential significance of gas-fired commercial cogeneration. The 1985 GRI projection includes 1.7 quadrillion Btu of gas-fired commercial cogeneration in 2010. Although cogeneration will displace some gas consumption which would otherwise occur, the projected growth in total commercial gas consumption without cogeneration would be reduced significantly.

INDUSTRIAL SECTOR

Table 4 presents the projection of industrial sector energy demand.

Table 4. Industrial Sector Delivered Energy Consumption (quadrillion Btu)

	Actual 1984	1990	2000	2010
Petroleum	8.0	9.1	10.3	11.8
Gas	7.4	8.2	8.4	6.1
Coal	2.9	3.4	4.7	5.6
Electricity	2.9	3.5	4.0	4.5
(Cogenerated elec.)[a]	(0.2)	(0.6)	(0.9)	(0.9)
Renewables	3.1	3.6	4.1	4.5
Total	24.3	27.8	31.5	32.5

[a]Energy consumed to produce cogenerated electricity has already been included in the totals for gas, petroleum and coal consumption.

Total industrial natural gas consumption is projected to progressively increase through 2000. This is the influence of real output growth in the industrial sector which exceeds the factors limiting gas consumption per dollar of real output. Between 1984 and 2000, real industrial output grows by 3.3 percent per year. Industrial gas consumption grows from 7.4 quadrillion Btu in 1984 to 8.4 quadrillion Btu in 2000, an average rate of 0.8 percent per year.

A substantial portion of the projected increased industrial gas consumption is the result of growth in gas-fired cogeneration. Consumption for industrial cogeneration grows from 0.4 quadrillion Btu in 1984 to 0.8 quadrillion Btu in 1990 and 1.2 quadrillion Btu in 2000.

After the year 2000, the projection indicates that, in the absence of new gas supply supplements which are competitive with low-cost alternative fuels, gas consumption in the industrial sector would be supply constrained to about 6.1 quadrillion Btu in 2010. An alternative supply slate is discussed in the supply presentation which could provide the necessary gas to sustain industrial demand at 7.7 quadrillion Btu.

ELECTRIC UTILITY SECTOR

Energy consumed in central station electricity generation is presented in table 5.

Table 5. Energy Consumption to Generate Electricity (quadrillion Btu)

	Actual 1984	1990	2000	2010
Petroleum	1.3	1.0	0.9	0.6
Gas	3.2	2.5	2.1	2.0
Coal	14.1	15.9	19.8	24.1
Nuclear	3.6	6.4	6.5	5.7
Hydro	3.7	4.0	4.0	4.0
Other	0.2	0.4	0.8	2.1
Total	26.1	30.2	34.1	38.5
Delivered electricity[a]	7.8	9.1	10.3	11.4
Canadian imports[b]	0.1	0.2	0.2	0.2
Purchases from cogenerators[b]	c	0.1	0.2	0.3

[a]"Delivered electricity" refers only to electricity purchased from electric utilities; it does not include cogeneration for self-use.

[b]Canadian imports and purchases for cogenerators are included in delivered electricity; both represent sources of electricity other than central station generation.

[c]Less than 0.05 quadrillion Btu.

The electric utility sector outlook reflects the projected impacts of cogeneration along with a reduced total end-use demand for electricity compared with previous projections. Between 1984 and 2010 total electricity demand, including cogeneration, is projected to grow at 1.8 percent per year or at 72 percent of the rate of growth in GNP.

An increasing portion of total end-use electricity demand is projected to be provided from non-utility generation, including cogeneration and imports. Between 1984 and 2010 electricity generated by U.S. utility powerplants is projected to decline from 95 percent to 84 percent of total end-use electricity.

Despite the fact that centrally generated electricity is a declining portion of total electricity supply, utility consumption of total primary energy consumption grows from 33.5 percent in 1984 to 37.7 percent in 2010.

The projection assumes that gas and petroleum are used increasingly for peaking purposes. This trend, combined with retirement of older generating capacity, results in a steady decline in both petroleum and gas consumption in the electric utility sector.

Assuming that the growth in demand for electricity will track economic expansion in the range of 50 to 100 percent of the rate of GNP growth, there are uncertainties about the ability of utility systems to meet the requirement for increased generating capacity.

While the addition of cogeneration in the industrial and commercial sectors reduces the projected requirement for central station powerplant capacity, it does not necessarily provide any greater assurance that the required capacity will be provided. Short lead times are associated with most cogeneration ventures, only one to three years from commitment to completion. There are few short-lead-time fallbacks available to a utility if demand should exceed expectations or if non-utility generators should fail to materialize. Gas-fired, combined-cycle powerplants could provide an economical form of short lead-time capacity additions if public policy were revised to enable utilities to plan for their use. Combined-cycle powerplants would be a particularly valuable option if unanticipated capacity shortfalls were to occur. However, the projection does not currently include gas-fired combined cycle powerplants as an option.

NATURAL GAS SUPPLY AND PRICE OUTLOOK

The natural gas and supply outlook through 2000 is presented in table 6.

Gas Supply and Price Analysis

Natural gas prices and supplies are based on analyses using the GRI Hydrocarbon Model.

The first line of table 6 presents the outlook for the supply and prices of natural gas from lower-48 production. This analysis is based upon the projected costs of production including the rate of return on producer investment. In other words, it is a cost-based analysis.

Currently, in the real world, prices for new gas are being set by market conditions in an oversupply situation. The persistent excess deliverability of gas is probably depressing spot market prices and some new contract prices below the level that would provide producers with a healthy rate of return. Some of the lowest prices currently being reported for new gas purchases almost certainly reflect distressed sales by producers who are forced to view their earlier investments as sunk costs and to obtain whatever cash flow can be gotten in a slack market.

Table 6. Gas Supply and Price Trends Base Technology

	1990		2000	
	Supply (quads)	Acquisition price[a] (1984$/MMBtu)	Supply (quads)	Acquisition price[a] (1984$/MMBtu)
Natural gas[b]	16.5	2.83	14.0	4.74
ANGTS	--	--	0.7	10.03
Pipeline imports	1.2	3.36	3.1	5.01
LNG	0.2	5.22	0.7	6.27
Coal gas	c	7.55	0.1	9.38
SNG fr. petroleum	0.1	4.08	0.2	6.03
Total purchases	18.0	2.91	18.8	5.09
Lease and plant fuel	1.0		0.8	
Total supply	19.0		19.6	
Less losses and exports	0.6		0.6	
Total demand	18.4		19.0	

[a]Weighted average price at wellhead, border of plant gate.

[b]Includes natural gas consumed in Alaska, lower-48 conventional and unconventional natural gas.

[c]Less than 0.05 quadrillion Btu.

The short-run outlook for gas prices, extending one or two years, must account for the extraordinary effects of the existing overhang. Meanwhile, however, current reserves under contract to pipelines are being depleted, and producer activity is low. As pipelines begin to bid more actively for new reserves to replace depleting holdings, competition for gas at the wellhead will begin to reveal the true cost of production. Our supply analyses indicate that for the next few years, wellhead price escalation need not be very great to support continued production at current levels. The price levels over the long term, however, must be sufficiently high to return the true costs of production, including a return on investment adequate to attract new capital in competition with other investment opportunities.

Outlook to 2000

Table 6 shows that, at prices competitive with alternative energy sources, total gas supply could remain essentially constant through 2000. In later years, however, lower-48 production must increasingly be supplemented by other supply sources. In 1984, supplements accounted for 5.7 percent of total gas supply. The share is projected to grow to 7.9 percent by 1990 and to 24.5 percent by 2000. The major share of the increase in supplemental supplies comes from pipeline imports.

The 1990 average acquisition price is slightly lower than the average price of gas in 1984. This is as a result of the increased competitive pressures which prevent lower-48 gas prices from escalating to marginal costs, more competitive pricing of pipeline imports, and lower drilling costs.

Between 1990 and 2000, the real price escalates quite rapidly, growing an average of 5.8 percent per year. This escalation arises principally from the rapid growth in the marginal cost of lower-48 production.

SUPPLY OUTLOOK 2000-2010

After the year 2000, rapidly declining lower-48 natural gas production puts increasing pressure on the supplemental gas sources. By 2010, supplemental sources are projected to provide 42 percent of U.S. gas supply. Despite the large increase in supplemental supplies, the demand for gas projected at the prices in the 1985 Baseline Projection begins to exceed the available supply by about 2000.

However, increased supplies of gas could be made available at competitive prices, using new technologies. We have analyzed the effects of introducing incremental natural gas production from tight sands, Devonian shale, coal seams, and co-production of gas and water to meet this excess demand.

Table 7 presents the supply outlook including the increment which results from advanced technologies.

Table 7. Gas Supply and Price Trends Advanced Technology

	2000		2010	
	Supply (quads)	Acquisition price[a] (1984$/MMBtu)	Supply (quads)	Acquisition price[a] (1984$/MMBtu)
Natural gas[b]	15.1	4.40	12.1	4.98
advanced Technology	(2.5)	--	(4.0)	--
ANGTS	--	--	1.2	6.10
Pipeline imports	3.1	4.63	3.9	5.43
LNG	0.7	5.76	1.0	6.92
Coal Gas	c	5.52	0.3	8.15
SNG fr. petroleum	0.2	6.03	0.2	8.93
Total purchases	19.1	4.50	18.7	5.33
Lease and plant fuel	0.9		0.7	
Total supply	20.0		19.4	
Less losses and exports	0.6		0.6	
Total demand	18.4		19.0	

[a]Weighted average price at wellhead, border of plant gate.

[b]Includes natural gas consumed in Alaska, lower-48 conventional and unconventional natural gas.

[c]Less than 0.05 quadrillion Btu.

36
Long-Run Forecasts of Regional Energy Prices With the Argonne Regional Energy Price Simulator (AREPS)

David W. South, Donald A. Hanson,
Argonne National Laboratory

1. INTRODUCTION

Since the early 1970s, energy prices have played an increasingly important role in determining future energy consumption patterns and levels of energy and economic activity. As a result, forecasts of energy prices are regularly required in the broad array of energy-related analyses conducted by public- and private-sector organizations. Unfortunately, there is often a need for energy price forecasts with different spatial or temporal details than those reported in published sources. For example, published projections of energy prices may have the required spatial, sectoral, and fuel-type dimensions but only be a short-run (1-5 year) or intermediate-term (5-15 year) forecast, when a longer-run outlook is needed. Alternatively, an appropriate set of energy prices may have a long-run time horizon but only at the national level. This paper describes a means to resolve these two data problems.

If projected energy prices in published sources do not correspond with the analytical requirements of a study, two alternatives are available. One is to assemble a set of projected energy prices with the requisite dimensions by using several different data sources. Even if these projected prices were normalized, this method has several inherent problems, namely, it is time-consuming and could introduce inconsistencies. Inconsistencies could be incorporated because assumptions and methods for projecting future energy prices would (more than likely) differ between data sources. In addition, the preparation dates of the various forecasts would differ, thereby decoupling the price forecasts from a common world oil price trajectory and set of economic factors. The second alternative is to employ a systematic method of generating a consistent set of projected energy prices through the use of available data. This method would entail the linking of spatial trends inherent in historic data with projected patterns in future energy prices. This paper documents a systematic method devised to translate national energy price projections by fuel type and sector into regional and state-level prices.

The Argonne Regional Energy Price Simulator (AREPS) was developed at Argonne National Laboratory to prepare regional and state-level projections of delivered energy prices by fuel type and end-use sector starting in 1980.[1] The AREPS system can produce a forecast of energy prices to the year 2030. Using national price levels by fuel type and sector, AREPS transforms these values into regional or state prices with an expected weighted average price differential (state-to-nation or region-to-nation, depending on the application) specific to each fuel and sector. The initial price differential is based on a three-year weighted average of historical price differentials. This differential is scaled over time to reflect a tendency for the expected value of projected prices to generally regress toward the national mean. This convergence is consistent with recent trends discovered through empirical examination. The scale factors applied to the price differentials account for these phenomena, although they do not cause complete convergence with national prices, even in the long run. Some spatial price differentiation is preserved.

Section 2 of this paper describes the methodological premise and basic design features of AREPS. The algorithm employed in AREPS is delineated in section 3. This is followed in section 4 by an illustrative set of projected prices produced by AREPS. A full set of projections (by fuel type and end-use sector) could not be presented due to space limitations.[2] The examples show regional projections for delivered industrial fuel prices for selected years from 1980 to 2010. The summary and conclusions are contained in Section 5.

2. METHODOLOGICAL PREMISE

Detailed price projections were needed as input to energy models representing each fuel-consuming sector (in some cases more than one model represents a sector). The AREPS system and these sector models are part of a larger modeling system that is being used to (1) project energy use and emissions by fuel-consuming sector under different scenarios, and (2) examine the effects of different control policies on these projections.[3]

The system was conceived in response to (1) the need to supply regional fuel price forecasts to the set of energy sector models and (2) the need for these price forecasts to be consistent with national prices in the National Energy Policy Plan (NEPP). (For convenience, the term "regional" refers here to either a single state or a multistate region.) Hence, a top-down method of preparing fuel price forecasts was devised. Three aspects make up the methodological premise in AREPS:

- National fuel prices would function as control variables,

- Historic differentials would capture the spatial price effects.

- A scale factor would be employed to induce continued convergence of the expected regional prices towards the national mean.

In the first aspect, the role of national prices is to capture overall price trends and the expected interaction between different fuel markets. These effects are reflected in the NEPP because national prices are projected by taking into account energy-market equilibrium conditions. These market effects are not explicitly modeled by AREPS in determining regional energy prices; interfuel competition and shifts in supply patterns at the subnational level are only partially captured, as will be discussed later. Instead, these market effects are presumed to be accounted for in the national price levels and the historic regional price differentials used to spatially disaggregate the projected national prices.

The means to disaggregate the projected fuel price trends to the regional and state level is incorporated in the second aspect of the methodological premise. A number of procedures were investigated; most were dismissed as impractical or infeasible, given the study's constraints.[4] The procedure finally selected to disaggregate national prices to the regional level employed fuel price differentials. Absolute and percentage price differentials (region-to-nation) were examined for each year from 1970 to 1981. The State Energy Price and Expenditure System (SEPES) data base assembled by the U.S. Department of Energy's Energy Information Administration was used for this exercise (U.S. Dept. of Energy, 1984). After a thorough examination of the data under each alternative, the use of absolute price differentials was decided upon. Moreover, a three-year weighted-average price differential was proposed, to better capture the subtle convergence properties inherent in the price differentials and to negate abnormal one-year price movements in the historic data. The years 1979-1981 were selected because they bounded the benchmark year (1980) used in the overall modeling system and represented the most current SEPES data available.

The use of three-year weighted-average price differentials in AREPS to derive subnational fuel prices presumes that the historic (1979-1981) relationship between national and regional prices would be fixed (i.e., static) over time. In our examination of the 1970-1981 price differentials, we observed some evidence that regional prices were gradually tending toward the national mean.[5] In addition, we found some dispersal in highly concentrated sources of regional fuel supply. Demand regions are less reliant on a single supply region. Instead, most demand regions receive fuel supplies from more than one supply source, selected (presumably) on a least-cost basis in the current (and evolving) deregulated environment. An examination of future supply patterns indicates a continuation of this trend and thereby a gradual contraction of the large historic regional disparities in fuel prices. These observations, together with the need to forecast long-run regional prices with a top-down procedure (i.e., disaggregate a national fuel price projection without explicitly accounting for local supply and demand considerations), implied that the best systematic approach to estimating future expected regional prices is through their regression toward the national mean. Consequently, expected price differentials are scaled over time to reflect factors that cause future state price projections to generally regress toward the national mean. Scale factors are used to account for this phenomenon, although they do not cause complete convergence to national prices by 2030. Some spatial price differentiation is preserved because of inherent differences in regional transportation.

3. AREPS ALGORITHM

The AREPS system was developed as a computer model that systematically produces price projections at the regional level by fuel type and end-use sector. These prices cover the time period 1980-2030, usually in five-year increments.[6] Delivered fuel prices for natural gas, distillate oil, residual fuel oil, liquefied petroleum gas (LPG), and electricity[7] are determined for the residential, commercial, and industrial sectors. Residual fuel oil prices in the industrial sector are also adjusted by sulfur content.

Regional fuel price projections are produced in AREPS by applying a generic regionalization algorithm. The algorithm is based on a weighted-average difference between regional and national prices, by fuel type and sector. Beginning with a three-year (1979-1981) weighted-average difference in fuel prices, and linearly tapering the difference so that it approaches the national average price, AREPS produces regional fuel prices by adding the estimated price differential to the national fuel price projection.

The procedural steps that make up the algorithm employed in AREPS are delineated below. The variables are defined in generic terms and are applicable to any fuel price or sector. A more thorough explanation of this regional fuel price projection methodology, together with the empirical basis for its selection, is documented in South et al. (1985).

STEP 1 COMPUTATION OF AVERAGE PRICE DIFFERENTIAL

$$\bar{D}^{r}_{i,s} = W_{79}\Delta P^{r}_{i,s}(79) + W_{80}\Delta P^{r}_{i,s}(80) + W_{81}\Delta P^{r}_{i,s}(81) \qquad (1)$$

where:

W = annual fuel price weights, with W_{79} = 0.2 W_{80} = 0.3 and W_{81} = 0.5,

ΔP^{r} = region-to-nation fuel price difference by year (1979-81), fuel type i, and sector s,

$\bar{D}^{r}_{i,s}$ = weighted-average region-to-nation price differential by fuel type i and sector s,

i = fuel types: residual fuel oil, distillate fuel, natural gas, LPG, electricity and

s = sectors: residential, commercial, and industrial.

The weights W are assumed, with higher weights assigned to the more recent years. The fuel price differentials are based on data reported in the State Energy Price and Expenditure System (SEPES). This data file is assembled by the Office of End Use Markets in the Energy Information Administration of the U.S. Department of Energy (U.S. Dept. of Energy, 1984). The SEPES contains annual data on prices, expenditures, and consumption by fuel type and sector for 1970 to 1981. The data are updated annually, with approximately a two-year lag.

STEP 2 SCALING OF AVERAGE PRICE DIFFERENTIAL BY TIME PERIOD

$$D^r_{i,s}(t) = [S(t)]*[\bar{D}^r_{i,s}] \qquad (2)$$

where:

$S(t)$ = a time-specific scale factor to taper the price differential toward the national mean.[8] Three future time points were assigned fixed scale factors; intermediate years were determined by linear interpolation. The fixed time points and scale factors are as follows:

Time Period	Scale Factor
1979-1981 (weighted average)	1.0
2000	0.9
2030	0.7

$D^r_{i,s}(t)$ = the scaled fuel price difference by fuel type i and sector s in time period t.

STEP 3 COMPUTATION OF FORECASTED REGIONAL (STATE) PRICE

$$P^r_{i,s}(t) = P^N_{i,s}(t) + D^r_{i,s}(t) \qquad (3)$$

where:

$P^N_{i,s}(t)$ = the projected national fuel price by fuel type i and sector s.

Hence, according to the regionalization algorithm outlined above, a regional price $P_{i,s}^{r}(t)$ is obtained from the projected national price plus a regional differential term calculated according to equations (1) and (2).

4. INDUSTRIAL FUEL PRICE PROJECTIONS

The AREPS system has recently generated fuel price projections by census region, federal region, and state in five-year time increments for the period 1980-2030. These projections were generated as part of a test exercise. For this test, national price projections by sector and fuel type were supplied by the draft National Energy Policy Plan; preliminary projections were dated April 1985 (U.S. Dept. of Energy, 1985). Three scenarios are normally produced as part of the biannual NEPP. In this paper only the middle world oil price track scenario, referred to as the reference case, is considered.[9] Furthermore, due to space limitations, only the projections of delivered industrial prices by fuel type and federal region are presented for selected years. A complete presentation of the recent projections produced by AREPS is contained in South et al. (1985). Figure 1 shows the federal regions and their component states.

Tables 1 and 2 present industrial price projections at the national and regional level for residual fuel oil and distillate fuel. All prices are reported in 1980 dollars per million Btu. National prices for both fuels are projected to decline between 1980 and 1990 in constant terms, residual fuel oil by -9.4% and distillate by -12.8%. After 1990, prices for both fuels are projected to increase steadily through 2010. Residual fuel prices escalate by 108.3% from 1990 to 2010, or at an average annual rate of 3.74%, while distillate prices increase by 125.7%, or 4.15% per year. Excess capacity in the domestic

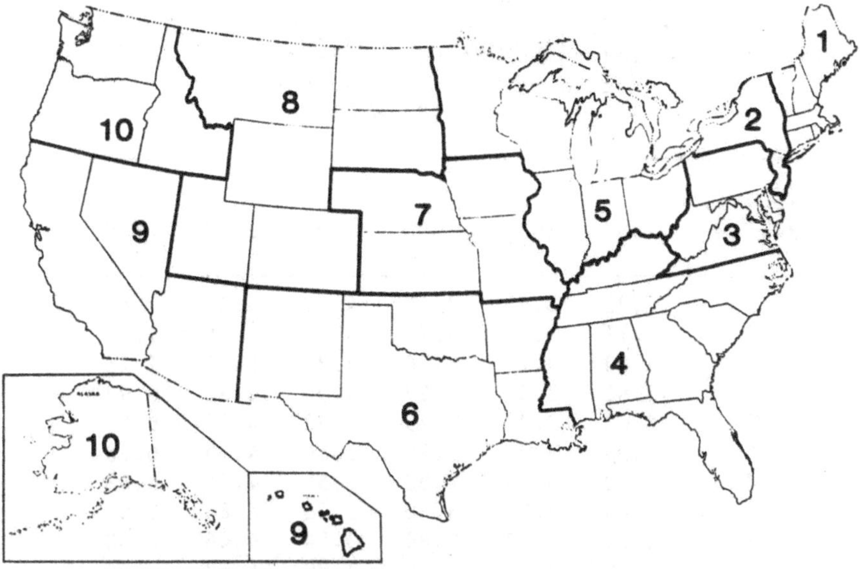

Figure 1. Federal Regions of the United States

and international crude oil supply markets precipitates the real price reductions projected until 1990. The supply tightens thereafter, causing prices to increase and new, higher-cost supply sources to be introduced.

At the federal region level, the projected national fuel price patterns are replicated due to the top-down procedure employed in AREPS. The projected price shifts in 1980-1990 and 1990-2010 are captured and reflected in the regional prices presented in tables 1 and 2. The actual percentage changes, however, vary slightly from those projected at the national level; differences in 1980 regional values and the effect of the scale factors on the expected price differential influence the projected price levels and percentage changes. Consequently, the national price patterns are reflected at the regional level but are not duplicated.

Table 1. AREPS Preliminary Projections of Residual Fuel Oil Prices for the Industrial Sector by Federal Region -- Reference Scenario (1980 $/10^6 Btu)

Federal Region	1980	1985	1990	1995	2000	2010
1	4.22	3.95	3.85	4.47	5.36	7.44
2	4.11	3.84	3.74	4.36	5.26	7.35
3	4.03	3.76	3.66	4.29	5.19	7.28
4	3.61	3.35	3.27	3.90	4.82	6.93
5	3.63	3.37	3.29	3.92	4.83	6.95
6	3.54	3.29	3.20	3.84	4.75	6.88
7	3.30	3.05	2.98	3.62	4.54	6.68
8	3.64	3.38	3.30	3.93	4.84	6.96
9	3.21	2.97	2.89	3.54	4.46	6.60
10	3.29	3.04	2.96	3.60	4.52	6.66
U.S.	3.72	3.46	3.37	4.00	4.91	7.02

Table 2. AREPS Preliminary Projections of Distillate Fuel Oil Prices for the Industrial Sector by Federal Region -- Reference Scenario (1980 $/10^6 Btu)

Federal Region	1980	1985	1990	1995	2000	2010
1	5.71	5.08	4.99	6.06	7.59	11.15
2	5.55	4.92	4.83	5.91	7.44	11.01
3	5.64	5.01	4.93	6.00	7.53	11.09
4	5.47	4.84	4.76	5.83	7.37	10.95
5	5.53	4.90	4.82	5.89	7.43	11.00
6	5.63	5.00	4.91	5.98	7.52	11.08
7	5.35	4.73	4.65	5.73	7.27	10.85
8	6.58	5.92	5.81	6.86	8.37	11.87
9	5.45	4.82	4.74	5.81	7.35	10.93
10	5.81	5.17	5.08	6.15	7.68	11.23
U.S.	5.63	5.00	4.91	5.99	7.52	11.08

In 1980, federal region 1 had the highest average price in the U.S. for residual fuel oil ($4.22/10^6 Btu, or $0.50/10^6 Btu higher than the national price). Federal region 9 had the lowest average price in 1980 ($3.21/10^6 Btu, or $0.51/10^6 Btu lower than the national price). The range of regional prices in 1980 thus varied by $1.01/10^6 Btu. The regional fuel prices projected by AREPS for 2010 through its scaling procedure were closer to the projected national prices. By 2010 federal region 1 still had the highest regional price at $7.44/10^6 Btu, but it was only $0.42/10^6 Btu higher than the national price. Similarly, federal region 9 also retained the lowest average price ($6.60/10^6 Btu), but its margin of difference with the national price narrowed to only $0.42/10^6 Btu. The overall regional distribution of fuel prices in 2010 was $0.84/10^6 Btu. Therefore, two observations can be made. First, the AREPS procedure caused regional price differentials for residual fuel oil to contract by approximately $0.08/10^6 Btu from 1980 to 2010 for the regions with the greatest original price differentials (negative or positive); regions with smaller price differentials regressed less during this time period. Second, the regional distribution of residual fuel oil prices contracted by $0.17/10^6 Btu ($1.01-0.84/10^6 Btu) from 1980 to 2010.

A similar pattern can be described for distillate fuel. For both 1980 and 2010, region 7 had the lowest average price and region 8 had the highest. Regional price differentials contracted more in region 8 than in region 7 due to the size of the original price differentials. In addition, the distribution of regional price differentials narrowed by $0.21/10^6 Btu ($1.23-1.02/10^6 Btu) from 1980 to 2010.

Tables 3 and 4 show national and federal region price projections for LPG and natural gas. At the national level, LPG prices decline in

Table 3. AREPS Preliminary Projections of LPG Prices for the Industrial Sector by Federal Region -- Reference Scenario (1980 $/$10^6$ Btu)

Federal Region	1980	1985	1990	1995	2000	2010
1	5.54	5.56	5.21	6.11	7.39	10.39
2	5.35	5.38	5.04	5.94	7.23	10.23
3	5.42	5.44	5.10	6.00	7.29	10.29
4	5.74	5.75	5.40	6.29	7.57	10.55
5	5.12	5.15	4.81	5.72	7.02	10.04
6	5.26	5.29	4.95	5.85	7.15	10.16
7	4.80	4.84	4.51	5.42	6.73	9.77
8	5.13	5.16	4.82	5.73	7.02	10.04
9	5.45	5.47	5.13	6.03	7.31	10.31
10	5.69	5.70	5.35	6.24	7.53	10.51
U.S.	5.25	5.28	4.94	5.84	7.14	10.15

Table 4. AREPS Preliminary Projections of Natural Gas Prices for the Industrial Sector by Federal Region -- Reference Case (1980 $/$10^6$ Btu)

Federal Region	1980	1985	1990	1995	2000	2010
1	4.18	5.12	4.99	6.08	6.83	9.48
2	3.55	4.51	4.40	5.49	6.27	8.96
3	2.96	3.94	3.84	4.95	5.74	8.47
4	2.75	3.73	3.64	4.76	5.55	8.29
5	2.87	3.85	3.75	4.87	5.66	8.39
6	1.83	2.84	2.76	3.91	4.72	7.52
7	2.48	3.47	3.38	4.51	5.30	8.07
8	2.31	3.30	3.22	4.35	5.15	7.92
9	3.16	4.13	4.03	5.13	5.91	8.63
10	3.70	4.66	4.54	5.64	6.40	9.08
U.S.	2.43	3.42	3.33	4.46	5.26	8.02

real terms from 1980 to 1990 (-5.90%), but not as rapidly as the prices projected for distillate and residual fuel oil. In the subsequent 20-year period (1990-2010), LPG prices are projected to increase by 105.5% (3.67% per year). Natural gas prices are projected to increase throughout the 30-year period; 37.0% from 1980 and 1990 (3.20%/year) and 140.8% from 1990 to 2010 (4.49%/year). Depletion effects and more costly supplies are precipitating the rapid escalation in natural gas prices.

There is a fairly symmetrical distribution of regional prices for LPG around the national mean; in 1980, federal region 4 has the highest LPG price ($5.74/10^6$ Btu), while region 7 has the lowest price ($4.80/10^6$ Btu). These prices translate into price differentials of $0.49/10^6$ Btu and -$0.45/10^6$ Btu, respectively. By 2010, the price differentials contract to $0.40 and -$0.38, respectively. Consequently, in 1980 the distribution of regional price differentials is $0.94/10^6$ Btu, whereas in 2010 it is $0.78/10^6$ Btu. This is a reduction in the overall distribution of $0.16/10^6$ Btu, and of approximately $0.08/10^6$ Btu for the greatest (individual) regional price differentials.

Regional prices for natural gas exhibit the greatest deviation from the national value. This pattern is due to the historic concentration of supply principally in one area of the country, the Southwest, as well as to the high transportation costs associated with the distance to major markets. Federal region 1 had the highest regional natural gas price in 1980 ($4.18/10^6$ Btu) and thereby the largest price differential, $1.75/10^6$ Btu (41.8% of its real delivered price is attributable to transportation). The smallest regional price in 1980 was in federal region 6 ($1.83/10^6$ Btu); its regional price differential was -$0.60/10^6$ Btu. These two regions reflect a difference in regional prices of $2.35/10^6$ Btu.

By 2010, the price differential in federal region 1 declines to $\$1.46/10^6$ Btu, a reduction of $\$0.29/10^6$ Btu. Correspondingly, but less dramatically, the price differential in region 6 declines to $-\$0.50/10^6$ Btu in 2010, a drop of $\$0.10/10^6$ Btu. The distribution in regional price differentials consequently declines to $\$1.96/10^6$ Btu ($1.46 to -$0.50). As a result of the scale factors in AREPS that account for the regression of regional prices toward the national mean, the distribution of regional natural gas prices contracts by $\$0.39/10^6$ Btu from 1980 to 2010. This difference in the regional distribution of natural gas prices is noticeable in table 4.

5. SUMMARY AND CONCLUSIONS

A forecast of energy prices is usually required in most studies of energy and economic activity. The problem, however, is in matching the assumptions and dimensions (temporal, spatial, and sectoral) of available published forecasts with the requirements of each study. This paper documents a systematic method to translate national energy price projections by fuel type and sector into regional and state prices. This procedure is accomplished through the Argonne Regional Energy Price Simulator (AREPS). The paper delineates the methodological premise underlying AREPS, together with its algorithm. It is shown that AREPS is a flexible model that employs a systematic and transparent method to produce regional and state fuel prices. The model retains spatial price differences between regions or states, although it accounts for an observed pattern, subnational prices regressing toward the national mean. The rate at which prices regress toward the national mean is variable and can be exogenously specified.

To illustrate the capabilities and results of AREPS, a set of sample projections are presented.

Industrial fuel price projections at the federal region level are reported for selected years from 1980 to 2010. The facility in AREPS to taper regional price differences toward zero (i.e., regress regional prices toward the national mean) is documented for each of four fuel types. It is observed that the greater the price differential, the larger and faster is the contraction in regional prices toward the national mean. Because natural gas had the largest regional price differentials, it exhibited the most dramatic shifts toward the national mean.

In conclusion, although AREPS was designed and developed for a particular project, it is a very flexible and adaptive system for the generation of regional and state fuel prices. Because AREPS uses a top-down approach to produce these subnational prices, we do not purport that these prices are truly reflective of regional conditions. Instead, the projected prices generated by AREPS establish a basis on which to (1) compare prices generated at a lower geographic level for consistency and reasonableness, (2) produce regional or state fuel prices by adjusting the AREPS prices for local conditions, (3) analyze regionally the relative price effects of a change in national prices, and (4) provide input to regional models where consistency with a national energy projection is most important.

NOTES

1. Work supported by the U.S. Department of Energy, Assistant Secretary for Fossil Energy, under Contract W-31-109-Eng-38.

2. The present set of regional price projections by fuel type and end-use sector is undergoing internal review. These projections would be available upon request pending the completion of this review.

3. AREPS is part of the Task Group B (TG-B) model set, a collection of forecasting models that develop projections of acid rain precursor emissions from the various fuel-consuming sectors. Development of the model set is administered by the Office of Planning and Environment within the Office of Fossil Energy, U.S. Department of Energy. The overall project is carried out in conjunction with the National Acid Precipitation Assessment Program (NAPAP). The preliminary results in this paper have not been reviewed by TG-B and are not official projections of the task group.

4. A complete discussion of the procedures examined is contained in South et al. (1985).

5. Various statistical tests were performed on the price differentials and absolute price levels. The Spearman rank correlation proved that, in general, states were not shifting in their rank over time, for a particular fuel type and sector. In other words, if state prices changed in a particular year, either all state prices changed so that they retained the same rank order, or if only particular state prices increased (decreased), they did so within their "neighborhood" price cushion. The state price differentials for a particular fuel and sector were also examined for their movement over time. It was discovered that state-to-nation price differentials were generally narrowing throughout the 1970s. A summary of these findings is available on request.

6. The NEPP national fuel prices are provided in five-year increments; therefore, AREPS produces its projections in the same increments. Interpolation could be employed to generate annual price forecasts from the standard set of AREPS projections if desired. Alternatively, if the national projection used has greater temporal detail, AREPS will produce a regional (state) forecast at the corresponding level.

7. The procedure used to produce regional (state-level) electricity price projections differs somewhat from the

standard AREPS algorithm, taking into account relative regional price projections from DRI for the 11 DRI regions.

8. It was discovered, through an empirical analysis of historic price differentials, that the best estimates of future state prices are those that tend to regress toward the national mean. In addition, preliminary investigation of the data indicates that the distribution of state fuel prices around the national average is becoming less dispersed. For these reasons, scale factors were adopted to retain the pattern exhibited by regional (state) fuel prices of regression toward the national mean. Currently, the values used as scale factors are assumed, although it is hoped that empirical measurement could be undertaken to calibrate the scale factors to historic (and expected) trends.

9. The world oil prices assumed under the reference case, expressed in 1984 $/bbl, are 1980, $42.36; 1990, $28.30; 1995, $34.63; 2000, $43.67; and 2010, $64.75. These prices and all projections prepared in conjunction with the 1985 NEPP are considered to be preliminary and subject to change before final publication (U.S. Dept. of Energy, 1985).

REFERENCES

South, D.W. et al. 1985. Unpublished information. Argonne National Laboratory. October.

U.S. Dept. of Energy. 1984. State Energy Price and Expenditure Data System: 1981 Update. Energy Information Administration. June.

U.S. Dept. of Energy. 1985. Unpublished draft energy projections prepared in conjunction with the National Energy Policy Plan. Office of Policy Evaluation. April.

37 Long-Run Projections of State-Level Commercial and Residential Energy Use

John F. McDonald, David W. South,
Argonne National Laboratory

1. INTRODUCTION

Forecasts of energy use at the state level and for the long run (1980-2030) are not usually prepared for the residential and commercial sectors by either public or private organizations. In addition, most energy forecasting models of the residential or commercial sectors are not designed to generate such forecasts. This paper describes a modeling system that has these features: the Commercial and Residential Energy Use and Emissions Simulation System, or CRESS.

CRESS is a new model that has been under development since mid-1984.[1] A test version of the modeling system is now operating and preliminary results have been generated. These results are being used to validate the system and verify its long-run forecasting capabilities. This paper, which provides the first documentation of the structure, development, and output of CRESS, is both an abbreviated summary of model development and a status report.

Section 2 of the paper describes the modular structure of CRESS and highlights the development of the state-level energy forecasting modules. Details of these modules are given in Sections 3 and 4. Preliminary energy projections generated by these modules are then reported. The paper closes with a summary and some concluding remarks.

2. MODEL STRUCTURE AND DEVELOPMENT

The CRESS model can generate energy projections by fuel type at the census-region and state-level for the period 1980-2030. It can also forecast emissions from the combustion and conversion of these fuels, by pollutant (SO_x, NO_x, VOC, TSP, and CO)[2] and source category, with the same spatial and temporal detail. CRESS represents the residential and commercial sectors in a larger modeling system used to (1) project energy use and emissions by fuel-consuming sectors under different scenarios and (2) examine the effect of different control policies on these projections.[3]

CRESS is composed of three modules (figure 1). This paper focuses on two of these modules: the energy module (and its component models [HOME and CSEM]) and the regionalization module. CRESS was designed and developed in modules because we were instructed to use existing models to perform the requisite tasks whenever possible. This

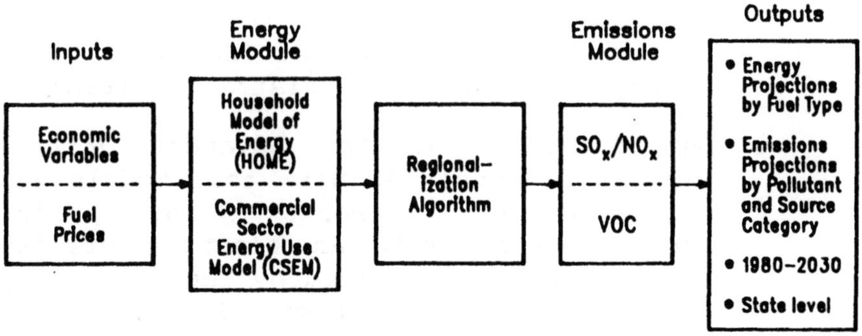

Figure 1. Modular Structure of CRESS

allowed us to insert existing energy use forecasting models, representing the residential and commercial sectors, into the modeling structure. However, original regionalization and emissions modules were designed for CRESS because suitable models did not exist.

The first development step was selection of an energy forecasting model (or set of models) to represent the residential and commercial sectors. The candidate models were to be capable of (1) projecting energy use by major fuel type, at the state level, for the period 1980-2030; and (2) simulating alternative scenarios and control policies. After an extensive review of residential- and commercial-sector energy use models, the following candidates were selected:

- Buildings Energy Conservation Optimization Model (BECOM): built by Brookhaven National Laboratory in 1978 and previously operated by Applied Energy Services for the U.S. Department of Energy (DOE) in preparing the biannual National Energy Policy Plan (NEPP).

- Hirst/ORNL residential model and Jackson/ORNL commercial model: both developed while Hirst and Jackson were at Oak Ridge National Laboratory in 1977-1978 and previously incorporated in the Mid-term Energy Forecasting System (MEFS) of DOE's Energy Information Administration (EIA).

- Demand module in the Advanced Utility Simulation Model (AUSM): this module was estimated by T. Mount (Cornell) for inclusion in AUSM, an electric utility industry model developed by the University Research Group on Energy (URGE) for the U.S. Environmental Protection Agency between 1980 and 1985.

- Household Model of Energy (HOME): developed by John Holte in 1983 for inclusion in the Intermediate Futures Forecasting System (IFFS), DOE/EIA.

- Commercial Sector Energy Model (CSEM): developed by S. Wade in 1983 for inclusion in IFFS, DOE/EIA.

Each of these models was examined with respect to the following evaluation criteria:

1. The input requirements for the models should be simple because projections must be made to 2030.

2. The models should operate (both in terms of inputs and outputs) at the subnational level because state projections are needed.

3. The models should disaggregate energy use by major fuel type, including electricity.

4. The models should be capable of being extended in time to 2030 without unreasonable effort.

Clearly, a model with a lengthy and complex set of input requirements would be difficult to use in preparing long-range projections. Also, a model with regional detail built in from the start would, in general, be preferable to ad hoc regionalization procedures applied to models that operate at the national level. Finally, given the criteria stated above, a model with substantial engineering detail would not be appropriate because its input requirements would be extensive, thus entailing the preparation of long-run forecasts for each parameter.

After a preliminary screening for general appropriateness, the review and selection of the residential and commercial energy use forecasting models was based on how closely the models related to the theory of derived demand. Demand for energy in the residential and commercial sectors is an example of derived demand, i.e., demand derived from basic needs such as heating, cooling, etc. Both HOME and CSEM were selected because they best satisfied the evaluation criteria and represented the theory of derived demand.[4] A further discussion leading to the recommendation of HOME and CSEM is given in McDonald and South (1984).

3. THE ENERGY MODULE

This section briefly describes the models used to project fuel use in the residential and commercial sectors. More extensive discussions of these models are contained in McDonald and South (1984) and Holte (1984a, 1984b).

3.1 HOME

The Household Model of Energy (HOME) is an econometric model designed to make intermediate-range forecasts of energy use in occupied residential structures. Energy use is determined in the accounting equation

$$Q = U \times S \times H \qquad (1)$$

where:

Q = energy consumption indexed by fuel, end use, housing structure type and vintage, region, and projection year,

U = utilization (use per household) indexed as for Q,

S = share of fuel in use, indexed as for Q, and

H = number of households indexed by housing structure type and vintage, region, and year.

HOME was estimated and operates at the regional level; inputs are at the four-region (census-region) level, and the outputs are produced at the four-region and 10-region (federal-region) levels. The model projects four end-uses, up to seven fuel/technology types (depending on end-use), two housing types, and four housing vintages. Exogenous inputs are housing starts (at the national level), population, household income, and fuel prices (all at the regional level).

The forecast of U (utilization) uses price and income elasticities estimated from recent (1980) data in the Residential Energy Consumption Survey (RECS). Elasticities were estimated for each end-use and fuel type in each of the four census regions. Utilization is assumed to adjust over time with a lag. The projection of S (fuel shares) starts with 1980 fuel shares by region from the RECS data base; the fuel shares for space heating then change over time as a function of the price of the fuel in question relative to a weighted average price of all fuels. Fuel shares in existing structures do not change except for some conversion from oil to natural gas for space heating. The final component is H (number of households, derived from a forecast of future housing structures). New construction and retirement rates are applied to the stock of existing structures (1980 data). HOME uses housing starts at the national level, but the model has been modified to use housing starts at the four-region level. Exogenous retirement rates that vary by vintage are used.

For the test runs reported in this paper, all inputs and outputs are specified at the census-region level; only fuel-use projections are produced (detailed projections by end-use and housing type and vintage are suppressed); and the time horizon was extended to 2030.

3.2 CSEM

The Commercial Sector Energy Model (CSEM) is also an econometric model designed to make intermediate-range forecasts of commercial energy use by building category. The model also was estimated and operates at the four-region (census-region) level. The fundamental equation in CSEM for the projection of a particular fuel and end use in a specific type of commercial building is:

$$A = SQFT \times PCT \times FU/SQFT \tag{2}$$

where:

A = energy consumption indexed by fuel, end use, building type, region, and projection year,

SQFT = amount of floor space in that end use and building type in the region,

PCT = percentage of floor space indexed by end use, building type, and region that uses the fuel in question, and

FU/SQFT = fuel consumption per square foot (given that the fuel in question is used).

Both SQFT and FU/SQFT are projected with equations estimated by econometric methods. SQFT in a region depends on population and income, while FU/SQFT depends on several variables, including fuel price and heating (and cooling) degree-days. The Nonresidential Buildings Energy Consumption Survey (NBECS) data collected in 1979 were used for the FU/SQFT equations. The value of FU/SQFT is assumed to adjust over time with a lag. PCT for added floor space is assumed to be the same as that for buildings constructed during 1974-1980. The CSEM projects four fuels used in six building categories and three end uses at the four- and 10-region levels. The exogenous data requirements for CSEM are real disposable income, population, and fuel prices at the four-region level.

For the test runs reported in this paper, all outputs are specified at the four-region level, the time horizon was extended to 2030, and only fuel use projections are produced (detailed projections by end use and building type are suppressed). To extend the time horizon to 2030, we added the assumption that fuel choice (PCT above) in new buildings is sensitive to fuel prices. We did this only for space heating because the fuel choice for air conditioning (the other major end use) was already 98.3% electricity (as of 1980). In space heating, the 1980 shares for the U.S. are:

Fuel Type	Share (%)
Electricity	20.0
Natural Gas	43.9
Oil	13.7
Other	7.2
None	15.2

Fuel choice for space heating in new buildings is specified as a three-way logistic model in which electricity, natural gas, and oil are the choices. In the logistic model, it is assumed that the own-price elasticities for each of the three fuels is -0.4, or that

$$\frac{d \ln S_i}{d \ln P_i} = -0.4,$$

where

S_i = the share of floor space heated by fuel i in time t, and

P_i = price of fuel i at time t.

The elasticity value of -0.4 is consistent with the empirical findings of Dubin and McFadden (1984) for the residential sector and Baughman et al. (1979) for the residential and commercial sectors. The logistic model exhibits the usual property of independence from irrelevant alternatives in the sense that $d \ln S_i/d \ln P_j = 0$, where P_j is the price of either of the other two fuels.

3.3 Energy Conservation in HOME and CSEM

A key question in projections of residential and commercial energy use is the extent to which the models capture the trend toward energy conservation. Both HOME and CSEM are based on standard production theory in which R ("real estate") is produced by capital, K, and energy, E, or

$$R = R\ (K,\ E). \tag{3}$$

This production model implies that the elasticity of derived demand for energy ε_{EE} is

$$\varepsilon_{EE} = S_E\ \eta^R + (1 - S_E)\ \sigma_{KE}, \tag{4}$$

where:

S_E = share of energy in the production of R,

η^R = elasticity of demand for R, and

σ_{KE} = elasticity of substitution of K for E in the production of R.

Energy conservation arises through the impacts of rising energy price on

1. The quantity and quality of R demanded (smaller structures, less heat, etc.) -- $S_E\eta^R$.

2. The substitution of K for E (insulation, etc.) so that more K and less E are used to produce a given R -- $(1 - S_E)\sigma_{KE}$.

In effect, the model (via the σ_{KE} parameter) presumes that technologies exist (and will exist in the future) to permit K/E to increase according to

$$\sigma_{KE} = \frac{\text{percentage change in K/E}}{\text{percentage change in } P_E}, \tag{5}$$

where P_E = price of energy.

HOME and CSEM are based on a <u>given</u> production function R(K, E); no shifts in this function are included (i.e., increases in R for given levels of K and E). However, it is assumed in HOME and CSEM that K/E can be increased whenever P_E increases. Indeed, all of the long-run values for ϵ_{EE} in CSEM indicate elastic demand ($\epsilon_{EE} < -1.0$), and most of the long-run demand elasticities for space heating in HOME are in the range of -0.50 to -1.07.

4. REGIONALIZATION MODULE

As indicated above, the fuel use projections produced by HOME and CSEM are now generated at the four-region (census-region) level. A regionalization method was devised to disaggregate these projections to the state level.

The regionalization method was designed to meet the following criteria: (1) fuel use in a state must reflect the size of the state as a part of the region, (2) fuel use in a state should be sensitive to the fuel price in the state relative to the regional average fuel price, and (3) fuel use in the states of a region must add to the total regional fuel use. To meet these objectives for the residential sector, fuel use in state s at time t [$F_s(t)$] relative to fuel use in the region [$F(t)$] is specified as

$$\frac{F_s(t)}{F(t)} = \frac{Pop_s(t)}{Pop(t)} \left[\frac{P_s(t)}{P(t)}\right]^{\varepsilon} Z(t) \qquad (6)$$

where:

$Pop_s(t)$ = population for state s at time t,

$Pop(t)$ = population for the region at time t,

$P_s(t)$ = fuel price in state s at time t,

$P(t)$ = regional average fuel price at time t,

ε = price elasticity of demand for that fuel in that region (as provided in HOME and CSEM), and

$Z(t)$ = factor that ensures that state fuel shares add to 1.0.

When the regionalization method is applied to fuel use projections for the commercial sector, the share variable in equation 5 [$POP_s(t)/POP(t)$] is changed to commercial sector employment. The values of Z(t) are defined by

$$Z(t) = \frac{1}{\sum_j \frac{Pop_j(t)}{Pop(t)} \left[\frac{P_j(t)}{P(t)}\right]^{\varepsilon}}$$

when equation 5 is expressed in terms of residential sector fuel use. The denominator of Z(t) is simply the sum of the shares for the states j in the region as projected, with no correction to ensure that these shares add to 1.0. If these "uncorrected" shares add to 1.1, for example, all shares are scaled down by the factor 1/1.1.

The population and employment projections at the regional and state level are discussed in detail by McDonald and South (1985a, 1985b), and the regional and state fuel price projections are provided by South et al. (1985) and described in South and Hanson (1985).

5. SELECTED PRELIMINARY PROJECTIONS

This section contains some preliminary projections generated by the energy and regionalization modules in CRESS. Two alternative macroeconomic scenarios were used as basic input data; these are discussed first. Projections of energy use at the four-region level are presented next, and an example of energy use projections at the state level concludes this section.

5.1 Projections from the Energy Module

The two models that comprise the energy module (HOME and CSEM) operate at the four-region level in terms of both inputs and outputs. Our input requirements included regional projections of real disposable income, population, and housing starts. These projections were based on two alternative macroeconomic forecasts provided by the Data Resources, Inc., (DRI) macroeconomic model. See McDonald and South (1985b) for an extensive discussion of these macroeconomic and regional projections. The two macroeconomic projections are the lower (or "Pessimistic") DRI case for Fall 1984 and a more optimistic projection that is consistent with the economic growth objectives of the Reagan administration. This latter scenario is referred to as the DOE Reference Case. National and regional fuel price projections employed are consistent with these two macroeconomic scenarios. The national fuel price projections are preliminary and were developed for the draft 1985 National Energy Policy Plan (U.S. Dept. of Energy, 1985).

Tables 1 and 2 summarizes selected input data for HOME and CSEM. Actual values for the benchmark year (1980) are reported, along with projected values for 1990 and 2000 for both the DOE Reference Case and the DRI Pessimistic Case. The population projections show a slightly greater proportion of the population residing in the Northeast and North Central regions in the DOE

Table 1. Selected Economic and Demographic Input Data for HOME and CSEM by Region and Macroeconomic Scenario, 1990 and 2000

Input Variable and Region	1980	DOE Reference Case 1990	DOE Reference Case 2000	DRI Pessimistic Case 1990	DRI Pessimistic Case 2000
Population (10^6)					
U.S.	226.3	249.2	267.4	249.2	267.4
Northeast	49.2	51.6	53.6	51.6	53.2
North Central	58.9	60.0	60.6	59.7	60.0
South	75.0	85.9	94.6	86.1	95.3
West	43.3	51.7	58.6	51.8	58.8
Disposal Income (1979$, 10^9)					
U.S.	1658	2239	2817	2191	2613
Northeast	383	511	627	500	571
North Central	436	537	644	517	582
South	497	698	897	689	852
West	343	494	649	485	607

Table 2. Selected Fuel Price Input Data for HOME and CSEM by Region and Macroeconomic Scenario, 1990 and 2000

Input Variable and Region	1980	DOE Reference Case 1990	DOE Reference Case 2000	DRI Pessimistic Case 1990	DRI Pessimistic Case 2000
Residential Sector Fuel Prices (1979$/$10^6$ Btu)					
Fuel Oil					
Northeast	6.54	5.47	7.71	5.02	6.74
North Central	6.28	5.22	7.48	4.77	6.50
South	6.42	5.36	7.61	4.91	6.64
West	6.27	5.22	7.47	4.76	6.50
Natural Gas					
Northeast	4.22	5.08	6.82	4.90	6.38
North Central	3.06	3.99	5.79	3.81	5.34
South	3.19	4.11	5.90	3.93	5.46
West	3.00	3.93	5.73	3.74	5.28
Electricity					
Northeast	19.78	16.71	17.95	16.84	17.46
North Central	14.36	14.51	15.74	14.63	15.30
South	13.29	14.51	16.74	14.63	16.27
West	12.64	12.85	14.74	12.95	14.33
Commercial Sector Fuel Prices (1979$/$10^6$ Btu)					
Fuel Oil					
Northeast	6.17	5.12	7.31	4.66	6.36
North Central	6.07	5.02	7.22	4.57	6.27
South	5.99	4.95	7.15	4.50	6.20
West	5.86	4.83	7.04	4.37	6.08
Natural Gas					
Northeast	3.77	4.58	6.33	4.40	5.89
North Central	2.78	3.69	5.44	3.46	5.00
South	2.86	3.72	5.51	3.54	5.07
West	3.16	4.00	5.78	3.82	5.34
Electricity					
Northeast	19.99	16.24	16.73	16.37	16.28
North Central	14.32	14.28	15.07	14.40	14.66
South	13.25	14.06	17.08	14.18	16.61
West	13.72	14.09	15.49	14.20	15.07

Reference Case scenario. Real disposable income for the U.S. is 7.8% higher for 2000 in the DOE Reference Case. Because of higher demand, fuel prices in both sectors are generally higher in the DOE Reference Case.

Table 3 presents national and regional projections of residential fuel consumption produced by HOME. These preliminary results are reported for two years, 1990 and 2000, and for both macroeconomic scenarios. Projections are shown only for fuel oil, natural gas, and electricity because these three fuels account for 96% of conventional fuel use in the residential sector. Substantial growth in residential energy use is projected for 1990 and 2000. Because of the generally lower fuel prices, total U.S. residential energy consumption is projected to be slightly higher in the DRI Pessimistic Case than in the DOE Reference Case. Fuel oil consumption generally declines (except for 1990-2000 in the DRI Pessimistic Case), while that of natural gas and electricity increase. Electricity use grows especially rapidly (43% from 1980 to 1990, and 30% from 1990 to 2000) in the DOE Reference Case, for example.

As shown in table 3, substantial growth in residential fuel consumption is projected for all four regions. This is primarily a reflection of the growth in electricity consumption in all four regions, although the growth of natural gas consumption in the West is also substantial. Regional fuel consumption is not very sensitive to the macroeconomic scenario used; the greatest difference between the two scenarios is a 10% shift in fuel oil use in the North Central region. Most other differences in table 3 are substantially less than 10%.

Table 4 shows national and regional projections of commercial fuel consumption from CSEM for 1990 and 2000. Only fuel oil, natural gas, and

Table 3. Preliminary Projections of Residential Fuel Consumption (10^{12} Btu)

Region and Fuel Type	1980	DOE Reference Case 1990	DOE Reference Case 2000	DRI Pessimistic Case 1990	DRI Pessimistic Case 2000
U.S.					
Total[1]	9127	11031	12470	11079	12491
Fuel Oil	1423	1408	1321	1453	1399
Natural Gas	4866	5470	5889	5498	5922
Electricity	2448	3510	4565	3481	4441
Northeast					
Total	2202	2655	2882	2678	2871
Fuel Oil	855	919	896	946	937
Natural Gas	927	1076	1143	1079	1132
Electricity	367	582	763	574	717
North Central					
Total	3102	3496	3702	3523	3763
Fuel Oil	278	273	238	286	266
Natural Gas	2081	2157	2143	2180	2200
Electricity	603	809	1044	799	1008
South					
Total	2423	2624	2934	2631	2961
Fuel Oil	241	160	139	165	149
Natural Gas	996	927	931	933	946
Electricity	1042	1341	1672	1337	1665
West					
Total	1400	2257	2952	2246	2896
Fuel Oil	48	56	48	56	47
Natural Gas	862	1310	1672	1306	1644
Electricity	436	778	1085	771	1051

[1]Total includes liquefied petroleum gas, fuel oil, natural gas, coal, and electricity. Projections of wood consumption were computed, but are not included in the total.

Table 4. Preliminary Projections of Commercial Fuel Consumption (10^{12} Btu)

Region and Fuel Type	1980	DOE Reference Case 1990	DOE Reference Case 2000	DRI Pessimistic Case 1990	DRI Pessimistic Case 2000
U.S.					
Total[1]	5962	7293	8304	7261	8197
Fuel Oil	1123	1242	1442	1271	1549
Natural Gas	2674	2952	2916	2936	2897
Electricity	1907	2854	3719	2809	3524
Northeast					
Total	1387	1604	1806	1592	1727
Fuel Oil	545	487	530	493	542
Natural Gas	437	535	522	530	504
Electricity	364	537	715	522	641
North Central					
Total	1731	1907	1955	1864	1852
Fuel Oil	140	124	132	123	132
Natural Gas	1069	1108	1035	1088	999
Electricity	440	587	702	565	634
South					
Total	1773	2326	2776	2357	2897
Fuel Oil	312	441	554	459	627
Natural Gas	679	758	775	767	816
Electricity	688	1056	1386	1059	1393
West					
Total	1071	1456	1767	1449	1722
Fuel Oil	126	190	226	196	247
Natural Gas	488	552	585	550	579
Electricity	414	674	916	663	856

[1]Total includes liquefied petroleum gas, motor gasoline, fuel oil, natural gas, coal, and electricity.

electricity are reported because these three fuels constitute 96% of conventional energy use. Substantial growth is projected for commercial fuel use (except for natural gas) in the U.S. during 1990-2000. Total fuel use is slightly higher in the DOE Reference Case; electricity use is higher and fuel oil use is lower than in the DRI Pessimistic Case. As in the residential sector, use of electricity by the commercial sector is projected to grow substantially (95% from 1980 to 2000 in the DOE Reference Case).

The regional projections in table 4 show substantial growth during 1980-2000 in the South (57%) and West (65%) in the DOE Reference Case. Less growth is projected for the same period in the Northeast (30%) and North Central (13%) regions in the DOE Reference Case. These results primarily reflect the increased use of commercial electricity. As in the residential sector, the regional fuel use projections are generally not very sensitive to the choice of macroeconomic scenario.

5.2 Projections from the Regionalization Module

As indicated above, CRESS has produced state-level fuel consumption projections for the two macroeconomic scenarios. What follows is an example of how the regionalization module allocates regional fuel use to the states in that region. More complete results are available from the authors.

Recall that the regionalization module allocates regional residential fuel consumption to the states in the region using population and fuel prices (relative to the regional average fuel prices). Table 5 presents these (input) data for the states in the Northeast for 2000. The share of regional fuel use in a state can be thought of as equal to the state's share of regional

Table 5. State-Level Residential Fuel Prices and Consumption in the Northeast in 2000; Regional Shares Shown in Parentheses

Input and Output Variables	Connecti-cut	Maine	Massa-chusetts	New Hampshire	Rhode Island	Vermont	New Jersey	New York	Pennsyl-vania
Inputs									
Population (10^6)	3.6 (6.7%)	1.3 (2.4%)	6.6 (12.3%)	1.2 (2.2%)	1.0 (1.9%)	0.6 (1.1%)	8.1 (15.1%)	18.8 (35.1%)	12.4 (23.1%)
Fuel Prices ($1979/$10^6$ Btu)									
Fuel Oil	7.79	7.69	7.79	7.69	7.77	7.88	7.68	7.78	7.54
Natural Gas	7.79	8.40	7.50	6.90	7.48	7.93	7.11	6.97	6.15
Electricity	17.23	14.64	18.38	18.09	19.25	12.69	20.33	20.69	14.66
Outputs									
Fuel Consumption (10^{12} Btu)									
Fuel Oil	58.7 (6.8%)	20.8 (2.4%)	108.2 (12.6%)	18.3 (2.1%)	16.4 (1.9%)	9.2 (1.1%)	134.1 (15.6%)	299.6 (34.9%)	193.0 (22.5%)
Natural Gas	72.2 (6.3%)	25.6 (2.2%)	135.3 (11.80%)	25.4 (2.2%)	20.6 (1.8%)	12.2 (1.1%)	170.6 (14.9%)	400.3 (35.0%)	280.3 (24.5%)
Electricity	53.9 (7.1%)	24.6 (3.2%)	91.1 (11.9%)	16.7 (2.2%)	13.0 (1.7%)	13.8 (1.8%)	98.0 (12.8%)	222.5 (29.2%)	229.6 (30.1%)
Total[1]	190.6 (6.6%)	72.6 (2.6%)	344.2 (12.1%)	62.2 (2.2%)	51.6 (1.8%)	36.1 (1.3%)	413.0 (14.5%)	952.6 (33.5%)	722.0 (25.4%)

[1]Total fuel consumption includes liquefied petroleum gas, fuel oil, natural gas, coal, and electricity.

population plus an adjustment for the fuel price in the state relative to the regional average fuel price. Table 5 also presents state-level consumption projections by fuel type for the Northeast in 2000. Because of relatively high electricity prices, New Jersey and New York display low electricity consumption relative to population, while Maine, Vermont, and Pennsylvania have relatively low electricity prices and correspondingly higher electricity consumption relative to population. Also, natural gas consumption in Pennsylvania is higher in proportion to population, while regional shares of natural gas consumption in Connecticut, Maine, and Massachusetts are lower.

6. SUMMARY AND CONCLUSIONS

In this paper we have described the basic features of a new modeling system (CRESS) that can generate long-run, state-level forecasts of energy use in the residential and commercial sectors. CRESS can also provide a corresponding forecast of emissions, by pollutant and source category, with the same spatial and temporal dimensions as the energy forecast. This paper focused on the capabilities of CRESS to forecast energy use; a description of the energy and regionalization modules was provided. The reasons for selecting HOME and CSEM were summarized, and the modifications undertaken for their inclusion in CRESS were highlighted. Thereafter, the methodology for the regionalization algorithm was described.

Preliminary projections for 1990 and 2000 were made at the regional and state level for two macroeconomic scenarios. Both energy models were determined to be sensitive to regional differences in fuel prices and the other economic and demographic inputs. However, differences in results between the two scenarios tended to be negligible (in most cases less than 10%). The state-level fuel use projections produced by the regionalization module accurately reflect the methodological premise. Fuel use in a state is approximately equal to the state's share of regional population with a relative fuel price adjustment. The regional share values in table 5 confirm this approach.

In conclusion, despite the preliminary nature of the reported projections, CRESS represents a systematic, well-documented method to forecast state-level energy consumption in the long term (1980-2030) for the residential and commercial sectors. The input requirements are simple and readily available from published sources. Test runs of CRESS indicate that reasonable results are produced; moreover, the results are "reproducible." We are now examining the preliminary projections reported herein and are using these results to validate the system and verify its long-run forecasting capability. We are also attempting to learn why the CRESS projections (in aggregate and by fuel type) are somewhat higher than those of alternative forecasts. We plan to examine differences in model inputs and parameters, and whether structural differences affect the projections. Previous efforts to discover whether structural differences affect consumption patterns revealed that

> substantial differences exist between population groups with respect to energy consumption, energy expenditures and fuel prices, both at the national and regional levels... Therefore, differentiation of population groups and their related characteristics would, we believe, substantially improve the forecasting efficiency of residential energy demand models. It is also widely recognized that there are <u>regional</u> differences that should be included in residential demand models. (South and McDonald, 1984.)

NOTES

1. Work supported by the U.S. Department of Energy, Assistant Secretary for Fossil Energy, under Contract W-31-109-Eng-38.

2. Sulfur dioxide and sulfates (SO_x), nitrogen oxides (NO_x), volatile organic compounds (VOC), total suspended particulates (TSP), and carbon monoxide (CO).

3. CRESS is part of the Task Group B (TG-B) emissions model set, a collection of forecasting models that develop projections of acid rain precursor emissions from the various fuel consuming sectors. Development of the model set is administered by the Office of Planning and Environment within the Office of Fossil Energy, U.S. Department of Energy. The overall project operates in conjunction with the National Acid Precipitation Assessment Program (NAPAP). The preliminary results in this paper have not been reviewed by TG-B and are not official projections of the task group.

4. Neither HOME nor CSEM complies fully with the theory of derived demand, but they capture the principal elements of the theory more closely than do the other models reviewed. A description of how the models are deficient in this regard is documented in McDonald and South (1984).

REFERENCES

Baughman, M.L., P.L. Joskow, and D.P. Kamat. 1979. Electric Power in the United States: Models and Policy Analysis. Cambridge, Mass.: MIT Press.

Dubin J. and D. McFadden. 1984. "An Econometric Analysis of Residential Electric Appliance Holdings and Consumption." Econometrica, 52:345-362, March.

Holte, J. 1984a. Model Documentation: Household Model of Energy, Energy Information Administration, U.S. Dept. of Energy, DOE/EIA-0409. February.

_______. 1984b. Model Documentation: Commercial Sector Energy Model, Energy Information Administration, U.S. Dept. of Energy, DOE/EIA-0453. August.

McDonald, J.F. and D.W. South. 1984. Unpublished information, Argonne National Laboratory, October.

_______. 1985a. Unpublished information, Argonne National Laboratory, January.

_______. 1985b. Unpublished information, Argonne National Laboratory, June.

South, D.W. et al. 1985. Unpublished information, Argonne National Laboratory, October.

South, D.W. and J.F. McDonald. 1984. "Residential Energy Consumption Characteristics of Minority Population Groups: Trends in Demand and Patterns of Use," Proceedings, The Energy Industries in Transition: 1984-2000, Sixth Annual North American Meeting, International Association of Energy Economists, San Francisco. November 5-7.

South, D.W. and D.A. Hanson. 1985. "Long-Run Forecasts of Regional Energy Prices Using the Argonne Regional Energy Price Simulator (AREPS)," Proceedings, World Energy Markets: Stability or Continued Cycle, Seventh Annual North American Meeting, International Association of Energy Economists, Philadelphia. December 10-13.

U.S. Dept. of Energy. 1985b. Unpublished draft energy projections prepared in conjunction with the National Energy Policy Plan. Office of Policy and Evaluation. April.

38
Choice of Technology and Long-Run Technical Change in Energy Intensive Industries

Finn R. Foersund, University of Oslo, Norway
Lennart Hjalmarsson, University of Gothenburg, Sweden

INTRODUCTION

The purpose of this paper is to analyze long run technical change in energy intensive industries on the basis of a vintage approach. The analysis is mainly based on the short-run industry production function introduced by Johansen (1972).

The vintage approach is concerned with the dynamic process of structural change in an industry producing a homogeneous good. Of particular interest is the difference between best-practice productivity and average productivity and the origin of differences in the structure with regard to capacity and input coefficients, the development of the structure over time through the process of choice of new technique and investments from the ex ante production function and the closing down of old equipment.

The basic idea may be presented in the following way. Let us consider an industry producing a homogeneous product. The firms in this industry face the same ex ante or choice of technique production function when new investments are performed. Ex ante there are large substitutions possibilities between different inputs and free choice of capacity. Ex post, when a new plant has been erected, capacity is fixed and substitution possibilities limited. This ex post rigidity creates a rigid capital structure in the industry, in the short run. In the long run, this structure may be changed through a, usually gradual, process of investments in new capital and closing down of old capital, embodied technical progress being assumed.

THE SHORT-RUN INDUSTRY PRODUCTION FUNCTION

The concept of the short-run industry production function rests on the assumption that each plant or a main piece of capital equipment is characterized by fixed production coefficients with regard to variable inputs, and the presence of fixed factors in the form of capital. The function is defined by maximizing the industry's total production for given amounts of total inputs. This also means that the industry's total production costs are minimized for any factor price ratio and any level of production, assuming that all units of production face the same prices.

Consider now an industry consisting of a certain number of micro units. The short-run production function of the industry as a whole is established on the basis of an ex ante production function, determining the full capacity values $\bar{x}$, $\bar{v}_j (j = 1,...n)$ of output x, and the current inputs v_j, $(j = 1,...,n)$. For the ex post function at the micro level, following Johansen (1972), a limitational law is assumed to hold:

$$x = \text{Min}\left[\frac{v_1}{\xi_1}, \ldots, \frac{v_n}{\xi_n}, \bar{x}\right], \tag{1}$$

where the input coefficients $\xi_j = \frac{v_j}{x}$ $(j = 1,\ldots,n)$ are assumed constant, that is independent of the rate of capacity utilization.

In the following, we assume that all plants or micro units have the simple structure given by (1). The input coefficients, ξ_j, are estimated by the observed coefficients.

The short-run industry function $X = F(V_1,\ldots,V_n)$ is obtained by solving the following problem:

$$\underset{x^i}{\text{Max}}\ X = \sum_{n=1}^{N} x^i \qquad \text{subject to} \tag{2a}$$

$$\sum_{i=1}^{N} \xi^i x^i \leq V_j \qquad j = 1,\ldots n \tag{2b}$$

$$x^i \in [0,\bar{x}^i], \tag{2c}$$

where X denotes output and $V_1,\ldots,V_n$ current inputs for the industry as a whole, and where $i = 1,,,N$ refers to plants with a capacity of $\bar{x}^i$. Since for our purpose, we are only interested in the economic region, it has been natural to assume free disposal of inputs as expressed by equation (2b).

In principle, the short-run function can be derived by solving a number of linear programming

(LP) problems. However, when the aim is to establish a reasonably interesting number of isoquants, in order to reveal all the corners of the piecewise linear isoquants, solving the LP problems (2a-c) is not a practical procedure. Instead an algorithm is used suggested in Foersund and Hjalmarsson (1983). A complete description of this algorithm is presented in Foersund and Hjalmarsson (1985).

DATA

In the following industries we have obtained data for almost all micro units (kilns for cement and plants in the other cases) during selected years. The data cover the following variables: (1) output is measured in tonnes per year; (2) capacity, reflecting potential output, is also measured in tonnes per year; (3) the labor input variable (L) is defined as the hours worked by production and maintenance workers, and (4) energy (E) is measured in calories or kWhs.

Industry	Period	Energy type
Swed. cement	1960-80	Fuel
Norweg. cement	1960-80	"
Finnish cement	1960-80	"
Swed. mechanical pulp	1920-74	Electricity
Swed. sulphite pulp	1920-74	Total energy
Swed. sulphate pulp	1920-74	"
Swed. pig iron	1850-1975	Fuel
Norweg. aluminium	1966-78	Electricity

During the periods covered by data there has been an increasing long run trend of a higher labor-energy relative price ratio, though this trend was temporarily broken in the mid-seventies.

THE DEVELOPMENT OF THE SHORT-RUN INDUSTRY PRODUCTION FUNCTION AND TECHNICAL CHANGE

The region of substitution and isoquant map of the short-run industry production function for some industries is presented in figures 1 to 5.

Cement

In the cement industry there are two basic technologies: wet and dry technology. In the dry process limestone powder is fed directly into the kiln where it is calcined to form clinker. In the wet process water is added to form a slurry which is then fed into the kiln. In the Swedish cement industry the dry technology has substituted for the wet one, the main reasons being energy conservation and increased utilization of economies of scale. Dry kilns are in general more energy efficient and there seem to be greater possibilities to achieve scale economies in dry kilns.

Against this background the steady shift of the substitution region in figure 1 toward the energy axis should be expected and is due to the simultaneous influence of the development of relative prices, shown in table 1, the scale properties of the ex ante function, and the shift in technology from the wet to the dry process. The development of the substitution region has been most rapid between 1960 and 1970 parallel to the very rapid increase in the relative price of labor.

During this period the average factor ratio between energy and labor doubled and capacity increased by 68 percent.

For all years the distance between the isoquants in figure 1 is 500 ktonnes. The productivity improvements can be seen by following any isoquant representing the same output level from year to year. In figure 1 three isoquant levels are indicated by arrows. For all levels there is a marked movement toward the energy axis. There is also a substantial shift toward the origin, which is somewhat stronger the higher the levels of output.

In the case of Norway we see that the development from 1960-1970 was marked by a strong movement of the substitution region in the direction of the energy axis; see figure 2. In the 1970s we have a complete reversal: The 1980 industry production function has swung back toward the energy axis. Following the same isoquant we see that technical progress from 1960-1970 turns into regress between 1970 and 1980.

Mechanical Pulp

Mechanical pulp is produced by grinding the wood while water is added, in order to free the cellulosa fibres. The other components of the wood (mainly lignin) remain in the pulp. Thus the pulp yield is very high. A modern version of this process is thermo mechanical pulp. The motive power of the pulp mills is electricity though earlier some plants used water power directly.

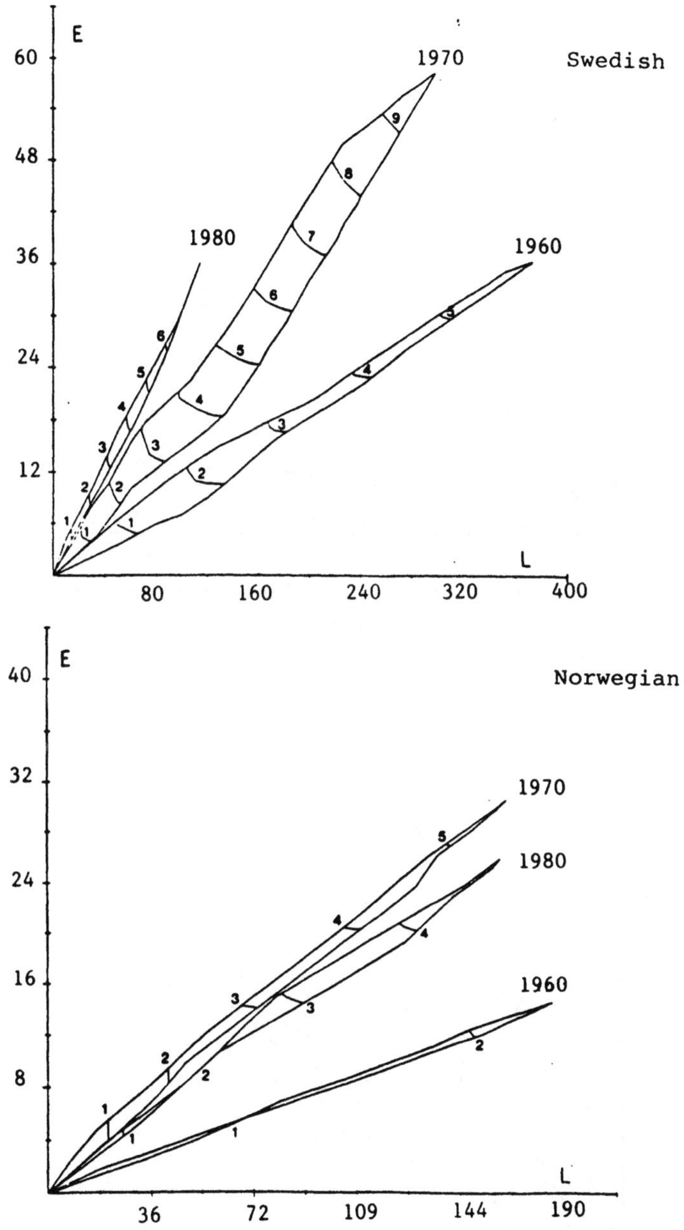

Figures 1 and 2. The development of the short-run industry production function of the Swedish and Norwegian cement industries between 1960 and 1980 (the distance between the isoquants is 500 ktonnes)

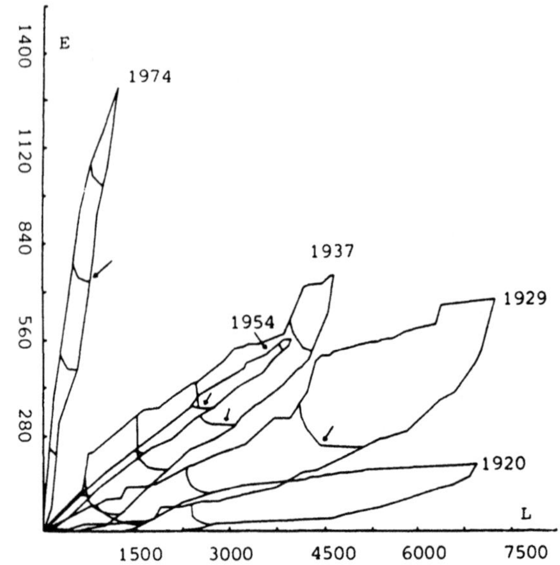

Figure 3. Short-run industry production functions for Swedish Mechanical Pulp 1920-1974 (isoquant distance 50 ktonnes)

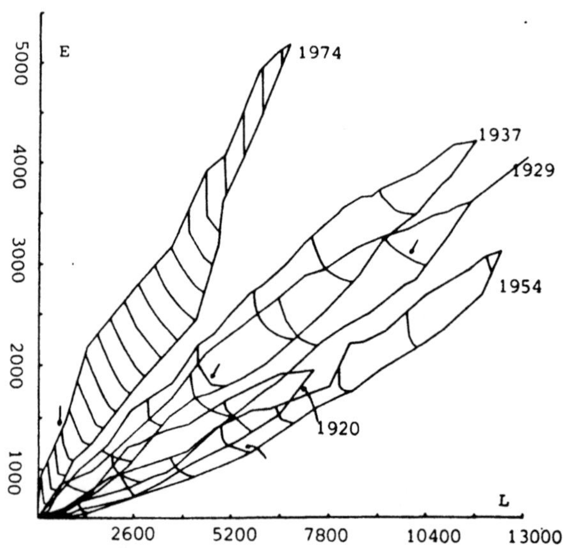

Figure 4. Short-run industry production functions for Swedish Sulphate Pulp 1920-1974 (isoquant distance 400 ktonnes)

The development of the short-run function, shown in figure 3, is characterized by a gradual change of the substitution region toward the energy axis. The isoquant of 50 ktonnes is marked by arrows. The shift of the isoquant between 1929 and 1974 reveals that technical change has been limited to a substitution between labor and electricity without any overall improvement in productivity. In our experience this is a rather rare case since technical change in most industries seems to be characterized by a simultaneous process of substitution and overall productivity improvements shifting (although not along a straight line) the isoquants toward the origin.

One explanation for these differences in structural change may be due to the fact that basically the production process for mechanical pulp has remained unaltered through time except for the size which has increased. This increase in size has mainly affected the unit requirements of labor, not electricity. On the other hand for chemical pulp it is easy to find major process innovations which have saved both labor and energy.

Chemical Pulp

In the sulphite and sulphate mills the wood is chipped into small pieces, which are boiled under pressure in an alkaline or acid solution. The lower yield, compared to mechanical pulp, is due to the fact that the chemical processes dissolve the lignin and hemicelluloses, leaving only the pure cellulose fibres, which represent about half of the dry weight of the wood. Since chemical pulps are more or less pure cellulose fibres, they are stronger than wood pulp and can be used for a variety of purposes.

Figure 4 shows the development of the sulphate pulp process and the shifts in one isoquant, 400 ktonnes, are marked by arrows.

The development of both processes may be divided into three phases. During the first phase, 1920-1937, both labor and energy productivity increased rapidly, during the second, between 1937 and 1954, energy was substituted for labor, while during the last period, 1954-1974, an overall productivity improvement took place.

Pig Iron

Three basic techniques were employed during the period 1850-1975: charcoal, coke and electric combined with charcoal and later coke blast furnaces. Charcoal was the only technique in 1850 and 1880, while all three techniques were in use in 1913, 1935 and 1950. Only coke furnaces were in use in 1975. Total production has increased from 100 ktonnes in 1850 to 3500 ktonnes in 1975. The development of the short-run function is shown in figure 5.

There was almost no change in the charcoal technique between 1850 and 1880. From 1880 onward the substitution region has shifted steadily toward the energy axis. The distance between the isoquants is 50 ktonnes for 1850-1935 and 100 ktonnes for 1950 and 1975. The movement of the isoquant for 300 ktonnes is indicated by arrows. After 1880 there is a uniform labor saving bias.

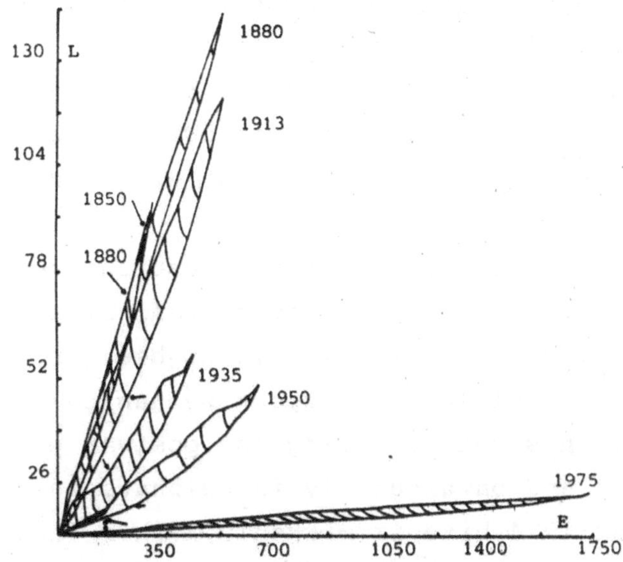

Figure 5. Short-run industry production functions for Swedish Pig Iron 1850-1974 (isoquant distance 1850-1935 50 ktonnes, 1950-1974 100 ktonnes)

TECHNICAL ADVANCE AND BIAS MEASURES

In all industries there has been a significant change in the substitution regions and isoquant maps during the periods. As regards numerical measures of these changes, we shall here adopt Salter's measures of technical advance and factor bias. The short-run industry production function provides us with the variable unit costs, along the expansion path. Salter's measure of technical advance shows the ratio between minimized unit costs in year t and t+1 and the factor bias measure shows the relative change in optimal factor ratios between year t and t+1; see Salter (1960). In all cases we have used the factor prices of the last year in the set of observations (Paasche index). The results are presented in table 1. Due to limited space we present the results for the entire periods for which we have data and in addition we also present the results for the last period in the data set. (Frontier output means a low output level produced by the most efficient plant(s).)

Generally the factor bias measures show a strong labor saving bias. The overall bias for the entire period of observation is highest in mechanical pulp. In all cases, except mechanical pulp, bias is much stronger during the postwar period up to 1974 and particularly in sulphate pulp.

After 1974 bias is markedly weaker (and even turns into energy saving at higher output levels in the Norwegian and Finnish cement industries). This variation in the degree of bias is consistent with the variation in the development of the relative factor prices.

The reduction in variable unit costs varies a lot between the industries and between different periods. This way of measuring technical advance confirms and quantifies the impressions from figures 1-5 that technical progress has been rapid during the postwar period up to 1974 in the cement and pulp industries. The very strong productivity growth in sulphate pulp is to a great extent explained by the investments in large modern units in the 1960s.

Table 1. The Salter Factor Bias and Technical Advance Measures in Last Year Prices. Yearly Percentage Changes Within the Parentheses

Industry	Period	Bias at Frontier	Techn. Advance at Frontier	Techn. Advance at Q
Swedish cement	1960-80	4.41	0.41	0.40
Q=500 ktonnes		(6.2)	(3.7)	(3.8)
	1975-80	1.31	0.90	0.89
		(5.4)	(2.1)	(2.3)
Norwegian cement	1960-80	2.19	0.42	0.35
Q=1000 ktonnes		(3.9)	(4.3)	(5.2)
	1975-80	1.03	1.02	1.02
		(0.6)	(-0.4)	(-0.4)
Finnish cement	1960-80	1.39	0.64	0.52
Q=2000 ktonnes		(1.6)	(2.2)	(3.3)
	1975-80	1.00	1.00	0.99
		(0.0)	(0.0)	(0.2)
Mechanical pulp	1920-74	127.47	0.06	0.05
Q=50 ktonnes		(17.5)	(5.2)	(5.5)
	1954-74	17.98	0.23	0.20
		(14.4)	(7.3)	(8.0)
Sulhpite pulp	1920-74	1.35	0.22	0.12
Q=100 ktonnes		(0.6)	(2.8)	(3.9)
	1954-74	1.75	0.25	0.24
		(2.8)	(6.9)	(6.8)
Sulphate pulp	1920-74	22.24	0.02	-
Q=100 ktonnes		(5.7)	(7.2)	
	1954-74	83.88	0.09	0.09
		(22.1)	(12.0)	(12.0)
Pig iron	1850-1975	21.01	0.28	0.22
Q=50 ktonnes		(2.0)	(1.0)	(1.2)
	1950-75	5.54	0.69	0.69
		(6.8)	(1.5)	(1.5)
Aluminium	1966-78	1.32	0.85	0.72
Q=150 ktonnes		(2.3)	(0.7)	(2.7)
	1974-78	1.01	1.04	1.01
		(0.2)	(-0.9)	(-0.2)

For those industries for which data after 1974 are available, cement and aluminium, technical advance slowed down markedly particularly on the frontier, in the case of Swedish cement. This means a smaller distance between the average and best-practice performance indicating that productivity growth was obtained by a rationalization or scrapping of the least efficient equipment. In Finnish cement it was a stand still and in Norwegian aluminium there was even a technical regress during this period mainly due to a low degree of capacity utilization, in combination with labor hoarding.

Technical progress is here measured in terms of reduction in variable costs. To complete the picture, capital costs should, of course, also be taken into consideration.

CONCLUSIONS

The main results of the paper may be summarized as follows:

In all industries up to midseventies there is a uniform labor saving bias and in most industries a fairly rapid technical progress. After 1974/75, however, bias is markedly weaker and in a few cases even energy saving. At the same time technical progress is slowed down and in a few cases went into technical regress.

REFERENCES

Foersund, F. R. and L. Hjalmarsson. 1983. "Technical progress and structural change in the Swedish cement industry 1955-1979." Econometrica September.

_____. 1985. "Analysis of industrial structure. A production function approach." IUI Working Paper. Stockholm.

Johansen, L. 1972. Production functions. Amsterdam: North-Holland Publishing Company.

Salter, W. E. G. 1969. Productivity and technical Change. Cambridge: University Press.

39
A Weather Index for International Heating Oil Consumption

Robert J. Leffler, Jerry Sullivan, Henry E. Warren,
U.S. Department of Commerce

INTRODUCTION

The Assessment and Information Services Center (AISC) within the National Environmental Satellite, Data and Information Service (NESDIS) is the lead National Oceanic and Atmospheric Administration (NOAA) organization responsible for determining, assessing and reporting the social and economic impact of climate anomalies and weather events on various sectors of the economy. Energy is one important sector. AISC obtains current weather data products from the Climatic Analysis Center (CAC) and historical data products from the National Climatic Data Center (NCDC). These observed meteorological data, monthly and seasonal outlook data from the National Weather Service (NWS) and geographic, demographic and economic data are used to derive short-term impact assessment products. The products are produced monthly, with annual summaries and special reports as required. In support of the assessment function of AISC, the Models Branch develops analytical models that can quantatively and qualitatively evaluate the effect of weather events on the economy.

Temperature fluctuations have a significant influence on the amount of oil consumed for heating in many developed countries, and the magnitude of the variations can result in substantial economic consequences (Quirk 1981). Assessing the impact of temperature fluctuations (for example, a cold winter in Europe) on international oil use for heating on a real time basis has, until this time, been handled in a subjective manner. AISC/NOAA, has developed a method for near real time assessment of the impact of international temperature variations on oil consumption in seven free world developed countries. These seven countries, Canada, France, Italy, Japan, the United Kingdom, the United States, and West Germany (Figure 1), consume an estimated 80% of the free world's heating oil. The assessment, prepared operationally for each month during the October through May heating season, is available with only a five to ten day lag.

The objective of this AISC product is to provide governmental, industrial, and other energy analysts concerned with global oil supply and demand a near real-time quantitative assessment on the impact of international temperature variations on global heating oil consumption. The objective was achieved by developing an international heating oil consumption index, available at the country, continent and international levels; a twenty-year time series of monthly index values useable for ranking the unusualness of the index; models which correlate the index values with oil consumed for heating; and an operational impact assessment.

INTERNATIONAL HEATING OIL CONSUMPTION INDEX

The basic input for the index values is the heating degree day (HDD), a unit developed to reflect temperature related heating fuel demand (Warren and LeDuc,1981). Index values were developed for the country, continent, and international (seven-country) total for the northern hemisphere heating season (October-May) in the following manner. Using a procedure previously developed to produce a national U.S. index value (Warren and LeDuc, 1981), cities in each of the six foreign countries were selected for use in producing the country level index values (table 1). The choices were governed by the following criteria: 1) the city had to be one which routinely reports monthly mean temperature to the World Meteorological Organization (WMO) network, thus making that data electronically available to NOAA, about two days after the end of each month; 2) the city represents an important temperature regime possible in the country, and; 3) the temperature of the city had to be representative of temperatures affecting at least three percent of the country's population. A total of 39 cities were chosen.

Temperature anomalies in the more heavily populated areas (where more heating fuel is used) were weighted to get more consideration than those representing less populated areas. The index reflects the average temperature related heating needs for the total population in that country.

The real-time operational foreign city HDD's are estimated from the monthly HDD's because the actual totals based on daily temperatures are not immediately available . Monthly estimates are computed using Wendland's procedure (Wendland, 1983) which produces accurate results in winter months with only the mean monthly temperature as input. The base temperature chosen for HDD computations in all cities located in Europe (France, Italy, West Germany, and United Kingdom) and Japan was 15.6^{0}C (60^{0}F). A base of 18.3° C (65° F) was used for North American (Canadian and U.S.) cities.

Country level index values were next aggregated to form multi-national (continent and international) index values by multiplying oil-use weights (derived from the first generation oil-use versus heating oil consumption models) by each country's monthly population-weighted HDD total and summing to the appropiate level.

TABLE 1. Countries and the Cities in the HDD Indices (non-U.S.)

France	Pop. Wt.	United Kingdom	Pop. Wt.
Bordeaux	.067	Glasgow	.092
Clermont-Ferrand	.056	London	.434
Lyon	.118	Manchester	.474
Marseille	.076		
Nantes	.145	**Japan**	
Paris	.399	Fukuoka	.087
Strasbourg	.084	Kagoshima	.073
Toulouse	.055	Maebashi	.042
		Niigata	.071
West Germany		Osaka	.248
Essen	.288	Sapporo	.049
Hamburg	.187	Sendai	.062
Munich	.325	Tokyo	.368
Offenbach	.167		
West Berlin	.033	**Canada**	
		Calgary	.050
Italy		Edmonton	.030
Catania	.117	Montreal	.234
Cagliari	.026	Quebec	.044
Milan	.276	Regina	.040
Pescara	.123	Sydney	.095
Rome	.332	Toronto	.360
		Vancouver	.107
		Winnipeg	.040

HISTORICAL TIME SERIES OF THE INDEX

Historical monthly temperature data for the 39 foreign cities chosen for the index were not readily available through NOAA. Instead, 19 heating seasons (1965-66 to 1983-84) of monthly HDD data (base 18.3° C) for 37 similar cities available

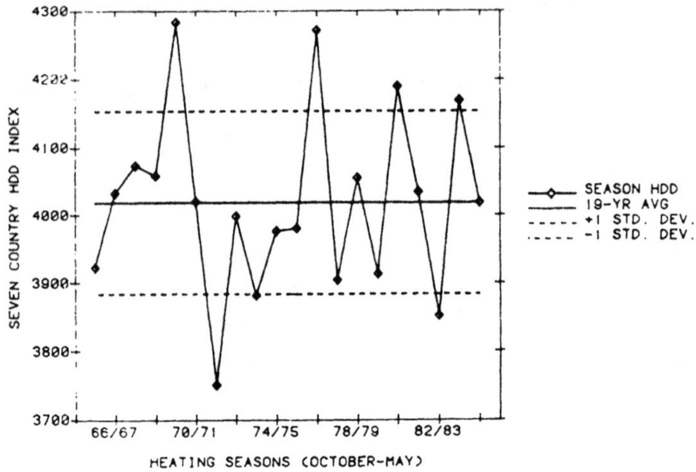

Figure 1. Time Series of Seven-Nation Oil Based HDD Index

from the United States Air Force Environmental Technical Applications Center (ETAC) were used. The European and Japanese indices were then adjusted from the 18.3° C base to our base of 15.6° C. This gave us a historical time series of monthly HDD index values based on the chosen temperatures. ETAC did not use the same cities that we did. A linear adjustment made the historical time series compatible with our HDD index values. This adjustment yielded a monthly time series of index values at the country, continent, and international levels which could be used to rank the unusualness of the NOAA/AISC real-time monthly index values (figure 1).

SPECIFICATION OF THE MODELS

The results of the evaluation of the simple models of monthly oil sales based on the country HDD index and time trend indicated that in most countries there was a significant relationship between HDD's and monthly oil sales. The overall model preformance was not consistent. Consequently we propose a more comprehensive model specification that will more accurately determine monthly oil sales. We speculate that a significant proportion of the difference between the simple model estimate and actual monthly oil sales is due to the divergence between oil sales and oil consumption. We propose to improve the model performance through the use of time related variables to 1) adjust for the cyclical (non-temperature related) buying patterns between months within the year and, 2) adjust for the inter-year downward trends in consumption patterns due to consumer conservation and government policies to promote lower consumption. The comprehensive model is a relationship between monthly oil sales in a country, population (customer) weighted heating degree days, and additional variables to more accurately estimate monthly sales which may not directly reflect consumption.

During the model development, an independent reviewer suggested that the cyclical variation in monthly oil sales that correlates with HDDs needed to be analyzed separately as the response to normal monthly heating degree days and monthly deviation from normal (Granzer, 1985). This would indicate to what extent the sales pattern was consistently cyclical and to what extent monthly sales actually responded to concurrent variations in HDDs. The hypothesis, that the relationship between monthly oil sales and monthly heating degree days is with the actual HDDs, was tested against the alternative hypothesis that monthly consumption is related only to normal HDDs. To do the test, the observed HDDs, H_m, were removed from the equation 1 models and models respecified. The respecified models contained the variables with statistically significant coefficients in equation 1.

$$S_m = f(H_m, I_y, D_n, D_d, D_j, D_f, D_{mr}, D_a, D_p, S_{m-12}, S_{y-1}) \quad (1)$$

$$S_m = f(N_m, F_m, I_y, D_n, D_d, D_j, D_f, D_{mr}, D_a, D_p, S_{m-12}, S_{y-1}) \quad (2)$$

S_m -- Monthly sales of light oil in the country for October to May (our chosen heating season).

H_m-- Monthly population weighted Heating Degree Days (customer weighted in U.S., Base 65^0 F in U.S. and Canada, Base 60^0F in U.K., France, W. Germany, Italy, and Japan).

N_m--Monthly normal population weighted HDDs for the country

F_m--Monthly deviation from normal HDDs for the country.

I_y-- Index of heating seasons over the period of the data, 1973-74 = 1,..., 1983-84 = 11.

$D_n,...,D_{my}$-- Discrete (Dummy) variable for the respective month (November,...,May). Equals one for the specified month, otherwise equals zero.

D_p-- Discrete (Dummy) variable for a set of heating seasons. Equals one for the specified seasons, otherwise equals zero.

S_{m-12}-- Sales of light oil in the country in the same month of the previous heating season.

S_{y-1}-- Sales of light oil in the country in the previous Oct.-May heating season.

Additional variables are derived from D_p in combination with I_y, N_m, and F_m. The purpose of the additional variables is to more accurately estimate monthly sales which may not directly reflect consumption. On the basis of previous analysis of the use of gas and electricity for space heating it is hypothisized that the consumption of oil for space heating is determined primarily by the population weighted heating degree day variable, H_m. The variables D_n-D_{my} and S_{m-12} are shift and autoregressive variables, respectively, that adjust for the intrinsic pattern in sales that is related to the intra-annual pattern in monthly consumption. The variables I_y, D_p, and S_{y-1} are related to changes in consumption and sales related trends and shifts that are associated with responses to changes in prices and government policies whose effects are interannual. The interactive variables D_pH_m and D_pI_y are hypothesized to be related to variations in interannual consumption rates and trend patterns.

It is anticipated that only some of the coefficients, of the variables in the formulas will be statistically significant. Also, some subjectivity is involved in the specification of the time period for the shift term D_p. D_p is associated with the 1978-79 increases in the price of OPEC oil. The response to this increase in price is seen in the time series of annual sales as a decrease in sales in several countries. In Canada the decrease occurred in the 78-79 season. In other countries the decrease was not until two or three years later. In developing the country models monthy price was introduced as a potential explanatory variable in place of the dummy variables trend variables but price was not statistically significant in the countries where it was tried. Apparently government policy was more important than OPEC prices in determining domestic sales and prices.

Theoretically, because $H_m=N_m+F_m$, the coefficients of N_m and F_m should be the same as a_1, the coefficient of H_m. The general model is below. For any specific country only the variables with statistically significant coefficients in equation 1 are used in equation 2. The linear form of equation 2 is equation 3. The coefficients of equation 3 were estimated using multiple linear regression analysis.

$$S_m = b_0 + b_1N_m + b_2F_m + b_3I_y + b_4D_n + b_5D_d + b_6D_j + b_7D_f + b_8D_a + b_9D_{my} + b_{10}S_{m-12} + b_{11}S_{y-1} + b_{12}D_p + b_{13}D_pN_m + b_{14}D_pF_m + b_{15}D_pI_y + b_{16}D_pS_{y-1} \quad (3)$$

EVALUATION OF THE MODELS.

The coefficients for the linear form of equation 1 were estimated and their statistical significance evaluated using the statistical analysis program RS/1 (BNN Research Systems, 1983). This was accomplished using a stepwise analysis for variable entry. Variable's coefficients whose explanatory power was low (generally those whose coefficient's t-statistic significance level was greater than 0.1) were deleted from the equation for the country.

The results of the regressions and variable selection for the linear form of equation 1 are not presented due to space limitations. Each country model was unique. The model for France had eight significant variable coefficients while West Germany had only two significant coefficients besides intercept. Every variable proposed in equation 1 was significant in at least one country except D_{mr}, the dummy variable for March. The model with the most explained variations is for Canada with an R^2 of 0.96. The model with the least explained variation is for West Germany with an R^2 of 0.67.

Table 2. Equation 3 Regression Results for each Country's Monthly Light Oil Sales (mmbbl)
Heating Season: October thru April Years: 1974/75 thru 1983/84

	Variable (S_m, N_m) Means and Standard Deviations						Estimated Coefficients (b_i) and Standard Errors					
	S_m	b_0	N_m	b_1	F_m	b_2	$b_3 I_y$	$b_4 D_n$	$b_5 D_d$	$b_6 D_j$	$b_7 D_f$	$b_8 D_a$
Country	(a)	(a)	(b)	(c)	(b)	(c)	(a)	(a)	(a)	(a)	(a)	(a)
Canada	10.3	2.86	.956	11.64	.008	6.81	-.47		1.00		1.25	
	(4.7)		(.368)	(.50)	(.101)	(1.10)	(.15)		(.36)		(.36)	
France	20.9	9.09	.396	26.49	.004	18.70	.72		4.69	3.68	2.83	
	(6.7)		(.165)	(3.32)	(.068)	(4.09)	(.27)		(1.18)	(1.23)	(1.03)	
Italy	8.3	4.69	.287	4.32	.006	3.93 [d]			1.77	1.96	1.66	-2.13
	(3.3)		(.164)	(2.31)	(.049)	(2.70)			(.74)	(.85)	(.64)	(.52)
Japan	27.2	7.51	.312	21.60	-.004	22.04				-4.17	-2.12	
	(7.9)		(.220)	(4.26)	(.051)	(5.55)				(1.22)	(1.01)	
U.K.	8.7	5.09	.472	6.17	.001	4.72	-.13					
	(1.7)		(.133)	(.95)	(.074)	(.97)	(.04)					
U.S.	99.7	-24.01	.698	28.49	.005	41.99						
	(19.5)		(.314)	(4.32)	(.090)	(9.59)						
W. Ger.	26.3	23.43	.513	11.83	.001	12.30						
	(5.9)		(.208)	(1.88)	(.091)	(4.32)						

Units--(a) MMBBL, (b) thousands of HDD, (c)mbbl/HDD (d) Not significant at the 0.1 t-statistic level

Table 2. (Continued)

Country	b_9D_{my} (a)	S_{m-12} (a)	b_{10}	S_{y-1}	b_{11} (a)	$b_{12}D_p$	$b_{13}D_pN_m$ (c)	$b_{14}D_pF_m$ (a)	$b_{15}D_pI_y$ (a)	$b_{16}D_pS_{y-1}$ (a)	R^2 std. error
Canada						6.84[e] (1.07)	-3.27[e] (.60)		-.62[e] (.17)		.96 (.96)
France				158.04 (27.77)		-22.66[f] (4.34)	-10.89[f] (3.30)			.11[f] (.02)	.88 (2.42)
Italy	-2.65 (.67)	8.37 3.24	.28 (.11)								.89 (1.15)
Japan		26.92 (7.52)	.52 (.10)								.92 (2.28)
U.K.	-.69 (.29)	8.97 (1.64)	.22 (.09)				-2.07[g] (.58)				.87 (.64)
U.S.		100.47 (19.63)	.30 (.07)	797.92 (86.23)	.92 (.01)						.86 (7.49)
W. Ger.										-.04[h] (.004)	.67 (3.45)

Dp=1 for (e) 1978/79 through 1983/84, (f) 1979/80 through 1983/84, (g) 1981/82 through 1983/84, (h) 1980/81 through 1983/84, Otherwise Dp=0

The results of the estimated equation 1 were better than the simple models in terms of having higher R^2 for all countries using more of the entire time series of oil data.

Table 2 contains the results of estimating equation 3. The values of b_1 and b_2 are similar for Italy, Japan, U. K. and W. Germany. They are relatively divergent for Canada, France and the United States. However, when the interaction of the sales rate shift terms, b_{13}, for Canada and France are considered the difference is much less. Also, the confidence intervals around the estimates of b_1 and b_2 are large enough that they cannot be said to be significantly different from each other, even for the U. S. The 90% confidence interval for estimates of b_1 and b_2 for the U. S. are:

$$b_1 = 28.49 + \text{or} - 1.70(4.32) = (21.16, 35.82)$$

$$b_2 = 41.99 + \text{or} - 1.70(9.59) = (25.71, 58.27).$$

Although estimates of b_1 and b_2 differ by a relatively large amount the overlap of their confidence intervals indicates that they are not statistically different. In all countries but Italy both the estimated coefficients of N_m and F_m are statistically significant at the 0.1 t-level. The fact that these variables are significant separately indicates that monthly oil sales are responding to both the normal cycle of degree days in the heating season and the corresponding HDD deviation from normal in the month. Thus, the current monthly HDD index for a country improves the model estimate over the estimate using only normal HDDs. The current HDD index also improves the estimate for Italy. If F_m is deleted from the Italy model N_m becomes non-significant at the 0.1 t-level and the deletion of N_m results in a much lower R^2 for the model. In some countries such as the U. S. replacing H_m with N_m and F_m caused other variable's coefficients to become non-significant.

U.S. coefficients of the dummy variables for November and February became non-sigificant. When these variables were deleted the R^2 only decreased by 0.007. In Canada, France, and the U. K., which had significant coefficients for D_pH_m, a_{13}, new variables, D_pN_m, and D_pF_m, were included in the equation 3 models. In all three countries the coefficient of D_pN_m was significant while the coefficent of D_pF_m was not.

The interpretation of the equation 3 models becomes easier if the coefficients associated with N_m are defined as normal or average rates of sales per thousand HDD and the coefficients of F_m are defined as marginal rates of sales of oil per thousand HDD. The coefficient of D_pN_m, b_{13}, is interpreted as a change in the average rate of sales per thousand HDD in the countries while the marginal rate of sale remains the same because the coefficients of D_pF_m are not significant.

CONCLUSION

The development of an assessment incorporating HDD indices, and their estimated effect on light heating oil consumption and sales, will provide useful information on the impact of climate on the international oil consumption. These data can subsequently be input by users in their quantative analysis of the international oil market.

The regression analysis was an effective method to quantitatively relate data on sales of light heating oil in major oil consuming countries to the HDD index developed for the countries. These regression models demonstrate that monthly consumption and monthly sales of light heating oil are dependent on current deviations from the normal monthly HDD index as well as the normal monthly index values. The time series of the aggregate seven-country HDD index had a sizable variation indicating that in the countries included that the aggregate index values did not average out across countries. Consequently, variations in winter weather can have a significant impact on the seven-country total heating oil consumption, and the HDD index captures that weather variation.

REFERENCES

BBN Research Systems. 1983. RS/1 User's Manual. Cambridge.

Quirk, William J., 1981. "Climate and the International Response to Oil Supply Disruptions." Technical Note No. UCRL-85686. Livermore, Ca.: Lawrence Livermore National Laboratory, January.

Granzer, R., 1985. "Seasonal Adjustment of Monthly Data on Apparent Oil Demand." Personal Communication, Paris: International Energy Agency, OECD, April.

Warren, H. E. and S. K. LeDuc., 1981. "Impact of Climate on Energy Sector in Economic Analysis." Journal of Applied Meteorology, 20(12): 1431-1439.

Wendland, Wayne M., 1983. "A Fast Method to Calculate Monthly Degree Days." Bulletin American Meteorological Society, 64 (3): 279-281.

APPENDIX--Sources and Definitions of Oil Data

The oil sales data used for our models orginated from the publications listed below. A major problem was determining what types of oil were included in the sales data, and whether the sales were to a consumer or an intermediary.

oil, as best as we can determine, generally fall into the category known in the U.S. as light oil. The actual definitions, as described in the orginial publications, are also given below. The sales (versus consumption) appear to be national totals at the refinery and/or wholesale dealers level.

Canada:	Refined Petroleum Products, catalogue # 45-004. Sales are for stove oil kerosene and light fuel oil (# 2 & 3).
France:	The Bulletin Mensuel, published by the Comite Professionnel de Petrole. Sales are for fuel-oil domestique (home fuel oil and industrial light).
Italy:	The Bulletin Mensuel, published by the Comite Professionnel de Petrole. Sales are for Gasolio Chauffage Gasolio Riscaidamento (heating oil).
Japan:	Oil Information Monthly, Sekiyo Shiryo Geppo. Sales are for light fuel oil and kerosene.
United Kingdom:	The Bulletin of Energy Trends, published by the Department of Energy. Sales are for Gas/Diesel Oil (other).
West Germany:	Data are from The Bulletin Mensuel, published by the Comite Professionnel de Petrole. Sales are for heizol leicht (heating oil).
United States:	Data are from the Petroleum Supply Monthly, published by the Department of Energy. Sales are for light fuel oil.

40
Decision Making Under Uncertainty in Thailand's Energy Sector[1]

G. Anandalingam, V. Mubayi, J. Lee, P. M. Meier,
International Development & Energy Associates Inc.

1. INTRODUCTION

In recent years Thailand has had major natural gas, oil and lignite discoveries and has oriented its energy and economic development plans to utilize these resources. These activities are subject to considerable uncertainties. The quantity and timing of resource supply are stochastic as is the demand for natural gas and lignite due to the capacity expansion plans of the Electricity Generating Authority of Thailand (EGAT) and the fuel based industrialization plans of the Eastern Seaboard Development (ESDB) project. Given these uncertainties, the important decisions that have to be made are the speed of implementing the EGAT and ESDB plans, the fuels to be used in future power plants, the rate of development of the supply of natural gas and lignite, and associated plans for infrastructural investment in NG pipelines.

In this paper we use an integrated modeling framework to analyze optimal decisions under uncertainty in Thailand's energy sector. The models consist of RESGEN, an energy network that captures the energy flows through the economy and estimates energy balances for different end-use energy demand projections, and EFAM, a financial network that estimates annual financial flows in the economy due to investment decisions in the energy sector[2]. Demand and supply uncertainties are translated into scenarios for RESGEN model runs which then provide import costs of these scenarios. Decision making under uncertainty is analyzed in a Game Theory framework-the payoff matrix consists of the present value of investment, importation and opportunity costs. We derive optimal policies for different criteria in order to arrive at a robust and flexible energy strategy for Thailand for the next decade.

It should be noted that the primary objective of this paper is to present a methodology for analyzing energy sector investment decisions under uncertainty. The methodology is applied to some real energy strategy issues in Thailand. However for proprietary reasons we have neither reported all the information on the Thai energy sector, nor all the policies examined.

2. SOURCES OF UNCERTAINTY

In this study we characterize uncertainty by two demand scenarios (Reference and Low cases) and by two supply scenarios (Reference and High). High supply and low demand will not affect investment decisions in this study and thus were considered uninteresting. We also do not address price uncertainties although our framework can handle it.

2.1 Domestic Supply Uncertainty

The most important variables subject to uncertainty are the domestic supply of natural gas and lignite (Table 1). The timing of NG supply depends primarily on when the Texas Pacific field in the gulf of Thailand comes on line, and whether there will be a significant increase in gas production in the Union and Exxon fields from new discoveries. The "Reference" NG supply case is based on predictions of the World Bank and PTT of the most likely outcome of these events. The low supply case assumes that none of the new developments (including TP) will be on line by 1994, which is the

Table 1. Resource Supply Scenarios

	Natural Gas (MMCFD)		Lignite (MTonnes)	
Year	Ref.	Low	Ref.	Low
1983	150	150	2.31	2.31
1984	225	225	3.62	3.62
1985	400	400	4.65	4.65
1986	495	495	5.92	5.92
1987	575	575	6.12	6.12
1988	575	575	6.29	6.29
1989	622	622	6.88	6.88
1990	795	795	9.81	5.55
1991	875	470	11.70	7.44
1992	935	445	12.23	7.97
1993	1050	480	12.23	7.97

Source: National Energy Administration, Govt. of Thailand

Note: All figures are based on 1984 estimates

study horizon. EGAT controls lignite mining and production depends on a variety of factors such as the price and availability of fuel oil and natural gas. The "Reference" lignite supply scenario is based on the Recommended EGAT Power Development Plan (PDP) of May 1985. In the low supply scenario it is assumed that due to a drop in fuel oil prices there will be no investment in two lignite based power plants (Mae Moh 9 and 10) and thus delayed development of new lignite mines.

2.2 Demand Uncertainty

Uncertainty in demand forecasts (Table 2) is from two sources: (i) energy demand from the NG based industries of the ESDB project, and (ii) forecasts of petroleum product consumption.

There is uncertainty in industrial demand for NG due to the timing of projects, and for lignite depending on whether a "lignite intensive" industrialization plan is followed or not. The ESDB plan consists of investment in two industries (Petrochemicals and Fertilizer) in the short-run (by 1987) and a third (Soda Ash) in the long-run (by 2000). The high demand case is based on the assumption that all industrial projects will come on line as scheduled. The "Reference" case assumes (more realistically) a construction delay of two years.

Variance of the petroleum product forecast is based on econometric considerations. Product demand (D_i) is estimated using the equation:

$$D_i = a_i + \sum_j b_{ij} P_j + \sum_k c_{ik} Y_k \quad (1)$$

Table 2. Industrial Demand Scenarios

	Natural Gas (MMCFD)		Lignite (TTonnes)	
Year	Ref.	High	Ref.	High
1983	22	22	484	484
1984	22	22	490	490
1985	30	100	576	590
1986	30	100	550	645
1987	110	110	586	735
1988	140	140	625	895
1989	150	230	666	950
1990	150	230	710	1085
1991	240	240	757	1165
1992	240	240	807	1235
1993	240	240	860	1380

where P_j is the price of product j, Y_k is the index of income of type k (for example GDP), and b_{ij}, c_{ik} are parameters of the model. Equation 1 is then used to forecast the demand for petroleum products given forecasts of product prices ($\hat{P}$) and income ($\hat{Y}$). The variance of the forecast is given by (Johnston [1972]):

$$\sigma_D^2 = \sigma_u^2 \, [1/n + (\hat{X} - \bar{X})^2 / \sum_{i=1}^{n} x_i^2] \qquad (2)$$

where $\hat{X} = (\hat{P}, \hat{Y})$, n is the number of data points, $x = \hat{X} - \bar{X}$, and σ_u^2 the variance of the error term in the estimated equation.

The high demand scenario assumes that product forecasts will be one standard deviation higher than that in the Reference case.

3. THE ANALYTICAL FRAMEWORK

The sources of uncertainty characterized in the previous section would affect decision making in the energy sector in Thailand. The methodology for incorporating uncertainty into the decision making process consists of the following steps: (1) Development of the scenarios based on the estimated ranges of the stochastic variables, (2) Simulations using the RESGEN/EFAM models for these scenarios, (3) Estimation of the impact of the stochastic scenarios in terms of import, investment and opportunity costs, (4) Construction of a payoff matrix to reflect the impact of different scenarios on decisions in the energy sector, and (5) formulation of investment strategies based on risk analysis using the payoff matrix. The framework for analyzing decision making under uncertainty is given in Figure 1.

3.1 Game Theory Fundamentals

In this paper DUU is modeled using the concepts of two-person zero-sum games with the energy sector policy maker as one player and "nature" as the other. The different combinations of supply-demand scenarios are assumed to be the different strategies that "nature" employs in the game, which are not known beforehand to the decision maker (DM). Given these uncertain states (strategies) of nature the DM has to decide on an energy strategy that is optimal according to some criterion. The chosen policy together with the actual realization of the state-of-nature will lead to some net benefit

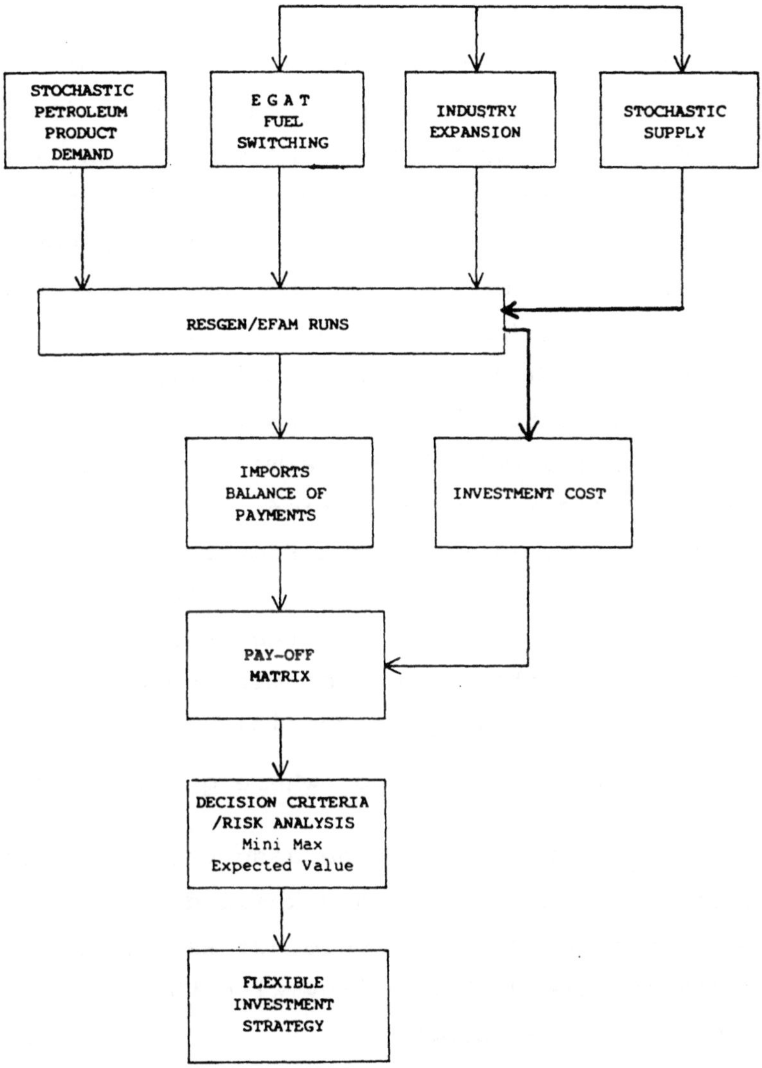

Figure 1. Framework for Decision Making Under Uncertainty

("payoff") to the economy. There will be different payoffs for different combinations of policies of the DM and states of nature. These payoffs are represented by a payoff matrix, p(i, j) where i is the strategy of the DM and j the state-of-nature.

The optimal strategy depends on the criterion of the decision maker which depends on risk aversion characteristics of the DM and on the (probabilistic) information available on the states-of-nature. In this paper we examine the policy consequences of using the following criteria: Wald's [1950] Maximin Criterion, Laplace's principle of insufficient reason (Luce and Raiffa [1957]), Hurwicz [1951]'s optimism-pessimism criterion, and Savage [1951]'s regret criterion.

Wald's Criterion. The assumption underlying this criterion is that the worst state of nature is the most likely outcome. Thus the (pessimistic) DM tries to obtain the maximum of minimum payoffs for each policy. The policy chosen is:

$$a^* = [i^*: q_{i^*} = \underset{i}{\text{Max}}\ q_i \text{ where } q_i = \underset{j}{\text{Min}}\ p_{ij}] \quad (3)$$

Laplace's Criterion. The assumption here is that the DM does not have any knowledge of the state-of-nature and thus would act as though each was equally likely. The policy with the maximum expected value is chosen:

$$a^* = [i^*: k_{i^*} = \underset{i}{\text{Max}}\ k_i = m^{-1} \sum_j p_{ij}] \quad (4)$$

Hurwicz's Criterion. In this criterion the DM attaches a prior probability r, based on his experience and level of risk aversion, on the best outcome for each policy. Then the probability (1-r) is attached to the worst outcome. Optimal policy is chosen as the one with maximum expected value:

$$a^* = [i^*: C_{i^*} = \underset{i}{\text{Max}}\ C_i \text{ where } C_i = r.\underset{j}{\text{Max}}\ p_{ij} + (1-r).\underset{j}{\text{Min}}\ p_{ij}] \quad (5)$$

<u>Savage's Criterion</u>. The assumption here is that the DM always tries to minimize <u>regret</u>. The "regret" to the DM if he uses the ith strategy and if the jth state-of-nature prevails is defined as:

$$r_{ij} = p_{ij} - \underset{i}{\text{Max}}\ p_{ij} \quad (6)$$

In order to select the optimal policy, the Maximin (Wald) criterion is used; only now, the regret matrix is used instead of the payoff matrix. The optimal policy is:

$$a^* = [i^*: s_{i^*} = \underset{i}{\text{Max}}\ s_i \text{ where } s_i = \underset{j}{\text{Min}}\ r_{ij}] \quad (7)$$

<u>Estimating the Payoff Matrix</u>. The payoff matrix consists of the present value of the annual stream of import, investment and opportunity costs. Estimates of costs are obtained by modeling energy and financial flows through the economy for different combinations (ie. scenarios) of states-of-nature and policy decisions. The energy flows and the resulting import costs are estimated by the RESGEN model, and annual investment flow required to sustain the energy flows are estimated by the EFAM model.

<u>Opportunity cost</u> is defined as the <u>value</u> of output not produced by the ESDB industries. Opportunity cost arises when the industries are ready to produce but there is no natural gas to sustain

production, or when there is NG available for the industries, but investment in the industries has not been completed.

3.2 Reference Energy System Generator-RESGEN

The Reference Energy System (RES) is a graphical representation of the more usual energy balance table; it captures energy flows through the economy with the accounting of energy losses at each stage of the system: conversion, distribution and end-use (figure 2). RESGEN is a software package that generates RESs for specified years in order to reconcile supply and demand. Mathematically the RES is most easily manipulated as a series of equations:

$$V(j + 1) = F(j, j+1).V(j) \tag{8}$$

where the j's are the different stages of the energy system, j+1 preceding j, and F is the transformation matrix defined so as to provide the proper fuel shares and conversion efficiencies. At each stage there can be a number of links (say n_j) in the system; thus F is an $n_{j+1}xn_j$ matrix. RESGEN contains all the elements of F(j, j+1); given end-use energy demand projections, RESGEN can generate all the intermediate steps and estimate energy flows. Imports are estimated as the difference between domestic supply and resource requirements.

3.3 Energy Finance Assessment Model-EFAM

EFAM is a microcomputer model that simulates year-by-year estimates of the income statement, balance sheet, and sources and applications of funds for all energy institutions in a country. For

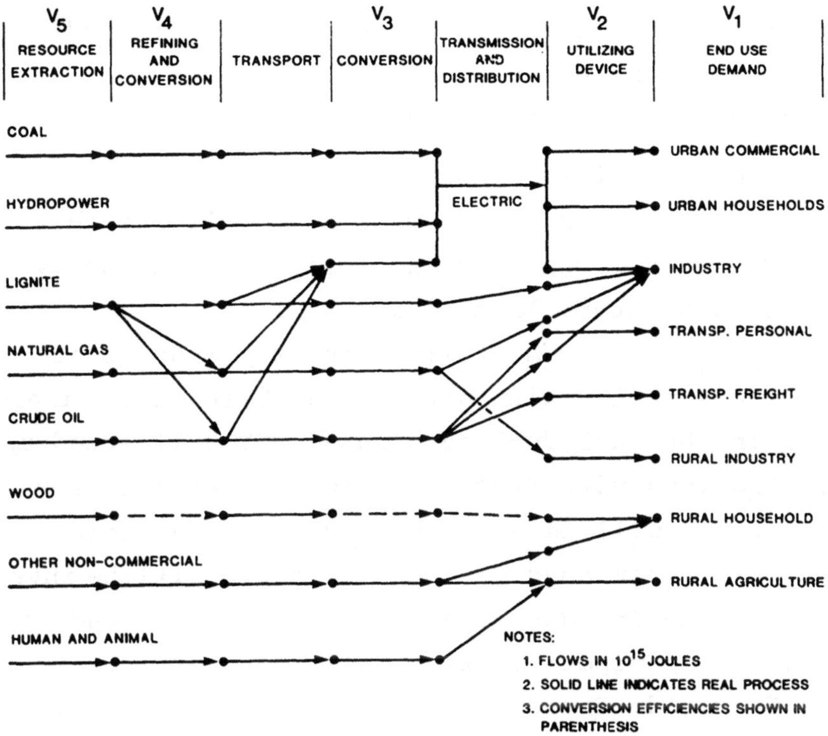

Figure 2. The Reference Energy System

the purposes of this study, only EFAM generated annual financial flows that result from energy sector investment are used.

The annual payments (CP) are obtained by multiplying capital investment (CC) by the capital recovery factor (CRF):

$$CP = CRF*CC, \text{ where} \tag{9}$$

$$CRF = r/[1 - (1 + r)^{-N}] \tag{10}$$

and where r is the rate of return on assets (or discount rate) and N is the useful equipment life.

For the different combinations of scenarios and decisions, annual financial flows (ie. payments) due to the different investments are estimated by EFAM using the above equations, and summed in order to obtain total annual investment costs.

4. RESULTS OF THE ANALYSIS

In this study we examine four policies that the Thailand government can follow in the energy sector and interrelated industries:

Policy A. EGAT follows the May 1985 Power Development Plan with natural gas being the primary fuel in the dual fuelled plants. PTT will speed up negotiations with Texas Pacific so that gas from that field will be available by 1990; in anticipation of increased gas supply, there will be investment in the 2nd gas separation plant (GSP) and in a couple of pipelines that will transport gas from the TP field. Investment in ESDB industries will proceed as scheduled.

Policy B. In anticipation of lower fuel oil prices in the future, EGAT will invest in a 600 MW fuel oil plant and not in the lignite based Mae Moh 9 and 10. More fuel oil (and less NG) will be used in the dual fuelled plants. Negotiations with TP will be slowed and thus NG supply from TP field will not be on line until after 1994. PTT will postpone investment in the 2nd GSP and the pipelines by 3-4 years. ESDB investment will be as in Policy A.

Policy C. Same as Policy A with 2 year speed up of the ESDB industrial development plan.

Policy D. Policy B with 2 year ESDB speed up.

Table 3 gives the foreign component of investment costs for these policies. Detailed RESGEN and EFAM results have not been presented, nor have opportunity cost calculations. The payoff matrix is given in Table 4. It should be noted that the matrix contains losses rather than gains.

The results of analyzing the outcome of the different criteria are given in Table 5. Clearly in all cases Policy A proves to be the best. It appears that if the Thailand government follows the investment package contained in Policy A (outlined above) it would satisfy all criteria from the most pessimistic (ie. Wald) to the most optimistic (ie. Laplace). In addition Policy A would minimize regret. Thus our analysis shows that among the limited alternatives examined, the most

Table 3. Investment Costs (Foreign Component)

Year	EGAT Policy		PTT Policy	
	A&C	B&D	A&C	B&D
1985	10.81	9.08	3.91	3.91
1986	10.78	9.05	0.53	0.51
1987	12.94	11.21	1.22	1.07
1988	13.48	11.76	3.89	0.37
1989	14.41	12.68	5.83	1.92
1990	12.92	12.92	3.22	3.22
1991	14.11	14.11	NU	NU
1992	17.90	17.90	NU	NU
1993	16.59	16.59	NU	NU

NOTE: All figures are in billion baht
NU = Investment in these years are not used in analysis.

Table 4. The Pay-off Matrix (PV of Economic Loss)*

	Scenarios			
	Reference	RD-LS	HD-RS	HD-LS
A	505.29	522.97	584.52	580.07
B	543.44	520.42	591.28	602.47
C	545.78	562.71	553.13	604.62
D	543.63	523.35	594.48	566.53

* Entries are in Billion Baht and abbreviations are as follows:
R = Reference, L = Low and H = High
D = Demand, & S = Supply.

flexible and robust energy strategy for Thailand would be to institute Policy A.

5. CONCLUDING REMARKS

The primary objective of this paper was to present a methodology for analyzing energy sector decisions under uncertainty. We applied the framework to a limited number of policies and supply-demand scenarios in Thailand. A more comprehensive analysis of the energy sector in Thailand would have addressed other issues such as energy conservation in industry, rationalization of the transportation sector, energy alternatives in the rural sector etc., and supply-demand scenarios that are intermediate to the ones that have been used. In addition, total costs, perhaps estimated at shadow prices, should be used in further analysis of the issues. These extensions are left for future work.

Table 5. Results of Game Theoretic Analysis

Policy	Wald (Maxmin)	Laplace (ExpLoss)	Hurwicz r=0.3	Hurwicz r=0.7	Savage (Regret)
A	584	548	561	529	31.39
B	602	564	578	545	35.94
C	605	567	587	563	42.29
D	594	557	573	545	41.35
"Best"	A	A	A	A	A

6. FOOTNOTES

1) The work for this paper was performed when the authors were consultants for International Development and Energy Associates Inc.,Washington DC The present affiliations are:
G. Anandalingam is at the Department of Systems Engineering, University of Virginia, Charlottesville, Virginia 22901;
V. Mubayi and J. Lee are at Brookhaven National Laboratory, Upton, New York 11973, and
P. M. Meier is at the Harriman School of Urban and Policy Sciences, State University of New York at Stony Brook, New York 11794.

2) RESGEN and EFAM are software packages created by IDEA Inc. which have been used for energy analysis in a number of countries.

7. REFERENCES

Hurwicz, L. [1951]. "Optimality Criteria for Decision Making Under Ignorance," Cowles Foundation Discussion Paper No. 350, Yale University.

Johnston, J. [1972]. Econometric Methods, Wiley, NY

Luce, R. D. and H. Raiffa [1957] Games and Decisions, John Wiley, NY.

Savage, L. J. [1951] "The Theory of Statistical Decision," J. American Statistical Association, vol. 46, pp 55-67.

Wald, A. [1950] Statistical Decision Functions,Wiley.

41
An Energy-Economy Model for Pakistan

Mary M. Chambers, Wen S. Chern,
University of Maryland

INTRODUCTION

The purpose of this study is to develop an energy-economy model for Pakistan. Multiple regression analysis is used to quantify the relationships of various energy-economy interactions. Once the system is estimated, it is used to conduct within-sample simulation to analyze the effects of the oil crisis and to perform a simulation to forecast future energy demand, economic growth, inflation, and balance of trade under alternative growth assumptions. The results of impact analysis have implications for programs relating to trade policies, environmental issues, conservation techniques and economic development strategies. The modeling framework is also applicable to other developing countries.

The model presented in this paper differs substantially from the models developed previously by Mukherjee and Rahman (1982) and Blitzer (1982). Our model may appear to be simpler in structure than theirs. However, our model is fully supported by the data from the country under study. That is, all structural parameters are estimated statistically. For the other studies, most parameters were constructed with few observations and some were not even estimated statistically for the country under study.

ECONOMETRIC MODELS

The basic hypothesis for constructing the energy-economy model for Pakistan is that there exist significant interactions between the energy sector and the rest of the economy. Economic conditions (growth and development) affect demand for energy. On the other hand, energy is a factor of production. At the macro-level, aggregate production is measured by gross domestic product (GDP). Thus, changes in energy prices have direct impacts on energy demand and GDP growth and consequently, inflation, imports, and exports. Although, the energy-economy interactions are likely more complicated than those represented in this model, we face tremendous constraints by the length of the available data series. The degrees of freedom problem prevents us from expanding the model to include more equations and from including more exogenous variables. Nevertheless, the model presented in this paper appears to capture the essence of these energy-economy interactions.

This model consists of six structural equations and one identity. The first is per capita primary energy demand which is specified to be a function of per capita real GDP, weighted average of fuel prices deflated by the wholesale price index, the share of GDP in the manufacturing sector, and the ratio of petroleum price to natural gas price. A partial adjustment model is adopted for modeling the dynamics of energy demand.

The GDP equation is an aggregate output function. Energy and capital stocks are the two major explanatory variables for aggregate output. Labor is not included because several proxy variables such as unemployment and population did not produce any sensible result. It can also be legitimately excluded because of a surplus of labor in Pakistan. The same dynamic specification used for energy demand is also adopted for the aggregate output equation.

The inflation is measured by wholesale price index in this model. The ratio of money supply to GDP, and energy price are the explanatory variables. Energy imports is the next structural equation with explanatory variables including GDP, price of energy imports, price of Middle East light crude oil, and domestic energy production. To explain the trade balance, total exports are specified as a function of GDP, price index of exports, and the ratio of the price of Pakistan exports to the export price in developing countries. Total imports are specified to be dependent upon GDP, price of imports and the export price of developing countries. The final equation is an identity equation to convert per capita energy demand to aggregate energy demand. There are additional dummy variables included in various equations. It should be mentioned also, that there were many more variables that were tried for in the preliminary analysis. For example, several economic structure related variables were tried for the energy demand equation. They were dropped because they did not significantly enhance the explanatory power and, furthermore, the degrees of freedom problem constrains the number of exogenous variables in the system.

All econometric variables are defined as follows (as standard notations, T.=Thousand, M.=Million, B.=Billion, and BBL=barrels of oil equivalent). First, the seven endogenous variables are:

EN = Total per capita end-use energy consumption (BBL per day per T.persons),
TEN = Total end-use energy consumption (T.BBL per day),
RGDP = Real GDP (B.Rupees, in 1975 base value),
EIM = Energy Imports, (T.BBL per day),
WPI = Wholesale price index (1975=100)
TOEX = Total exports (M.Rupees),
TOIM = Total imports (M.Rupees).

The following 19 exogenous variables are included:

POP = Population (M.Persons),
WPE = Weighted average price of energy (Rupees per BBL),
RGDPM = Real GDP in the manufacturing sector (B.Rupees, in 1975 base value),
PPNG = Ratio of petroleum price of natural gas price,
CAPT = Real capital stocks lagged for one year (M.Rupees, in 1975 base value),
PEIM = Price index of energy imports (1975=100),
POIL = Middle East light petroleum price (US$ per BBL),
EPRO = Total energy production (T.BBL per day),
M1 = Money supply (B.Rupees),
PEX = Export price index for Pakistan (1975=100),
PEEX = Ratio of export price index in Pakistan to developing countries (1975=100),
DEEX = Export price index for developing countries (1975=100),
D79 = Dummy variable having the value of 1.0 for the years after 1978, and 0 otherwise,
D74 = Dummy variable having the value of 1.0 for the years after 1973, and 0 otherwise,
D71 = Dummy variable having the value of 1.0 for the years after 1970, and 0 otherwise,
D80 = Dummy variable having the value of 1.0 for the years after 1979, and 0 otherwise,
D75 = Dummy variable having the value of 1.0 for the years after 1974, and 0 otherwise,
D68 = Dummy variable having the value of 1.0 for the years after 1967 and years before 1972, and 0 otherwise,
D78 = Dummy variable having the value of 1.0 for the years after 1977, and 0 otherwise.

DATA BASE

Data on end-use energy consumption and prices were obtained from the Government of Pakistan's Energy Year Book. Macroeconomic and demographic data were gathered from the World Tape, released by the World Bank, and Pakistan Statistical Year Book published by the Central Statistical Office of Pakistan. International Financial Statistics, published by the International Monetary Fund, was another statistical source.

Capital is one of the determinants of GDP. Capital stocks were computed following the procedure used by Taylor (1979). Numerous procedures were constructed to reach an appropriate measure of initial capital stocks. In addition, the collection of data for Pakistan required careful evaluation of the time series since the separation of East and West Pakistan in 1971. For the most part, the time series collected were adjusted for this separation, but some variables, such as energy imports, were not, so a dummy variable had to be used to account for this separation. The detailed procedures for data base construction and data sources are discussed in Chambers (1985).

ESTIMATION PROCEDURES AND RESULTS

The method of analysis for this system of equations is nonlinear three-stage least squares (3SLS) since OLS does not produce consistent estimators. Several functional forms including log-log, semi-log, and linear were examined. The linear form gives the best results in terms of the sign and significance of the coefficient estimates. Although all structural equations are linear (except the identity equation), nonlinearity arises because of the variable ratios present in the model.

The six structural equations as estimated by nonlinear 3SLS, are presented below (t-ratios are in parentheses, DW is Durbin-Watson statistic, and H is Durbin H-statistic).

(1) $$EN = \underset{(-2.22)}{-0.372} + \underset{(2.73)}{0.376} * EN_{t-1} + \underset{(4.51)}{0.773} * (RGDP/POP) - \underset{(-1.71)}{0.0024} * (WPE/WPI) + \underset{(2.33)}{2.846} * (RGDPM/RGDP) + \underset{(2.58)}{0.043} * PPNG + \underset{(4.17)}{0.158}\, D79$$

$R^2 = 0.992$, $DW = 2.41$, $H = 1.26$.

(2) $$TEN = EN * POP$$

(3) $$RGDP = \underset{(0.77)}{2.84} + \underset{(3.38)}{0.324}\, TEN + \underset{(1.52)}{0.101}\, CAPT + \underset{(4.17)}{5.94}\, D74 + \underset{(2.58)}{0.449}\, RGDP_{t-1}$$

$R^2 = 0.994$, $DW = 2.15$, $H = 0.610$.

(4) $$WPI = \underset{(0.97)}{0.121} + \underset{(3.27)}{1.72}\, (M1/RGDP) + \underset{(2.72)}{0.0021}\, WPE + \underset{(4.65)}{0.253}\, D75$$

$R^2 = 0.986$, $DW = 1.59$

$$(5) \quad EIM = \underset{(2.93)}{31.02} + \underset{(2.09)}{0.641}\ RGDP - \underset{(-4.42)}{0.200}\ PEIM$$

$$\underset{(-3.18)}{23.83}\ D71 + \underset{(4.25)}{41.48}\ D80$$

$$- \underset{(-0.47)}{0.346}\ (POIL/WPI) + \underset{(0.90)}{0.224}\ EPRO$$

$$R^2 = 0.833,\ DW = 2.39.$$

$$(6) \quad TOEX = \underset{(3.75)}{67.80} + \underset{(2.56)}{67.80}\ RGDP + \underset{(3.75)}{61.44}\ PEX$$

$$\underset{(-1.19)}{-1284}\ PEEX + \underset{(6.62)}{6856}\ D79 \underset{(-2.86)}{-2477}\ D68$$

$$R^2 = 0.989,\ DW = 2.09.$$

$$(7) \quad TOIM = \underset{(-1.93)}{3391} + \underset{(1.73)}{47.17}\ RGDP + \underset{(4.29)}{33.79}\ PEIM +$$

$$\underset{(8.13)}{151.11}\ DEEX + \underset{(5.30)}{9118}\ D78 \underset{(-1.99)}{-2012}\ D68$$

$$R^2 = 0.992,\ DW = 2.56.$$

The results show that all the exogenous variables are significant in explaining per-capita energy consumption. The short-run and long-run GDP elasticities are calculated at the sample means and the resulting values are 0.635 and 1.018, respectively. These estimates reveal the increased energy requirements given increases in Pakistan's GDP. Both the short-run and long-run price elasticities are inelastic at -0.125 and -0.20, respectively. These estimates reflect Pakistan's relative inability to decrease consumption of energy given a price increase.

The estimated real GDP equation shows that the lagged dependent variable and total energy consumption are the two most significant determinants of GDP. These results reveal a significant relationship between energy use and production. The calculated energy elasticities reveal an inelastic value of 0.398 in the short run and 0.722 in the long run. The capital variable, though having the expected sign, is significant only at the 20% level.

The estimation results for other structural equations are all satisfactory. The results indicate that the inflation indicator is quite responsive to changes in both the money ratio and energy price, as the corresponding elasticities are 5.14 and 2.24, respectively. Furthermore, real GDP is a significant explanatory variable for energy imports, total imports, and total exports.

MODEL APPLICATIONS

The major purpose of developing the energy-economy model for Pakistan is to apply the estimated equations to various simulation schemes. The first application involves the analysis of "within-sample" simulation. The purpose of the analysis is to evaluate the impacts of the 1973 oil embargo. In order to generate a reasonable assumption on energy price, growth rates of energy price for various periods were calculated and reviewed. For the 1970-71 period, the average annual growth of nominal energy price was 7.28%, and for the 1973-82 period, the growth rate was 19.26%. It is assumed that the annual growth rate of nominal energy price would have been 7.28% if the 1973 oil embargo did not happen. The resulting values for energy price were inputted into the system with all other exogenous variables assumed unchanged.

The simulated values for 1982 under the actual and assumed price of energy as well as the actual data are presented in Table 1. Based on these results, it is appropriate to conclude that the 1973 oil embargo impacted Pakistan in terms of decreases in total and per-capita energy consumption, real GDP, and total exports and increases in the inflation rate, energy imports, total imports and trade deficit. Therefore, Pakistan's economy is deemed worse off due to the oil crisis with respect to numerous aspects of the economy.

The dynamic simulation with actual prices produced very reasonable projection of all the endogenous variables. The predictive errors are generally less than 5%. These simulation results indicate that the model performs very well.

The second application involves the projection of the endogenous variables to the year 2000. Since Pakistan is a developing nation, the increase of demand for energy in this economy could significantly impinge energy supplies in the future. Therefore, an analysis of the growth of energy demand as well as the structure of Pakistan's economy could prove to be informative

Table 1. Estimated Energy-Economy Interactions Given a Reduced Growth of Energy Price (Assumed Growth rate of energy price for 1973-82: 7.28%)

Endogenous Variables[a]	1982 Actual Values	1982 Simulated Values Actual Price	1982 Simulated Values Assumed Price
EN (BBL/person)	0.97	0.95	1.13
TEN (T.BBL/day)	231.92	227.49	269.59
Real GDP (B.Rupees)	167.07	170.22	192.26
WPI (1975=1.00)	1.86	1.78	1.36
Energy Imports (T.BBL/day)	118.16	113.21	125.28
Total exports (M.Rupees)	27,647.00	27,821.20	29,315.50
Total imports (M.Rupees)	63,796.00	60,371.10	61,410.60
Trade Balance (M.Rupees)	-36,149.00	-32,549.80	-32,095.10

[a]EN=Total per-capita end-use energy consumption, TEN=Total end-use energy consumption, WPI=Wholesale price index.

and helpful in accessing the needs of this economy.

In order to generate values for the endogenous variables, assumptions on exogenous variables have to be specified. For forecasting, the assumed annual growth rates for 1983-2000 are 3% (population), 5.7% (manufacturing GDP), 0.5% (ratio of petroleum price to natural gas price), 6% (capital stocks), 17% (money supply), and 4.5% (total energy production). Two sets of assumptions are made for energy price related variables. Specifically, the assumed growth rates under the Medium and Low scenarios, respectively, are 3% and 8% (energy price), 2% and 5% (price of energy imports), 2% and 5% (light crude oil price), and 5% and 7% (price of exports). The bases for these assumptions are discussed in Chambers (1985).

Table 2 presents the results of the two simulations. The results show that the model is sensitive to the assumptions placed on energy and export prices. Assumptions of lower energy and export prices used in the Medium Growth scenario result in higher growth of per-capita and total energy demand than under the Low Energy Growth scenario. Also, real GDP and energy imports experience a higher growth under the Medium Growth scenario indicating the increase in aggregate production given lower energy prices. The inflation indicator and trade deficit both exhibit a decline under the Medium Growth scenario revealing the increased welfare of Pakistan's economy under lower energy and export prices. Total exports and total imports also generate a lower growth under the Medium scenario, due primarily to the growth in export prices. Given the larger percentage increase in price of exports, under the Low scenario, results in an increase in expenditure on both exports and imports. But the trade deficit is smaller in the Medium scenario thus, Pakistan's economy is better off with lower export prices as well as lower energy prices.

Table 3 presents the forecasted average annual growth rates of the endogenous variables for 1982-2000 under the two scenarios. The growth rates presented for aggregate energy demand are consistent with the findings of Chern

Table 2. Forecasted Endogenous Variables

Endogenous Variables	Unit of Measurement	1982 Actual	2000 Medium Scenario	2000 Low Scenario
EN	BBL/person	0.97	1.48	1.33
TEN	T.BBL/day	232	603	538
RGDP	B.Rupees (base 1975)	167	440	405
WPI	Base 1975	1.86	6.89	8.62
EIM	T.BBL/day	118	306	204
TOEX	B.Rupees	27.6	63.8	73.59
TOIM	B.Rupees	63.8	128.8	173.1
Trade Balance	B.Rupees	-36.1	-64.04	-99.5

et al. (1984). Their study documents Pakistan's primary energy demand growth for the period 1983-2000 as 5.2% under the Medium scenario and 4.1% under the Low scenario. The minor difference between this study and Chern's is the result of different assumptions and also the use of end-use versus primary energy demand.

In conclusion, the two scenarios developed for forecasting the energy-economy situation in Pakistan show that energy demand will continue to grow in the future. Also, the growing energy prices, under the Low scenario, cause real GDP to grow at a slower rate than under the Medium case assumptions. Note that the inflation rate

Table 3. Forecasted Annual Growth Rates (%) for 1982-2000

Endogenous Variables	Medium Scenario	Low Scenario
EN	2.42	1.77
TEN	5.45	4.78
RGDP	5.54	5.04
WPI	7.54	8.88
EIM	5.43	3.09
TOEX	4.76	5.59
TOIM	3.94	5.70
Trade Deficit	3.22	5.79

will be higher if the energy prices maintain a higher rate of growth. Further, since the model is sensitive to the input assumptions of the prices of energy and exports, the validity of the forecasts is dependent upon these assumptions.

CONCLUSIONS

This study shows that the energy-economy interactions are indeed significant in Pakistan. The first simulation of the model shows that the 1973 oil embargo signifcantly impacted Pakistan's economy. The rise in the weighted average energy prices (resulting from the two oil shocks) lowered not only energy consumption but also Pakistan's real income. This fall in real income resulted in the decline of total energy imports and the increase in the trade deficit. Also, the increase in weighted price of energy coupled with the fall in real GDP, significantly increased inflation in Pakistan.

The second simulation involved forecasting the endogenous variables to the year 2000. Two growth scenarios, Low and Medium, were generated based on the growth assumptions of exogenous variables. The results not only reveal the degree of uncertainty in predicting energy demand in Pakistan, but also show that the energy demand is likely to grow at a relatively high rate from now to the year 2000. Energy prices are also shown to have significant impacts on GDP growth, inflation, and trade balance in the future. The forecasted results reveal that Pakistan's economy will be significantly better off if the assumptions under the Medium Growth scenario hold.

REFERENCES

Blitzer, C. R. (1982). "Modelling energy-economy interactions in developing countries." Paper presented at the North American meetings of the International Association of Energy Economists, Denver, Colorado, November 19, 1982.

Chambers, M. M. "A General Equilibrium Energy - Economy Model for Pakistan." Unpublished Master Thesis, University of Maryland, College Park, 1985.

Chern, W. S., and S. Y. Lii, and H. Soberon-Ferrer (1984). "Impacts of economic growth and energy prices on energy demand in less developed countries." Paper presented at the sixth Annual North American Meeting of the International Association of Energy Economists, San Francisco, California, November 5-7, 1984.

Islam, Nurel (1981). Foreign Trade and Economic Controls in Development, The Case of United Pakistan. New Haven and London: Yale University Press.

Mukherjee, S. K., and G. H. Rahman (1982). "Energy Economy simulation model for oil-importing developing countries: an application to India." Paper presented at the Fourth Annual North American Meeting of the International Association of Energy Economists, Denver, Colorado, November 17-19, 1982.

Taylor, L. (1979). Macro Models for Developing Countries. New York: McGraw-Hill Company.

42
Urban Energy Use in the Developing Countries

Jayant Sathaye, Stephen Meyers,
Lawrence Berkeley Laboratory

The movement of people from the countryside to cities is a significant feature of the recent development process of many Asian, African, and Latin American countries. In many of the poorest countries (mostly in Africa), the growth rate of the urban population averaged more than 6% per year during the 1970s. Together, the developing countries now contain more than 250 cities with population over 500,000. Urbanization brings with it changes in the ways resources are collected, distributed, and used. In rural areas, people are more directly involved in these activities. In cities, there is greater dependence on a supply network to meet these needs. With many cities growing very rapidly, there is increasing pressure upon these networks, and in many cases, concern about whether they will be able to cope with the growing demand. Understanding the nature of urban resource consumption, and in particular, the changes that take place as a country's population becomes more urban, is an important element in planning supply networks that will be able to accomodate future demands.

This work was supported in part by the Office of Policy, Planning and Analysis, U.S. Department of Energy, under Contract No. DE-AC03-76SF00098, in part by grants from the Exxon Corporation, Standard Oil Company of California, Standard Oil Company of Ohio, and Statoil of Norway, and in part by the International Development Research Centre, Ottawa, Canada.

While the rural energy situation in developing countries has been the object of a large amount of study, there has been comparatively little research on the nature of urban energy use. Because of the importance of this area to understanding energy demand in the developing countries, we undertook a review of the literature on energy use in urban areas of the developing countries.

Urbanization has brought with it a transition from traditional energy sources to modern ("commercial") ones like petroleum fuels and electricity. The growth in income that has taken place in urban areas has also facilitated demand for new services, such as refrigeration, air-conditioning, and personal vehicle transportation, that require modern fuels. In most countries, the use of modern fuels is highly concentrated in the cities, and urban growth and rising demand for modern fuels are highly correlated.[1]

The patterns of energy use in the cities of developing countries exhibit great variety across socioeconomic groups. There are pockets in the cities where the energy use patterns are similar to those found in warm-climate European cites. There are also areas where the patterns resemble more closely those of the rural areas from which many urban dwellers are recently arrived. The important difference is that energy resources are rarely available for free in the urban area, and the need to purchase energy creates problems for the urban poor.

The information we found in our literature review largely dealt with energy use by households, either in the home itself or in personal transportation. We discuss our findings in these areas below.

Energy Use in the Home

As households take on a more modern way of life, demands for new services arise, and there are changes in the manner in which old services are performed. In some cases, a new demand arises which traditionally did not exist (such as refrigeration of food). In others, a traditional service (such as lighting or space cooling) is performed more adequately by the modern device/fuel combination. Replacement of human labor by non-human-powered machines is also a characteristic of the transition (especially in clothes care). Convenience, the desire for more service (e.g., more cooling than ventilation provides, more entertainment than radio provides), and considerations of style and image have led to growing use of electric appliances and changes in cooking habits in urban homes. Such changes are very much dependent on household income. The majority of Third World urban households makes use of a combination of traditional and modern methods. The mix varies widely among cities, but in most, there are probably more households living in a largely traditional manner than in a fully modern one.

Cooking is the primary energy-consuming activity in the majority of Third World homes in both rural and urban areas. Results from a survey of semi-urban households in India show that over 90% of total energy use in both low and middle-income homes went for cooking.[2] A survey of households in three Chinese cities found an even higher share of energy use for cooking.[3]

The predominance of cooking in these cases is a result of both the absence of other energy demands and the low efficiency of energy conversion associated with use of traditional cooking fuels. As household income rises, these conditions change. Households are able to purchase new energy-using devices to meet various demands, and also to acquire different, more energy-efficient devices for cooking.

The choice of cooking fuels depends on preference, ability to afford to use a particular fuel, and the availability of fuels and devices. Urban areas are a fertile setting for change in cooking fuels both because of their income-earning opportunities and the availability of different fuels. The type of fuel used for cooking is usually a good indicator of economic status. As income rises, the main cooking fuel tends to move from firewood or charcoal to kerosene to liquefied petroleum gas (LPG) or electricity. One pattern that emerges is a rise in use of kerosene with income within the lower-income groups. As income increases further, however, use of kerosene gives way to use of LPG and/or electricity.

A recent survey of 1800 households in Hyderabad, India,[4] found that, as expected, firewood consumption fell (by 8%) as income rose (by 10%). For LPG, the income coefficient was almost 1. Kerosene use showed a less continuous pattern than wood and LPG. Its use rose very sharply from the lowest income group and then fell off as income increased further.

Availability of fuels plays a key role in shaping patterns of change. It strongly influences use of firewood, which remains a common fuel for the urban poor in many places. Where it is available for free or at low cost, it tends to be used – both for reasons of cost and habit. Recent surveys of energy use in Kenya found that fuelwood accounted for 60% of total energy consumption among the lowest income group of urban households.[5] In the Philippines, reliance on wood is much higher among households in the poorer socio-economic class in provincial urban areas, where wood is relatively cheaper and more available than kerosene and LPG, than it is in Manila, the primary city.[6] Lack of wood resources around the urban area has become a serious problem in many places, particularly in Africa. Scarcity of wood contributes to the shift to charcoal, which has become a common cooking fuel for the poor in many African cities. Lack of wood can also accelerate the transition to modern fuels, especially where they are locally available at a low price. This has been the case with kerosene in Indonesia, and with coal in

China.

Ownership and use of more than one cooking device is common in urban areas. This is partly because different kinds of foods are best prepared with different types of fuel. Households generally do not discard their old cooking device when they acquire a new, more modern, one. Among upper-income households in Kuala Lumpur, 87% used LP gas, 45% used electricity, 23% used kerosene, and 19% used charcoal.[7] In Hyderabad, the proportion of households using both wood and kerosene ranged from 24% in the lowest income group to 7-9% in the upper-income groups. The proportion using both kerosene and LPG ranged from 1% in the lowest income group to 35-40% in the upper-middle-income groups. The percentage dropped for the highest income groups, as use of only LPG becomes very common. Use of more than one cooking device and fuel is not restricted to middle and upper-income households. Among the Hyderabad lower-income households, 21% used wood and kerosene, and 10% used kerosene and LPG.

Fuel switching can be either temporary or permanent. Households that own more than one cooking device have flexibility in responding to changes in the cost or availability of particular fuels. The acquisition of new cooking devices when poorer households gain more income may lead to a more permanent change, although going back to the old fuel often remains a possibility. The initial cost of new cooking devices can be an important barrier to the use of a new fuel, even when the price of the fuel itself is comparatively attractive.

The amount of energy households use for cooking depends very much upon the efficiency of energy conversion, which can vary greatly depending upon the kind of fuel and device used. In the Hyderabad survey, average monthly energy use per person for cooking fell from 0.239 million Btu among very-low income households, who rely heavily on wood, to 0.165 in the highest income households, who mainly use LPG. The effect of use of more efficient devices can also be seen among the Chinese households. Average monthly cooking fuel consumption per person was lowest in the homes where town gas was used (180 MJ) and highest where bituminous coal was used (630 MJ). It is possible to use measured or estimated conversion efficiencies to calculate the approximate amount of energy that is actually providing the cooking service. Among the Hyderabad households, "useful" energy consumption per person for cooking increased only slightly as income rose.

The use of electricity for lighting is now widespread in urban areas. Where electrification has not yet reached -- in the peripheral areas of large cities and in small cities and towns -- kerosene is still used for lighting in many homes. The quantity of lighting service demanded by households varies considerably. Wealthier families, living in larger homes, demand much more lighting than low-income households, who often only have one or two bulbs.

A key feature of the urban scene is the growing ownership of electric appliances. Three activities in particular could have a major impact on residential electricity demand in Third World cities: refrigeration, water heating, and air-conditioning. The percentage of urban homes with refrigerators varies from almost zero in China to over three-quarter in the wealthier cities of Asia (see Table 1). A refrigerator is usually the first electricity-intensive appliance acquired when urban families have sufficient income to do so. (Black and white televisions, which are often the first major electric appliance purchased, are much smaller consumers of electricity.) Data from the Philippines and Malaysia show that ownership of refrigerators increases sharply from the lowest income group to the next highest. In the upper-income groups, refrigerator ownership is nearly universal.

Water heating for purposes of hygiene is similar to refrigeration in that it is usually not found or is seldom used in a traditional setting. In the Third World, most modern water heaters use electricity. Malaysian survey data, which show low levels of water heater ownership for most income groups, indicate that it is a lesser priority for households than refrigeration. This is no doubt in part a consequence of the warm, humid climate of most Third World cities. The tropical climate works in the other direction with respect to home cooling, the demand for which could have a major effect on electricity use. At present, air conditioning is uncommon except among the wealthiest households. Determining the income level at which households tend to acquire air conditioning is an important task for electric utility planning.

Other home appliances are mostly not heavy electricity users. In places where household electricity use is very low, however, increasing use of appliances such as TV sets and clothes washers could have a significant proportional effect on electricity demand. While ownership of TV sets has become common in many cities, and is nearly universal in the more modernized cities of Asia, clotheswashers are still relatively uncommon.

Increased use of electric appliances and use of more efficient devices for cooking as income rises have opposing effects on overall energy consumption. In urban areas where the modernization process is not so far along, the result may be only a small increase in overall household energy use as income grows. Greater efficiency of energy use in cooking by middle-income families balances their use of more electric appliances. As overall income levels increase, and as the middle and upper classes become wealthier, the situation changes. Use of very low efficiency device/fuel combinations for cooking becomes less common among the poor, and ownership of electric appliances by wealthy households becomes significant. In this situation, there is greater increase in energy consumption from the lowest to the highest income groups.

The growth rate in residential demand for modern fuels will depend largely on the movement of families to cities, the rate at which poor households move from traditional methods of meeting services to modern ones, and the extent to which middle-class households expand their appliance holdings. The fastest growth is taking place in use of electricity, and room for growth in its use exists at nearly all income levels.

Energy Use in Transportation

Energy use in transportation is influenced both by the spatial environment in which people live and by the activities that entail movement, such as work, shopping, social interaction, and distribution of products. While the traditional human and animal-powered forms of transportation predominate in rural areas of developing countries, the use of motor-powered vehicles -- motorcycles, cars, buses -- has become an important feature of urban life. A wide range of transport options is often available in cities, and the amount of energy used to accomplish the movement of people and goods is very much dependent on the transport mode chosen.

The various transport modes provide different types of service, measured in terms of speed and comfort of movement, and also require differing amounts of economic resources in order to make use of them. Walking, the least expensive mode of travel, remains an important one in cities of developing countries. In Lae, Papua New Guinea, it was estimated that walking was the major transport mode for 20% of the people, compared to 15% for cars.[8] Where longer distances are involved, buses are the primary transport mode for the urban poor and middle class.

The mode most commonly used in personal transport varies with household income. As average income has grown, the use of personal motorized vehicles has risen. In Kuala Lumpur and Kajang in Malaysia, 40% of the surveyed households reported the car as their mode of travel to work. Among the poor households, very few used a car, but in the wealthiest group, over 90% did so (see Table 2). Philippines data also show that automobile ownership is very dependent on household income. In the upper 9% of households, 44% owned a car, 19% owned a jeep, and 13% owned utility vehicles. In the middle-income group, only 5% owned a car and 6% owned a jeep. In the two lowest groups, comprising half of the sampled households, there was no car ownership at all.

Car ownership also varies between large and smaller cities. In Manila, 11% of households owned a car. In provincial urban areas of the Philippines, the number was 3-4%. Higher incomes, a well-developed road system, and the greater distances to be travelled for daily activities probably account for this phenomenon. Once a car is owned, the household tends to use it for much of their transport needs. In Nairobi, the share of total travel mileage accounted for by automobile travel increased from 3% in the lowest income group to 90% in the highest group.[9]

Growing use of cars has an important effect on energy use because they tend to be an inefficient mode of transport relative to others available in the urban setting. In three Latin American countries, for example, automobiles are responsible for 65-75% of energy use in passenger transportation, but carry only 25-35% of the total volume of traffic.[10] Energy efficiencies calculated for Hong Kong show the automobile to be some 10 to 15 times more energy-intensive than buses.

The amount of energy used in a particular mode depends largely on the number and length of trips taken. Studies of energy use in Nairobi and Mexico City[11] show that the number of trips per day increases rapidly with rising incomes. Average trip length is affected by particular features of the urban landscape, such as the degree of urban sprawl. Automobile ownership encourages the undertaking of longer trips: The average car trip in Nairobi was almost twice as long as the average foot or bicycle trip. Traffic conditions affect the length of trips in terms of time. Congestion, which has become severe in many Third World cities, leads to slower travel and less efficient operation of fuel-powered vehicles.

Because of the differences in mode choice, trip length, and number of trips, energy use in transportation varies enormously among income groups. In Hong Kong in 1974, Newcombe[12] found a forty-fold increase in per capita energy use for transportation between the lowest and highest income groups (see Table 3). Most of this increase was accounted for by purchases of gasoline and diesel for private use. Consumption in this category showed a big jump from the second highest to the highest income group, reflecting frequent car use by the wealthiest families. Estimates of transport energy use by households in Nairobi and Mexico City show a similar trend. In Nairobi, research indicated a 60-fold increase in energy use per household from the lowest to highest income groups. As in Hong Kong, most of the increase occured in energy used for car travel, which accounts for 30 percent of the energy used in the lowest income group compared to 95 percent in the highest income group. For Mexico City, there was a forty-fold increase in the energy use per household; the automobile emerges again as the major contributor to this increase. If households are at a point where automobile ownership is a possibility, moderate increases in household income may lead to very substantial growth in the consumption of transport fuels. The price and availability of automobiles, the ability of city dwellers to purchase them, and the existence and adequacy of alternatives to private automobile use, will be major determining factors of energy use in urban passenger transportation.

Conclusions

Patterns of energy use in the cities of the developing countries have undergone considerable change during the past two decades. These changes are closely linked to growth in household income, which has allowed the acquisition of devices that use modern fuels. A major area of change has been in cooking, where use of traditional fuels like wood has given way to use of kerosene, LPG, and electricity. The other key development in homes has been the growth in ownership of electric appliances. These include some devices, like refrigerators, water heaters, and air conditioners, that substantially increase household electricity demand.

A striking feature of both energy use in the home and in transportation is the large difference in the amount of energy used by households at different socio-economic levels. Major segments of the urban population in many cities own few appliances, and use most of their energy for cooking. For transport they either walk or use mass transit. In many cities, a small proportion of the households account for a large share of the use of modern fuels, especially electricity. The extent to which lower-income households move into more electricity-intensive lifestyles will depend very much upon both general income growth and income distribution.

REFERENCES

1. LBL International Studies Group (1984), *Summary of Results and Progress Report for the Study of Energy Use in Developing Countries,* LBL-17842.

2. Gupta, C.L., Rao, K., Vasudevaraju, V. (1980), "Domestic Energy Consumption in India (Pondicherry Region)," *Energy* 5: 1213-1222.

3. Zhu, H., Brambley, M., Morgan, R. (1983), "Household Energy Consumption in the People's Republic of China," *Energy* 8: 763-774.

4. Alam, M., Dunkerley, J., Gopi, K., Ramsay, W. (1983), *Fuelwood Survey of Hyderabad.* Resources for the Future, Washington, D.C.

5. Beijer Institute (1984), *Energy and Development in Kenya: Opportunities and Constraints,* Stockholm.

6. Philippines Ministry of Energy (1982), *Energy Sectoral Survey Series: 1979 Urban Household Energy Demand,* Manila.

7. Socio-Economic Research Unit (1981), *The Use of Energy and Attitudes towards Energy Conservation among Urban Households*, Kuala Lumpur.

8. Newcombe, K. (1980), *Energy for Development: the energy policy papers of the Lae Project.* Australian National University.

9. McGranahan, G., Chubb, S., Nathanns, R., Mbeche, O. (1979), *Patterns of Urban Household Energy Use in Developing Countries: The Case of Nairobi*, Institute for Energy Research, Stony Brook, NY.

10. Inter-American Development Bank (1982), *The Impact of Energy Costs on the Transport Sector in Latin America*, Washington, D.C.

11. McGranahan, G., Taylor, M. (1977), *Urban Energy Use Patterns in Developing Countries: A Preliminary Study of Mexico City*, Institute for Energy Research, Stony Brook, NY.

12. Newcombe, K. (1979), "Energy use in Hong Kong: Part IV," *Urban Ecology* 4: 179-205.

Table 1. Electric appliances ownership and income in urban areas.

Income group	Refrigerator	AC	Water heater
	(percent of households in group)		
Malaysia (1980)[a]			
150-299	13	0	0
300-599	50	0	0
600-999	65	1	6
1000-1999	79	10	14
2000-4999	87	23	31
5000+	96	79	50
Philippines (1979)			
Low	15	0	-
Middle	66	2	-
High	93	20	-

[a]Kuala Lumpur and Kajang.

Table 2. Mode of travel to work in Kuala Lumpur and Kajang (1980)

Monthly Income[a]	Car	Taxi	Bus	Motorcycle	Others
150-299 (3%)	-	-	27	13	60
300-599 (20%)	8	2	30	22	39
600-999 (28%)	3	2	27	19	18
1000-1999 (29%)	48	4	11	18	18
2000-4999 (15%)	73	1	3	15	9
5000+ (5%)	92	-	-	-	8
Total	40	2	18	18	22

[a]Values in parentheses refer to percentage of sample population.

Table 3. Transport energy use in income in Hong Kong (1974).

Monthly income[a] (HK$/cap-month)	Public	Private (MJ/capita-day)	Total
<100 (3%)	0.13	0.13	0.26
101-150 (11%)	0.07	0.25	0.32
151-200 (18%)	0.21	0.05	0.26
201-250 (16%)	0.34	0.60	0.94
251-300 (10%)	0.49	1.38	1.87
301-350 (7%)	0.67	1.11	1.78
351-400 (4%)	0.49	1.58	2.07
401-550 (9%)	0.92	3.52	4.44
550+ (18%)	1.78	9.26	11.04

[a]Values in parathenses refer to percentage of sample population.

For Product Safety Concerns and Information please contact our EU representative GPSR@taylorandfrancis.com Taylor & Francis Verlag GmbH, Kaufingerstraße 24, 80331 München, Germany

Batch number: 10725931

Printed by Printforce, the Netherlands